STUDIES IN ECONOMIC DESIGN

Series Editor Murat R. Sertel
Turkish Academy of Sciences

Springer

Berlin
Heidelberg
New York
Barcelona
Hong Kong
London
Milan
Paris
Tokyo

Titles in the Series

V. I. Danilov and A. I. Sotskov
Social Choice Mechanisms
VI, 191 pages. 2002. ISBN 3-540-43105-5

B. Dutta and M. O. Jackson (Eds.)
Networks and Groups
VIII, 496 pages. 2003. ISBN 3-540-43113-6
(in preparation)

Tatsuro Ichiishi
Thomas Marschak
Editors

Markets, Games, and Organizations

Essays in Honor of Roy Radner

With 9 Figures
and 28 Tables

Springer

Professor Tatsuro Ichiishi

The Ohio State University
Department of Economics
1945 North High Street
Columbus, Ohio 43210-1172, USA
Email: ichiishi.1@osu.edu

Professor Thomas Marschak

University of California
Haas School of Business
Berkeley, CA 94720, USA

First published in "Review of Economic Design, Volume 6, Issue 2, 3, 4, 2001

ISBN 3-540-43897-1 Springer-Verlag Berlin Heidelberg New York

Library of Congress Cataloging-in-Publication Data applied for
Die Deutsche Bibliothek – CIP-Einheitsaufnahme

Markets, Games, and Organizations: Essays in Honor of Roy Radner /
Ed.: Tatsuro Ichiishi, Thomas Marschak. –
Berlin; Heidelberg; New York; Barcelona; Hong Kong; London; Milan;
Paris; Tokyo: Springer, 2002
(Studies in Economic Design)
ISBN 3-540-43897-1

Springer-Verlag Berlin Heidelberg New York
a member of BertelsmannSpringer Science + Business Media GmbH

http://www.springer.de

Printed in Germany

Cover design: Erich Kirchner, Heidelberg

SPIN 10886149 43/2202-5 4 3 2 1 0 – Printed on acid free paper

Table of Contents

Introduction

We are pleased to help celebrate Roy Radner's 75th birthday, by issuing in one volume the papers that originally appeared in his honor in two special issues of *Review of Economic Design* (Vol. 6/2 and 6/3–4, 2001). Through his truly original ideas and lucid writing, Roy has influenced and guided the theory community for decades. Many colleagues and students have found their own work shaped and improved by Roy's wide-ranging curiosity, his encouragement, and his keen insights.

In soliciting contributions to the *Review of Economic Design* Radner issues, we decided to approach his former students at the University of California, Berkeley, his former post-doctoral fellows at Bell Laboratories, and his published co-authors. We express our sincere apology to any potential authors who fit these categories and whom we may have unintentionally failed to approach.

Our job as editors of the *Review of Economic Design* Radner issues turned out to be easy, thanks to the enthusiastic response we received from authors and the quality of their submissions.

The papers in this volume cover quite diverse areas, ranging over general equilibrium analysis of the market mechanism, economies undergoing transition, satisficing behavior, markets with asymmetric information, organizational resource allocation and information processing, incentives and implementation, stable sets and the core, stochastic sequential bargaining games, perfect equilibria in a macro growth model, repeated games, and evolutionary games. Roy's research interests cover all those topics. He has made seminal contributions to most of them, and indeed to so many areas that we shall not attempt a survey. In what follows, we briefly introduce the seventeen papers.

General equilibrium analysis of the market mechanism. The paper by Rabi N. Bhattacharya and Mukul K. Majumdar, "On characterizing the probability of survival in a large competitive economy," introduces a survival constraint into the random pure exchange economy, and studies the competitive equilibrium price vector (a random variable) and the probability of ruin, as the size of the economy (the number of consumers) becomes infinitely large. It provides a sensitivity analysis of the survival probability with respect to a change in the limiting averages of the endowments over the agents. The paper by Rose-Anne Dana, "Uniqueness of Arrow-Debreu and Arrow-Radner equilibria when utilities are additively separable," surveys various approaches to the unique existence of a competitive equilibrium (called the Arrow-Debreu equilibrium) of a pure exchange economy when consumers' utility functions are additively separable, and to the unique existence of a competitive equilibrium (called the Arrow-Radner equilibrium) of a one-commodity two-period pure exchange economy with securities. The author has been one of the key players in this research area, especially for the economy with infinitely many commodities (or with infinitely many states for the economy with securities).

Economies undergoing transition. In the paper by Kenneth J. Arrow, "Entry, production, and investment," the author first points out two modes of transition from the government controlled economy to the free market economy, by privatization and by free entry, and argues that the latter mode is more efficient. The paper concerns the latter mode, and provides policy guidance. The problems are caused by two basic facts: limited financial resources and uncertainty about the productivity of new entrants. The issue here is, therefore, how many entrants are to be financed. The author's first conclusion is that if the same adequate support level is given to all the supported entrants, then it is optimal to encourage multiple entry, although that may be constrained by resource availabilities. He then considers differentiated financing strategies; his second conclusion is that there is a gain by including a possibly inadequate level of financing of a firm. Finally, he analyzes the effect of entry on savings for the situation in which the marginal returns of the entrants are initially higher than the market return. In the paper by Richard E. Ericson and Barry W. Ickes, "A model of Russia's 'virtual economy'," the authors first point out that the Russian economy has evolved into the so-called virtual economy, a partially monetized quasi-market system. Here, inefficient enterprises engage in barter. The authors construct a simple partial equilibrium model of the energy market, in which there are an energy-supplying monopolist and a continuum of energy-demanding enterprises with differing degrees of efficiency. The main results of the paper concern an equilibrium (a "trap") in which inefficient enterprises decline to restructure, and hence they hinder the transition to a free-market economy.

Satisficing behavior. The paper by Itzhak Gilboa and David Schmeidler, "Reaction to price changes and aspiration level adjustments," studies examples of a consumer's satisficing behavior, in which his past actions and his observed market prices determine an aspiration level, and his aspiration level in turn determines his preference relation, and so influences his action. Implications for a comparative statics problem (the study of the consumer's responses to several modes of changes in a price) are explored. In particular, results contradictory to the neoclassical results (which are based on the postulate of consumer's optimizing behavior) are obtained.

Markets with asymmetric information. The paper by Peter Linhart, "Bargaining equilibria with non-standard objectives," studies a model of sealed-bid bargaining of one item with one seller and one buyer. The seller knows the cost of the item, but cannot observe the buyer's action (bid), and there is a symmetric scenario for the buyer. Two alternative objectives are proposed, and the associated noncooperative equilibria in pure strategies are studied: one objective is minimization of maximal regret, and the other objective is maximization of maximal profit. Given the former objective, the author's equilibrium is close in spirit to an α-individually rational strategy bundle, and he shows it to be unique in some important special cases.

Organizational resource allocation and information processing. The paper by Harold Cole, George J. Mailath and Andrew Postlewaite, "Investment and concern for relative position," studies the effect of non-market considerations (marriage) on decision-making in the market (investment), given a continuum of females and a continuum of males: A female first makes an investment decision, and after realization of the return of her investment, she plays a matching game for marriage. A female's first decision influences her position in the marriage game. The paper by Stanley Reiter, "Coordination of economic activity: An example," constructs a formal model to address coordination of managers' decisions either through a market mechanism or through a direct (nonmarket) mechanism, when managers' pursuit of self interest is abstracted away. The author examines two examples. In one example, the market mechanism does not result in efficient coordination, and so it is ruled out. In the other example, both the market and the nonmarket mechanism bring about efficient coordination, so the two mechanisms are compared in order to identify the one that has lower informational cost. The paper by Leonid Hurwicz and Stanley Reiter, "On transversals and systems of distinct representatives," establishes a necessary and sufficient condition for a family $\mathscr{C}$ of subsets of a set W to have a system of distinct representatives (that is, there exists a 1–1 mapping $\Lambda : \mathscr{C} \to \Theta$, $\Theta \subset W$, such that $\Lambda(K) \in K$ for every $K \in \mathscr{C}$). The question of existence of a system of distinct representatives arises in designing decentralized mechanisms to meet a given optimality criterion, as well as in matching games. The authors also establish several necessary and sufficient conditions for a family $\mathscr{C}$ to be a partition of the set W.

Incentives and Implementation. The paper by Eric S. Maskin, "Roy Radner and incentive theory," provides a self-contained integrate survey of some incentives issues when individuals are endowed with private information. These issues include: implementation in dominant strategies in the presence of adverse selection; welfare loss due to moral hazard in a one-principal, one-agent model; its approximate recovery as a perfect Bayesian equilibrium of the associated repeated game (in which players maximize their discounted sum of payoffs); and welfare loss due to double moral hazard in a partnership model. Brief comments on implementation in Nash or Bayesian equilibrium are also given. The original version of the paper by Steve Williams, "Sufficient conditions for Nash implementation," was written in Spring 1984, and had been circulated as a well-known discussion paper since then. It clarifies some difficulties inherent in Maskin's conjecture on Nash implementation, and settles the matter positively. Given a social choice correspondence F which satisfies monotonicity and no veto power, the paper first presents Maskin's sufficient condition on a game form (S, g) under which (S, g) implements F in Nash equilibrium. The paper then quotes the author's own published result establishing a sufficient condition for F to be Nash implementable. Here, Maskin's assumption of finiteness of the outcome space is replaced by a new condition on the cardinality of $F^{-1}(a)$ for each outcome a. The paper points out that given an objective F satisfying these assumptions, Maskin's procedure produces a game form which satisfies Maskin's sufficient condition for Nash implementation of F. The paper also provides an example of an F which satisfies monotonicity and no veto power, fails to satisfy the author's condition on cardinality of $F^{-1}(a)$, and cannot be implemented by the game form produced by Maskin's procedure. Finally the paper establishes that the author's condition on cardinality of $F^{-1}(a)$ is not needed after all for Nash implementability (if one is not required to use the game form obtained by Maskin's procedure).

Stable sets and the core. The paper by James S. Jordan, "Majority rule with dollar voting," considers a society whose total wealth is allocated to its members. Given any allocation, a coalition whose members have been allocated, in total, more than a half of the society's wealth is considered a majority, and is empowered to re-distribute the society's total wealth to its members. Thus, the concept of dominance relative to an allocation is well-defined (although the model cannot be reduced to a game in characteristic function form). Only extreme concentration of wealth, in which one player owns everything or two players each own half of the total wealth are undominated, and thus constitute the core. However, the stable set (the Von Neumann-Morgenstern solution) is significantly larger. Allocations in which one player has half the wealth, or which divide the total wealth equally among a number of players equal to a power of two, constitute the unique stable set. The stable set thus provides a formal model of an endogenous balance of power.

Stochastic sequential bargaining games. The paper by Charles A. Wilson, "Mediation and the Nash bargaining solution," studies the following two-person sequential bargaining game with a mediator, and shows that as the discount rates become arbitrarily small, the subgame perfect payoffs converge to the asymmetric Nash bargaining solution, with weights determined by the relative discount rates of the players. The mediator announces a payoff allocation to the two players according to an exogenously given density function f (hence a proposed payoff allocation is not an endogenous variable in the game), and then the two players sequentially choose either to accept it or reject it. If both players accept it, then the game is over. If one player rejects it, another round of the game is played, in which the mediator proposes a payoff allocation according to the same function f.

Perfect equilibria in a macro growth model. The paper by Jess Benhabib, Aldo Rustichini and Andres Velasco, "Public spending and optimal taxes without commitment," constructs a simple macro growth model with one representative agent (among a continuum of agents) and the government. The government imposes a tax on the agent, and uses 100% of the tax for provision of public goods. The public goods and the accumulated capital net of consumption are used to produce the output. The government and the agent play a game, in which the government's strategy is a history-contingent tax rate for each period, and the agent's strategy is history-contingent future savings for each period. A perfect equilibrium is proposed and studied.

Repeated games. In the paper by Roger Lagunoff and Akihiko Matsui, "Are 'anti folk theorems' in repeated games nongeneric?", the authors consider the space of repeated games, each associated with a stage game of pure coordination, in which players move at different times as determined by an external stochastic process. They establish the following genericity theorem: Fix any stage game of pure coordination, and let u^* be its unique Pareto dominant Nash equilibrium payoff vector. Given any $\varepsilon > 0$, if the players are sufficiently patient, there exists an open neighborhood of the given stage game such that every perfect equilibrium payoff of the repeated game associated with any stage game in this neighborhood is within ε of u^*.

Evolutionary games. The paper by Robert W. Rosenthal, "Trust and social efficiencies," constructs an evolutionary-game model based on a modified repeated prisoner's dilemma, proposes cost-effective policies for selecting and maintaining an efficient equilibrium, and discusses difficulties that arise when the population is divided into several groups, or when nonuniform matchings prevail. Here, there are three equilibria. The *stability* concept for an equilibrium was defined in the literature; in the present model, the unique stable equilibrium consists in everybody always defecting, so it is inefficient. The author proposes the *weak stability* concept, and shows that the completely mixed equilibrium, which is more efficient than the "always defecting" equilibrium, is weakly stable. The main argument of the paper is that adoption of social policies to achieve and maintain this weakly stable equilibrium is cost-efficient. He then reconsiders the same problem within the framework of modified evolutionary games, either by introducing several population groups, or by introducing nonuniform matchings, and points out some difficulties that arise in the modified games. The paper by Prajit K. Dutta and Rangarajan K. Sundaram, "Survival and the art of profit maximization," constructs a simple evolutionary game in which there are two symmetric groups of people. Each player of group I maximizes the expected profit, each player of group II maximizes the probability of survival, and a higher-level action increases the profit but decreases the probability of survival. The main results of the paper are the computation in several specific cases of the eventual population ratio and the eventual wealth ratio of the two groups.

Tatsuro Ichiishi, Ohio State University, Columbus, USA
Tom Marschak, University of California, Berkeley, USA

On characterizing the probability of survival in a large competitive economy

Rabi N. Bhattacharya[1], **Mukul Majumdar**[2]

[1] Department of Mathematics, Indiana University, Rawles Hall, Bloomington, IN 47405, USA (e-mail: bhattach@indiana.edu)

[2] Department of Economics, Cornell University, Uris Hall 460, Ithaca, NY 14853-7601, USA (e-mail: mkm5@cornell.edu)

Abstract. We consider a Walrasian exchange economy in which an agent is characterized by a utility function, a random endowment vector, and a function that specifies the minimum expenditure necessary for survival at a given price system. If at any equilibrium price system, the income of the agent is no more than the minimum expenditure for survival, it is ruined. The main results characterize the probability of ruin when the number of agents is large. The implications of stochastic dependence among agents are explored.

0 Introduction

In his Schwartz Memorial Lecture (1995) on *Economic Survival*, Radner started out with the following observations:

> "Standard textbooks on microeconomic theory typically ascribes to consumers the goal of maximizing "utility" and to firms the goal of maximizing "profit" or the "value of the firm". Explicit consideration of the survival and failure of firms has scarcely been recognized by general equilibrium theory, in spite of the sophisticated development of the subject in the past forty years. The recent reawakening of interest in the evolution of economic behavior, especially among game theorists, implicitly brings with it a concern for the goal of "survival" but thus far most game-theoretic models of evolution do not bear much resemblance to even stylized pictures of economic institutions. Nevertheless, failure is a common occurrence ..."

Radner noted that the "connections between survival and uncertainty are particularly interesting" and went on to review some issues involving *individual*

We would like to thank Professors Kaushik Basu, Tatsuro Ichiishi, Debraj Ray, Santanu Roy, Roy Radner and Amartya Sen for helpful comments on earlier drafts. We acknowledge that we have not been able to deal with most of the issues raised by Professor Debraj Ray.

firms and investors in a class of models that had their roots in the celebrated "Gambler's Ruin Problem" of probability theory.

Among earlier writers on Walrasian equilibrium analysis, Koopmans (1957, pp. 62–63) observed that sufficient conditions ensuring the survival of consumers in equilibrium posed a "considerable challenge to further research". This challenge was not taken up seriously, and Newman (1989) provides an insightful commentary on the proper interpretation of a consumption possibility set and some of the difficulties of incorporating the survival problem in the Walrasian equilibrium theory. On the other hand, one can argue that "survival" has remained a basic issue in development economics, and, to take an influential example, it has figured prominently in the work of Amartya Sen and others (see Sen 1981 and Ghose 1989) on understanding the causes of some major famines and appropriateness of policy measures to mitigate the impact of a famine. Sen has emphasized the link between the wealth of a consumer at equilibrium prices and the minimum expenditure necessary for survival (see Appendix A, pp. 167–168 in Sen 1981, and the formal Walrasian equilibrium model of Coles and Hammond 1993: both are deterministic models).

In this paper we explore some connections between uncertainty and survival in a simple Walrasian equilibrium model. We consider an exchange economy in which an agent is characterized by its preferences (described by a utility or demand function), a random endowment vector and a function that specifies the minimum expenditure necessary for survival at a price system (see Sen 1981, pp. 167–181). To be precise, assume that there are ℓ commodities. The set of all possible states of the environment is denoted by Ω, and the *exogenous* stochastic law determining the occurrence of states is denoted by P (defined on a σ-field $\mathcal{F}$ of subsets of Ω). The endowment of an agent $e(\cdot)$ is a (measurable) mapping from Ω into the strictly positive orthrant of R^{ℓ}. The demand function f describing the preferences of an agent is assumed to be deterministic. The wealth $w(\cdot)$ of an agent $\alpha(\cdot) = (f, e(\cdot))$ at a (random) equilibrium price system $p^*(\cdot)$ is defined as

$$w(\cdot) = \sum_{k=1}^{\ell} p_k^*(\cdot) e_k(\cdot)$$

An agent is *ruined* (fails to survive) at a particular state ω of the environment ($\omega \in \Omega$) if

$$w(\omega) \leqq m(p^*(\omega))$$

where $m(p^*(\omega))$ is the minimum expenditure that the agent $\alpha(\cdot)$ must incur for survival at the equilibrium price system $p^*(\omega)$. Observe that the equilibrium price system typically depends on the preference-endowment patterns of *all* the agents in the economy. Hence, if there are n agents, we consider the event defined as

$$\mathfrak{R}_n = \{\omega : w(\omega) \leqq m(p_n^*(\omega))\}$$

and interpret it as the set of environments in which the agent is ruined (we stress the dependence of equilibrium price system on the number of agents by writing

$p_n^*(\cdot)$ explicitly). It is clear that 'ruin' can occur due to a meager endowment in a particular state. This is a 'direct' effect of endowment uncertainty. But 'ruin' can also be due to an equilibrium price system $p_n^*(\cdot)$ at which the value of the endowment falls short of the minimum needed for survival. This is an 'indirect' terms-of-trade effect of endowment uncertainty.

Our first task is to characterize $P(\mathfrak{R}_n)$ when – in the Walrasian tradition – n is 'large'. In Sect. 1, we consider in detail a simple example that captures the main issues formally without too much technicalities involving measure theory. Here, there are two commodities and n agents with identical Cobb-Douglas utility functions. An explicit computation and some routine algebraic manipulations enable us to express the unique random price equilibrium $p_n^*(\omega)$ in a form that involves sums of random variables. Hence, if a "non correlation" property (see A2 in Sect. 1c) holds (and some mild restrictions on endowments are satisfied) one can show by a direct appeal to the law of large numbers that as n, the number of agents, goes to infinity, the sequence $p_n^*(\omega)$ converges in probability to a constant p_0 (see (1.12)). It follows that for *all* "sufficiently large" n, $P(\mathfrak{R}_n)$ is approximately the same as the probability of an event that depends on the distribution of the agent's random endowment and the constant p_0 (see (1.13)). In the special case when all the agents have the same distribution of endowments, the probability of ruin is *entirely* determined by the distribution of endowments of the individual agent. But, in general, the constant p_0 can be computed only if the information about the distributions of *all* the agents is available. Next we see that – even in this example – the risk of ruin due to the "indirect" or terms of trade effect may remain significant even for a large economy if the family of endowments satisfies a "conditional independence" or "exchangeability condition". In this case the sequence $p_n^*(\cdot)$ can be shown to converge to a random variable $p_0(\cdot)$. The probability of ruin $P(\mathfrak{R}_n)$ still converges, but the limiting expression is more complicated (see Proposition 1.4).

The example is deceptively simple in one important respect: in a more general framework, one can neither hope for an explicit computation of an equilibrium price system nor for expressing an equilibrium price system in a form that involves sums of random parameters in the model. The framework developed in Sect. 2 relies on the measure theoretic model of an exchange economy (see the definitive account of Hildenbrand 1974) and is unavoidably technical. Here, following Bhattacharya and Majumdar (1973) we consider a particular way of changing the size of the economy and obtain asymptotic results on the probability of ruin (although there is an important distinction between our present model and the earlier one in Bhattacharya and Majumdar 1973 regarding role of independence as noted in Sect. 2d). A uniqueness assumption ((U.1) and (U.2)) leads to a particularly sharp characterization of the survival probability of an agent in a large economy (see (2.12)). (A general treatment of exchangeability leads to Proposition 2.4). Even with independence, the probability of ruin in a large economy depends not only on the distribution of the individual endowment but also on a constant that is interpreted as an equilibrium price system of a deterministic "average" economy.

In Sect. 3 we explore the general model further without the uniqueness assumption. The main results are on estimating bounds on $P(\mathfrak{R}_n)$ as n goes to infinity.

In addition to characterization of $P(\mathfrak{R}_n)$, one would like to throw light on the basic question: "how can one improve the chance of survival of an agent through appropriate interventions?" It seems to us that in order to answer this question one needs to have an idea of how sensitive $P(\mathfrak{R}_n)$ is with respect to changes in the distribution of endowments. In Sect. 4 we return to explicit computations in the Cobb-Douglas-Sen economy and report some results on a special case. A more thorough investigation is perhaps the most important direction for future research.

While we are primarily motivated by questions of economic survival, the formal analysis has its links to another theme in the literature on risk and uncertainty. Economists have long been interested in the implications and applicability of the law of large numbers in different contexts (see, for example, Arrow 1951 for references to earlier writings in the 1920s and also Malinvaud 1972 on individual and collective risks), and our analysis relies upon an application of this basic law in probability theory.

We recognize that, as a framework for dealing with "uncertainty", a static formal model of an exchange economy has its essential limitations. We also feel that our model cannot capture the sweep of Sen's "entitlement approach": as he correctly noted (p. 46), this framework is "perhaps the simplest case" of his approach. It is our hope that the present exercise is a step towards filling the gap in the equilibrium theory literature that Radner and others so rightly pointed out.

1 A Cobb-Douglas-Sen economy with random endowments

1a Equilibrium

Consider, first, a deterministic Walrasian exchange economy with two goods (we shall often refer to the first good as "food"). Assume that an agent i has an initial endowment $\mathbf{e}_i = (e_{i1}, e_{i2}) >> 0$, and a Cobb-Douglas utility function

$$u(x_{i1}, x_{i2}) = x_{i1}^{r} x_{i2}^{1-\gamma} \tag{1.1}$$

where $0 < \gamma < 1$ and the pair (x_{i1}, x_{i2}) denotes the quantities of goods 1 and 2 consumed by agent i. Thus an agent i is described by a pair $\alpha_i = (\gamma, \mathbf{e}_i)$.

Let p be the price of the first good. The Walrasian agent accepts the price vector $(p, 1-p)$ as given and solves the following maximization problem (P):

$$\text{maximize } u(x_{i1}, x_{i2})$$

subject to the "budget constraint"

$$px_{i1} + (1-p)x_{i2} = w_i$$

where the income or wealth w_i of the i-th agent is defined as

$$w_i(p) = pe_{i1} + (1-p)e_{i2}\,. \tag{1.2}$$

Solving the problem (P) one obtains the excess demand for the first good as:

$$\zeta_i(p) = [(1-p)/p]\gamma e_{i2} - (1-\gamma)e_{i1} \tag{1.3}$$

The total excess demand for the first good at the prices $(p, 1-p)$ in a Walrasian exchange economy with n agents is given by:

$$\zeta(p) = \sum_{i=1}^{n} \zeta_i(p) \tag{1.4}$$

Hence, the Walrasian equilibrium price can be computed by solving the equation;

$$\zeta(p) = 0 \tag{1.5}$$

and this gives us the equilibrium price as:

$$p_n^* = \left[\sum_{i=1}^{n} X_i\right] \Big/ \left[\sum_{i=1}^{n} X_i + \sum_{i=1}^{n} Y_i\right] \tag{1.6}$$

where

$$X_i = \gamma e_{i2},\; Y_i = (1-\gamma)e_{i1}\,. \tag{1.7}$$

To be sure, by Walras' law, demand equals supply in the market for the second good when the excess demand for the first good is zero.

Recall that a Walrasian economy is "informationally decentralized" in the sense that agent i has no information about $(\mathbf{e}_j)$ for $i \neq j$. Thus it is *not* possible for agent i to compute the equilibrium price p_n^*.

1b Survival

In order to provide the motivation for our formal approach, we recall the basic elements of Amartya Sen's analysis (1981, Appendix A) in our notation. Let F_i be a (nonempty) closed subset of R^2_{++}. We interpret F_i as the set of all combinations of the two goods that enable the i-th agent to survive. Now, given a price system $(p, 1-p)$, one can define a function $m_i(p)$ as

$$m_i(p) = \min_{(x_{i1}, x_{i2}) \in F_i} \{px_{i1} + (1-p)x_{i2}\} \tag{1.8}$$

Thus, $m_i(p)$ is readily interpreted as the minimum expenditure needed for survival at prices $(p, 1-p)$. In Sect. 4 we study in detail the following:

Example 1.1. Let $(a_{i1}, a_{i2}) >> 0$ be a fixed element of R^2_{++}. Let

$$F_i = \{(x_{i1}, x_{i2}) \in R^2_{++} : x_{i1} \geq a_{i1},\; x_{i2} \geq a_{i2}\} \tag{1.9}$$

Here $m_i(p) = pa_{i1} + (1-p)a_{i2}$.

In our approach we do not deal with the set F_i explicitly. Instead, let us suppose that, in addition to its utility function and endowment vector, each agent i is characterized by a continuous function $m_i(p) : [0, 1] \to R_{++}$, and say that for an agent to *survive* at prices $(p, 1-p)$, its wealth $w_i(p)$ (see (1.2)) must exceed $m_i(p)$. Hence, the i-th agent *fails to survive* (or, *is ruined*) at the Walrasian equilibrium $(p_n^*, 1-p_n^*)$ if

$$[p_n^* e_{i1} + (1-p_n^*) e_{i2}] \leq m_i(p_n^*) \tag{1.10}$$

or, using the definition (1.2)

$$w_i(p_n^*) \leq m_i(p_n^*) \tag{1.11}$$

Observe that in our economy even with an exact information of the total endowment ($\sum_{i=1}^{n} e_{i1}$) of the first good ("food"), it is not possible to figure out how many agents may starve in equilibrium, in the absence of detailed information on the pattern of $(\mathbf{e}_i, m_i)$, (and the formula (1.6)). This is related to one of the main points stressed by Sen (1981).[1]

1c Random endowments: computing the probability of ruin

Let us suppose that the endowments $\mathbf{e}_i$ of the agents $(i = 1, 2, \ldots n)$ are random variables. In other words, each $\mathbf{e}_i(\cdot)$ is a (measurable) mapping from a probability space $(\Omega, \mathscr{F}, P)$ into the non-negative orthant of R^2. One interprets Ω as the set of all possible states of the environment, and $\mathbf{e}_i(\omega)$ is the endowment of agent i in the particular state ω. The distribution of $\mathbf{e}_i(\cdot)$ is denoted by μ_i [formally each μ_i is a probability measure on the Borel σ field of R^2, its support being a nonempty subset of the strictly positive orthant of R^2]. From the expression (1.6), the equilibrium price $p_n^*(\omega)$ is random, i.e., depends on ω. So is the wealth $w_i\ (p_n^*(\omega))$ at $p_n^*(\omega)$). The event

$$\mathfrak{R}_n^i = \{\omega \in \Omega : w_i(p_n^*(\omega)) \leq m_i(p_n^*(\omega)))\}$$

is the set of all states of the environment in which agent i does not survive. From the definition of the event $\mathfrak{R}_a^i$ it is clear that an agent may be ruined due to a meager endowment vector in a particular state of the environment. In what follows, we shall refer to this situation as a "direct" effect of endowment uncertainty or as an "individual" risk of ruin. But it is also possible for ruin to occur through an unfavorable movement of the equilibrium prices (terms of trade) even when there is no change (or perhaps an increase!) in the endowment vector. A Walrasian equilibrium price system reflects the entire pattern of endowments

[1] It is useful to recall the following from Sen (1981, p. 17): "Starvation – as discussed – is a function of entitlements and not of food availability as such. Indeed, some of the worst famines have taken place with no significant decline in food availability per head. To say that starvation depends 'not merely' on food supply but also on its 'distribution' would be correct enough, though not remarkably helpful. The important question then would be: what determines distribution of food between different sections of the community?"

that emerges in a particular state of the environment. Given the role of the price system in determining the wealth of an agent and the minimum expenditure needed for survival, this possibility of ruin through adverse terms of trade can be viewed as an "indirect" ("terms of trade") effect of endowment uncertainty. This issue is linked to the literature on the "price" and "welfare" effects of a change in the endowment on a deterministic Walrasian equilibrium (see the review of the transfer problem by Majumdar and Mitra 1993) and has also been stressed by Sen (1987, p. 47).[2]

To begin with let us make the following assumptions:

A1. $\lim_{n\to\infty} \left[\sum_{i=1}^{n} \operatorname{Var} X_i\right] \Big/ n^2 = 0, \quad \lim_{n\to\infty} \left[\sum_{i=1}^{n} \operatorname{Var} Y_i\right] \Big/ n^2 = 0 \quad \text{as } n \to \infty.$

A2. $\{X_i\}$ are uncorrelated, $\{Y_i\}$ are uncorrelated.

A3. $[(1/n)\Sigma_i EX_i]$ converges to some $\pi_1 > 0$, $[(1/n)\Sigma_i EY_i]$ converges to some $\pi_2 > 0$ as n tends to infinity.

In the special case when the distributions of $\mathbf{e}_i$ are the same for all i (so that $1/n\Sigma_i EX_i = \pi_1$, where π_1 is the common expectation of all X_i; similarly for π_2), A3 is satisfied.

Under A1–A3, if the number n of agents increases to infinity, as a consequence of the weak law of large numbers we have the following property of equilibrium prices p_n^*:

Proposition 1.1. *Under A1–A3, as n tends to infinity, $p_n^*(\omega)$ converges in probability to the constant*

$$p_0 = \pi_1/[\pi_1 + \pi_2] \tag{1.12}$$

Proof. This result is a direct consequence of the statement in Lamperti (1966, p. 22). Q.E.D.

Roughly, one interprets (1.12) as follows: for large values of n, the equilibrium price will not vary much from one state of the environment to another, and will be insensitive to the exact value of n, the number of agents.

For the constant p_0 defined by (1.12), we have the following characterization of the probability of ruin in a large Walrasian economy:

Proposition 1.2. *If $p_0e_{i1}(\omega)+(1-p_0)e_{i2}(\omega)$ has a continuous distribution function,*

$$\lim_{n\to\infty} [P(\mathfrak{R}_n^i] = P\{\omega : p_0e_{i1}(\omega) + (1-p_0)e_{i2}(\omega) \leq m_i(p_0)\} \tag{1.13}$$

Proof. The sequence of random variables $w_i(p_n^*(\omega)) - m_i(p_n^*(\omega))$ converges in probability, hence, in distribution to the random variable $V_i(\omega) = p_0e_{i1}(\omega) + (1 - p_0)e_{i2}(\omega) - m_i(p_0)$. Hence, as n tends to infinity,

[2] "Starvation can develop for the group of people as its endowment vector collapses, and there are indeed many accounts of such endowment declines on the part of sections of poor rural population in developing countries ... but starvation can also develop with *unchanged* asset ownership through movement of exchange entitlement mapping" (Sen 1981, pp. 47–48). In our Walrasian exchange economy the entitlement mapping associates with each (p, e) the budget set of the agent (see Sen 1981, p. 46). In his analysis of the Ethiopian famine (1972–1974), Sen gave an example of a group of agents "decimated by the market mechanism" (p. 112).

$$P(\mathfrak{R}_n^i) = P\{\omega : w_i(p_n^*(\omega)) - m_i(p_n^*(\omega)) \leq 0\}$$

converges to $P\{\omega : V_i(\omega) \leq 0\}$, given the assumed continuity property of the distribution function of $p_0 e_{i1}(\omega) + (1 - p_0)e_{i2}(\omega)$. Q.E.D.

Remarks 1.1. The probability on the right side of (1.13) does not depend on n, and is determined by μ_i, a characteristic of agent i, and p_0.

1.2. $p_n^*(\omega)$ does not vary too much over the states ω, so a central planner can approximate p_0 by p_n^*.

1.3. For the proof of Proposition 1.2, one requires continuity of the distribution function of $p_0 e_{2i} + (1 - p_0)e_{i2}$ only at the point $m_i(p_0)$.

One is tempted to conjecture that the convergence property of Proposition 1.1 will continue to hold if correlation among agents becomes 'negligible' as the size of the economy increases. We shall indicate a 'typical' result that captures such intuition.

Proposition 1.3. *Let the assumptions (A1) and (A3) hold. Moreover, assume*

(A.2') There exist two non-negative sequences $(\mathscr{L}_k)_{k\geq 0}$, $(\mathscr{L}'_k)_{k\geq 0}$ both converging to zero such that for all i, k

$$\begin{aligned} |\mathrm{Cov}(X_i, X_{i+k})| &\leq \mathscr{L}_k \\ |\mathrm{Cov}(Y_i, Y_{i+k})| &\leq \mathscr{L}'_k \end{aligned}$$

Then, as n tends to infinity, $p_n^*(\omega)$ converges in probability to the constant

$$p_0 = \pi_1/[\pi_1 + \pi_2]$$

Proof. Write

$$\left(\sum_{i=1}^n X_i\right) \Big/ n = \overline{X} \quad \text{and} \quad \left(\sum_{i=1}^n Y_i\right) \Big/ n = \overline{Y}$$

By (A.2'),

$$\begin{aligned} E(\overline{X} - E\overline{X})^2 &\equiv \text{variance } \overline{X} \\ &= \frac{1}{n^2}\sum_{i=1}^n \text{variance } X_i + \frac{2}{n^2}\sum_{k=1}^{n-1}\sum_{i=1}^{n-k} \mathrm{Cov}\ (X_i, X_{i+k}) \\ &\leq \frac{1}{n^2}\sum_{k=1}^n \mathscr{L}_0 + \frac{2}{n^2}\sum_{k=1}^{n-1}\sum_{i=1}^{n-k} \mathscr{L}_k \\ &= \frac{\mathscr{L}_0}{n} + \frac{2}{n^2}\sum_{k=1}^{n-1}(n-k)\mathscr{L}_k \\ &\leq \frac{\mathscr{L}_0}{n} + \frac{2}{n}\sum_{k=1}^{n-1}\mathscr{L}_k \to 0 \quad \text{as} \quad n \to \infty\,. \end{aligned}$$

Therefore, by Chevyshev's inequality, for every $\varepsilon > 0$ one has

$$P(|\overline{X} - E\overline{X}| \geq \varepsilon) \leq \frac{\mathrm{var}\overline{X}}{\varepsilon^2} \to 0 \quad \text{as} \quad n \to \infty\,.$$

In other words, $\overline{X} - E\overline{X} \to 0$ in probability. Since $E\overline{X} \to \pi_1$, $\overline{X} \to \pi_1$ in probability. The same argument leads to "$\overline{y} \to \pi_2$ in probability". Q.E.D.

Remark 1.4. It is important to note that the assumptions on X_i and Y_i in Propositions 1.1 and 1.3 are really assumptions on the endowments e_{i1} and e_{i2} (see (1.7)); so their averages converge in probability to, say $\overline{e}_1$ and $\overline{e}_2$.

1d Dependence: Exchangeability

We shall now see that if dependence among agents does not "disappear" even when the economy is large, the risk of ruin due to the "indirect" terms of trade effect of uncertainty may remain significant. To capture this in a simple manner, let us say that μ and ν are two possible probability laws of $\{\mathbf{e}_i(\cdot)\}_{i\geq 1}$. Think of Nature conducting an experiment with two outcomes "H" and "T" with probabilities $(\theta, 1-\theta)$, $0 < \theta < 1$. Conditionally, given that "H" shows up, the sequence $\{\mathbf{e}_i(\cdot)_{i\geq 1}\}$ is independent and identically distributed with common distribution μ. On the other hand, conditionally given that "T" shows up, the sequence $\{\mathbf{e}_i(\cdot)\}_{i\geq 1}$ is independent and identically distributed with common distribution ν. Let $\pi_{1\mu}$ and $\pi_{1\nu}$ be the expected values of X_1 under μ and ν respectively. Similarly, let $\pi_{2\mu}$ and $\pi_{2\nu}$ be the expected values of Y_1 under μ and ν. It follows that $p_n(\cdot)$ converges to $p_0(\cdot)$ almost surely, where $p_0(\cdot) = \pi_{1\mu}/[\pi_{1\mu} + \pi_{2\mu}] = p_{0\mu}$ with probability θ and $p_0(\cdot) = \pi_{1\nu}/[\pi_{1\nu} + \pi_{2\nu}] = p_{0\nu}$ with probability $1-\theta$. We now have a precise characterization of the probabilities of ruin as n tends to infinity. To state it, write

$$\begin{aligned} J &= \{(u_1, u_2) \in R_+^2 : p_{0\mu}u_1 + (1 - p_{0\mu}u_2 \leq m_i(p_{0\mu})\}\,; \\ r_i(\mu) &= \int_J \mu(du_1, du_2)\,. \end{aligned} \tag{1.14}$$

Similarly, define $r_i(\nu)$ obtained on replacing μ by ν in (1.14).

Proposition 1.4. *Assume that $p_0e_{i1}(\omega) + (1 - p_0)e_{i2}(\omega)$ has a continuous distribution function under each distribution μ and ν of $\mathbf{e}_i = (e_{i1}, e_{i2})$.*

(a) Then, as the number of agents n goes to infinity, the probability of ruin of the i-th agent converges to $r_i(\mu)$, with probability θ, when "H" occurs and to $r_i(\nu)$, with probability $1-\theta$, when "T" occurs.

(b) The overall, or unconditional, probability of ruin converges to $\theta r_i(\mu) + (1 - \theta)r_i(\nu)$.

Here, the precise limit distribution is slightly more complicated, but the important distinction from the case of independence (or, "near independence") is that the limit depends not just on the individual uncertainties captured by the distributions μ and ν of an agent's endowments, but also on θ that retains an influence on the distribution of prices even with large n.

2 A general model

We shall now describe a more general model and show how the survival probability can be characterized in large Walrasian economies without explicit computation of equilibrium prices (i.e., without a formula like (1.6)).

2a Notation

There are ℓ commodities in the economies we consider. A vector $x = (x^{(i)})$ is *non negative* (written $x \geq 0$) if $x^{(i)} \geq 0$ for all i. We write $R_+^\ell = \{x \in R^\ell : x \geq 0\}$. Let R_{++} be the set of *strictly positive reals*, and call a vector $x = (x^{(i)})$ *strictly positive* (written $x >> 0$) if $x^{(i)} > 0$ for all i. We write $R_{++}^\ell = \{x \in R^\ell : x >> 0\}$. For any $x \in R^\ell$, define the norm $|x| = \sum_{i=1}^{\ell} |x^{(i)}|$. For any two vectors a, b we write $\langle a, b\rangle = \sum_{i=1}^{\ell} a^{(i)}b^{(i)}$. Furthermore, let

$$S = \{p : p \in R_{++}^\ell,\ |p| = 1\} \tag{2.1}$$

We interpret S as the set of all (normalized) prices. The closure of S is denoted by $\overline{S}$. Let $C(S)$ be the set of all real valued bounded continuous functions on S.

2b Characteristics of an agent

Let T be a (nonempty) compact subset of R_{++}^ℓ. The *endowment* of any agent is an element e of T. Let β be a positive number such that

$$\text{for all } x \in T, \quad |x| \leq \beta \tag{2.2}$$

Given a price vector $p \in S$, the *income* or *wealth* of an agent with endowment $e \in T$ is defined as:

$$w = \langle p, e\rangle \tag{2.3}$$

A function f defined on $S \times R_{++}$ with values in R_+^ℓ is a *demand function* if it satisfies

(a) f is continuous on $S \times R_{++}$;
(b) $\langle p, f(p, w)\rangle = w$ for all $p \in S$, $w \in R_{++}$;
(c) If $p_n \in S$, $w_n \in R_{++}$ are such that $p_n \to p \in \overline{S} - S$, $w_n \to w > 0$, then $|f(p_n, w_n)| \to \infty$.

An element m of $C(S)$ is called a *minimum expenditure function* if $m(p) > 0$ for all $p \in S$.

In a deterministic framework, an agent is specified formally by an element $a \equiv (f, m, e)$ of $D \times C(S) \times T$. Corresponding to a price vector $p \in S$, the *demand vector* of the agent $a \equiv (f, m, e)$ is computed as

$$\xi(a, p) = f(p, w) = f(p, \langle p, e\rangle) \tag{2.4}$$

where $w = \langle p, e\rangle$ is the wealth of a (see (2.3)). The excess demand vector of the agent a is given by

$$\zeta(a,p) = \xi(p,w) - e \tag{2.5}$$

observe that $\langle p, \zeta(a,p)\rangle = 0$. If an exchange economy $\mathscr{E}$ consists of n agents $a_1, \ldots a_n$, the total excess demand vector in $\mathscr{E}$ at $p \in S$ is

$$\zeta(p) \equiv \sum_{i=1}^{n} \zeta(a_i, p) \tag{2.6}$$

2c A random economy

We shall consider exchange economies in which the endowments of the agents are subject to random shocks. Thus, for an agent $a = (f, m, e)$ we keep the pair (f, m) fixed (deterministic) but view e as a random vector. Formally, let $(\Omega, \mathscr{F}, P)$ be a probability space where Ω is the set of all possible states of the environment, and $\mathbf{e}(\cdot)$ be a measurable map from Ω into (T, τ) where τ is the Borel σ-field of T. We shall indicate a *random agent* by $\alpha(\cdot) \equiv (f, m, \mathbf{e}(\cdot))$, again stressing that (f, m) does not change from one state of the environment ω to another state ω'. The *distribution* of $\mathbf{e}(\cdot)$ is the induced probability measure on $\mu = P\cdot\mathbf{e}^{-1}(\cdot)$ on τ (for any B in τ, $\mu(B) = P[\omega : \mathbf{e}(\omega) \in B]$).

The demand vector of a random agent $\alpha(\cdot) = (f, m, \mathbf{e}(\cdot))$ at a price $p \in S$ is given by

$$\xi(\alpha(\cdot), p) = f(p, \langle p, \mathbf{e}(\cdot)\rangle) \tag{2.7}$$

Its excess demand vector at $p \in S$ is simply

$$\zeta(\alpha(\cdot), p) = \xi(\alpha(\cdot), p) - \mathbf{e}(\cdot) \tag{2.8}$$

Consider a *random economy* $\mathscr{E}$ consisting of n random agents $\{\alpha_1(\cdot), \ldots \alpha_n(\cdot)\}$. The total excess demand vector corresponding to $p \in S$ in the state of the environment ω is given by

$$\zeta_{\mathscr{E}}(\omega, p) = \sum_{i=1}^{n} \zeta(\alpha_i(\omega), p) \tag{2.9}$$

A *random Walrasian price equilibrium* $p^*(\cdot)$ is a (measurable) mapping from $(\Omega, \mathscr{F}, P)$ into S such that for a.e.ω.,

$$\xi_{\mathscr{E}}(\omega, p^*(\omega)) = 0 \tag{2.10}$$

We say that the agent $\alpha(\cdot)$ *fails to survive* (or, is ruined) when the state of the environment is ω, and a random Walrasian equilibrium $p^*(\omega)$ prevails, if

$$\langle p^*(\omega), \mathbf{e}(\omega)\rangle \leq m(p^*(\omega))$$

Given a random Walrasian price equilibrium $p^*(\cdot)$ and an agent $\alpha(\cdot) = (f, m, \mathbf{e}(\cdot))$ consider the event $\mathfrak{R}$ defined by

$$\mathfrak{R}_n^\alpha = \{\omega \in \Omega : \langle p^*(\omega), \mathbf{e}(\omega))\rangle \leq m(p^*(\omega)\}$$

$\mathfrak{R}_n^\alpha$ is the set of all states in which the agent $\alpha(\cdot)$ fails to survive at a random Walrasian equilibrium $p^*(\cdot)$ (with n agents).

2d Large economies: Independent agents

We shall now explore the implications of increasing the size of the economy. First, in this section we examine the case in which there are different types of agents, and within each type the *random agents are stochastically independent.* We shall say that two random agents are of the same 'type' k if they have the same demand function f_k, the same minimum expenditure function m_k, and the same probability distribution μ_k of endowments (over τ). A sequence of economies $\mathscr{E}_n$ is called *steadily expanding* if

(i) $\mathscr{E}_n$ consists of N_n random agents, of whom there are C_n^k independent agents of type $k (k \geq 1)$.
(ii) $\mathscr{E}_n \subset \mathscr{E}_{n+1}$, and N_n goes to infinity as n tends to infinity;
(iii) there is a countable set $\mathscr{M} = \{\mu_k, k = 1, 2, \ldots\}$ of probability measures on τ such that the distribution of (endowments of) each agent in each economy is in $\mathscr{M}$, and the fractions C_n^k / N_n of agents in $\mathscr{E}_n$ of type k (with distribution μ_k) converges to c_k as $n \to \infty$ with $\sum_{k=1}^{\infty} c_k = 1$.

Remarks 2.1. The definition of a 'steadily expanding' sequence of economies $\mathscr{E}_n (n \geq 1)$ given here differs with that given in Bhattacharya and Majumdar (1973), p. 41, in one aspect. Unlike the latter, in this article we do not assume independence among groups of agents belonging to different types.

2.2. Observe that we can choose $\mathscr{M}$ to be a (countable) set that is a dense (in the weak topology) subset of the set of all probability measures on τ.

Write $\mu = \sum_{k=1}^{\infty} c_k \mu_k$, and call μ the *asymptotic distribution* of the sequence $\mathscr{E}_n$. As explained in Hildenbrand (1974), this asymptotic distribution μ can also be interpreted as a deterministic pure exchange economy. Let $\zeta_k(a, p)$ be the excess demand of an agent $a \equiv (f_k, e)$ at $p \in S$. Define

$$W(\mu) = \left\{ p \in S : \sum_{k=1}^{\infty} c_k \int_T \zeta_k(a, p) d\mu_k = 0 \right\}.$$

We shall now make a uniqueness assumption that is admittedly restrictive, but leads to a sharp result

U.1. *$W(\mu)$ has a single element p.*

We can now state the following:

Proposition 2.1. *Let $\mathscr{E}_n$ be a strictly expanding sequence of economies. Assume that the asymptotic distribution μ of $\mathscr{E}_n$ satisfies U.1. Then every sequence $p_n^*(\cdot)$ of random price equilibria for $\mathscr{E}_n$ converges to p almost surely.*

Proof. Let $\nu_{n,k}(\omega)$ denote the empirical distribution of (the endowments of) agents of type k in $\mathscr{E}_n$. That is, $\nu_{n,k}(\omega)$ assigns a mass $1/C_n^k$ to each of the C_n^k endowments of the agents of type k. By the assumption of stochastic independence among these agents, the sequence $\nu_{n,k}(\omega)$ converges weakly to μ_k as

$n \to \infty$, for every ω outside a set M_k of probability zero (see, e.g., Parthasarathy 1967, p. 52). Let $M = \cup_{k=1}^{\infty} M_k$. Then M has probability zero. Let $\nu_n(\omega)$ denote the empirical distribution of (the endowments of) agents in M_n, assigning a mass $1/M_n$ to each of the M_n values. We will show that for every $\omega \notin M$, $\nu_n(\omega)$ converges weakly to μ. For this, fix $\omega \notin M$. Let f be an arbitrary bounded continuous function on R_{++}^{ℓ}. Then

$$\nu_n(\omega) = \sum_{k=1}^{\infty} (C_n^k / N_n) \nu_{n,k}(\omega),$$

and

$$\begin{aligned}
&\left| \int f(e) d\nu_n(\omega)(e) - \int f(e) d\mu(e) \right| \\
&= \left| \sum_{k=1}^{\infty} \left(\frac{C_n^k}{N_n} - c_k \right) \int f(e) d\nu_{n,k}(\omega)(e) \right. \\
&\quad \left. + \sum_{k=1}^{\infty} c_k \left(\int f(e) d\nu_{n,k}(\omega)(e) - \int f(e) d\mu_k(e) \right) \right| \\
&\le \sum_{k=1}^{\infty} \left| \frac{C_n^k}{N_n} - c_k \right| \|f\|_\infty \\
&\quad + \sum_{k=1}^{\infty} c_k \left| \int f(e) d\nu_{n,k}(\omega) - \int f(e) d\mu_k(e) \right|
\end{aligned} \tag{2.11}$$

where $\|f\|_\infty := \sup\{|f(e)| : e \in R_{++}^{\ell}\}$. By Scheffe's Theorem (see, e.g., Billingsley 1968, p. 224), $\Sigma |C_n^k / N_n - c_k| \to 0$ as $n \to \infty$. Also, by Lebesgue's Dominated Convergence Theorem, the second sum on the right of the inequality above goes to zero, since each term $\int f(e) d\nu_{n,k}(\omega)(e) - \int f(e) d\mu_k(e) (k = 1, 2, \ldots)$ is bounded by $2\|f\|_\infty$ and goes to zero as $n \to \infty$.

Let $p_n^*(\omega) \in W(\nu_n(\omega))$, be a measurable selection of Walras equilibrium of the economy $\mathscr{E}_n$. Then $p_n^*(\omega) \to p$ as $n \to \infty$, for every $\omega \notin M$, by a well-known continuity property of Walrasian equilibrium correspondence according to which "$\nu_n(\omega) \to \mu$ weakly" implies "the limit points of $p_n^*(\omega)$ are in $W(\mu)$" (see Hildenbrand 1974). By U.1, $p_n(\omega) \to p$, for every $\omega \notin M$. Q.E.D.

As a consequence of Proposition 2.1 we derive, as in the proof of Proposition 1.2.

Proposition 2.2. *Assume the hypothesis of Proposition 2.1. For an agent of type k in $\mathscr{E}_n$, with random endowment $\mathbf{e}(\cdot)$, let $\mathfrak{R}_n$ denote 'ruin', i.e., $\mathfrak{R}_n := \{\omega : \langle p_n^*(\omega), \mathbf{e}(\omega)\rangle \le m_k(p_n^*(\omega)\}$ where $p_n^*(\omega) \in W(\nu_n(\omega))$ is measurable. Assume that $\langle p, \mathbf{e}(\cdot)\rangle$ has a continuous distribution function when $\mathbf{e}(\cdot)$ has distribution μ_k. Then, if $J_1 = \{e \in T : \langle p, e\rangle \le m_k(p)\}$,*

$$\lim_{n\to\infty} P(\mathfrak{R}_n) = \int_{J_1} \mu_k(de) \tag{2.12}$$

Proof. Since $p_n(\cdot)\langle, \mathbf{e}(\cdot)\rangle$ converges almost everywhere to $\langle p, \mathbf{e}(\cdot)\rangle$, the convergence is also in distribution. Hence $P(\langle p_n(\cdot), \mathbf{e}(\cdot)\rangle \leq mkp_n^*(\cdot)) \to P(\langle p, \mathbf{e}(\cdot)\rangle \leq m_k(p))$, since $m_k(p)$ is a point of continuity of the distribution function of $\langle p, \mathbf{e}(\cdot)\rangle$, by assumption. The right side of (2.12) is just this last probability, since $\mathbf{e}(\cdot)$ has distribution μ_k. Q.E.D.

2e Dependence in the general model: Exchangeability

As in Sect. 2d consider a sequence of economies $\mathscr{E}_n$, $\mathscr{E}_n \subset \mathscr{E}_{n+1}$, such that there are C_n^k agents of type k in $\mathscr{E}_n(k = 1, 2, \ldots)$, $\sum_{k=1}^{\infty} C_n^k = N_n \to \infty$ as $n \to \infty$. The C_n^k type k agents have the same nonrandom demand function f_k and nonrandom minimum expenditure function $m_k (k \geq 1)$. But the endowments $\mathbf{e}_k^{(j)}(\cdot)$, $j \geq 1$, of these agents are not independent, but rather *symmetrically dependent*, or *exchangeable*. That is, their joint distribution is unchanged under permutations. By a well known characterization due to De Finetti (see, e.g., Hewitt and Savage 1955) this means that, conditionally given a random 'parameter' ω', the $\mathbf{e}_k^{(j)}(\cdot)(j \geq 1)$ are i.i.d. with a common distribution $\mu_k^{\omega'}$, say $(k = 1, 2, \ldots)$. Note that, as in the case of Sect. 2d, *no restriction is imposed on the nature of dependence among different types*. Assume, as in 2d, $C_n^k/N_n \to c_k$ as $n \to \infty$ $(k \geq 1)$, where $\sum_{k=1}^{\infty} c_K = 1$. Define

$$\mu^{\omega'} := \sum_{k=1}^{\infty} c_k \mu_k^{\omega'}, \tag{2.13}$$

and assume that the support of $\mu^{\omega'}$ is contained in a compact subset $T \subset R_{++}^{\ell}$, for all ω' outside a set M_1 of probability zero. Finally assume

U.2. *$W(\mu^{\omega'})$ is a singleton $\{p^{\omega'}\}$ for $\omega' \notin M_1$.*

Proceeding as in the proof of Proposition 2.1, *but conditionally given ω'*, we arrive at the following result concerning market clearing prices $p_n(\cdot) \in W(\nu_n(\cdot))(n \geq 1)$.

Proposition 2.3. *Under the above assumptions, outside a set of zero probability $p_n(\omega) \to p^{\omega'}$ as $n \to \infty$.*

From this one obtains an analog of Proposition 2.2. Note that the event $\mathfrak{R}_n$ of ruin of an agent of type k may be expressed in this case as

$$\mathfrak{R}_n = \{\omega \in \Omega : \langle p_n(\omega), \mathbf{e}(\omega)\rangle \leq m_k(p_n(\omega))\} \tag{2.14}$$

We will write, for an agent of type k,

$$J_2^{\omega'} = \{e \in T : \langle p^{\omega'}, e\rangle \leq m_k(p^{\omega'})\} \text{ and } r_k^{\omega'} := \int_{J_2^{\omega'}} \mu_k^{\omega'}(de) \tag{2.15}$$

Proposition 2.4. *In addition to the assumptions above, assume that the conditional distribution function of $\langle p, e(\cdot)\rangle$, given ω', is continuous for every $p \in S$. Then the conditional probability of ruin, given ω', of an agent of type k in the* *economy $\mathscr{E}_n$ converges to the random variable $r_k^{\omega'}$ in (2.15). The overall, or unconditional, probability of ruin, $P(\mathfrak{R}_n)$, converges to $E(r_k^{\omega'})$, as $n \to \infty$.*

Remark 2.3. Note that if $\mu_k^{\omega'}$ is absolutely continuous for every ω' outside a null set, then the assumption of continuity of the distribution function ($d.f$) in Proposition 2.4 is satisfied. However, the continuity of the $d.f.$ of $\langle p^{\omega'}, \mathbf{e}(\cdot)\rangle$ under $\mu_k^{\omega'}$ is only needed at the point $m_k(p^{\omega'})$. Without the assumption of such continuity, one can still derive appropriate inequalities (see Billingsley 1968, Theorem 2.1).

It is perhaps worth emphasizing that under the symmetric dependence assumption made in this section, a particular value ω' of the random parameter is realized. Therefore, the ruin probability of an agent of type k is really reflected by the random quantity $r_k^{\omega'}$ in a large economy at any particular instance. The expected value $E(r_K^{\omega'})$ is an idealized average over all parameter values, ω' that can arise. Of course, in the special case in which $\mu_k^{\omega'}$ ($k \geq 1$) do not depend on ω' (i.e., have degenerate distributions) one has the case of independence among members of type k, for every k. Thus Propositions 2.1, 2.2, are special cases of Propositions 2.3, 2.4, respectively.

3 Nonuniqueness of equilibrium

We consider now the implications on the ruin probability of dropping the uniqueness assumptions (U.1), (U.2) in our general model.

First consider the case of the steadily expanding sequence of economies $\mathscr{E}_n$. Under assumptions (i)–(iii) in Sect. 2d the empirical distribution $\nu_n(\omega)$ of endowments of agents in $\mathscr{E}_n$ converges weakly to μ, as $n \to \infty$, for all ω outside a null set M. Therefore, by the upper semicontinuity property (Hildenbrand 1974), if $p_n(\omega) \in W(\nu_n(\omega))$, $n \geq 1 (\omega \notin M)$, then all limit points of $\{p_n(\omega)\}_{n\geq 1}$ belong to $W(\mu)$. This implies that for every $\varepsilon > 0$

$$\eta_n(\varepsilon) := P(p_n(\cdot) \notin W^{\varepsilon}(\mu)) \to 0 \quad \text{as} \quad n \to \infty\,, \tag{3.1}$$

for every measurable selection $p_n(\cdot) \in W(\nu_n(\cdot))$, $n \geq 1$. Here $A^{\varepsilon} = \{p \in S : \|p - q\| < \varepsilon \text{ for some } q \in A\}$, $\|\|$ denoting Euclidean norm. For if this is not true then there exist $\varepsilon > 0$, $\delta > 0$, and a sequence $1 < n_1 < n_2 < \ldots$ such that $P(B_k) \geq \delta \forall k$, where $B_k = \{\omega : p_{n_k}(\omega) \notin W^{\varepsilon}(\mu)\}$. This implies $P(B) \geq \delta$ where $B = \{\omega : \omega \in B_k \text{ for infinitely many } k\} = \cap_{m=1}^{\infty} \cup_{k=m}^{\infty} B_k$. But for $\omega \in B$, the limit points of $p_{n_k}(\omega)$ do not belong to $W(\mu)$. This is a contradiction.

For an agent of type k, with endowment $\mathbf{e}(\cdot)$, the event $\mathfrak{R}_n$ of ruin satisfies

$$\begin{aligned} \mathfrak{R}_n &= \{\langle p_n(\cdot), \mathbf{e}(\cdot)\rangle - m_k(p_n(\cdot)) \leq 0\} \\ &\subset \left\{ \min_{p\in W(\mu)} (\langle p, \mathbf{e}(\cdot)\rangle - m_k(p)) \leq \delta(\varepsilon) \right\} \cup \{p_n(\cdot) \notin W^{\varepsilon}(\mu)\} \end{aligned} \tag{3.2}$$

where $\delta(\varepsilon) = \sup\{|(\langle q, e\rangle - m_k(q)) - (\langle p, e\rangle - m_k(p))| : p \in W(\mu), \|q - p\| < \varepsilon,\ e \in T\} \downarrow 0$ as $\varepsilon \downarrow 0$. It follows from (3.2) that

$$P(\mathfrak{R}_n) \leq P\left(\min_{p\in W(\mu)}(\langle p, \mathbf{e}(\cdot)\rangle - m_k(p)) \leq \delta(\varepsilon)\right) + \eta_n(\varepsilon) \tag{3.3}$$

Using (3.1) in (3.2) we get

$$\limsup_{n\to\infty} R(\mathfrak{R}_n) \leq P\left(\min_{p\in W(\mu)}(\langle p, \mathbf{e}(\cdot)\rangle - m_k(p)) \leq \delta(\varepsilon)\right),$$

and letting $\varepsilon \downarrow 0$ one has

$$\limsup_{n\to\infty} R(\mathfrak{R}_n) \leq P\left(\min_{p\in W(\mu)}(\langle p, \mathbf{e}(\cdot)\rangle - m_k(p)) \leq 0\right). \tag{3.4}$$

Similarly, one has

$$\left\{\max_{p\in W(\mu)}(\langle p, \mathbf{e}(\cdot)\rangle - m_k(p)) \leq -\delta(\varepsilon)\right\} \subset \mathfrak{R}_n \cup \{p_n(\cdot) \notin W^{\varepsilon}(\mu)\},$$

so that

$$P(\mathfrak{R}_n) + \eta_n(\varepsilon) \geq P\left(\max_{p\in W(\mu)}(\langle p, \mathbf{e}(\cdot)\rangle - m_k(p)) \leq -\delta(\varepsilon)\right) \tag{3.5}$$

Letting $n \to \infty$ one gets

$$\liminf_{n\to\infty} P(\mathfrak{R}_n) \geq P\left(\max_{p\in W(\mu)}(\langle p, \mathbf{e}(\cdot)\rangle - m_k(p)) \leq -\delta(\varepsilon)\right) \tag{3.6}$$

Letting $\varepsilon \downarrow 0$ in (3.6) one finally obtains

$$\liminf_{n\to\infty} P(\mathfrak{R}_n) \geq P\left(\max_{p\in W(\mu)}(\langle p, \mathbf{e}(\cdot)\rangle - m_k(p)) < o\right) \tag{3.7}$$

Thus we have arrived at

Proposition 3.1. *Under the assumptions (i)–(iii) for a steadily expanding sequence of economies, the probability of ruin of an agent of type k satisfies (3.4) and (3.7), with* $\mathbf{e}(\cdot)$ *having distribution* μ_k.

In exactly the same fashion, under symmetric dependence one obtains, by conditioning on the random parameter ω', the following result.

Proposition 3.2. *Assume symmetric dependence for an expanding sequence of economies as in Sect. 2e, but without requiring (U.2). (a) Then the conditional probability of ruin of an agent of type k, given* ω'*, satisfies for all* ω' *outside a null set the following relations:*

$$\limsup_{n\to\infty} P(\mathfrak{R}_n|\omega') \leq P\left(\min_{p\in W(\mu^{\omega'})}(\langle p, \mathbf{e}(\cdot)\rangle - m_k(p)) < 0|\omega'\right) \tag{3.8}$$

$$\liminf_{n\to\infty} P(\mathfrak{R}_n|\omega') \geq P\left(\max_{p\in W(\mu^{\omega'})}(\langle p, \mathbf{e}(\cdot)\rangle - m_k(p)) < 0|\omega'\right) \tag{3.9}$$

Here the probabilities on the right are to be computed using the conditional distribution $\mu_k^{\omega'}$ *of* $\mathbf{e}(\cdot)$ *given* ω'.

(b) The overall, or unconditional, probability of ruin satisfies

$$\limsup_{n\to\infty} P(\mathfrak{R}_n) \leq E\left[P\left(\min_{p\in W(\mu^{\omega'})}(\langle p, \mathbf{e}(\cdot)\rangle - m_k(p)) < 0|\omega'\right)\right], \quad (3.10)$$

$$\liminf_{n\to\infty} P(\mathfrak{R}_n) \geq E\left[P\left(\max_{p\in W(\mu^{\omega'})}(\langle p, \mathbf{e}(\cdot)\rangle - m_k(p)) < 0|\omega'\right)\right]. \quad (3.11)$$

Proof. (a) Let $\eta_n^{\omega'}(\varepsilon)$ denote the conditional probability of $\{p_n(\cdot) \notin W^{\varepsilon}(\mu^{\omega'})\}$, given ω'. For every ω' outside a null set N_1, this conditional probability goes to zero. One may similarly obtain an analog of (3.2), with μ replaced by $\mu^{\omega'}$ and $\delta^{\omega'}(\varepsilon)$ on the right side of (3.2). In this way one arrives at

$$P(\mathfrak{R}_n|\omega') \leq P\left(\min_{p\in W(\mu^{\omega'})}(\langle p, \mathbf{e}(\cdot)\rangle - m_k(p)) \leq \delta^{\omega'}(\varepsilon)|\omega'\right) + \eta_n^{\omega'}(\varepsilon). \quad (3.12)$$

From this (3.8) follows. Similarly, one obtains (an analog of (3.5))

$$P(\mathfrak{R}_n|\omega') + \eta_n^{\omega'}(\varepsilon) \geq P\left(\max_{p\in W(\mu^{\omega'})}(\langle p, \mathbf{e}(\cdot)\rangle - m_k(p)) \leq -\delta^{\omega'}(\varepsilon)|\omega'\right). \quad (3.13)$$

(b) Relations (3.10), (3.11) follow on applying Fatou's Lemma to the left sides of (3.8), (3.9), respectively. Q.E.D.

Note that Propositions 2.2, 2.4 are immediate consequences of Propositions 3.2 and 3.3, respectively.

It may be pointed out that Propositions 3.1, 3.2 provide asymptotic lower and upper bounds to the ruin probability of an agent.

4 An analysis of the survival probability in the Cobb-Douglas-Sen economy

We now turn to the question of obvious practical importance: "how does one improve the chance of survival of an agent"? Here, we report on some computations in the context of a special example. It is our hope that the insights gained from explicit computations will lead to more general results.

We return to the Cobb-Douglas-Sen economy of Sect. 1 and focus on a single agent i. Our basic assumptions on the endowments of agents are the same as in Proposition 1.1 and 1.3 (see Remark 1.4). In particular, these imply the existence of limiting averages of the endowments of all agents in the economy. To simplify notation we drop the subscript i. Our computation is based on the assumption that the minimum expenditure function $m(p)$ is linear (in prices), i.e.,

$$m(p) = a_1 p + (1-p)a_2 \quad (a_i > 0,\ i = 1, 2) \quad (4.1)$$

We point out that in Example 1.1, this is indeed the case. The right side of the equality in (1.13) provides us with the asymptotic or limiting probability of ruin. We shall refer to

$$P\{\omega : p_0\mathbf{e}_1(\omega) + (1-p_0)e_2(\omega) > m(p_0)\} \tag{4.2}$$

as the *asymptotic probability of survival* of the agent, and sometimes drop the term ‘asymptotic’ in the subsequent paragraphs.

Let $\overline{e}_1$ and $\overline{e}_2$ denote the limiting averages over all agents of the endowments of commodities 1 and 2 respectively. Then from (1.12) we get:

$$p_0 = \gamma\overline{e}_2/[\gamma\overline{e}_2 + (1-\gamma)\overline{e}_1] \tag{4.3}$$

From (4.1)–(4.3), the asymptotic probability of survival is given by

$$\begin{aligned} &P\{\omega : p_0e_1(\cdot) + (1-p_0)e_2(\cdot) > a_1p_0 + (1-p_0)a_2\} \\ &= P\left\{\omega : e_1(\cdot) - a_1 > \left(\frac{1-p_0}{p_0}\right)(a_2 - e_2(\cdot)\right\} \\ &= P\left\{\omega : \frac{e_1(\cdot) - a_1}{\overline{e}_1} > \left(\frac{(1-\gamma)\overline{e}_1}{\gamma\overline{e}_2}\right)(a_2 - e_2(\cdot))\right\} \\ &= P\left\{\omega : \frac{e_1(\cdot) - a_1}{\overline{e}_1} > \left(\frac{1-\gamma}{\gamma}\right)\left[\frac{a_2 - e_2(\cdot)}{\overline{e}_2}\right]\right\} \\ &= P\left\{\omega : \frac{e_1(\cdot)}{\overline{e}_1} + \left(\frac{1-\gamma}{\gamma}\right)\frac{e_2(\cdot)}{\overline{e}_2} > \frac{a_1}{\overline{e}_1} + \left(\frac{1-\gamma}{\gamma}\right)\frac{a_2}{\overline{e}_2}\right\} \end{aligned} \tag{4.4}$$

To state Proposition 4.1, we recall that (σ_1, σ_2) are said to be *scale parameters* for the joint distribution of $(e_1(\cdot), e_2(\cdot))$ if the distribution of $\frac{e_1(\cdot)}{\sigma_1}, \frac{e_2(\cdot)}{\sigma_2})$ does not depend on $(\sigma_1, \sigma_2) \in (0, \infty)^2$. From (4.4) we can derive the following:

Proposition 4.1. *Assume that* $\overline{e}_1 (i = 1, 2)$ *are scale parameters for the joint distribution of* $(e_1(\cdot), e_2(\cdot))$ *and that* $\frac{e_1(\cdot)}{\overline{e}_1} + (\frac{1-\gamma}{\gamma})\frac{e_2(\cdot)}{\overline{e}_2}$ *has a continuous distribution function* F. *Assume also that the asymptotic probability of survival is given by (4.2) (with* $m(p)$ *and* p_0 *as in (4.1) and (4.3)). Then*

(a) the asymptotic probability of survival is given by

$$\phi(\overline{e}_1, \overline{e}_2) = 1 - F(f(\overline{e}_1, \overline{e}_2)) \tag{4.5}$$

where

$$f(\overline{e}_1, \overline{e}_2) = \frac{a_1}{\overline{e}_1} + \left(\frac{1-\gamma}{\gamma}\right)\frac{a_2}{\overline{e}_2} \tag{4.6}$$

and $\phi(\overline{e}_1, \overline{e}_2)$ *is increasing in* $(\overline{e}_1, \overline{e}_2)$.

(b) $\phi(\overline{e}_1, \overline{e}_2) \to 1$ *if both* $\overline{e}_1$, $\overline{e}_2$ *go to infinity. If* $F(x) > 0$ *for all* $x > 0$, *then* $\phi(\overline{e}_1, \overline{e}_2) \to 1$ *if and only if both* $\overline{e}_1$, $\overline{e}_2$ *go to infinity.*

(c) If one of the parameters $\overline{e}_1$, $\overline{e}_2$ *goes to zero then the asymptotic probability of survival goes to zero irrespective of whether the other parameter remains bounded or goes to infinity.*

Proof.

(a) (4.5) is the same as (4.4). Also, $f(\overline{e}_1, \overline{e}_2)$ is a decreasing function of $(\overline{e}_1, \overline{e}_2)$.
(b) $\lim_{\overline{e}_1, \to \overline{e}_2 \to \infty} f(\overline{e}_1, \overline{e}_2) = 0$. Hence, due to the assumed continuity of F, $\lim_{\overline{e}_1, \to \infty \overline{e}_2 \to \infty} \phi(\overline{e}_1, \overline{e}_2) = 1 - F(0) = 1$. Conversely, if one of the $\overline{e}_i$'s, say $\overline{e}_2$ is bounded by $\delta_2 < \infty$, then $f(\overline{e}_1, \overline{e}_2) > (\frac{1-\gamma}{\gamma})\frac{a_2}{\delta} > 0$. Hence $\phi(\overline{e}_1, \overline{e}_2) < 1 - F(\frac{1-\gamma}{\gamma}) \cdot \frac{a_2}{\delta} < 1$.
(c) $f(\overline{e}_1, \overline{e}_2) > \frac{a_1}{\overline{e}_1} \to \infty$ as $\overline{e}_1 \to 0, f(\overline{e}_1, \overline{e}_2) > \frac{1-\gamma}{\gamma} \cdot \frac{a_2}{\overline{e}_2} \to \infty$ as $\overline{e}_2 \to 0$. Hence $1 - F(f(\overline{e}_1, \overline{e}_2)) \to 0$ in either case. Q.E.D.

It may be noted that if $g(x_1, x_2)$ is an arbitrary probability density function (p.d.f.) on $R_+^2 = [0, \infty)^2$, then

$$h(x_1, x_2; \sigma_1, \sigma_2) := \frac{1}{\sigma_1 \sigma_2} g\left(\frac{x_1}{\sigma_1}, \frac{x_2}{\sigma_2}\right), \; (\sigma_1 > 0, \sigma_2 > 0) \tag{4.7}$$

defines a one-parameter family of p.d.f.s, with σ_1, σ_2 as scale parameters.

To carry out an explicit computation, suppose that $e_1(\cdot)$ and $e_2(\cdot)$ are *independent exponential* random variables with means $\overline{e}_1, \overline{e}_2$, respectively.

From (4.5), (4.6) the survival probability may be expressed as

$$\phi(\overline{e}_1, \overline{e}_2) = P\left(\frac{e_1}{\overline{e}_1} > -\frac{1-\gamma}{\gamma}\frac{e_2}{\overline{e}_2} + f(\overline{e}_1, \overline{e}_2)\right) \tag{4.8}$$

If $(1-\gamma)e_2/\gamma\overline{e}_2 \geq f(\overline{e}_1, \overline{e}_2)$, then the conditional probability of the inequality within parentheses in (4.8), given e_2, is 1. Therefore,

$$\begin{aligned}
\phi(\overline{e}_1, \overline{e}_2) &= P\left(\frac{1-\gamma}{\gamma}\frac{e_2}{\overline{e}_2} \geq f(\overline{e}_1, \overline{e}_2)\right) \\
&\quad + P\left(\frac{e_1}{\overline{e}_1} > -\frac{1-\gamma}{\gamma}\frac{e_2}{\overline{e}_2} + f(\overline{e}_1, \overline{e}_2) \text{ and } \frac{1-\gamma}{\gamma}\frac{e_2}{\overline{e}_2} < f(\overline{e}_1, \overline{e}_2)\right) \\
&= \exp\left\{-\frac{\gamma}{1-\gamma} f(\overline{e}_1, \overline{e}_2)\right\} + \\
&\quad \int_0^{\frac{\gamma}{1-\gamma} f(\overline{e}_1, \overline{e}_2)} \exp\left\{\frac{1-\gamma}{\gamma} u - f(\overline{e}_1, \overline{e}_2)\right\} e^{-u} du \\
&= \exp\left\{-\frac{\gamma}{1-\gamma} f(\overline{e}_1, \overline{e}_2)\right\} + \exp\{-f(\overline{e}_1, \overline{e}_2)\} \times \\
&\quad \int_0^{\frac{\gamma}{1-\gamma} f(\overline{e}_1, \overline{e}_2)} \exp\left\{\frac{1-2\gamma}{\gamma} u\right\} du .
\end{aligned} \tag{4.9}$$

For $\gamma = \frac{1}{2}$, the last integral equals $\gamma f(\overline{e}_1, \overline{e}_2)/(1-\gamma) = f(\overline{e}_1, \overline{e}_2)$, so that

$$\begin{aligned}
\phi(\overline{e}_1, \overline{e}_2) &= \exp\{-f(\overline{e}_1, \overline{e}_2)[1 + f(\overline{e}_1, \overline{e}_2)] \\
&= \exp\left\{-\frac{a1}{\overline{e}1} - \frac{a_2}{\overline{e}_2}\right\}\left[1 + \frac{a1}{\overline{e}1} + \frac{a_2}{\overline{e}_2}\right], \quad \left(\gamma = \frac{1}{2}\right).
\end{aligned} \tag{4.10}$$

If $\gamma \neq \frac{1}{2}$, then the integral in (4.9) equals

$$\frac{\gamma}{1-2\gamma}\left[\exp\left\{\frac{1-2\gamma}{1-\gamma}f(\overline{e}_1,\overline{e}_2)\right\}-1\right]$$

so that

$$\begin{aligned}\phi(\overline{e}_1,\overline{e}_2) &= \exp\left\{-\frac{\gamma}{1-\gamma}f(\overline{e}_1,\overline{e}_2)\right\}+\frac{\gamma}{1-2\gamma}\\ &\quad\times\exp\left\{-\frac{\gamma}{1-\gamma}f(\overline{e}_1,\overline{e}_2)\right\}-\frac{\gamma}{1-2\gamma}\exp\{-f(\overline{e}_1,\overline{e}_2)\}\\ &= \frac{1-\gamma}{1-2\gamma}\exp\left\{-\frac{\gamma}{1-\gamma}f(\overline{e}_1,\overline{e}_2)\right\}\\ &\quad-\frac{\gamma}{1-2\gamma}\exp\{-f(\overline{e}_1,\overline{e}_2)\},\quad\left(\gamma\neq\frac{1}{2}\right).\end{aligned}\tag{4.11}$$

It is simple to check directly that in both cases (4.10), (4.11), the survival probability $\phi(\overline{e}_1,\overline{e}_2)$ is *strictly increasing* in $(\overline{e}_1,\overline{e}_2)$, approaches one as $\overline{e}_1\to\infty$ and $\overline{e}_2\to\infty$, and goes to zero if at least one of $\overline{e}_1$, $\overline{e}_2$ goes to zero.

Note that in this example one may take $Ee_i(\cdot)=\eta_i\overline{e}_i$ where η_i are arbitrary positive constants ($i=1,2$). In (4.10) one would then multiply the exponents by η_1 and η_2. A similar modification may be made for (4.11). The calculation of survival probability in this situation are completely analogous to those carried out for the case $\eta_i=1$, $i=1,2$.

Thus, we can explicitly study the implications of improving the means of the endowments $(\mathbf{e}_1(\cdot),\mathbf{e}_2(\cdot))$ for an agent. As we stated above, a thorough sensitivity analysis for the survival probability in a more general situation is left for future research.

References

Arrow, K.J. (1951) Alternative approaches to the theory of choice in risk-taking situations. *Econometrica* 19: 404–437

Bhattacharya, R.N., Majumdar, M. (1973) Random exchange economies. *Journal of Economic Theory* 6: 37–67

Billingsley, P. (1968) *Convergence of Probability Measures*. Wiley, New York

Coles, J.L., Hammond, P.J. (1995) Walrasian equilibrium without survival: Existence, efficiency and remedial policy. In: Basu, K. et al. (eds.) *Choice Welfare and Development*. Clarendon Press, Oxford, pp. 32–64

Ghose, A.K. (1989) Famine. In: Eatwell, J., Milgate, M., Newman, P. (eds.) *The New Palgrave: Economic Development*. Macmillan, London, pp. 122–129

Hewitt E., Savage, L. (1955) Symmetric measures on cartesian products. *Transactions of the American Mathematical Society* 80: 470–501

Hildenbrand, W. (1974) *Core and Equilibria of a Large Economy*. Princeton University Press, Princeton

Koopmans, T.C. (1957) *Three Essays on the State of Economic Science*. McGraw Hill, New York

Lamperti, J. (1966) *Probability*. Benjamin, New York

Majumdar, M., Mitra, T. (1983) Some results on the transfer problem in an exchange economy. In: Dutta, B. et al. (eds.) *Theoretical Issues in Development Economics*. Oxford University Press, New Delhi, pp. 221–244

Malinvaud, E. (1972) The allocation of individual risks in large markets. *Journal of Economic Theory* 4: 312–328

Newman, P. (1989) Consumption sets. In: *The New Palgrave: General Equilibrium* Eatwell, J., Milgate, M., Newman, P. (eds.) Macmillan, London, pp. 108–111

Parthasarathy, K. (1967) *Probability Measures on Metric Spaces.* Academic Press, New York

Radner, R. (1995) *Economic Survival.* Nancy L. Schwartz Memorial Lecture. J.L. Kellog School of Management, Northwestern University, Evanston

Sen, A. (1981) *Poverty and Famines.* Clarendon Press, Oxford

Uniqueness of Arrow-Debreu and Arrow-Radner equilibrium when utilities are additively separable

Rose-Anne Dana

Ceremade, Université Paris IX - Dauphine, Place du maréchal De Lattre de Tassigny, 75775 Paris, France (e-mail: dana@ceremade.dauphine.fr)

Abstract. This survey paper has three purposes: We first present in finite dimension, different approaches to the problem of uniqueness of Arrow-Debreu equilibrium when agents have additively separable utilities. We then study how, in the specific framework of a two period contingent good economy the results obtained generalize to infinite dimension. We consider economies where agents' consumption space is $L^p_+(\mu)$ $1 \leq p \leq \infty$ and agents' utilities are additively separable. Lastly, we show that in some restricted settings, some results may be used to prove uniqueness of Arrow-Radner equilibria when there are incomplete financial markets.

1 Introduction

When there is a finite number of states of the world, it is well known that if agents' utilities are von-Neumann Morgenstern and their relative risk aversion cœfficients are smaller than one, then their demands for contingent goods are gross substitute and therefore Arrow-Debreu equilibrium is unique. It is also known, that if agents' relative risk aversion cœfficients are smaller than four, then demands with fixed income are "monotone"(or obey the law of demand) and therefore Arrow-Debreu equilibrium is unique whenever agents have collinear endowments (see Milleron 1974; Mitjushin-Polterovich 1978; or Mas-Colell 1991). The purpose of this survey paper is triple: We first present in finite dimension, different approaches to the problem of uniqueness of Arrow-Debreu equilibrium when agents have additively separable utilities. Then, in the specific framework of a two period contingent good economy, we study how the results obtained generalize to infinite dimension (we consider economies where agents' consumption space is $L^p_+(\mu)$ $1 \leq p \leq \infty$ and agents' utilities are additively separable). Lastly, we show that in some restricted settings, some results may be used to prove uniqueness of Arrow-Radner equilibria when there are incomplete financial markets. As a special case, we obtain sufficient conditions for uniqueness of Arrow-Debreu equilibrium and Arrow-Radner equilibrium when agents have either the same probabilities over future states of the world or different probabilities with same sets of measure zero and von-Neumann Morgenstern utilities. Although we only consider two dates economies here, the results presented in infinite dimension can trivially be extended to continuous time economies with complete financial markets.

The paper is organised in a symmetrical way: part one is devoted to the finite dimension and part two to the infinite dimension and we have tried to use the same type of proof in both cases. Some methods of proofs are borrowed from the continuous time literature on optimal consumption and investment (see Karatzas and Shreve (1998)). In part one, after having recalled sufficient conditions to obtain gross substitution of aggregate demand and that one could then give an easy existence proof of equilibrium without using a fixed point theorem, we show that one can fruitfully work in the space of utility weights. As Mas-Colell (1985), we introduce the "excess-utility map" and show the symmetry between the demand approach and the excess-utility approach: the excess-utility is gross substitute under the same conditions that aggregate demand is gross substitute. Then, bearing in mind an application to incomplete financial markets, we reconsider the problem of "monotonicity" of aggregate demand and generalize Mitjushin-Polterovich's conditions to the case where agents consumption sets are closed convex cones.

As mentionned before, part two deals with infinite dimension. As prices for which aggregate demand exists may not be characterized, the demand approach may not easily be followed to obtain existence results. The space of utility weights and the Negishi map (or Negishi correspondence) have therefore been extensively used to prove existence of equilibrium (see Mas-Colell Zame (1991)) and determinacy of equilibria (see Kehoe-Levine (1985)). We go one step further. We show that, if agent' relative risk aversion cœfficients are smaller than one, then the excess utility map is gross substitute. Uniqueness of equilibrium follows as well as existence ,without using a fixed point theorem. We also show that one can generalize the concept of gross substitution of demand to the infinite dimension and that sufficient conditions for gross substitution of demand and uniqueness of equilibrium may be given. We further show that Mitjushin-Poltrovich's conditions for monotonicty of demand generalize to $L^p_+(\mu)$. Finally, we end the paper with an example of unique Arrow-Radner equilibrium with incomplete markets in infinite dimension.

2 Additively separable utilities in finite dimension

2.1 Notation

Let $x = ((x^1, \ldots, x^k) \in \mathbb{R}^k$. $x \geq 0$ means that $x^j \geq 0,\ \forall\, j,\ \ x > 0$ means $x \geq 0,\ x \neq 0,$ and $x \gg 0$ means $x^j > 0,\ \forall\, j.$ $\mathbb{R}^k_+$ is the positive cone of $\mathbb{R}^k$ while $\mathbb{R}^k_{++}$ is its interior.

Let $(U^j)_{j=1}^k, U^j : \mathbb{R}_+ \to \mathbb{R}$ be k strictly increasing, strictly concave, C^2 functions and let

$$u(x^1, \ldots, x^k) = \sum_{j=1}^{k} U^j(x^j).$$

We denote by ∇u and H_u the gradient and the hessian of u, by $U^{j'}$ (resp $U^{j''}$) the first (resp second) derivative of U^j. We assume furthermore that $U^{j'}(0) = \infty$ for $j = 1, \ldots, k$ and refer to these assumptions as Inada's conditions.

There are two important particular cases: the von-Neumann Morgenstern one good utility where $U^j(x^j) = \pi^j U(x^j)$, and π^j is the probability of state j, and the time-independent intertemporal additively separable one good utility where $U^j(x^j) = \delta^j U(x^j)$ and δ is the discount factor.

Let us define the cœfficients $\sigma^j(x) = -\dfrac{xU^{j''}(x)}{U^{j'}(x)}$, $x \in \mathbb{R}_+$. In the particular cases mentionned before, $\sigma^j(x)$ is independent of j and in the v.N.M. case is the Arrow-Pratt relative risk aversion cœfficient: $\sigma^j(x) = \sigma(x) = -\dfrac{xU''(x)}{U'(x)}$ $\forall x \in \mathbb{R}_+, j = 1, \ldots, k$.

Let $I^j :]U^{j'}(\infty), \infty[\to \mathbb{R}_+$ denote the inverse of the strictly decreasing map $U^{j'}$. The map I^j is continuous, strictly decreasing and fulfills the following boundary conditions: $I^j(\infty) = 0$ and $I^j(U^{j'}(\infty)) = \infty$. The following lemma will turn out to be very useful in the sequel.

Lemma 2.1

1) The following statements are equivalent:
   a) $\sigma^j(x) < 1, \forall x \geq 0$ (resp $\sigma^j(x) \leq 1$),
   b) the function $x \to U^{j'}(x)x$ is strictly increasing (resp nondecreasing),
   c) the function $x \to I^j(x)x$ is strictly decreasing (resp nonincreasing).

2) If $\sigma^j(x) \leq 1$, then for any $a > 0$, the function $x \to (x - a)U^{j'}(x)$ is strictly increasing.

Proof. The fact that 1.a) is equivalent to 1.b) is obvious. To prove that 1.b) is equivalent to 1.c) it suffices to remark that $(I^j(x)x)' = \dfrac{x}{U^{j''}(I^j(x))} + I^j(x) = \dfrac{[U^{j''}(I^j(x))I^j(x) + x]}{U^{j''}(I^j(x))}$. □

2.2 Individual demand

Consider an agent with additively separable utility, wealth $w \in \mathbb{R}_+$ (resp endowment $\varepsilon \in \mathbb{R}^k_+$). Let $p \in \mathbb{R}^k_{++}$ be given. Let $f(p, w)$ (resp $f(p, p \cdot \varepsilon)$) denote his demand, optimal solution to the problem

$$\max \sum_{j=1}^{k} U^j(x^j),$$
$$\sum_{j=1}^{k} p^j x^j = w \qquad\qquad (\text{ resp } p \cdot \varepsilon)$$
$$x^j \geq 0, \ \forall j = 1, ..., k.$$

Since $U^{j'}(0) = \infty$ for every $j = 1, \ldots, k$, there exists a unique multiplier $\lambda(p, w) > 0$ such that

$$\lambda(p, w) U^{j'}(x^j) = p^j \qquad j = 1, \ldots, k \tag{1}$$

Let us recall a pair of definitions:

Definitions. A map $h : \mathbb{R}^h_{++} \to \mathbb{R}^l_{++}$ is strictly isotone if $x > x'$ implies $h(x) \gg h(x')$.
A map $h : \mathbb{R}^k_{++} \to \mathbb{R}^k_{++}$ is strictly gross substitute (S.G.S.) if for every $(i,j), i \neq j, h^j$ is strictly increasing in p^i.

Propositon 2.2.
1) *If $\sigma^j(x) < 1$, for every $j = 1, \ldots, k$, $\forall x \geq 0$, the function $\lambda(., w)$ is strictly isotone and the function $f(., w)$ is S.G.S.*
2) *If $\sigma^j(x) \leq 1$ and $\varepsilon^j > 0$ for every $j = 1, \ldots, k$,, the function $p \to \lambda(p, p \cdot \varepsilon)$ is strictly isotone and $p \to f(p, p \cdot \varepsilon)$ is strictly S.G.S.*

Proof. We now on write λ instead of $\lambda(p, w)$. The f.o.c. (1) and the budget equation can equivalently be written

$$x^j = I^j(\frac{p^j}{\lambda}) \quad j = 1, \ldots, k, \tag{1'}$$

$$\sum_{j=1}^{k} p^j I^j(\frac{p^j}{\lambda}) = w. \tag{2}$$

As the function $\lambda \to \sum_{j=1}^{k} p^j I^j(\frac{p^j}{\lambda})$ is defined on $]\max_j \frac{p^j}{U^{j'}(\infty)}, \infty[$ to $]0, \infty[$ and is continuous and strictly increasing, for a given p, (2) has a unique solution which is a continuous function of p. By Lemma 2.1., if $\sigma^j(x) < 1$, the function $x \to I^j(x)x$ is strictly decreasing, hence λ is strictly increasing in p^j which proves that the function $\lambda(., w)$ is strictly isotone. It follows from (1') that x^j is a strictly increasing function of λ, hence x^j is a strictly increasing function of $p^i, i \neq j$.
It follows from Lemma 2.1 that a similar proof may be given for $\lambda(p, p \cdot \varepsilon)$ and $f(p, p \cdot \varepsilon)$. □

Definition. A map $f : \mathbb{R}^k_{++} \to \mathbb{R}^k_{++}$ is monotone (resp strictly monotone) if

$[f(p) - f(p')] \cdot [p - p'] \leq 0, \quad \forall (p, p') \in (\mathbb{R}^k_{++})^2 \quad (\text{ resp } < 0, \text{ if } f(p) \neq f(p'))$

A correspondence $\Gamma : \mathbb{R}^k_{++} \to \mathbb{R}^k_{++}$ is monotone (resp strictly monotone) if

$$[y - y'] \cdot [p - p'] \leq 0, \quad \forall (y, y') \in \Gamma(p) \times \Gamma(p'), \ (p, p') \in (\mathbb{R}^k_{++})^2$$
$$(\text{ resp } < 0, \text{ if } \Gamma(p) \neq \Gamma(p'))$$

Milleron (1974) and Mitjushin-Polterovich (1978) gave a necessary and sufficient condition (resp sufficient condition) on a utility function so that the associated demand with fixed income be monotone (resp strictly monotone). The following result is a particular case in that utility is assumed to be additively separable. Agent's consumption space is assumed to be a closed convex cone $C \subseteq \mathbb{R}^k_+$.

Proposition 2.3. *Let C be a closed convex cone of $\mathbb{R}^k_+$ Let $f(p, w)$ denote the optimal solution to the problem*

$$\begin{array}{l} \max \sum_{j=1}^{k} U^j(x^j) \\ p \cdot x \leq w \\ x \in C \end{array}$$

. If $\sigma^j(x) < 4$ for every $j = 1, \ldots, k$ (resp $\sigma^j(x) \leq 4$, $j = 1, \ldots, k$), then for any w, $f(., w)$ is strictly monotone :

$$[f(p, w) - f(p', w)] \cdot [p - p'] < 0, \quad \forall (p, p') \in (\mathbb{R}^k_{++})^2$$
$$\text{such that } f(p, w) \neq f(p', w)$$

and $f(p, p \cdot \varepsilon)$ is strictly monotone for every (p, p'), $p \neq p'$ such that $p \cdot \varepsilon = p' \cdot \varepsilon$

Proof. Since demand exists, it follows from f.o.c. that there exists $\lambda > 0$ and $\nu \in N_C(f(p, w))$, the normal cone to C at $f(p, w)$, such that

$$\nabla u(f(p, w)) = \lambda p + \nu. \tag{3}$$

Since C is a cone, $\nu \cdot f(p, w) = 0$, hence $\nabla u(f(p, w)) \cdot f(p, w) = \lambda p \cdot f(p, w)) = \lambda w$. Therefore eliminating λ and using (3), we get

$$p = \frac{w(\nabla u(f(p, w)) - \nu)}{\nabla u(f(p, w)) \cdot f(p, w)} \tag{4}$$

Let us show that the correspondence $\dfrac{(\nabla u(x) - N_C(x))}{\nabla u(x) \cdot x}$ is strictly monotone.

Since $\sigma^j(x) < 4, \forall\, j = 1, \ldots, k$ is equivalent to $-\dfrac{< H_u(x)x, x >}{\nabla u(x) \cdot x} < 4,$, it follows from Mitjushin-Polterovich's proof (see for example Mas-Colell (1991)) that

$$\left[\frac{\nabla u(x)}{\nabla u(x) \cdot x} - \frac{\nabla u(y)}{\nabla u(y) \cdot y} \right] \cdot \left[x - y \right] < 0, \quad \forall (x, y) \in C^2.$$

Moreover if $\nu(x) \in N_C(x)$ and $\nu(y) \in N_C(y)$, $\left[\frac{\nu(x)}{\nabla u(x) \cdot x}\right] \cdot \left[y - x\right] \leq 0$ and $\left[\frac{\nu(y)}{\nabla u(y) \cdot y}\right] \cdot \left[x - y\right] \leq 0$, $\forall y \in C$, hence the correspondence $\frac{(\nabla u(x) - N_C(x))}{\nabla u(x) \cdot x}$ is strictly monotone. Setting $x = f(p, w)$, we obtain strict monotony of demand. □

2.3 Aggregate excess demand

Let us now consider a pure exchange economy E with n agents described by the list:
$E = \left(\mathbb{R}^k_+, u_i : \mathbb{R}^k_+ \to \mathbb{R},\ \varepsilon_i \in \mathbb{R}^k_+, i = 1, \ldots, n\right)$ where $\varepsilon_i \gg 0$, and $u_i(x_i) = \sum_{j=1}^{k} U_i^j(x_i^j)$ with U_i fullfilling the hypotheses of paragraph 1.2. Let $I_i^j :]U_i^{j'}(\infty), \infty[\to \mathbb{R}_+$ denote the inverse of the strictly decreasing map $U_i^{j'}$.

Let $f_i(p, p \cdot \varepsilon_i)$ denote agent i's demand, $\varepsilon = \sum_{i=1}^{n} \varepsilon_i$ aggregate endowment and $F(p) = \sum_{i=1}^{n} f_i(p, p \cdot \varepsilon_i) - \varepsilon$ aggregate excess demand. The following results are easily obtained by aggregation:

Proposition 2.4.
1) If $\sigma_i^j(x) \leq 1$ for every $i = 1, \ldots, n,\ \ j = 1, \ldots, k$ and $x \geq 0$, $F(p)$ is S.G.S.,
2) If agents' consumption space is a closed convex cone $C \subseteq \mathbb{R}^k_+$ and $\varepsilon_i = \beta_i \varepsilon$, $\forall i = 1, \ldots, n$ with $1 = \sum_{i=1}^{n} \beta_i$ and $\sigma_i^j(x) < 4$ for every $i = 1, \ldots, n,\ \ j = 1, \ldots, k$ and $x \geq 0, F$ is strictly monotone, i.e.

$$[F(p) - F(p')] \cdot [p - p'] < 0$$

for normalised prices satisfying $p \cdot \varepsilon = 1, p' \cdot \varepsilon = 1,\ p \neq p'$.

2.4 Existence and uniqueness of Arrow-Debreu equilibrium

In this section, we recall two existence results of Arrow-Debreu Equilibrium which do not require the use of a fixed point theorem and three uniqueness results.

Proposition 2.5. *If $\sigma_i^j(x) \leq 1$ for every $i = 1, \ldots, n, j = 1, \ldots, k$ and $x \geq 0$, then there exists a unique equilibrium.*

Proof. The existence proof originally due to Greenberg (1977) is borrowed from Mas-Colell (1985) p.222. One shows the existence of an equilibrium without using a fixed point theorem as follows: Let Δ^k denote the non negative simplex of $\mathbb{R}^k$ and let $G(p) = \max_j F^j(p)$. As $G(p)$ is continuous in the relative interior of Δ^k and tends to infinity at the boundary, G has a minimum for some $p_0 \gg 0$. Assume that $G(p_0) > 0$. Then by Walras law, for some $i, F^i(p_0) < 0$. Assume $F^1(p_0) < 0$. If p^1 decreases, $\max_j F^j(p)$ decreases strictly by G.S., which leads to a contradiction with the definition of p_0. The proof of uniqueness is standard and is not recalled. □

Proposition 2.6. *Assume that agents' consumption space is a closed convex cone $C \subseteq \mathbb{R}^k_+$. If endowments are collinear and if $\sigma^j_i(x) < 4$ for every $i = 1, \dots, n, j = 1, \dots, k$ and $x \geq 0$, then there exists a unique equilibrium.*

The uniqueness result follows immediately from Proposition 2.4.

Proposition 2.7. *Let agents' consumption space be a closed convex cone $C \subseteq \mathbb{R}^k_+$ and $\varepsilon_i = \beta_i \varepsilon \quad \forall i = 1, \dots, n$ with $1 = \sum_{i=1}^{n} \beta_i$. If utilities are homogeneous, then there exists unique equilibrium consumptions.*

Proof. Assume utilities are homogeneous of degree t_i, for every $i = 1, \dots, n$. We shall prove that: $\left((x_i)_{i=1}^n, p\right)$ is an equilibrium iff $(x_i)_{i=1}^n$ is the optimal solution to the problem:

$$\max \sum_{i=1}^n \beta_i w_i(x_i) \quad \text{s.t.} \quad \sum_{i=1}^n x_i \leq \varepsilon, \quad x_i \in C, \ \forall i$$

where $w_i(x_i) = \frac{\log u_i(x_i)}{t_i}$ and $\beta_i \nabla w_i(x_i) - p \in N_C(x_i)$, for every $i = 1, \dots, n$.

Indeed for every $t > 0$, $w_i(tx_i) = w_i(x_i) + \log(t)$, hence $\nabla w_i(x_i) \cdot x_i = 1, \quad \forall x_i$. From the first order conditions, the problem:

$$\max \sum_{i=1}^n \beta_i w_i(x_i) \quad \text{s.t.} \quad \sum_{i=1}^{n} x_i \leq \varepsilon, \quad x_i \in C, \ \forall i$$

has a solution $(x_i)_{i=1}^n$ iff there exists $p \in \mathbb{R}^n_+$ and $\nu_i \in N_C(x_i)\ \forall i$, such that $\beta_i \nabla w_i(x_i) = p + \nu_i \quad \forall i$. Since C is a cone, $\forall i, \ \nu_i \cdot x_i = 0$, thus $p \cdot x_i = \beta_i$ and $p \cdot \varepsilon = 1$. Hence x_i is the optimal solution to the problem:

$$\max w_i(x_i) \quad \text{s.t.} \quad p \cdot x_i \leq p \cdot \varepsilon_i, \quad x_i \in C$$

and $((x_i)_{i=1}^n, p)$ is an equilibrium.

Conversely if $((x_i)_{i=1}^n, p)$ is an equilibrium, the f.o.c. imply that there exists $\forall i, \lambda_i \geq 0$ and $\nu_i \in N_C(x_i)$ such that $\nabla w_i(x_i) = \lambda_i p + \nu_i$. As $\nabla w_i(x_i) \cdot x_i = 1$ and $\nu_i \cdot x_i = 0, \lambda_i = \beta_i^{-1}$, hence $\beta_i \nabla w_i(x_i) = p + \nu_i$. Thus $(x_i)_{i=1}^n$ is the optimal solution to the problem:

$$\max \sum_{i=1}^n \beta_i w_i(x_i). \quad \text{s.t.} \quad \sum_{i=1}^n x_i \leq \varepsilon, \quad x_i \in C, \ \forall i$$

□

2.5 The weight approach

As shown extensively in Mas-Colell[1985], there is a function, in the space of utility weights, the excess utility map which has the same properties as an excess demand function. While Mas-Colell takes a differentiable point of view and use the result to obtain qualitative properties of equilibria, we only deal here with the topological properties of the excess utility map. This will turn out to be fruitful in infinite dimension. Let us recall the construction of the excess utility function.

Let $\lambda \in \mathbb{R}^n_+$. Let $x(\lambda) = (x_i^j(\lambda), \quad i = 1, \ldots, n,\ j = 1, \ldots, k)$ denote the P.O. associated with λ, as follows: It is the solution to the problem

$$\begin{aligned} \max \quad & \sum_{i=1}^{n} \sum_{j=1}^{k} \lambda_i U_i^j(x_i^j) \\ & \sum_{i=1}^{n} x_i^j = \varepsilon^j, \quad j = 1, \ldots, k \\ & x_i^j \geq 0, \forall\, i, j. \end{aligned}$$

Let aggregate utility for good j be $\bar{U}^j(x^j, \lambda) = \max \left\{ \sum_{i=1}^{n} \lambda_i U_i^j(x_i^j), x_i^j \geq 0, \sum_{i=1}^{n} x_i^j = x^j \right\}$ and aggregate utility be the additively separable function defined by: $\bar{U}(x, \lambda) = \sum_{j=1}^{k} \bar{U}^j(x^j, \lambda)$.

Under the boundary assumptions made, the functions $\bar{U}^j(., \lambda),\ j = 1, ..., k$ are differentiable and $\bar{U}^{j'}(\varepsilon^j, \lambda) = \lambda_i U_i^{j'}(x_i^j(\lambda))\ \forall i$ such that $\lambda_i > 0$. Thus $\bar{U}$ is differentiable and the P.O. associated to λ is supported by the price $\nabla \bar{U}(\varepsilon, \lambda)$.

Let us define the **excess utility** $e : \mathbb{R}^n_+ \to \mathbb{R}^n$ by $e_i(\lambda) = \frac{1}{\lambda_i}[\nabla \bar{U}(\varepsilon, \lambda) \cdot (x_i(\lambda) - \varepsilon_i)],\ \forall\, i = 1, ..., n$.

An equilibrium is a P.O. for which transfer payments are zero thus corresponds to a utility weight λ such that $e(\lambda) = 0$. Let us next recall the properties of e.

Proposition 2.8.

a) e is continuous in $\mathbb{R}^n_{++}$, homogeneous of degree 0, bounded above,

b) verifies Walras law, $\sum_{i=1}^{n} \lambda_i e_i(\lambda) = 0$,

c) if $\lambda_i \to 0$, then $e_i \to -\infty$,

d) if $\sigma_i^j(x) \leq 1$ for every $i = 1, \ldots, n, \quad j = 1, \ldots, k$ and $x \geq 0$, then e is strictly gross substitute: In other words $\forall (i \neq h)$, e_i is a strictly decreasing function of λ_h.

Proof. We shall only prove d). Let $\lambda >> 0$ be given and let $x(\lambda) = (x_i^j(\lambda) \quad i = 1, \ldots, n,\ j = 1, \ldots, k)$ denote the P.O. associated to λ. We have:

$$\begin{aligned} & \lambda_1 U_1^{j'}(x_1^j(\lambda)) = \ldots = \lambda_n U_n^{j'}(x_n^j(\lambda)) \text{ and} \\ & \sum_{i=1}^{n} x_i^j = \varepsilon^j \end{aligned}$$

Differentiating with respect to λ_h, $h \neq i$, we get

$$\frac{\partial x_i^j(\lambda)}{\partial \lambda_h} = \frac{U_h^{j'}(x_h^j(\lambda))}{\lambda_i \lambda_h U_h^{j''}(x_h^j(\lambda)) U_i^{j''}(x_i^j(\lambda)) \sum_{i=1}^n \frac{1}{\lambda_i U_i^{j''}(x_i^j(\lambda))}} \tag{5}$$

hence $\frac{\partial x_i^j(\lambda)}{\partial \lambda_h} < 0$. Since $\bar{U}^{j'}(\varepsilon^j, \lambda) = \lambda_i U_i^{j'}(x_i^j(\lambda))$,

$$e_i(\lambda) = \sum_{j=1}^k U_i^{j'}(x_i^j(\lambda))(x_i^j(\lambda) - \varepsilon_i^j), \; \forall\, i = 1, ..., n.$$

By Lemma 2.1, the functions $x \to U_i^{j'}(x)(x - \varepsilon_i^j)$ are strictly increasing for every j, hence $\forall (i \neq h)$, e_i is a strictly decreasing function of λ_h. □

Using the standard excess demand theory, it follows from a), b), c) that there exists an equilibrium. One may deduce from a), b), c), d) a proof of existence and uniqueness of equilibrium similar to that of Proposition 2.5 .

2.6 *Isotone fixed point theorems in equilibrium theory*

Isotone fixed point theorems (Banach-Tarski fixed point theorems) have not been used in equilibrium theory though they have been used in a large variety of other economic context. In the usual approach. equilibrium prices (resp weights) are fixed points of the map $F + Id$ (resp $e + Id$) which are not isotone. In this section, we show that equilibrium prices and equilibrium weights are indeed fixed points of strictly isotone maps.

Let us consider the equilibrium equations:

$$\lambda_i U_i^{j'}(x_i^j) = p^j, \quad i = 1, \ldots, n, \quad j = 1, \ldots, k, \text{ preference maximisation} \tag{6}$$

$$\frac{1}{\lambda_i} \sum_{j=1}^k p^j (x_i^j - \varepsilon_i^j) = 0, \quad i = 1, \ldots, n, \text{ budget constraint} \tag{7}$$

$$\sum_{i=1}^n x_i^j = \varepsilon^j \quad j = 1, \ldots, k \text{ attainability.} \tag{8}$$

Let us define $H : \mathbb{R}_{++}^n \to \mathbb{R}_{++}^k$, $G : \mathbb{R}_{++}^k \to \mathbb{R}_{++}^n$ by $H(\lambda) = \left[\nabla \bar{U}(\varepsilon, \lambda)\right]_{j=1}^k$ and $G(p) = \left[\lambda_i(p)\right]_{i=1}^n$ where $\lambda_i(p)$ is as in 2.1. The function $H(\lambda)$ is defined by the following implicit equations obtained by eliminating x between (6) and (8):

$$\sum_{i=1}^n I_i^j \left(\frac{H(\lambda)^j}{\lambda_i}\right) = \varepsilon^j \quad j = 1, \ldots, k. \tag{9}$$

while $G(p)$ is obtained by eliminating x between (6) and (7):

$$\sum_{j=1}^k p^j \left(I_i^j \left(\frac{p^j}{G_i(p)}\right) - \varepsilon_i^j\right) = 0 \quad i = 1, \ldots, n \tag{10}$$

Proposition 2.9.
a) H *is homogeneous of degree one and strictly isotone,*
b) G *is homogeneous of degree one and if* $\sigma_i^j(x) \leq 1$ *for every* $i = 1, \ldots, n, \quad j = 1, \ldots, k$ *and* $x \geq 0$, *then* G *is strictly isotone.*

Proof. a) Clearly $x(\lambda)$ the P.O. associated to λ, is homogeneous of degree zero, thus $\bar{U}^{j'}(\varepsilon^j, \lambda) = \lambda_i U_i^{j'}(x_i^j(\lambda)), \ \forall i$ such that $\lambda_i > 0$, is homogeneous of degree one. Furthermore, it follows from Proposition 2.8 that $\frac{\partial x_i^j(\lambda)}{\partial \lambda_h} < 0$, if $h \neq i$. Since $\bar{U}^{j'}(\varepsilon^j, \lambda) = \lambda_i U_i^{j'}(x_i^j(\lambda))$ and $U_i^{j'}$ is decreasing, H^j is a strictly increasing function of $\lambda_h, \ \forall\, h$ and therefore H is strictly isotone.
b) follows from the proof of Proposition 2.2.

Proposition 2.10.
a) p *is an equilibrium price iff* $H \circ G(p) = p$.
b) λ *is an equilibrium weight iff* $G \circ H(\lambda) = \lambda$,
c) If $\sigma_i^j(x) \leq 1$ *for every* $i = 1, \ldots, n, \quad j = 1, \ldots, k$, *and* $x \geq 0$, *then* $H \circ G$ *and* $G \circ H$ *have at most one fixed point.*

Proof. a) and b) follow from simple arguments. One shows that $H \circ G(p) = p$ holds iff (5), (6), (7) are fulfilled. To prove c) it suffices to remark that a strictly isotone homogeneous map of degree 1 map has a unique fixed point. Indeed suppose that there exists two non proportionnal fixed point p and $\tilde{p}$. By homogeneity, we can assume that $p \geq \tilde{p}$ and $p^k = \tilde{p}^k$. Since $H \circ G$ is strictly isotone, $H \circ G(p) = p > H \circ G(\tilde{p})$, a contradiction. □

2.7 Arrow Radner equilibria

We consider an exchange economy with n traders and two periods $t = 0, 1$. We assume here that at date $t = 0$, there is only trade in assets. At date one, there are $k < \infty$ states of the world and a single good available for consumption. Each agent is characterized by a couple (u_i, ε_i) where u_i satisfies the hypotheses of Sect. 2.1.

At date zero, there are d assets. Assets are specified by a matrix of returns A where a_j^s is the amount of the good to be delivred by asset j in state s. Without lost of generality, we assume A injective. When $\dim A = k$, markets are complete. Let $q \in \mathbb{R}^d$ denote a vector of assets prices.

Let us define the budget set af agent i:

$$B(q, \varepsilon_i) = \left\{ x_i \in \mathbb{R}_+^k, \ \exists \theta_i \in \mathbb{R}^d, \text{ s.t.} q \cdot \theta_i \leq 0 \text{ and } x_i = \varepsilon_i + A\theta_i \right\}.$$

Definition. An Arrow Radner Equilibrium is a triple $(\bar{x}, \bar{\theta}, \bar{q}) \in (\mathbb{R}_+^k)^n \times (\mathbb{R}^d)^n \times \mathbb{R}^d$, where $\bar{x} = (\bar{x}_1, \bar{x}_2 \ldots, \bar{x}_n)$ and
(i) $\bar{x}_i = \arg\max u_i(x_i)$,
$x_i \in B(\bar{q}, \varepsilon_i)$
(ii) $\sum_{i=1}^n \bar{\theta}_i = 0$

Definition. An allocation $x \in (\mathbb{R}^k_+)^n$ is A-feasible if

(i) $\sum_{i=1}^n x_i = \sum_{i=1}^n \varepsilon_i$,
(ii) For every $i = 1, \dots, n$, there exists $\theta_i \in \mathbb{R}^d$ such that $x_i - \varepsilon_i = A\theta_i$

We denote by $\mathcal{F}_A$ the set of feasible allocations.

Definition. An allocation $\bar{x} \in (\mathbb{R}^k_+)^n$ is a A-constrained Pareto-optimal (C.P.O.) if $\bar{x} \in \mathcal{F}_A$ and there does not exist $x \in \mathcal{F}_A$ such that $u_i(x_i) \geq u_i(\bar{x}_i)$ with strict inequality for at least one i.

In the case of complete markets, results on uniqueness of equilibrium follow trivially from the following fact: If $(\bar{x}, \bar{\theta}, \bar{q})$ is an Arrow Radner equilibrium, then there exists a unique $\sigma \in \mathbb{R}^k_{++}$ such that $\bar{q} = A^T\sigma$ and $(\bar{x}, \sigma)$ is an Arrow-Debreu equilibrium.

In the case of incomplete markets, it would seem natural to link asset demands and cœfficients $\sigma^j(x)$, but this may only be done in the two assets case (a riskless and a risky asset). We provide two results. The first is roughtly based on the assumption that C.P.O.and P.O. coincide while the second is based on the cone version of Milleron, Mitjushin and Polterovich's result.

Proposition 2.11. *If every Arrow Radner Equilibria of the economy is Pareto-optimal and if $\sigma_i^j(x) \leq 1$ for every $i = 1, \dots, n,\quad j = 1, \dots, k$ and $x \geq 0$, there exists at most one Arrow Radner equilibrium.*

The proof of Proposition 2.11 may be found in the appendix.

Example. Assume that $\varepsilon_i = A\theta_i$ for some θ_i, for every $1 = 1, \dots, n$, $u_i(x) = \sum_{j=1}^k \pi^j (x^j)^\alpha, 0 < \alpha < 1$ or $u_i(x) = \sum_{j=1}^k \pi^j \log(x^j)$ for every $i = 1, \dots, n$, then there exists a unique Arrow Radner Equilibrium. Indeed, any P.O. allocation is proportionnal to aggregate endowment and belongs to $\mathcal{F}_A$ (see Magill-Quinzii (1995)). Hence P.O. and C.P.O. coincide. Since any Arrow Radner equilibrium is C.P.O., it is P.O. and Proposition 2.11 applies. □

Proposition 2.12. *Assume that $\varepsilon = A\theta_0$ for some θ_0 and collinear endowments. If utilities are homogeneous or additively separable with $\sigma_i^j(x) < 4$ for every $i = 1, \dots, n,\quad j = 1, \dots, k$ and $x \geq 0$, then there exists a unique Arrow Radner Equilibria .*

Proof. If $(\bar{x}, \bar{\theta}, \bar{q})$ is a Arrow Radner equilibrium, then there is no arbitrage (no θ such that $\bar{q} \cdot \theta$ and $A\theta \geq 0$, thus there exists a σ such that $\bar{q} = A^T\sigma$. Let $X = \{x \in \mathbb{R}^k_+$ such that $\exists\ \theta \mid x = A\theta\}$. Clearly X is a convex cone. Since $(\bar{x}, \bar{\theta}, \bar{q})$ is an Arrow Radner Equilibrium ,

$$(i)\quad \bar{x}_i = \begin{array}{l} \arg\max u_i(x_i) \\ \sigma \cdot x_i \leq \sigma \cdot \varepsilon_i \\ x_i \in X \end{array}$$

(ii) $\sum_{i=1}^n \bar{x}_i = \sum_{i=1}^n \varepsilon_i$

It follows from Proposition 2.7 that $(\bar{x}, \sigma)$ is unique, thus $\bar{q}$ is unique. Since A is injective, $\bar{\theta}$ is unique. □

3 Additively separable utilities in infinite dimension

3.1 The model

Let us consider an n agent pure exchange economy in the case of uncertainty. In each state of the world, there is one good. Given as primitive is a measure space $(\Omega, \mathcal{A}, \mu)$. For $1 \leq p < \infty$, $L^p_+(\mu) = \{f \mid f \geq 0 \text{ a.e.}, \int f^p d\mu < \infty\}$, $L^\infty_+(\mu) = \{f, f \geq 0 \text{ a.e.}, \exists M > 0, f < M, \text{a.e.}\}$. For $f \geq g, f > g$ means that f is greater than g on a set of positive measure while $f \gg g$ means $f(s) > g(s)$ a.e.
We assume that agents trade contingent claims before uncertainty is resolved and that the economy E is described as follows:

$$E = \{X_i = L^p_+(\mu), 1 \leq p \leq \infty,\ u_i : X_i \to \mathbb{R} \cup \{-\infty\}, \varepsilon_i \in X_i,\ \ i = 1, \dots, n\}$$

We assume that agents have additively separable utilities

$$u_i(x) = \int U_i(x(s), s) d\mu(s) \quad \forall x \in L^p_+(\mu), \quad i = 1, \dots, n$$

where $U_i(., s)$ verifies the properties of part 2 and the following integrability condition:
For some $A \in L^q_+(\mu)$ and $B \in L^1_+(\mu)$, $U_i(c, s) \leq A(s)c + B(s)$; $\forall (c, s) \in \mathbb{R}_+ \times \Omega$.
We assume $U^{'}(0, s) = \infty$, $\forall\ s$. Let $I(., s) :]U^{'}((\infty), s), \infty[\to \mathbb{R}_+$ denote the inverse of the strictly decreasing map $U^{'}(., s)$. The map $I(., s)$ is continuous, strictly decreasing and fulfills the following boundary conditions: $I(U^{'}((\infty), s), s) = \infty$ and $I(\infty, s) = 0$, $\forall\ s$.

We further assume $\varepsilon_i \gg 0$, $\forall i$. Let $\varepsilon = \sum_{i=1}^n \varepsilon_i$.

We define

$$\sigma_i(x, s) = -\frac{x U_i^{''}(x, s)}{U_i^{'}(x, s)}, \quad i = 1, \dots, n, \quad x \geq 0.$$

3.2 Individual demand

For $p \geq 1$, let q be defined by $1/p + 1/q = 1$. Prices are assumed to belong to $L^q_+(\mu)$ if $p \neq \infty$ and to $L^1_+(\mu)$ if $p = \infty$. We use the following notation: $\psi \cdot x = \int \psi(s) x(s) d\mu(s)$.

As it is well known, the demand approach may not easily be followed to obtain existence of an equilibrium, since one cannot characterize prices for which demand exists. We shall show that, nevertheless, sufficient conditions for uniqueness of equilibrium may be given. Let $f(\psi, w)$ (resp. $f(\psi, \psi \cdot \varepsilon)$) denote an agent's demand **when it exists**, the optimal solution to the problem

$$\begin{array}{llll} \max & \int U(x(s), s) d\mu(s) & & \max\ \int U(x(s), s) d\mu(s), \\ & \int \psi(s) x(s) d\mu(s) \leq w & (\text{resp} & \int \psi(s) x(s) d\mu(s) \leq \int \psi(s) \varepsilon(s) d\mu(s)) \\ & x \in L^p_+(\mu) & & x \in L^p_+(\mu) \end{array}$$

Let $D(w)$ (resp $D(\varepsilon)$) denote the set of prices for which $f(\psi, w)$ exists (resp. $f(\psi, \psi \cdot \varepsilon)$ exists).

Let $\lambda(\psi, w)$ (resp $\bar{\lambda}_i(\psi)$) denote the inverse of the marginal utility of income of the agent at price income (ψ, w) (resp $(\psi, \psi \cdot \varepsilon)$) when it exists.

We first generalize the definitions recalled in Sect. 2.2.

Definition. A map $f : D \subseteq L^q_+(\mu) \to \mathbb{R}^n_{++}$ is strictly isotone if $\psi > \psi'$, implies $f(\psi) \gg f(\psi')$.
A map $f : D \subseteq L^q_+(\mu) \to L^p_+(\mu)$ is strictly gross substitute (S.G.S.) if for any $(\psi, \psi') \in D^2$, $A \subset D$ such that $\psi = \psi'$ on A and $\psi > \psi'$ on A^c, $f(\psi) > f(\psi')$ on A.

Proposition 3.1.

a) *If $\sigma(x, s) < 1$ for every $x \geq 0$ and a.e. s, then $\lambda(., w)$ is strictly isotone on $D(w)$ while $f(., w)$ is S.G.S..*

b) *If $\sigma(x, s) \leq 1$ for every $x \geq 0$ and a.e. s, $\bar{\lambda}(\psi)$ is strictly isotone on $D(\varepsilon)$ while $f(\psi, \psi \cdot \varepsilon)$ is S.G.S.*

Proof. Demand exists at price ψ iff there exists $\lambda(\psi, w) > 0$ such that $\int(\lambda(\psi, w)U(x(s), s) - \psi(s)x(s)d\mu(s)$ is maximized at $f(\psi, w)$. Equivalently $\lambda(\psi, w)U(x(s), s) - \psi(s)x(s)$ is maximized at $f(\psi(s), w(s))$ a.e. Since $U'(0, s) = \infty$, $\forall\ s$

$$\lambda(\psi, w)U'(x(s), s) = \psi(s) \quad \text{and} \tag{11}$$

$$\int \psi(s)x(s)d\mu(s) = w, \quad \text{Equivalently,} \tag{12}$$

$$\int \psi(s)I(\frac{\psi(s)}{\lambda(\psi, w)}, s)d\mu(s) = w \tag{13}$$

The function $\lambda \to \int \psi(s)I(\frac{\psi(s)}{\lambda}, s)d\mu(s)$ is strictly increasing on its domain. If $\sigma(x, s) < 1$, for every $x \geq 0$, the function $x \to I(x, s)x$ is strictly decreasing implying a). Using (11) one gets gross substitution of demand. The proof of b), which is similar, is omitted. □

For further use, let us introduce the following assumption:

$$(\mathbf{H})U(s, x) \;=\; a(s)x^r,\ 0 < r < 1 \text{ or } U(s, x) = -a(s)x^{-r},\ r > 0 \quad \text{for some } \in L^\infty_+(\mu)$$

Proposition 3.2. *Let ψ and ψ' belong to $D(w)$. If U fulfills* **(H)** *or if $\sigma(x, s) < 4$ for every $x \geq 0$ and a.e. s, then*

$$\int [f(\psi, w)(s) - f(\psi', w)(s)][\psi(s)) - \psi'(s)]d\mu(s)) < 0, \text{ if } f(\psi, w) \neq f(\psi', w)$$

and $\int [f(\psi, \psi \cdot \varepsilon)(s) - f(\psi', \psi' \cdot \varepsilon)(s)][\psi(s) - \psi'(s)]d\mu(s) < 0$ *if* $f(\psi, \psi \cdot \varepsilon) \neq f(\psi', \psi' \cdot \varepsilon)$ *and* $\psi \cdot \varepsilon = \psi' \cdot \varepsilon = 1$.

The proof may be found in Dana (1995).

3.3 Aggregate excess demand

Let $F(\psi)$ denote aggregate demand at price ψ whenever it exists. Let $D = \cap_i D(\varepsilon_i)$ denote its domain. The following result follows easily from Proposition 3.2.

Proposition 3.3.
1) If $\sigma_i(x,s) \leq 1$ for $\forall i = 1,\ldots,n$ and $x \geq 0$ and almost any s, F is S.G.S. on D.

2) Let $\varepsilon_i = \theta_i \varepsilon$, $\forall i = 1,\ldots,n$ with $\sum_{i=1}^{n} \theta_i = 1$. If U_i fulfills **(H)** *or if $\sigma_i(x,s) < 4$ for every $i = 1,\ldots,n$ and $x \geq 0$ and almost any s, then*

$$\int [F(\psi)(s) - F(\psi')(s)][\psi(s) - \psi'(s)]d\mu(s) < 0$$

for prices ψ and ψ' such that $\int [\psi)(s) - \psi')(s)][(s)]d\mu(s) = 0$ and $F(\psi) \neq F(\psi')$.

3.4 Uniqueness of Arrow-Debreu equilibrium

In infinite dimension, it is no longer the case that when aggregate demand is S.G.S., one can prove existence of equilibrium without using a fixed point theorem. One can however give sufficient conditions for uniqueness of equilibrium.

Proposition 3.4. *Assume that $\sigma_i(x,s) \leq 1$ for every $i = 1,\ldots,n$ and $x \geq 0$ and a.e. s. Assume that for any two equilibrium prices ψ and ψ', $F(\max(\psi,\psi'))$ or $F(\min(\psi,\psi'))$ exists, then there exists at most one equilibrium.*

Proof. Assume that there exist two equilibrium prices ψ and ψ' and that $F(\max(\psi,\psi'))$ exists. By S.G.S., $F(\max(\psi,\psi')) > 0$ a.e. contradicting Walras-Law.

Proposition 3.5. *Assume that endowments are collinear. If U_i fulfills* **(H)** *for every $i = 1,\ldots,n$ or if $\sigma_i(x,s) < 4$ for every $i = 1,\ldots,n$ and $x \geq 0$ and a.e. s, then there exists at most one equilibrium.*

3.5 The weight approach

Notation: Let $\lambda \in \mathbb{R}^n_+$. Let us define the aggregate utility:

$$\bar{U}(x,\lambda,s) = \max\left\{\sum_{i=1}^{n} \lambda_i U_i(x_i,s), x_i \geq 0, \sum_{i=1}^{n} x_i = x\right\} \text{ and}$$

$$(C_i(x,\lambda,s))_{i=1}^n = \arg\max\left\{\sum_{i=1}^{n} \lambda_i U_i(x_i,s), x_i \geq 0, \sum_{i=1}^{n} x_i = x\right\}$$

The function $C_i(.,.,s)$ is continuous in $\mathbb{R}_+ \times \mathbb{R}^n_+$, continuously differentiable in $\mathbb{R}_{++} \times \mathbb{R}^n_{++}$, $\frac{\partial C_i(x,\lambda,s)}{\partial x} > 0$, $\frac{\partial C_i(x,\lambda,s)}{\lambda_j} < 0$ for $i \neq j$, $\frac{\partial C_i(x,\lambda,s)}{\partial \lambda_i} > 0$. The function $C_i(x,.,s)$ is homogeneous of degree zero.
The function $\bar{U}(.,.,s)$ is continuous in $\mathbb{R}_+ \times \mathbb{R}^n_+$, $\forall \lambda \in \mathbb{R}^n_+, \bar{U}(.,\lambda,s)$ is continuously differentiable in $\mathbb{R}_{++}$ with $\bar{U}'_x(x,\lambda,s) = \lambda_i U'_i(C_i(x,\lambda,s)) \quad \forall i$ s.t. $\lambda_i > 0$.

In order to find prices that support P.O., let us introduce the following assumption

(E) if $1 \leq p < \infty$ $\max_{\lambda \in \Delta^{n-1}} \bar{U}'_x(\varepsilon(s),\lambda,s) \in L^q_+(\mu)$
if $p = \infty$ $\max_{\lambda \in \Delta^{n-1}} \bar{U}'_x(\varepsilon(s),\lambda,s) \in L^1_+(\mu)$.

Remark. This assumption turns out to be equivalent to the following assumption made in the literature to obtain existence of an A.D. equilibrium (see Mas-Colell-Zame Sect. 11).

(E') There exists a feasible allocation $(\alpha_i(s))^n_{i=1}$ such that $U'_i(\alpha_i(s),s) \in L^q_+$ for every $i = 1,\ldots,n$.

Indeed if **(E)** holds, pick any $\lambda \gg 0$. Then $U'_i(C_i(\varepsilon(s),\lambda,s) \in L^q_+(\mu)$ for every $i = 1,\ldots,n$ and $(C_i(\varepsilon(s),\lambda,s)^n_{i=1}$ is a feasible allocation, thus **(E')** is satisfied with $\alpha_i(s) = C_i(\varepsilon(s),\lambda,s)$. Conversely if **(E')** is satisfied , define for each k: $S_k = \{s \mid C_k(\varepsilon(s),\lambda,s) > \alpha_k(s)\}$. If $s \in S_k$, then $\bar{U}'_x(\varepsilon(s),\lambda,s) = \lambda_k U'_k(C_k(\varepsilon(s),\lambda,s)) \leq \lambda_k U'_k(\alpha_k(s),s)$. If $s \in \Omega - \cup_k S_k$, then for every $k, C_k(\varepsilon(s),\lambda,s) \leq \alpha_k(s)$. As $\sum^n_{i=1} C_k(\varepsilon(s),\lambda,s) = \sum^n_{i=1} \alpha_k(s) = \varepsilon(s)$, $C_k(\varepsilon(s),\lambda,s) = \alpha_k(s)$ and $\lambda_k U'_k(C_k(\varepsilon(s),\lambda,s) = \lambda_k U'_k(\alpha_k(s),s)$ for every k. Therefore for any λ and s, $\bar{U}'_x(\varepsilon(s),\lambda,s) \leq \max_i U'_i(\alpha_i(s),s)$ which imply that **(E)** is fulfilled. □

We recall that an allocation $(x_i(s))^n_{i=1} \in (L^p_+(\mu))^n$ is P.O. iff there exists $\lambda \in \mathbb{R}^n_+$ such that $x_i(s) = C_i(\varepsilon(s),\lambda,s)$ for every $i = 1,\ldots,n$ and $[(C_i(\varepsilon(s),\lambda,s)^n_{i=1}, \bar{U}'_x(\varepsilon(s),\lambda,s)]$ is an equilibrium with transfer payments. We may therefore define the excess utility $e : \mathbb{R}^n_+ \to \mathbb{R}^n$ by

$$e_i(\lambda) = \frac{1}{\lambda_i} \int \bar{U}'_x(\varepsilon(s),\lambda,s)(C_i(\varepsilon(s),\lambda,s) - \varepsilon_i(s))d\mu(s).$$

Proposition 3.6. *Assume* **(E)**

a) e is continuous in $\mathbb{R}^n_{++}$, *homogeneous of degree 0, bounded above,*
b) verifies Walras law $\sum^n_{i=1} \lambda_i e_i(\lambda) = 0$,
c) If $\lambda_i \to 0$, *then* $e_i \to -\infty$,
d) If $\sigma_i(x,s) \leq 1$ *for every* i, $x \geq 0$ *and a.e. s,* $\forall (i \neq j)$, e_i *is a strictly decreasing function of* λ_j.

The proof may be found in Dana (1993).

Theorem 3.7. *Assume* **(E)**.

a) There exists an equilibrium.
b) If $\sigma_i(x,s) \leq 1$ *for every* $i = 1,\ldots,n$ *and* $x \geq 0$ *and a.e. s, then there exists a unique equilibrium.*

Proof. Using finite dimension demand theory, one deduces from a), b), c) of Proposition 3.6 existence of an equilibrium. From a), b), c), d) of Proposition 3.6, one deduces existence and uniqueness of equilibrium. □

3.6 The price-weight, weight-price approach

In this section, we assume **(E)**.

We may define two maps $H : \mathbb{R}^n_+ \to L^q_+(\mu)$ and G: $D \subset L^q_+(\mu) \to \mathbb{R}^n_{++}$ by

$$H(\lambda) = \bar{U}'_x(\varepsilon(s), \lambda, s) \text{ and } G(\psi) = \left[\bar{\lambda}_i(\psi)\right]_{i=1}^n$$

where $\bar{\lambda}_i(\psi)$ denotes the inverse of agent's i multiplier as defined in 3.2.

Proposition 3.8.

a) *The function H is continuous, homogeneous of degree one and is strictly isotone (if $\lambda > \lambda'$, then $H(\lambda) > H(\lambda')$ a.e.).*

b) *G is homogeneous of degree one and if $\sigma_i(x,s) \leq 1$ for every $i = 1, \ldots, n$ and $x \geq 0$, then G is strictly isotone.*

c) *λ is an equilibrium weight iff $G \circ H(\lambda) = \lambda$. If $\sigma_i(x,s) \leq 1$ for every $i = 1, \ldots, n$, $x \geq 0$ and a.e. s, then for every λ, $H(\lambda) \in D$ and $G \circ H$ has at most one fixed point.*

Proof. a) The continuity of H follows from assumption **(E)** and Lebesgue dominated convergence theorem while its strict isotonicity follows from Proposition 3.6. Assertion b) follows from the proof of Proposition 3.1. In order to prove c), we have to show that aggregate demand exists at price $\bar{U}'_x(\varepsilon(s), \lambda, s)$ for every λ. Let

$$\Phi_i(\lambda, \mu) = \frac{1}{\mu} \int \bar{U}'_x(\varepsilon(s), \lambda, s)(I_i(s, \frac{\bar{U}'_x(\varepsilon(s), \lambda, s)}{\mu}) - \varepsilon_i(s))d\mu(s).$$

If $\sigma_i(x,s) < 1$, for every $x \geq 0$, and a.e. s, by Lemma 2.1, the function $x \to I(x,s)x$ is strictly decreasing, hence $\Phi_i(\lambda, .)$ is strictly increasing on its domain. We have $\Phi_i(\lambda, \lambda_i) = e_i(\lambda) < \infty$, hence $\Phi_i(\lambda, \mu) \leq \infty$, $0 < \mu \leq \lambda_i$. By Lebesgue dominated convergence theorem, $\Phi_i(\lambda, .)$ is continuous and strictly increasing on its domain and satisfies $\lim_{\mu \to 0} \Phi_i(\lambda, \mu) = -\infty$ and $\lim_{\mu \to \infty} \mu\Phi_i(\lambda, \mu) = \infty$. Hence there exists $\mu_i(\lambda)$ such that $\Phi_i(\lambda, \mu_i(\lambda)) = 0$. It follows from the first order condition that $I_i(s, \frac{\bar{U}'_x(\varepsilon(s),\lambda,s)}{\mu_i(\lambda)})$ is the demand at price $\bar{U}'_x(\varepsilon(s), \lambda, s)$, $\forall\lambda$. The proof of the rest of the assertion is identical to that of Proposition 3.10. □

3.7 Arrow Radner equilibria

We consider an exchange economy with n traders and two periods $t = 0, 1$. We assume here that at date 0, there is only trade in assets. We start by describing the economy at date one.

Given as primitive there is a finite measure space $(\Omega, \mathcal{A}, \mu)$. In each state of the world, there is a single good available for consumption. $L_+^\infty(\mu)$. Agent i is described by a pair (ε_i, u_i) $\varepsilon_i \in \text{int } L_+^\infty(\mu)$. In order to avoid integrability conditions, we assume here that utilities are von-Neumann Morgenstern: $u_i(x) = \int U_i(x(s))d\mu(s)$, $\forall x \in L_+^\infty(\mu)$. $i = 1, \ldots, n$ where U_i is strictly increasing, strictly concave and C^2 functions. Let $\sigma_i(x) = -\dfrac{xU_i''(x)}{U_i'(x)}$, $x \in \mathbb{R}_+$ denote agent's i relative risk aversion cœfficient.

At date zero, agents may buy a finite number of assets with payoffs $(r^j)_{j=1}^d \in (L_+^\infty)^d$ assumed to be linearly independent. Let H denote the asset span and $q \in \mathbb{R}^d$ be a vector of assets prices. Let $B_i(q) = \{x_i \in L_+^\infty(\mu) \mid \exists \theta_i \in \mathbb{R}^d,\ q \cdot \theta_i \leq 0 \text{ and } x_i = \varepsilon_i + \sum_{j=1}^d \theta_i^j r^j\}$ be the budget set of agent i.

Definition. An Arrow-Radner equilibrium is a triple $(\bar{x}, \bar{\theta}, \bar{q}) \in [L_+^\infty(\mu)]^n \times (\mathbb{R}^d)^n \times \mathbb{R}^d$ with $\bar{x} = (\bar{x}_1, \bar{x}_2, \ldots \bar{x}_n), \bar{\theta} = (\bar{\theta}_1, \bar{\theta}_2, \ldots, \theta_n)$ such that

(i) $\bar{x}_i = \arg\max u_i(x_i)$,
$x_i \in B(\bar{q})$,
(ii) $\sum_{i=1}^n \bar{\theta}_i = 0$.

In order to give a cone version of Proposition 3.5., let us introduce the following condition:

(G) $\qquad U'(0) < \infty$ and $\sup_{x \in \mathbb{R}_+} -U''(x) < \infty$

Lemma 3.9. *Assume that agents' consumption space is a convex cone $C \subseteq L_+^\infty$ and that endowments are collinear.*

1) Assume that U_i satisfies (G) and $\sigma_i(x) < 4$ for every i, then there exists at most one equilibrium.
2) If $\sigma_i(x) < 4$ for every i, then there exists at most one interior equilibrium.

The proof may be found in Dana (1995).

Proposition 3.10.

a) There exists a financial equilibrium.
b) Assume furthermore that endowments are collinear and that $\varepsilon \in H$. If U_i satisfies (G) and $\sigma_i(x) < 4$, for every $i = 1, \ldots, n$ and $x \geq 0$, then there exists a unique Arrow-Radner equilibrium. If $\sigma_i(x) < 4$, for every $i = 1, \ldots, n$ and $x \geq 0$, then there exists a unique interior Arrow-Radner equilibrium.

The proof of a) which can be done by Negishi's method is omitted. The proof of b) is similar to that of Proposition 2.12.

Appendix

The proof of Proposition 2.11 requires a preliminary lemma.

Lemma A.

1) *If* $(\bar{x}, \bar{\theta}, \bar{q})$ *is a financial market equilibrium, then* $\bar{x}$ *is C.P.O. and* $\bar{x}_i \gg 0$*, for every* $i = 1, \ldots, n$.
2) *An allocation* $\bar{x}$ *with* $\bar{x}_i \gg 0$*, for every* $1 = 1, \ldots, n$*, is C.P.O. iff there exists* $\alpha \in \Delta^{n-1}, \alpha \gg 0$ *such that* $\bar{x}$ *is the solution to the problem* $P_{(A,\alpha)}$

$$\max_{x \in \mathscr{F}_A} \sum_{i=1}^{n} \alpha_i u_i(x_i)$$

3) *If* $x(\alpha, A) = (\varepsilon_i + A\theta_i(\alpha, A))_{i=1}^n$ *is the solution to* $P_{(A,\alpha)}$ *with* $\alpha \gg 0$*, then* $\alpha_i u_i'(x_i(\alpha, A))A$ *is independent of* i*. Let* $q(\alpha, A) = \alpha_i u_i'(x_i(\alpha, A))A$*, for some* i*. Then*

(i) *For every* $i = 1, \ldots, n$.

$$x_i(\alpha, A) = \begin{array}{l} \arg\max u_i(x_i) \\ x_i - \varepsilon_i = A\theta_i \;\; \text{for some } \theta_i \in \mathbb{R}^d, x_i \in \mathbb{R}^k_+ \\ q(\alpha, A) \cdot \theta_i \leq q(\alpha, A) \cdot \theta_i(\alpha) \end{array}$$

(ii) $\sum_{i=1}^n \theta_i(\alpha, A) = 0$,

In other words $(x(\alpha, A), q(\alpha, A))$ *is an equilibrium with assets transfer.*

The proof of the lemma is omitted. It is similar to that of the first and second welfare theorems.

Proof of Proposition 2.11. It follows from the lemma above that an equilibrium with financial market is a strictly positive C.P.O. for which assets transfers are equal to zero. Define the A-constrained excess utility map: $E_A : \operatorname{int}\Delta^{n-1} \to \mathbb{R}^n$ by: $E_{i,A}(\alpha) = \frac{1}{\alpha_i} q(\alpha, A) \cdot \theta_i(\alpha, A) = u_i'(x_i(\alpha, A)) \cdot (x_i(\alpha, A) - \varepsilon_i)$, for every $i = 1, \ldots, n$. An equilibrium with financial market is therefore associated with a zero of E_A. Let $E : \operatorname{int}\Delta^{n-1} \to \mathbb{R}^n$ be the standard excess utility map defined by: $E_i(\alpha) = u_i'(x_i(\alpha)) \cdot (x_i(\alpha) - \varepsilon_i)$, for every $i = 1, \ldots, n$ where $x(\alpha)$ is the solution to $\max \begin{array}{l} \sum_{i=1}^n \alpha_i u_i(x_i) \\ \sum_{i=1}^n x_i = \varepsilon \end{array}$

By assumption, an equilibrium with financial market is P.O., hence it is associated to a zero of E. As E is strictly gross substitute, it has a unique zero, thus there exists a unique equilibrium. □

References

Dana, R.A. (1993) Existence and uniqueness of equilibria when preferences are additively separable and gross substitute. *Econometrica* 61: 953–957

Dana, R.A. (1995) An extension of Milleron, Mitjushin and Polterovich's result. *Journal of Mathematical Economics* 24: 259–269

Greenberg, I. (1977) An elementary proof of existence of a competitive equilibrium with weak gross substitute. *Quaterly Journal of Economics* 91(4): 513–516

Karatsas, I.; Shreve, S.E. (1998) Methods of Mathematical Finance. Springer, Berlin Heidelberg New York

Kehoe, T.J.; Levine, D.K. (1985) Comparative statics and perfect foresight in infinite horizon economies. *Econometrica* 53: 433–453

Magill, M.; Quinzii, M. (1996) Theory of Incomplete markets. MIT Press, Cambridge, London

Mas-Colell, A. (1991) On the uniqueness of equilibrium once again. In: Barnet, W.A.; Cornet, B.; d'Aspremont, C.; Gabszewicz, I.; Mas-Colell, A. (eds.) Equilibrium theory and applications. Cambridge University Press, Cambridge

Mas-Colell, A.; Zame, W. (1991) Equilibrium theory in infinite dimensional spaces. Handbook of Mathematical Economics, n°4

Mas-Colell, A. (1985) The theory of general economic equilibrium: a differentiable approach. Econometric Soc.Monograph, Cambridge University Press, Cambridge

Milleron, J.C. (1974) Unicité et stabilité de l'équilibre en économie de distribution. Séminaire d'Econométrie Roy-Malinvaud, mars 1974 (preprint)

Mitjushin, L.G.; Polterovich, V.W (1978) Criteria for monotonicity of demand functions (in Russian). *Ekonomika i Matematicheskie Metody* 14: 122–128

Entry, productivity, and investment

Kenneth J. Arrow

Stanford University, Department of Economics, Stanford, CA 94305-6072, USA
(e-mail: arrow@leland.stanford.edu)

1 Introduction and viewpoint

The transition in Eastern Europe from a planned and governmentally-owned economy to a free market system has been discussed primarily in terms of the transfer of ownership of existing firms and productive assets from the government sector to private hands. It appears to me that this process of privatization has proceeded more rapidly that is optimal and has eclipsed an alternative process of private capital acquisition and creation, namely through entry. The process of privatization implies retention of the capital structure and, to some extent at least, of the organizational structure of the previous regime.

There are several reasons for arguing that undue stress on privatization is inefficient. (1) It is unanimously accepted that the previous industrial organization was inefficient because it was created in the absence of a controlling market mechanism; therefore directing production in the old channels is very likely to be a slow way of getting to an efficient allocation. (2) As a special case of (1), it is noted in particular that the allocation of investment to industries differed considerably from that in advanced market economies; in particular, there was excessive capital in heavy industries and insufficient in areas such as distribution, transportation, and communication. (3) The organizational form of the state industries emphasized hierarchical structures which are highly insensitive to market pressures. The preservation of these structures in the reform period makes easy their domination by previous insiders who, in many cases, find it more profitable to drain existing resources than to develop profitable industries in the future. (4) In any economy, innovation is frequently (not universally) best developed by the entry of new firms, not merely the modernization of old ones, and the latter is frequently in response to the former.

Written as consultant to the European Bank for Reconstruction and Development under Contract C5128/JAP-94-05-15. The opinions are my own, and the Bank is not responsible for any of them. I am indebted to Philippe Aghion and to a referee for useful suggestions.

Development in any country is thus dependent on entry, and the special nature of transition from socialism requires positive policy to encourage entry. This paper broaches some of the questions and outlooks which are needed to guide such a policy.

In this note, I hope simply to open up the subject by stressing two themes, the limited knowledge of good productive opportunities by investors, and the need for savings to permit more rapid economic growth. Given limited knowledge, there is a clear preference for trying as many entrants as possible. In the initial phase, there are limited financial resources for supporting entry. If productivity can be observed at small scales, then it is clearly a preferred policy to support many entrants to find out which is the best. Models to analyze this will be developed in Sects. 2 and 3.

The prospect of successful entry generally means supernormal profits for at least some period. We will demonstrate that an optimal savings program will lead, under these conditions, to an increase in the total volume of capital formation. The example of the individual entrepreneur who saves a very large fraction of his or her income, possibly by investing time with little immediate reward, is very familiar. The model of Sect. 4 formalizes this everyday observation.

Privatization *per se* creates no new capital. Either the capital stock is simply given away to a narrower or wider circle or it is paid for by a transfer of capital from some other part of the economy. Entry can, on the other hand, have a direct effect on individual savings. As in the evolution of capitalist societies, the savings generated in entering firms can ultimately be used to modernize the heavy industrial sectors which had been the center of state ownership.

2 Optimal entry: A simple model

Suppose that there are many potential entrants for an industry and that there is a fixed amount of capital available for financing them. There is uncertainty about the production function for each firm. I will assume this uncertainty is public; the would-be entrepreneur knows no more about his or her production function than does the source of finance (the "banker"). The production function is (possibly) revealed after one period's production, and subsequent financing can then use this information optimally.

For simplicity, assume that the production functions of the potential firms are random draws from a known distribution. (I think that the extension to the case of correlated draws, as when there is a common factor in all firms' productivities, is not difficult). Then, in the second period, the bank can find the firm or firms with the best production function given the amount of financing which will be then available.

Let,

$$K^t = \text{ amount of capital available at time } t = 1, 2.$$

If all production functions satisfy the condition of constant returns, then the output of any one firm is proportional to the capital invested. The relevant production function is determined by one parameter, the capital productivity. This can be determined with arbitrarily small investment. In this case, the optimal first-period policy is clearly to finance as many different firms as possible. Since *ex ante* all firms have the same expected capital productivity, the expected output in the first period is independent of the capital allocation. For the second period, let,

$Y_i =$ output of firm i in period 2 if it receives the entire capital allotment, K^2.

Then if r firms have been financed in the first period and their production functions revealed, the banker can calculated Y_i for each $i = 1, \ldots r$, and choose the firm that maximizes Y_i. Let,

$$M_r = \max\{Y_i | i = 1, \ldots, r\}.$$

Then expected output in period 2 is $E(M_r)$. It is easy to see that, by definition, M_{r+1} is greater than or equal to M_r in every realization, and that except for degenerate cases $M_{r+1} > M_r$ with positive probability, so that $E(M_{r+1}) > E(M_r)$. Under constant returns, then, there is no expected loss to increasing r in period 1 and an expected gain (a purchase of information) in period 2.

Theorem 1. *Under constant returns to scale, it pays (in this model) to divide the available capital among as many firms as exist.*

A more severe test of the virtues of entry occurs when increasing returns are possible. Then the gains from new information have to be weighed against the expected loss in the first period from spreading capital more widely (and thereby losing the benefits of increasing returns). We have therefore to specify more exactly the terms of trade between present and expected future outputs.

I have used the phrase, "second period," but in fact the second period has to be interpreted as a long perhaps indefinite future. The weight to be applied to the second period is therefore really the sum of the discount rates for for one, two, ..., periods. If d is the discount rate for output one period ahead, then, if the future were to last forever, the discount rate for the entire future is,

$$D = d + d^2 + d^3 + \ldots = d/(1 - d),$$

and therefore is, in general, a large number, perhaps between 10 and 20.

Let X_i be the output of firm i in period 1. X_i will, of course, depend on x_I, the amount of capital allocated to firm i in period 1, where,

$$\sum x_i = K^1. \tag{1}$$

I now propose a simple functional form to represent increasing returns, a fixed cost to produce anything plus constant marginal costs. Then the possibility of learning depends on the scale of investment. If there is insufficient investment in a firm, there is no output, and in general there is no learning about the parameters of the production function of that firm except that they are such that, with the given investment, they do not permit any production. Since the parameters of the production function of a given firm are random variables from the point of view of the banker, any given investment defines a probability of yielding information. Let T be the set of firms about which learning has taken place in period 1; it is itself a random variable. Then in the second period the optimum firm among those for which learning takes place is chosen. That is, assume that the entire amount of capital available in the second period be devoted to one firm (as is optimal, given increasing returns). Let Y_i be the output of firm i if all period 2 resources were devoted to it. Then,

$$M_T = \max_{i \varepsilon T} Y_i$$

is the output in the second period. Even given T, M_T is a random variable from the viewpoint of the first period.

In the absence of risk aversion, the maximand is, then,

$$E(\sum X_i) + DE_T E(M_T|T). \tag{2}$$

The model for increasing returns (i.e., the presence of fixed costs) can be written, as follows:

$$X_i = p_i(x_i - F_i)^+ ,, \tag{3}$$

$$Y_i = p_i(K^2 - F_i)^+, \tag{4}$$

for suitable parameter values p_i, F_i, where, for any real number, $w^+ = w$ if $w > 0$, $w^+ = 0$ otherwise.

This is a well-defined optimization problem; since the functions in (3) and (4) are not concave, it is difficult to solve. In this section, I will first discuss the general problems and then make some observations on a related problem, with a restricted range of strategies, which affords some insight. In the next section, we show that violating the imposed constraint can improve performance.

Consider the first term in (2). The banker has to decide how to allocate the first-period financing available among the firms, i.e., determine the values of x_i for each of the potential firms i. In general, some or indeed many will be zero, because the existence of increasing firms means that there are costs to spreading the resources too thinly.

The output of a financed firm i will be zero if $x_i < F_i, p_i(x_i - F_i)$ otherwise. Therefore,

$$E(X_i) = \text{Prob}\,(F_i < x_i)E[p_i(x_i - F_i)|F_i < x_i].$$

Since all firms have the same distribution of the parameters, p_i, F_i, the subscripts on those variables can be omitted. For simplicity, assume that p and F are independently distributed. Then,

$$E(\sum X_i) = \sum \text{Prob}\,(F < x_i)E(p)[x_i - E(F|F < x_i)]. \tag{5}$$

Differentiation of (5) verifies that this is a convex function of the allocations, x_i. It would therefore achieve its maximum subject to (1) by concentrating all the available capital on one firm. If D were 0 or very small, then the same policy would maximize (2). But clearly, if D is at all sizeable, there is a gain in permitting experimentation with more than one firm. It is certainly clear from (2) that, if D is sufficiently large, the gain in the second term from having two firms with positive x_i would outweigh the loss in the first term. In general, then, we expect that increasing the number of firms financed to some extent will improve expected productivity over a long period of time, even though there will be an expected loss of output in the current period.

A considerable simplification occurs if we confine ourselves to policies in which each firm that is financed at all is financed to an extent that learning of productivity will take place with certainty. Under the production assumptions of (3-4), if $F_i > x_i$, then there is no output no matter what p_i is and therefore no possibility of estimating p_i. Indeed, it could be argued that we do not even learn the fixed cost, F_i , except the fact that it exceeds the amount of capital supplied, x_i. Suppose, as is reasonable, that the prior distribution of F_i is bounded above, say by F^m. We might choose to restrict ourselves to choices of the x_i's for which either $x_i > F^m$ or $x_i = 0$. Then, $F_i < x_i$ with probability 1 for the r firms financed, and (5) simplifies to,

$$E(\sum X_i) = E(p)[K^1 - rE(F)]. \tag{6}$$

Note that the first-period output is independent of the specific values of the x_i's provided the positive values exceed F^m. In this case, the set of firms whose productivity is learned is fixed to be the set financed. The second term in (2) depends only on the number, r, of firms financed. Let M_r be the maximum second-period output when r firms are financed, that is, the maximum of Y_i, as given by (4), over the financed firms whose values of p_i and F_i are known. It is well-known and easily proven that the expectation of the maximum of a set of independent and identically distributed variables is a concave function of the number of those variables. Thus the second term in (2) is a concave function, while, by (6), the first term is linear and therefore concave. The number of firms, r, is subject to the condition,

$$rF^m < \sum x_i = K^1. \tag{7}$$

Hence, we can state,

Theorem 2. *Assume that the parameters, p_i, F_i are independently distributed and that the distribution of F_i is bounded. Suppose in the above model we impose the condition that if a firm is financed at all, it is financed sufficiently to learn its parameters.*

Then the choice of the number of firms to be financed in the first period is a concave programming problem, so that the first-order conditions are sufficient.

To illustrate, take the special case where F is uniformly distributed between 0 and 1 and p is a constant, say 1. The conditions (7), then, is simply that $r < K^1$, with $x_i > 1$ for all i which are financed. Clearly, $E(F) = 1/2$. Assume further that $K^2 > 1$. From (4),

$$Y_i = K^2 - F_i,$$

so that,

$$\begin{aligned} M_r &= \max Y_i = K^2 - \min F_i, \\ E(M_r) &= K^2 - E(\min F_i). \end{aligned}$$

When F_i is uniformly distributed from 0 to 1, it is well known that,

$$E(\min F_i) = 1/(r+1).$$

The maximand (2) becomes,

$$K^1 - (r/2) + DK^2 - [D/(r+1)], \tag{8}$$

so that the optimum choice of r is easily found to be $(2D)^{1/2} - 1$ (more exactly, one of the two integers adjacent to this magnitude), provided, of course, that this value is less than K^1, in accordance with (7). Given the assumption that financing of each firm is large enough to permit learning with probability 1, the actual values of the x_i's is irrelevant. This result is enough to show that in general it is optimal to encourage multiple entry to an extent determined by the discount rate subject to a resource constraint.

3 Optimal entry: A more sophisticated strategy

So far, I have confined myself to the case where each firm receives enough financing to insure learning. We may consider more sophisticated strategies where, for some firms at least, $x_i < F^m$, so that there is a positive probability of not learning for those firms. I will illustrate by continuing the previous example, where p is the known constant 1 and F is uniformly distributed between 0 and 1. Since the problem is non-convex, it is not surprising that a full analytic characterization is difficult or impossible to attain. However, some properties of the solution can be derived. In particular, it can be established that the solution of the previous section is not optimal. That is, given the optimal number of firms financed enough to ensure learning about production, it pays to divert some resources to finance one firm at less than enough to guarantee learning.

We need to express the two terms of the maximand (2). To this end, let H (high level of financing) be the set of firms financed with $x_i \geq 1$ and L (low level of financing) be the set of firms financed with $0 < x_i < 1$. Let r and q be the numbers of members of H and L, respectively. Let $x_i^* = \min(x_i, 1)$. Then, Prob $(F_i < x_i^*) = x_i^*, E(F|F < x_i) = x_i^*/2$, so that, from (5),

$$E(\sum X_i) = \sum x_i^* x_i - (1/2) \sum (x_i^*)^2.$$

To simplify notation, let $x_i = z_i$ for $i \varepsilon L, = y_i$ for $i \varepsilon H$. In the first case, $x_i* = z_i$, in the second, $x_i* = 1$. Then,

$$E(\sum X_i) = \sum y_i - (r/2) + (1/2) \sum (z_i)^2. \tag{9}$$

Now let us consider the second term in (2). Among the members of L, we learn the production parameter, F_i, for the random subset, say L', for which $F_i < x_i$. Then F_i is known for all the firms in H and in L'. To determine the expectation,

$$E(\min F_i | i \varepsilon H \quad \text{or} \quad i \varepsilon L').$$

we need the distribution of $\min F_i$ conditional on i belonging to H or L'. Since the F_i's are independent,

$$\text{Prob }(\min F_i \geq t) = \prod_{i \varepsilon H} \text{Prob }(F_i \geq t) \prod_{i \varepsilon L'} \text{Prob }(F_i \geq t),$$

If $i \varepsilon H$, then F_i is uniformly distributed on (0, 1), so that Prob $(F_i \geq t) = 1 - t$ if $t < 1, 0$ otherwise. If $i \varepsilon L'$, then it must be that $F_i < z_i < 1$, and therefore F_i is uniformly distributed on $(0, z_i)$, so that,

$$\text{Prob }(F_i \geq t) = 1 - (t/z_i) \quad \text{if} \quad t < z_i, = 0 \quad \text{otherwise, for} \quad i \varepsilon L'.$$

It follows that if $t > \min z_i$, then Prob $(\min F_i \geq t) = 0$, i.e., the support of the random variable, $\min F_i$, is the range, $(0, \min z_i)$. Hence,

$$\begin{aligned} &\text{Prob }(\min F_i \geq t | i \varepsilon H \quad \text{or} \quad i \varepsilon L') \\ &\quad = (1-t)^r \quad \prod [1 - (t/z_i)], 0 < t < \min z_i, \\ &\quad = 0 \quad \text{otherwise.} \end{aligned}$$

From this, it is possible to derive the density function of $u = \min F_i$ conditional on H or L',

$$\begin{aligned} \phi(u|H, L') \quad &= \quad \prod_{i \varepsilon L'} [1 - (u/z_i)][r(1-u)^{r-1} + (1-u)^r \quad \sum_{i \varepsilon L'} (1/(z_i - u))], \\ &\qquad \text{if} \quad 0 < u < \min z_i, \\ &= \quad 0 \quad \text{otherwise.} \end{aligned} \tag{10}$$

Then, $E(\min F_i | H \quad \text{or} \quad L') = E(u | H \quad \text{or} \quad L')$ can be calculated. This expression still depends on the set L', which is a random variable. Obviously,

$$\text{Prob }(L' | z_1, \ldots, z_q) = \prod_{i \varepsilon L'} z_i \quad \prod_{i \varepsilon L \sim L'} (1 - z_i). \tag{11}$$

Then the expected fixed cost of the best firm in the second period is the expectation over $L'$of the expectation of minimum fixed cost given H and L'.

$$E_{L'}(M_{L'}) = \sum \text{Prob }(L' | z_1, \ldots, z_q) E(\min F_i | H \quad \text{or} \quad L'). \tag{12}$$

Thus, the payoff can be written down explicitly by substituting the expressions (9) and (12) into (2). This expression is a function of r, q, the y_i's and the z_i's.

I have not been able to do much with the general expression. One remark can be made. The values of the y_i's (provided there is at least one) enter only through their sum; see (9). Note that only the set H and not the values of the y_i's enters into the term (12).

However, it is interesting to ask the following question. Suppose that the value of r (the number of firms financed at a level sufficiently high to insure learning) is set at the optimal value when L is empty, that is, $q = 0$. This is the case discussed in Theorem 2, at the end of the last section. Now raise q from 0 to 1. Since there is only one element of L, call the corresponding z_i simply z. Can we choose z so that the payoff (2) is increased?

Since $q = 1$, the only possible sets L' are the empty set and the set consisting of the one firm in L. For simplicity, call these sets 0 and 1, respectively. If $L' = 0$, then, of course, learning takes place only for the firms in H, of which there are r, so that, as before,

$$E(\min F_i | H, 0) = 1/(r+1).$$

When $L' = 1$, the density of the minimum known fixed cost, (10), simplifies to,

$$\phi(u | H, 1) = (1/z)(1-u)^{r-1}[r(z-u) + (1-u)].$$

with support $(0, z)$. Direct calculation of the expectation shows that,

$$E(\min F_i | H, 1) = (1/z)\{-[1/(r+1)(r+2)] + [z/(r+1)] + [(1-z)^{r+2}/(r+1)(r+2)].$$

Obviously, Prob $(0|z) = 1 - z$, Prob $(1|z) = z$. Substitution into (12) yields,

$$E_{L'} E(\min F_i | H, L') = [(1/(r+2)] + [(1-z)^{r+2}/(r+1)(r+2)]. \qquad (13)$$

What is the optimal value of z, given that low-level entry takes place? Substitute (9) and (13) into (2), and omit terms not involving z. Recall that, by the budget constraint (1), we must have,

$$\sum y_i = K^1 - z.$$

Then $z$is to be chosen to maximize,

$$F(z) = -z + (z^2/2) - D(1-z)^{r+2}/(r+1)(r+2).$$

The first-order conditions are satisfied at,

$$z^0 = 1 - [(r+1)/D]^{1/r},$$

and at $z = 1$. Examination of the second derivative shows that the function $F(z)$ is concave from 0 to a point above z^0 and convex thereafter. It can be inferred from this that z^0 yields the maximum. It finally has to be shown that the maximum payoff with this strategy exceeds that when there is no low-level finance. Elaborate but elementary computations show that if r has been chosen to be optimal without low-level financing, i.e., $r = (2D)^{1/2} - 1$, as we have seen in Sect. 2, then there is a gain by low-level financing of one firm at the level just indicated.

4 The effect of entry on savings

Assume that entry takes place, with good information, so that the entrepreneur can realize a profit $F(K)$as a function of the stock of capital, K. For the purposes of this model, assume diminishing returns and further assume that initially (i.e., for low values of K), the marginal return is above the return available in the financial market, say, r. It is fairly clear but may be worth demonstrating that the savings of the entrepreneur are increased over what they would be if only the general financial market were available for investment.

Suppose first that the saver can only invest at a constant rate of return, r. The saver is maximizing,

$$\int_0^\infty e^{-\rho t} U[c(t)]dt, \tag{14}$$

subject to the capital accumulation condition,

$$dK/dt = rK(t) - c(t), \tag{15}$$

where ρ is the subjective rate of discount, c is consumption, and $U(c)$ is the instantaneous utility of the consumption flow. For a simple but useful case, assume that $U(c) = c^{1-\theta}/(1-\theta)$, with $\theta > 1$. In what follows, I let $\sigma = 1/\theta < 1$. It is well known that the optimal policy is,

$$c(K) = [\rho\sigma + r(1-\sigma)]K,$$

which implies that c and K both grow at the rate, $\sigma(r-\rho)$.

Now suppose that the entrepreneur can divide his or her capital, K, at any moment between the enterprise and the financial market. By assumption, the marginal return of the enterprise at the initial capital, K_0, is greater than the market return, $F'(K_0) > r$. Then, with the same maximand, the entrepreneur will invest in the enterprise until the marginal return falls to r, that is, when the capital in the enterprise reaches $K*$ defined by,

$$F'(K^*) = r.$$

After that point of time, additional capital is invested in the financial market, in accordance with the previous policy. Let T be the time at which $K(T) = K^*$. In the interval before T, the Pontryagin principle yields the pair of differential equations, (15) and,

$$dc/dt = \sigma[F'(K) - \rho]c.$$

Since $F'[K(t)] > r$ for $t < T, dc/dt$ is greater than in the period of investment at the return r, after T. Since $c(T)$ is given, this means that $c(t)$ must be less than it would be without the opportunity of investing in one's own enterprise, and therefore savings must be greater.

5 Conclusions

It is perhaps a bit presumptuous to advance any policy implications on the basis of some very simple and yet incompletely analyzed models. Still, some tentative conclusions may be drawn.

The importance of entry to any progressive economic system hardly needs stress; it is too familiar a statement. I am trying to outline the importance of encouraging entry because of the need for flexibility in picking entrants and because of what can easily be a positive effect of entry on the formation of capital.

Further, there are some tentative implications for the specifics of encouraging entry, particularly in situations where there are economies of scale. There are a variety of possible entrants; we will know the best choice only by experience. The existence of economies of scale has two implications, both of which must be attended to. One is that there are arguments against spreading the capital available to finance entry too thinly. The second is more subtle; to learn which entrant studied is likely to be most successful, we need to invest enough, for we will learn little about performance at the higher levels of capital formation in the future if we invest too little to begin with. On the other hand, we do not know *a priori* what the economies of scale are, and therefore we do not know for certain what is the appropriate level of support which will be adequate to measure the production function of the firm. We must make our financial support decisions under uncertainty.

One conclusion that is suggested by the analysis is that support for different firms should be at different levels, even though the financing agency has the same uncertainties about the two. It looks as if it should support some firms at a level high enough to ensure learning about the production function and others at a lower level where there is some chance of not learning.

A model of Russia's "virtual economy"

Richard E. Ericson[1], **Barry W. Ickes**[2]

[1] Department of Economics, Columbia University, 420 W. 118th Street, New York, NY10027, USA (e-mail: ree3@columbia.edu)
[2] Department of Economics, The Pennsylvania State University, University Park, PA. 16802, USA (e-mail: bwickes@psu.edu)

Abstract. The Russian Economy has evolved into a hybrid form, a partially monetized quasi-market system that has been called the *virtual economy*. In the virtual economy, barter and non-monetary transactions play a key role in transferring value from productive activities to the loss-making sectors of the economy. We show how this transfer takes place, and how it can be consistent with the incentives of economic agents. We analyze a simple partial-equilibrium model of the virtual economy, and show how it might prove an obstacle to industrial restructuring and hence marketizing transition.

1 Introduction

The Russian transition from a "demonetized command economy" to a "monetized market economy" has taken an unexpected detour. The Russian economy appears to be evolving a new hybrid system, a partially monetized quasi-market economy.[1] This hybrid has been called the "virtual economy."[2] The "virtual economy hypothesis" has been used to explain the lack of restructuring in Russian enterprises and the growth of barter and other non-monetary transactions. In particular, the virtual economy hypothesis implies that barter and non-monetary transactions play a key role in distributing value from productive sectors and activities to the loss-making sectors and enterprises in the economy. Without such transfers the virtual economy could not exist.

Here we begin an exploration of the heart of that redistribution of value through a simple model of the interaction between the principal actors in the 'virtual economy': the government, the primary value-adding sector, energy, and

[1] In his 1999 State of the Federation, Boris Yeltsin commented that, "We are stuck halfway between a planned, command economy and a normal, market one. And now we have an ugly model – a cross-breed of the two systems."

[2] See, for example, Gaddy and Ickes (1998b).

enterprises in the largely unrestructured, and hence low to negative value-added, industrial manufacturing sector. In this model we formalize the incentives of the key agents and the way those incentives support the 'virtual economy' as an equilibrium configuration of behaviors on the part of these economic actors. We also begin an exploration of some of the consequences of this economic system, in particular the additional barrier that it places before the restructuring and modernization of Russian industry.

1.1 Some Russian transition puzzles

The "Virtual Economy" hypothesis provides a potential explanation for a number of anomalies and puzzles of the Russian transition, characteristics which set its experience apart from the transition experience of the emerging market economies of east central Europe. The most important puzzle, of course, is the failure of a large number of enterprises to restructure. In addition are a set of phenomena, elsewhere considered a "passing part" of early transition,[3] that have become *characteristic* — embedded in the structure of the economic system — in Russia. Among these are:

- apparently permanent *Arrears* of payments, wages, taxes;[4]
- massive *Barter* among industrial enterprises, in elaborate chains, at 'idiosyncratic' (virtual) prices/rates of exchange;[5]
- substantial use of *Quasi-moneys* [*Vekseli*, offsets (*zachëty*), and local or enterprise script], with idiosyncratic values, for closing transactions within 'barter chains', for taxes and for wages.

These distortions indicate a substantial *re-demonetization* of economic interaction and exchange in the core industrial sectors of the Russian economy, a resort to non-monetized intermediation reminiscent of the Soviet period. They have been accompanied by a continuing, indeed growing, inability to cover costs in manufacturing,[6] despite (explicitly & implicitly) subsidized prices for fundamental inputs, including energy, transportation, basic metals and industrial materials, and even — due to the ability to reduce wages through arrears, script and in-kind payments — labor. This has been accompanied by a continuing absence/decline in investment in the production sector,[7] limiting restructuring in

[3] See, for example, the discussion in Blanchard (1977).

[4] Industrial arrears measured as a share of industrial sales increased from over 40% in early 1998 to 60% in August. Since the sharp devaluation of the ruble they have gradually returned to about 40%. They are comprised primarily of two items: arrears to suppliers, and arrears to the budget and off-budget funds (*Russian Economic Trends*, June 1999: 3.). Total arrears as a percentage of annualized GDP have followed the same pattern (Ivanova and Wyplosz 1999: 24).

[5] Barter increased from approximately 5% of sales in 1992 to over 45% of sales in 1997. See, for example, Hendley, et. al. (1998).

[6] For example, the share of industrial enterprises reporting net losses was 47.3 % in October 1997 (that is, before the crisis of August 1998), up from less than 27 % in 1995. Data are from Goskomstat as reported in Interfax Statistical Reports, nos. 14, 51/52: 1997, 4: 1998, and 5: 1998.

[7] Investment declined steadily throughout the period of transition, bringing the volume of capital investment for 1997 to less than 24% of its 1990 level (OECD 1997, 37). See also *Interfax Statistical*

core industry (despite massive debt accumulation, much from abroad), and by a surprising (given dramatic changes in economic and valuation environment) continuity/stability in business networks and relations. This state of transition has led to growing fiscal imbalances, at all levels, that culminated in the financial crisis of 1998.[8]

A large number of partially overlapping explanations are available for these phenomena. They include:

- insufficient liquidity due to misplaced 'monetarism' (Russian Academy 1997, Commander-Mumssen 1998, Woodruff 1999a);
- irrationally high (controlled) monetary prices, especially for energy, inducing barter as a means to effect price cuts (Woodruff 1999a, 1999b);
- tax evasion (Hendley et al. 1998, Yakovlev 1999);
- inefficient monetary and credit systems (Poser 1998);
- rent-seeking in monetized transactions by commercial and monetary intermediaries, raising transactions costs above those of barter and quasi-monies (Guriev-Pospelov 1998);
- a lack of serious industrial restructuring, implying an inability to reproduce value with the inherited configuration of technologies, production facilities, social obligations, etc. (Commander-Mumssen 1998, Gaddy-Ickes 1998b, Ericson 1998).

These explanations basically fall into two categories: (1) bad policy, and (2) bad structure. The "bad policy" arguments suggest that technical solutions could be devised that would eliminate barter.[9] In these explanations, barter is what needs to be explained. The "bad structure" explanations focus on more fundamental problems that plague the Russian transition. Barter is a side effect of agents' attempts to cope with the structural legacies of the previous system in the context of a quasi-market economy.

While both types of explanation are undoubtedly valid, the second seems to us more fundamental. Moreover, only the virtual economy hypothesis explains the lack of restructuring and the growth in barter as part of the same process. Specifically, it derives from the fact that much of inherited industry — the legacy of the Soviet Union — must avoid the monetized economy as it is not viable there. It can only survive in a "virtual economy."

Report, no. 4, 1998. In 1998 gross fixed investment declined 6.7%; during 1999 this finally showed an increase, 1% for the year. (*PlanEcon Report*, vol. XVI, 3, February 2000, 6) Although some decline in investment-GDP ratio was a necessary response to the excessive rates of the Soviet period, this seems to be an over-correction. This is evident in the aging of the capital stock. In 1980 the average age of plant and equipment was 9.5 years; in 1995 it was 14.1. This is all the more ominous given the fact that in the Soviet period replacement rates were very low, and capital was kept in place until physically obsolete.

[8] See, for example, Ericson (1998).

[9] These may be complex to implement, at least with respect to tax evasion, but in in principle they are feasible, technical solutions.

1.2 The virtual economy hypothesis

Much of the economic activity and the stock of assets in Russia, as measured in monetary terms, is more apparent than real. It reflects an exaggerated valuation of both production and capital in the core manufacturing sectors of the economy. These capacities reflect a structure of factor and input use inherited from the Soviet Union, despite sometimes substantial borrowing for investment in new equipment. They reflect a general lack of serious restructuring of facilities, processes and products, as well as little change in managerial practices.[10] Thus the core of industrial manufacturing contains many low (to negative) value-added enterprises at "market" [user/consumer value] prices. Particularly with import alternatives, much of manufacturing can't survive in an even partially competitive market. Yet the collapse/disappearance of this core is socially/politically unacceptable, even when it is economically rational (market-valued social surplus enhancing) to close and replace those enterprises. Indeed, in the extreme conditions of political, economic and institutional uncertainty that prevail in Russia, the replacement of closed enterprises would seem to be an extremely lengthy and uncertain process.[11] This helps explain why bankruptcy statutes have been effectively ignored.

It is not just governments that are reluctant to shut down loss-making enterprises. Enterprise directors have an incentive to keep them operating so that they can continue to appropriate cash flow on the basis of their control of enterprise assets.[12] The fact that the enterprise is not viable in the market economy means that some other way must be found to continue operation, allowing continued appropriation of cash flow. To make these enterprises *appear* viable (value-adding) they engage in specific strategies to keep output prices 'above market' and input costs held 'below market' through barter, arrears, or quasi-monetary instruments, generating "virtual prices."[13] Among such strategies are:

- trading industrial output at exaggerated value for energy, transportation, and basic material inputs (lowering their relative prices);
- forcing "natural" (in-kind) wages on, or ceasing to pay (i.e. imposing "arrears" on) workers, lowering the wage bill;

[10] This lack of restructuring, and the reasons behind it, are nicely summarized by a recent report of the McKinsey Global Institute (1999) to the Russian government on the situation in 10 critical sectors of the Russian economy in 1997–1998.

[11] One important factor is the peculiar geographic location of enterprises in Russia. Enterprises were located under Soviet conditions without regard to transportation costs. If L/NVA enterprises were shut down it is not at all clear that new enterprises will form in the same location. For regional officials this is an important consideration operating against enforcing bankruptcy statutes. See Ickes et. al. (1997).

[12] Even L/NVA enterprises have some cash flow, just not of a sufficient magnitude to cover costs. A director of such an enterprise can appropriate some of this cash flow if the operation can be maintained. This provides a good part of the explanation of the keen interest of directors in maintaining operation of loss-making enterprises. Notice the role of a regime where agents do not have to meet their fiduciary responsibilities to survive, e.g. a regime in which arrears to suppliers, government and workers is endemic.

[13] Note than none of these is possible in a legal environment in which property and contract rights are effectively enforced, providing recourse for creditors.

– bartering with, or using offsets/arrears on, governments at all levels to lower indirect/overhead costs and taxes.

Thus low/negative value added (L/NVA) enterprises can appear viable, able to cover costs, by pursuing these 'virtual' strategies. The only problem for them is how to get their hands on cash/money/credit [an apparent liquidity problem]; no one is willing to pay real money at these virtual prices. This provides a strong incentive for management, that would otherwise lose its (personally lucrative and politically powerful) position, to engage in this de-monetized "virtual economy." In addition, the total lack of transparency in the resulting system of valuation covers the massive extraction of "rents" under the illusion of performance. Thus both the government and L/NVA enterprises have an interest in preserving the fiction, a mutual interest that is reflected in some (now generally indirect) government subsidization through tax offsets, tacit acceptance of arrears on taxes, wages, etc.

The interests of the government and the L/NVA enterprises in maintaining the fiction that the core of the manufacturing sector is viable are clear. But these incentives are insufficient to maintain operation of these L/NVA enterprises; value must be transferred from the value-adding sectors of the economy to prop up loss-making enterprises. The primary source for the reallocation of value that preserves the virtual functioning of inefficient manufacturing is the same as it was in the Soviet Union — the energy and resource sectors.[14]

1.3 Is it real?

As participation in the "virtual economy" involves a sacrifice of (potential) wealth, the question arises as to why value-adding producers in the energy and resource sectors would willingly participate in such a transfer of value to other enterprises. The basic answer seems to lie in separation of the incentives of those who control the resource and energy industries from the value created in their operation. As discussed in Gaddy and Ickes (1998a, 1999) the government is able to offer incentives for "cooperation," and threaten punishments if the 'value adders' do not continue to provide support for manufacturing, in terms of access (or its denial) to lucrative export markets, political power and influence, the toleration of rent-seeking ("leakages"), and the threat of loss of control by independently voting its shares or redoing tainted privatizations.

In addition it has been argued (Woodruff 1999a,b) that these "natural monopolies" have an interest in using their market power to extract additional surplus through price discrimination.[15] This is reinforced if export (hard cash) markets

[14] This continuity is nicely observed and discussed in Tompson (1998). These are not, however, the only sources of value. In addition, new private enterprise contributes in the form of higher effective tax rates and other costs associated with operating in the monetary economy. See Gaddy and Ickes (1999).

[15] There are also incentives for price discrimination along "relational capital" lines within traditional inter-enterprise networks. See Gaddy and Ickes (1998a).

are quantity and price constrained and the domestic cash prices are supported by a (high) regulated floor. Under such circumstances, energy producers will try to increase domestic sales,[16] and by employing barter they can segment the domestic "for cash" and "for barter" markets. Hence barter for overpriced manufactures can generate a desired "price cut" maximizing profits from the L/NVA sector. However, the question remains as to whether these incentives are sufficiently strong and consistent for the configuration of behaviors required by the virtual economy hypothesis to be self-reinforcing, i.e. to comprise an equilibrium.

There is also a question of the consequences of the existence of the "virtual economy" for the Russian transition. Should it be considered just a reflection of a passing stage in a long and difficult transition process, one generated largely by misguided policy choices and the optimal response of economic agents thereto? Or is it representative of a much deeper problem, as much a cause as a consequence of the extraordinary difficulties of the Russian transition? We believe that the latter is closer to the truth as the roots of the "virtual economy" lie in the inherited inefficiencies and deformities of the Soviet industrial and factor-use structures. The "virtual economy" has become a means of survival for wasteful economic activity, removing the incentives and pressures for the radical restructuring of production activity that is essential to success of the transition to a tolerably well-functioning market economy. It has erected a barrier to investment in restructuring, further delaying the progress of transition.

Here we begin a formal analysis of this issue in a simple microeconomic model of the two key production sectors, energy (G) and manufacturing (M), their interaction through both monetized and barter/offset/*vekseli* markets, and the self-interested role of the government in supporting their interaction. In addition to providing a partial equilibrium model, we explore the conditions under which non-monetized interaction (aka "barter") supporting inefficient industrial enterprises is an optimal strategy for the energy sector, given government incentives, and then analyze conditions under which this optimal "barter" removes incentives for efficiency enhancing, surplus maximizing, and often Pareto improving restructuring of the manufacturing sector. Thus we take the first steps toward providing a general equilibrium model in which the "virtual economy" can be seen as a "bad" Nash equilibrium in comparison to a fully monetized and marketized equilibrium of a restructured economy.

2 The model

We model the "virtual economy" as consisting of two active (types of) agents: a monopolist energy sector (**G** — 'Gazprom') and a manufacturing sector, **M**, consisting of a continuum of producers with differing inherited efficiencies. The efficiency of manufacturing production is captured by an energy input coefficient, and the model is explicitly short run with fixed unit-input requirements up to an

[16] Alternatively, they could simply store the gas and sell it in the future if the expected growth in price exceeds the market rate of interest.

exogenously given capacity. We explicitly focus on the "energy" market where we model the determination of both monetized and 'barter' equilibrium prices and quantities; other market prices are taken as exogenously fixed. Enterprises in **M** are price-takers, while **G** is a monopolist who can discriminate between efficient and inefficient manufacturing enterprises.[17] The government participates in the equilibria of these markets through its (here fixed) choice of "incentive" parameters affecting the willingness of **G** to engage in 'barter' and hence the resulting transaction prices and quantities, the survival rate of manufacturing enterprises, and the revenues at the disposal of the state.

As a first approximation, we consider governmental behavior parameters, introduced in Sect. 2.2 below, to be fixed, and hence part of the environment faced by the active agents in the model. Although its support is critical to the existence and viability of the virtual economy, we take that support to be given in the parameters used here to influence the incentives of G. These parameters are assumed to result from the incentives of the government to support L/NVA manufacturers that were discussed in the Introduction. These include the (indirect) taxes that operating, even if unprofitable, firms still pay, and the avoidance of direct and indirect social and economic costs of shutdown and unemployment. These incentives are of course weakened when industry undertakes substantial restructuring, thereby increasing efficiency and taxable revenues but doing less for maintaining industrial operations and employment. Thus the support of barter and restructuring are to some extent substitutes in the preferences of the government. How they interact with the desire for tax revenue and the perceived need to maintain certain types of manufacturing capacity, regardless of efficiency, is the subject of further investigation and modeling that goes beyond the scope of this paper.

2.1 Manufacturing

We model L/NVA firms in the manufacturing sector, **M**, as those wasteful in their use of energy. Let the **M** sector consist of a continuum of non-atomic plants/enterprises, indexed $f \in [0,\bar{f}]$, each with a linear homogeneous technology and energy input requirement a_f. Each has the capacity to use at most 1 unit of (energy) inputs from **G,** thereby producing a_f^{-1} units of output. Let p_m be the market price of manufacturing output,[18] and p be the price of energy inputs. Letting $\eta_f \equiv w\ell_f + \gamma_f$ be other unit production costs, where w is the wage rate, ℓ_f — unit labor requirements, and γ_f — capital, tax and other overhead unit costs, the full unit cost of output becomes: $pa_f + \eta_f$. Let plants be ordered by *decreasing* energy efficiency, i.e. by *increasing* input coefficient, a_f, where the energy input coefficient is parametrized as follows:

$$a_f = \varphi + \sqrt{f},\ f \in [0,\bar{f}]\,.$$

[17] This ability comes from detailed knowledge of the rigid production networks and their planned energy requirements inherited from the Soviet Union.

[18] This might be considered the price at which import substitutes become available.

Assume that $\eta_f = \eta$, $\forall f$, and that plants are uniformly distributed on $[0,\bar{f}]$.[19] Then to produce, the plant with input requirement a_f must be able to cover unit costs:

$$p_m \geq pa_f + \eta. \tag{1}$$

This implies $p \leq (p_m - \eta)a_f^{-1}$ is necessary for the energy input to be purchased; for any p, only manufacturing enterprises with a_f sufficiently small will demand any energy input, as only they satisfy (1). As technology is linear, the plant f will use either 1 (i.e. up to capacity) or 0 units of energy; we will assume maximal output, i.e. $y_f = a_f^{-1}$ from 1 unit of energy input, whenever this condition is satisfied. This gives an inverse demand function for energy inputs of

$$P(f) = \frac{p_m - \eta}{\varphi + \sqrt{f}} \equiv D^{-1}(f) \tag{2}$$

where $D(p)$ denotes total demand at the price p, and f is the least efficient (marginal) enterprise demanding a unit of energy inputs. That is, $P(f)$ is the price at which each of the enterprises $\widetilde{f} \leq f$ would demand its capacity quantity of 1, while each enterprise with index greater than f would demand 0 energy inputs. Note that $\frac{p}{p_m}$ is the amount of manufactures that must be sold to pay for required energy inputs, while $\frac{\eta a_f^{-1}}{p_m}$ is the amount that must be sold to cover non-energy production costs. Thus a firm produces if and only if

$$\frac{p}{p_m} + \frac{\eta a_f^{-1}}{p_m} \leq a_f^{-1} \Leftrightarrow pa_f + \eta \leq p_m.$$

Enterprises with $p_m < pa_f + \eta$ are unable to pay for unit costs of production unless they can avoid paying some labor or capital costs, or can get a better price. This might be done by paying $q < p$ through bartering their output to **G** for $\theta p_m > p_m$, so that $q = \frac{p}{\theta}$. This barter can only reduce energy costs; other costs must still be covered by selling output $(a_f^{-1} - \frac{q}{p_m})$, beyond the amount $\frac{q}{p_m}$ required to purchase the unit of energy input, at the market price p_m.

Hence, enterprises f such that $P(f) < p$, or equivalently $D(p) > f$, produce insufficient value to cover their costs at prevailing market prices; their operation reduces the value produced in the economy if p is a competitive equilibrium market price. Such enterprises, unless they are subsidized, will have to cease production even if they cannot fully exit in the short run. It appears that Russian manufacturing is replete with such enterprises.[20]

It is among such enterprises that the search for "barter" alternatives, that effectively raise the price of their output above p_m, is urgent.

[19] This is inessential, but makes the analysis much more transparent.

[20] Many are kept alive by institutional imperfections such as the lack of effective bankruptcy. In 1997–1998, 40–60% of Russian manufacturing operated at a loss. See *Russian Economic Trends*, 7, 4, 1998: 45. Notice that precisely because of the 'virtual strategies' employed by enterprises it is notoriously difficult to interpret enterprise financial statements.

2.1.1 Barter[21]

We assume that **G**, from long prior experience, knows which enterprises/plants are sufficiently productive to be able to pay the market price, p, and which will cease operation if they can't get subsidized energy inputs. **G** will thus refuse to engage in subsidization through barter of those it knows able to pay. Thus a sufficiently efficient firm cannot engage in barter with the energy sector. Only those enterprises unable to afford the market price p can barter their product for a 'virtual' price θp_m, hence effectively paying only q per unit of energy input. This barter adds to the 'demand' for energy, expanding sales without cutting into effective monetized demand. The increment in energy 'demand', that is the quantity of 'energy' bartered for manufactures, then becomes:

$$D_b(q,p) = D(q) - D(p).$$

The reduction in its real energy costs from the ability to acquire inputs cheaply generates an increase in apparent ("virtual") value of a manufacturing enterprise's output. Let y_m be the share sold for the market (equilibrium) price of p_m, and y_b be the share bartered at an implicit price $\theta p_m > p_m$, with total output $y = y_m + y_b$. Since y_b is only used to acquire energy inputs, $\theta p_m y_b = p a_f y$ so $y_b = \frac{p}{\theta p_m} a_f y = \frac{q}{p_m} a_f y = \frac{q}{p_m}$ as $y = a_f^{-1}$, and $p_m y_m = p_m \left(1 - \frac{p}{\theta p_m} a_f\right) y \geq \eta y$ if barter makes the enterprise viable. This generates, for $\theta > 1$, "virtual revenues" of

$$\begin{aligned} \theta p_m y_b + p_m y_m &= p_m \left[1 + (p - q) a_f\right] y = \\ &= p_m y + \frac{p_m}{\theta} [\theta - 1] p a_f y > \\ &> (p a_f + \eta) y = p + \eta a_f^{-1}, \end{aligned} \tag{3}$$

which are necessary to appear viable.

For the rest of the paper we will normalize the (fixed by assumption) price of manufactures output to be 1. When $p_m = 1$, the manufacturing demand for energy input is

$$D(p) \equiv F(p) = \left(\frac{1 - \eta - \varphi p}{p}\right)^2. \tag{4}$$

It is a decreasing, convex function of price with an elasticity, $\frac{-2(1-\eta)}{1-\eta-\varphi p}$, which is increasing in p (decreasing in f, i.e. in quantity sold) and greater (in absolute value) than $\frac{2\left(\varphi + \sqrt{\bar{f}}\right)}{\sqrt{\bar{f}}} > 2$ [for all $f \leq \bar{f}$, i.e. $p \geq \frac{1-\eta}{\sqrt{\bar{f}} + \varphi}$]. Thus there is a well

[21] We use the term "barter" to refer to any of the quasi- and non-monetary ways of implementing idiosyncratic prices that overvalue the product of L/NVA producers and undervalue that of the value-adding sectors. This includes the use of commodity or services backed script, *vekseli*, re-traded promissory notes and debt, and offsets, as well as the direct and indirect exchange of products at 'virtual' prices (rates of exchange). On the many forms used, see Aukutsionek (1998), Commander and Mummsen (1998), Poser (1998) and Yakovlev (1998), as well as any of the papers of Gaddy and Ickes.

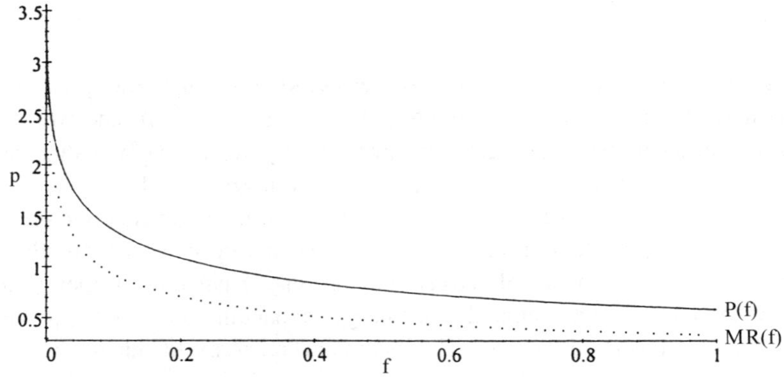

Fig. 1. Manufacturing demand for energy

defined optimum for the **G** monopolist selling to **M.** This demand function, and its associated marginal revenue curve, are illustrated in Fig. 1 where $\eta = 0.3$ and $\varphi = 0.2$ are assumed.[22]

This demand curve reflects the willingness to pay for energy inputs of the manufacturing sector. It is the true "value of marginal product" of energy in manufacturing, derived from the market demand for manufacturing output. It is relevant for determining the quantity transacted at any real "price," whether monetary or bartered.

2.1.2 Restructuring

An alternative to operating with current technology is to invest in restructuring. Restructuring by enterprises in **M** is assumed to involve raising investment funds through borrowing or surrender of equity, requiring opening the books of the enterprise, and establishing new economic relations, effectively breaking out of old relationships and barter networks. Restructuring investment has four primary consequences. For any enterprise f that restructures:

- energy efficiency rises: $\widehat{a}_f < a_f$;
- there is a rise in the other unit costs due to an increase in the "cost of capital" that exceeds any savings in unit costs from increasing factor/input productivity: $\widehat{\eta} > \eta$;
- the effective output (quality units) per unit bundle of inputs increases: $\varrho > 1$;
- the opportunity to barter output at more favorable than market rates is lost: network relations are broken and finances become transparent.[23]

These considerations are formalized as follows. Letting $\kappa > 0$ be the net increment of other unit costs per efficiency unit of output and $\varepsilon \in (0, 1)$

[22] Note marginal revenue (dotted line): $R(f) = p(f) \cdot f$ so $R'(f) = 1.75\frac{5.0\sqrt{f}+2.0}{\left(1.0+5.0\sqrt{f}\right)^2}$.

[23] Thus any restructured firm, regardless of its efficiency, is in the same position as a firm that **G** knows to be efficient: it must rely on arms-length market relations.

parametrize the relative energy-efficiency gain, we have $\widehat{\eta} = \varrho^{-1}(\eta + \kappa)$ and $\widehat{a}_f = \varrho^{-1}\left(\varphi + \varepsilon\sqrt{f}\right)$. This gives an f that restructures a new cost covering condition

$$p_m \geq p\widehat{a}_f + \widehat{\eta}, \tag{5}$$

and a new 'willingness to pay' (demand price) of

$$\widehat{P}(f) = \frac{\varrho p_m - (\eta + \kappa)}{\varphi + \varepsilon\sqrt{f}} = \frac{\varrho - (\eta + \kappa)}{\varphi + \varepsilon\sqrt{f}}, \tag{6}$$

as $p_m = 1$. Thus the restructuring opportunity is characterized by three fixed parameters: $\{\varepsilon, \kappa, \varrho\}$. Only ε interacts with the prior efficiency of the enterprise; the others are given by the characteristics of the technology.

This formulation implies that restructuring has very little effect on initially energy-efficient ("world class") enterprises, and brings the greatest benefit to the least efficient enterprises. Another implication is that the restructuring of all enterprises will result in a more elastic sectoral demand for energy as $\varepsilon < 1$. Finally, note that, due to the fixed increase in other costs, the willingness (ability) of some enterprises, those with sufficiently low index f, to pay for energy *can fall* with restructuring.[24] This demand for energy from a restructured manufacturing industry can be seen in Fig. 2, using the same parameters as in Fig. 1, with $\varepsilon = 0.7$, $\kappa = 0.1$, and $\varrho = 1$.

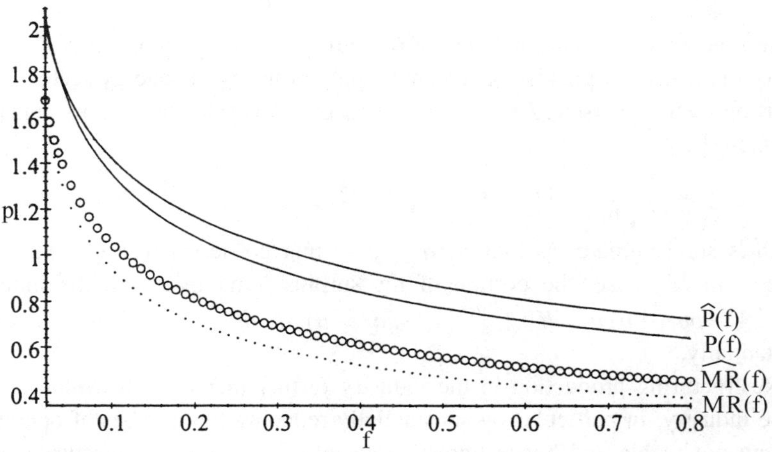

Fig. 2. Impact of restructuring on energy demand

Notice that marginal revenue (circles) from sales to the restructured industry also rises (above dotted MR curve) for sales above some minimal $\widetilde{f}$, and hence the monetized market can expand dramatically.

A enterprise that restructures can no longer engage in barter as it has broken old connections, and undertaken strong commitments to outsiders. Enterprises thus rationally restructure only when the surplus they receive after restructuring,

[24] Whether this occurs, and for which f, depends of course on the specific parameter values $\{\varepsilon, \kappa, \varrho\}$. This is discussed in Sect. 3 below.

$\widehat{s}_f = 1 - \widehat{p}\widehat{a}_f - \widehat{\eta}$, where $\widehat{p}$ is the new market price for energy, is greater than that in its absence: $s_f = 1 - pa_f - \eta$ or (if it is initially bartering for its input) $s_f = 1 - qa_f - \eta$. Otherwise there is no restructuring chosen. Notice, however, that when restructuring is taking place in some manufacturing firms other firms may no longer face the original price p or q as the monopolist adjusts to some $\widetilde{p}$ in order to optimally exploit the restructuring market. Thus the relevant comparison, at least for firms in the monetized market, may be between $\widehat{s}_f$ and $\widetilde{s}_f = 1 - \widetilde{p}a_f - \eta$, where $\widetilde{p} > p$.

2.1.3 Economic value in **M.**

To close this section we present the social surplus generated by the use of energy in the manufacturing sector. As the sector is competitive and technology linear homogeneous, each operating enterprise contributes $\left(p_m - c_f\right) a_f^{-1}$, where c_f is the unit cost of production in f that depends on the 'price' (p or q) paid for energy input. If a enterprise does not operate, then it imposes a fixed cost on society of $-\phi$.[25] Thus the surplus generated by the activity of the unrestructured industry with no barter and $p_m = 1$ is:

$$\int_0^{F(p)} \left(1 - ca_f - \eta\right) a_f^{-1} df - \phi \left[\overline{f} - F(p)\right],$$

where c is the social marginal cost of providing the energy input. If $p > c$, then part of this social surplus is taken as monopoly profit by the energy sector. When a portion of the industry, $F(q) - F(p)$, engages in barter, the surplus generated becomes:

$$\int_0^{F(q)} \left(1 - ca_f - \eta\right) a_f^{-1} df - \phi \left[\overline{f} - F(q)\right],$$

which is surely greater as long as $q \geq c$ so that no destruction of value takes place.[26] In any case, the portion of the surplus remaining with the industry, $\int_0^{F(p)} \left(1 - pa_f - \eta\right) a_f^{-1} df + \int_{F(p)}^{F(q)} \left(1 - qa_f - \eta\right) a_f^{-1} df - \phi \left[\overline{f} - F(q)\right]$, increases substantially.

Restructuring production in the industry further increases the value created in the industry, in particular by substantially reducing the number of operations that are not viable and hence impose a social cost ϕ. Thus restructuring is, in part, a substitute for barter in the eyes of the government. Letting $\widehat{F}(p)$ be the industry demand for energy after restructuring [the inverse of the willingness to pay function in (6)], we get

$$\int_0^{\widehat{F}(p)} \left(1 - c\widehat{a}_f - \widehat{\eta}\right) \widehat{a}_f^{-1} df - \phi \left[\overline{f} - \widehat{F}(p)\right],$$

[25] It is the avoidance of these costs that, in part, provides the reason for the government setting incentives to encourage barter.

[26] Even when $c > q$, there is an increase in net social value as long as the loss in value added is less than the gain from avoiding shutdown of operations, $\phi \left[f(q) - f(c)\right]$.

where $\widehat{F}(p) > F(p)$ and can be greater even than $F(q)$, depending on precise parameter values. In this case it is the largest social value that might be created by the manufacturing sector. When $\widehat{F}(p) < F(q)$, there is a trade-off between increased value produced in each firm, and the cost savings from the increased number of firms surviving under barter. In either case, individual enterprises may be less well off, as the increase in demand from restructuring allows the monopoly provider of energy inputs to raise its price to $\widehat{p}$.

In all cases, the maximal social value that could be generated from energy use in manufacturing is

$$\int_0^{F(c)} \left(1 - ca_f - \eta\right) a_f^{-1} df - \phi \left[\overline{f} - F(c)\right]$$

without restructuring, and

$$\int_0^{\widehat{F}(c)} \left(1 - c\widehat{a}_f - \widehat{\eta}\right) \widehat{a}_f^{-1} df - \phi \left[\overline{f} - \widehat{F}(c)\right]$$

after restructuring. The latter is easily seen to be substantially greater than the former, as $\left(1 - c\widehat{a}_f - \widehat{\eta}\right) \widehat{a}_f^{-1} > \left(1 - ca_f - \eta\right) a_f^{-1}$ for all firms that restructure, and $\widehat{F}(c) \gg F(c)$.[27]

2.2 Energy: Gazprom, UES, etc.

The energy sector is modelled as a unitary actor.[28] It is taken to be a price-taker in international markets, its primary source of serious revenue, and a discriminating monopolist in domestic markets.[29] The world market (dollar) price of energy in rubles is $\overline{p}$, but **G** is export-constrained, by transport capacity and through licensing by the government, to a quantity $E(\cdot)$. The constraint can be altered by the government, and is assumed to depend on **G**'s support for industry **M**.[30] Let that support be measured by the volume of sales/barter, B, at below market (i.e. "barter") prices. Thus revenues from the hard currency export market are $\overline{p}E(B)$.

The domestic market is segmented into those who can pay cash and those who must barter, with the boundary determined by the price chosen by **G,** and

27 We provide illustrative numbers in the continuation of our numerical example below.

28 While clearly an exaggeration, this assumption captures the substantial market power exercised by the gas monopoly, *Gazprom*, the electric network, *UES*, the pipeline monopoly, *Rosneft*, and the major oil producers such as *Lukoil* and *Sidanko*.

29 In 1997, for example, *Gazprom* exported 25% of its total production to Europe, receiving 100% cash in return, while 62% of total production was sold domestically with cash receipts constituting only 15% of the total. The remainder went to CIS countries which paid cash for 58% of deliveries. See Pinto et al., (1999).

30 This government policy can be derived as the optimal solution of government welfare in a more general model. That welfare will depend on tax revenues, the utility of maintaining a large manufacturing sector, the direct and social costs of entrerprise shutdown, etc.

the extent of the market determined by **G**'s choice of a barter 'price' q. Thus **G**'s total revenues are[31]

$$R(p,q) = \overline{p}E(B) + pD(p) + qD_b(q,p), \tag{7}$$

where the subscript b indicates the amount of energy bartered for manufactured goods. Those revenues are, however, subject to taxation leaving only some portion providing high-powered incentives to **G**. Assume that those incentives come from "leakages" from hard currency sales, $\alpha\overline{p}E(B)$, that are "overlooked" (i.e. implicitly allowed) by the government, and from (a share of) after tax profits, given by[32]

$$\beta\left[\begin{array}{c}(1-\alpha)\overline{p}E(B) + pD(p) + qD_b(q,p)\\ -C(E(B)+D+B)\end{array}\right],$$

where $B = D_b(q,p)$ and $D = D(p)$. Finally, we might suppose that there are direct, non-pecuniary, incentives provided by the government to encourage support of manufacturing through lower input prices (barter); let this be given by $\delta u(B)$, and δ is a parameter allowing variation in the strength of this incentive.[33] The cost function is assumed to contain a large fixed cost, **F** (the model is short-run), and a low, constant marginal cost, c: $C(Q) = \mathbf{F} + cQ$.

2.2.1 The monopoly optimum

Under these assumptions, **G**'s optimization problem is:

$$\max D,B\left\{\alpha\overline{p}E(B) + \delta u(B) + \beta\left[\begin{array}{c}(1-\alpha)\overline{p}E(B) + p(D)D + q(D+B)B\\ -c\cdot[E(B)+D+B] - \mathbf{F}\end{array}\right]\right\}, \tag{8}$$

Assume $E(B) = \overline{E} + \vartheta(B - \overline{B})$, and $\overline{pE} > \mathbf{F}$ so that the unit cost of domestic sales is just c. Then optimization yields FOC's,

$$\begin{aligned}(\alpha + (1-\alpha)\beta)\overline{p}\vartheta + \delta u'(B) + \beta\left[q'(D+B)B + q(D+B) - c(1+\vartheta)\right] &= 0\\ \beta\left[p'(D)D + p(D) - c\right] &= 0 \quad (9)\end{aligned}$$

The impact of these conditions, and how they exploit the segmentation of the market are easy to see in the analytic example introduced in the prior section. Letting $c = 0.7$,[34] we can explicitly solve for the monopoly optimum both with and without barter and with and without special government incentives. The basic monopoly optimum is $F(p) \approx 0.205$, with $p \approx 1.072$, as seen in Fig. 3.

Introducing the option to segment the market and barter energy to manufacturers at a lower real price, allows **G** to expand sales and seize more of the surplus generated by the operation of manufacturers, even without added government incentives. In that case, the first order conditions are:

[31] We assume that **G** only barters with manufacturers, while monetary sales are to the entire market including some manufacturers. This revenue function implicitly assumes that **G** sells all of the manufactured goods that it receives in barter, either to others or to itself, at the market price, p_m, thereby generating actual revenue per unit of bartered energy of $q = \frac{p}{\theta}$. If the price has to be

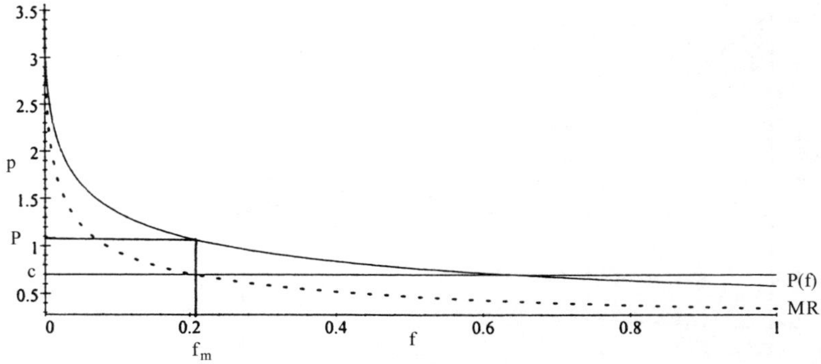

Fig. 3. Monopoly optimum without barter

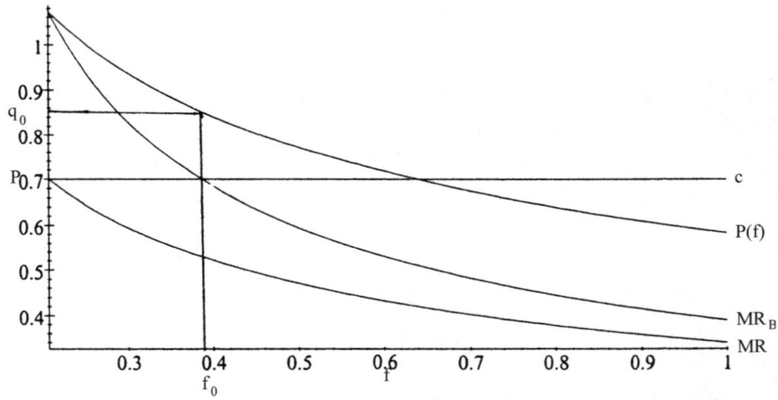

Fig. 4. Barter optimum without government incentives

$$MR_D(D) = c$$
$$MR_B(B,D) = c$$

as all of the terms involving the parameters $\alpha, \vartheta, \delta$ drop out of the first line of (9). In this case, the barter segment of the market is illustrated in Fig. 4. Here barter reduces the inefficiency of monopoly, although it may drive $P(f)$ below ATC (full unit, including average fixed, cost) of energy production.

The energy sector, **G,** however, faces strong incentives to further extend barter, due to government policy. The introduction of incentives for barter effectively lowers the marginal cost to **G** of providing energy to the barter segment of the market. Indeed, as its decision-relevant marginal cost, $c(1+\vartheta)-$

discounted below p_m for resale or further barter, then **G**'s (marginal) revenues are below what is calculated below, reducing **G**'s incentive to barter with **M.**

[32] This assumes that the government taxes actual revenues, and not the revenues that would have been received if the bartered output had actually been sold at price p.

[33] This might be justified in a more general model by threat/probability of expropriation and therefore losing the pecuniary incentives.

[34] And ignoring demand from other sectors, perhaps because their markets are further segmented and **G**'s marginal costs are constant.

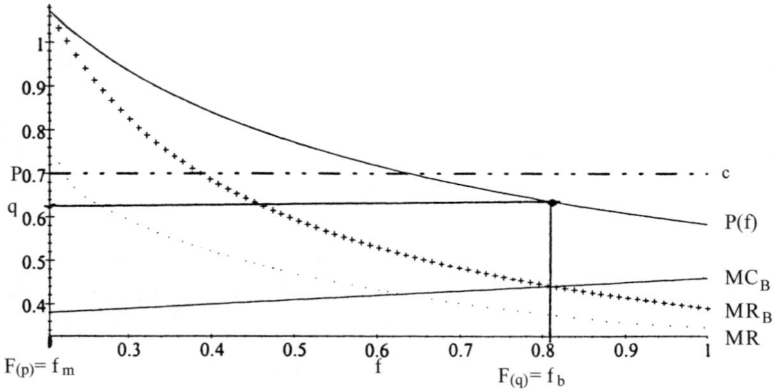

Fig. 5. Barter extension of monopoly optimum

$\beta^{-1}\left[(\alpha+(1-\alpha)\beta)\overline{p}\vartheta+\delta u'(B)\right]$, is below social marginal costs, c, **G** may find it optimal to supply manufacturing enterprises for whom $P(f) < c+\frac{\mathbf{F}}{\mathbf{Q}}$, and hence to support true NVA producers. This can be easily seen in the FOC's for our example,

$$\begin{aligned} MR_D(D) &= \frac{1-\eta}{2}\cdot\frac{2\varphi+\sqrt{D}}{\left(\varphi+\sqrt{D}\right)^2} = MC_D(D) = c \\ MR_B(B,D) &= MR_D(D+B) + \frac{(1-\eta)D}{2\sqrt{D+B}\left(\varphi+\sqrt{D+B}\right)^2} = \\ MC_B(B,D) &= (1+\vartheta)c - \frac{1}{\beta}\left\{[\alpha+(1-\alpha)\beta]\overline{p}\vartheta+\delta u'(B)\right\}, \end{aligned} \tag{10}$$

showing how political factors lower the real marginal cost of supplying to barter. The optimal solution in this case is illustrated in Fig. 5, where the politically determined marginal costs in our example are given by

$$\begin{aligned} MC_B(B,0.205) &= 0.38056+0.10B = \\ &= c(1+\vartheta) - \frac{1}{\beta}\left\{(\alpha+(1-\alpha)\beta)\overline{p}\vartheta+\delta u'(B)\right\} < c = 0.7, \end{aligned} \tag{11}$$

while the relevant marginal benefit is $MR_B(B,D) > MR_D(D)$ [given by '+++' line above the '· · ·' line].
Here the monopolists optimal decisions are:

$$\{p=1.072; F(p)\equiv D=0.205; q=0.6357; F(q)\equiv F(p)+B=0.812\}.$$

Note that almost three quarters of the energy inputs acquired by manufacturers are acquired through barter.

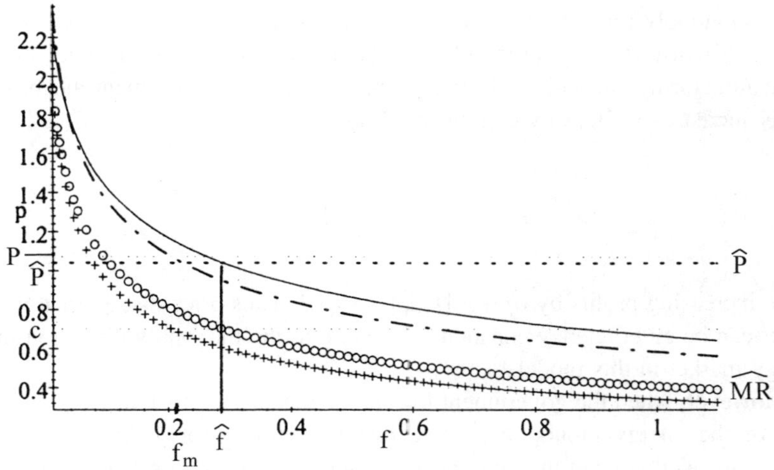

Fig. 6. Monopoly optimum in the restructured industry

When the manufacturing industry restructures, **G** loses its ability to distinguish the efficient from the inefficient among the "restructured" firms,[35] and hence the ability to segment the markets through barter. Thus it faces a single market with demand given by $\widehat{P}(f)$, and will choose an optimal $\{\widehat{p}, \widehat{D}\}$ such that $MR(\widehat{D}) = c$, where

$$MR(\widehat{D}) = \frac{\varrho - (\eta + \kappa)}{2} \cdot \frac{2\varphi + \varepsilon\sqrt{\widehat{D}}}{\left(\varphi + \varepsilon\sqrt{\widehat{D}}\right)^2}.$$

In the example with $c = 0.7$, $\epsilon = 0.7$, $\kappa = 0.1$, and $\varrho = 1$, optimal monopoly energy supply is $\widehat{D} = .2902 > D = 0.205$, and $\widehat{P}(\widehat{D}) = \frac{1-(\eta+\kappa)}{\varphi+\varepsilon\sqrt{0.2902}} = 1.0397 < P(0.205) = 1.072$. These results are illustrated in Fig. 6. Thus, in this example, the monopolist allows some growth of the market, but nowhere near as much as with barter, even without extra government incentives, would allow.

2.2.2 Welfare analysis

The monopolization of the energy sector clearly leads to a loss of welfare in the economy, due to the value of energy (its demand price $F(p)$) being greater than the social cost of its provision ($\approx c$). This is reflected in a restriction in energy use in the monetized market, generating a deadweight loss of

$$\int_{F(p)}^{F(c)} \left(1 - ca_f - \eta\right) a_f^{-1} df,$$

[35] Firms, from the other perspective, lose the ability to credibly distinguish themselves as barter partners, due to their breaking out of the old networks during restructuring. Firms that do not restructure, however, maintain their old relationships, including that with **G.**

and a monopoly rent of $(p - c)F(p)$. The introduction of barter, however, can reduce this distortion by profitably (for **G**) extending sales to a larger number of manufacturing enterprises. In the absence of special government incentives it surely increases welfare by cutting the deadweight loss to

$$\int_{F(q)}^{F(c)} \left(1 - ca_f - \eta\right) a_f^{-1} df,$$

while increasing profits by $(q - c)[F(q) - F(p)]$. Thus price discrimination cum barter can be an efficiency enhancing response to the monopoly distortion in the energy market in this model.

However, when the government lowers the incentive-effective marginal costs (11) of the energy monopolist, price discrimination through barter can drive energy use well beyond the point at which social marginal costs and benefits are equal, as is illustrated in Fig. 5. There the social optimum occurs at $P(f) = 0.7$, that is when $f = 0.640$, while the discriminating monopoly optimum is $F(q) = 0.812$, so that the firms indexed in $(0.64, 0.812]$ (over 21% of those operating) are truly negative value-added producers. Yet they appear to be viable, albeit cash constrained; a mirage of the virtual economy. This generates a deadweight loss of

$$\int_{F(c)}^{F(q)} \left(ca_f - (1 - \eta)\right) a_f^{-1} df,$$

while increasing the profits of the energy monopoly by $\int_{F(p)}^{F(q)} \left[q - MC_B(B, D)\right] df$ beyond the profits from monetized sales. This again illustrates the incentive that the monopolist has to transfer value to manufacturers, even when there is a net social loss; its private residual is thereby enhanced.

When manufacturing restructures, it suffers the full impact of the monopoly distortion. The deadweight loss imposed by monopoly restriction of output is

$$\int_{\widehat{F}(\widehat{p})}^{\widehat{F}(c)} \left(1 - c\widehat{a}_f - \widehat{\eta}\right) \widehat{a}_f^{-1} df,$$

which is substantially greater than in the original unrestructured case. In our numerical example, $\widehat{F}(c) = 0.8813 > F(c) = 0.64$, $\widehat{F}(\widehat{p}) = 0.2902 > F(p) = 0.205$, and $\left(1 - c\widehat{a}_f - \widehat{\eta}\right) \widehat{a}_f^{-1} > \left(1 - ca_f - \eta\right) a_f^{-1}$ as illustrated in Fig. 2. In addition, monopoly rents increase to $\left(\widehat{p} - c\right) \widehat{F}(\widehat{p}) = 0.09858 > 0.205 \times 0.2476 = 0.050758$, the market monopoly rents from the unrestructured industry. These, however, are swamped by the rents earnable from barter, due to the special incentives that the government provides: $0.050758 + \int_{0.205}^{0.812} (0.6357 - 0.38 - 0.15f) df = 0.0508 + 0.1089 = 0.1597$. Thus again there is a substantial divergence between private and social incentives, one that can be expected to stand in the way of socially optimal restructuring.

3 Equilibrium and the "virtual economy" trap

Let us now explore in greater depth the equilibrium interaction between **G** and **M**, when enterprises in **M** have an option to invest in significant "restructuring." As argued in Sect. 2.1.2, restructuring by enterprises in **M** involves investment, requiring opening the books of the enterprise, which raises their energy efficiency and perhaps also labor efficiency and the quality/quantity of output. This gives an enterprise, f, that restructures a new cost covering condition

$$1 \geq p\widehat{a}_f + \widehat{\eta} \tag{12}$$

where $\widehat{a}_f = \varrho^{-1}\left(\varphi + \varepsilon\sqrt{f}\right)$, $\varepsilon \in (0,1)$, and $\widehat{\eta} = \varrho^{-1}(\eta + \kappa)$, $\kappa > 0$, generating the demand price for a restructured enterprise of $\widehat{P}(f)$ (6). As also argued there, an enterprise that restructures can no longer engage in barter since it has broken old connections, and undertaken strong commitments to outsiders.

3.1 **M***'s response to the restructuring opportunity*

Whether an enterprise chooses to restructure depends on both how its "demand price," $\widehat{P}(f)$, changes and how the price it is paying will change. Because the improvement in energy productivity is assumed inversely proportional to initial efficiency, the demand price of the most efficient firm, $f = 0$, will rise only if $(\varrho - 1)p_m = \varrho - 1 > \kappa$, i.e. the increase in unit value of output exceeds the increase in unit capital costs, net of other factor input savings. Such a restructuring opportunity is essentially a 'free lunch' and will be assumed not to be available. This gives a simple characterization of the change in demand price:

Lemma 1. *Let $\kappa > \varrho - 1$. Then, if they restructure, the most efficient firms, $f \in [0,\widetilde{f})$, would experience a drop in the unit value of (their willingness to pay for) energy inputs, while the less efficient firms, $f \in (\widetilde{f},\overline{f}]$, would be willing to pay more for energy inputs after restructuring. The demand price of firm $\widetilde{f} = \left\{\frac{[(\varrho-1)-\kappa]\varphi}{[\kappa+(1-\varepsilon)\eta-(\varrho-\varepsilon)]}\right\}^2$ remains unchanged with restructuring: $\widehat{P}(\widetilde{f}) = P(\widetilde{f})$.*

Proof. The formula for $\widetilde{f}$ is the solution to the equation $\widehat{P}(\widetilde{f}) = P(\widetilde{f})$, i.e.

$$\frac{\varrho - (\eta + \kappa)}{\varphi + \varepsilon\sqrt{f}} = \frac{1 - \eta}{\varphi + \sqrt{f}}.$$

When the numerator is nonnegative, the demand price for all firms must increase. □

We will say that a firm, f, "has an incentive to restructure" if and only if restructuring increases the unit value of energy for it: $\widehat{P}(f) > P(f)$. Thus $\widetilde{f}$ and all $f < \widetilde{f}$ have no incentive to restructure, so only those firms $f > \widetilde{f}$ will consider restructuring. Each such enterprise rationally decides to restructure when the surplus it receives after restructuring is greater than that in its absence:

$$\widehat{s_f} > s_f, \tag{13}$$

where

$$\begin{aligned} \widehat{s_f} &= 1 - \widehat{p}\widehat{a_f} - \widehat{\eta}, \\ s_f &= \begin{cases} 1 - pa_f - \eta \\ 1 - qa_f - \eta \end{cases}, \end{aligned}$$

depending on whether the firm f had access to barter or not. Here $\widehat{p}$ is the new price set by **G**.[36] We assume that the restructuring decision is irrevocable, but taken in correct anticipation of **G**'s optimal pricing response to the changed demand that results.

The optimal restructuring decisions, i.e. the reaction functions, of manufacturing firms are straightforward to characterize:

Proposition 1. *Let $\widehat{p}$ be the anticipated price of* **G** *in response to restructuring by users, $p = P(f_m)$ — the market price to the unrestructured industry, and let $\overline{p} = \widehat{P}(f_m)$.*

1. *For all $\widehat{p}$, no firm $f \in [0,\widetilde{f}]$ will choose to restructure.*
2. *For all $\widehat{p}$, every firm $f \in \left(\widetilde{f},f_m\right]$ will restructure if it must pay $\widehat{p}$ even if it doesn't restructure.*
3. *For $\widehat{p} \geq \overline{p}$, no firm $f \in \left[0,f_m\right]$ will choose to restructure if not doing so leaves the price at p.*
4. *For $\widehat{p} \leq p$, all firms $f \in \left(\widetilde{f},f_m\right]$ will restructure: $\widehat{s_f} \geq s_f$ (13).*
5. *For each $\widehat{p} \in (p,\overline{p})$, there exists an $\widehat{f_p}$ such that $\widehat{s}_{\widehat{f_p}} = s_{\widehat{f_p}}$; i.e. $f < \widehat{f_p} \Rightarrow \widehat{s_f} < s_f$ and $f > \widehat{f_p} \Rightarrow \widehat{s_f} > s_f$. Hence the "no restructuring" set of efficient firms expands as $\widehat{p}$ increases, if not restructuring leaves the price at p.*
6. *Let $\underline{p} = \widehat{P}(f_b)$. Unless $\widehat{p} < \underline{p}$, no $f \in \left[f_m,f_b\right]$ will choose to restructure. If $\widehat{p} < \underline{p}$ then some firms $f > f_b$ will choose to renew operation by restructuring.*

Proof. Part 1 holds as there is, by Lemma 1, no incentive for these firms to restructure. Part 2 follows from (13) and the fact that $\widehat{P}(f) > P(f)$, $\forall f \in \left(\widetilde{f},f_m\right]$. Part 3 is a consequence of the fact that $\widehat{P}'(f) < P'(f)\ \forall f$. Hence the surplus of all but the least efficient firm, f_m, is less after restructuring and facing $\overline{p}$ than when facing p without restructuring. For prices above $\overline{p}$ all restructured firms generate a still smaller surplus, while those near f_m cannot survive. Part 4 is similarly clear, as $pa_f > \widehat{p}\widehat{a_f} + \kappa \Leftrightarrow \widehat{s_f} \geq s_f$. These can be easily seen from the relationship between $P(f)$ and $\widehat{P}(f)$ in Figs. 2, 6 and 8.

To see Part 5, note that for $\widehat{p} = p$, there is no change in the surplus of $\widetilde{f}$ from restructuring, while all firms $f \in \left(\widetilde{f},f_m\right]$ strictly gain. As $\widehat{p}$ increases above p, the surplus of all firms decreases, rendering that of $\widetilde{f}$, and all f such that

[36] The price a manufacturer faces after restructuring, $\widehat{p}$, may or may not differ from p, depending on whether, and how, **G** responds to its restructuring.

$\widehat{P}(\widetilde{f}) - \widehat{P}(f) < \widehat{p} - p$, less than it would have been with no restructuring at p. Clearly $\widehat{f_p} = \widehat{P}^{-1}\left(\widehat{P}(\widetilde{f}) - \widehat{p} + p\right)$ and the set of efficient firms that chooses not to restructure expands to $\left[0, \widehat{f_p}\right]$. Part 6 follows from the observation that, at $\widehat{p} = \underline{p}$, we have the same situation with respect to bartering firms as we have in Part 2 with respect to $\overline{p}$ for firms buying on the monetized market; only the least efficient firm maintains its (zero) surplus, and all others get a smaller surplus than they would if they continue to barter without restructuring at the rate of exchange q. Thus no firm, with an option to continue bartering, would consider restructuring, implying a return to the monetized market, at any $\widehat{p} \geq \underline{p}$. As $\widehat{p}$ drops below $\underline{p}$, firms on both sides of f_b, in particular those $f > f_b$ which without restructuring could not operate, will begin to find restructuring a desirable option. □

This proposition has as an immediate consequence: the opportunity to survive through "barter" creates a barrier to restructuring *if* **G** (e.g. for political reasons) fails to respond to restructuring by altering its terms of trade.

Corollary 1. *If* $\widehat{p} = p$, *then no bartering firm will choose to restructure, unless* $\underline{p} > p$.

Proof. Follows immediately from Part 5 of Proposition 1. □

Under our assumption that $\kappa > \varrho - 1$, the condition $\underline{p} > p$ can only hold for ε close to 0: $\varepsilon < \frac{q(\varrho-\eta-\kappa)-\varphi q p}{p(\varrho-\eta-\varphi q)}$.[37]

3.2 G's response to the restructuring possibility

To characterize the equilibrium restructuring decision, we now need to analyze the optimal response of **G** to restructuring by its users. **G** reacts to the demand function generated by restructuring decisions of firms in **M** and chooses a ex-post monopoly price. That response depends naturally on the number and type of firms in **M** that choose to restructure. The basic cases are outlined in the following:

Proposition 2. *Letting* $\widehat{P}(\cdot)$ *be the restructured demand price function, and* $\widehat{F}(\cdot)$ *be its inverse (the restructured industry's demand for energy), the optimal decision of* **G** *depends on restructuring as follows:*

1. *If no firm in* **M** *restructures, the market and barter price-quantity decisions of* **G** *remain unchanged.*
2. *The restructuring of any set of* **M**-*firms of measure zero has no impact on the monopoly price or quantity.*

[37] In our numerical example the right-hand side of this expression equals $0.399159 < \varepsilon = 0.7$.

3. *If all firms with an incentive to restructure in* **M** *do so, then no "barter" occurs and sales are made to* $\widehat{f} > f_m$ *firms, where* $\widehat{f}$ *solves*

$$\frac{d}{df}\left(f \cdot \widehat{P}(f)\right) = c,$$

and $\widehat{p} = \widehat{P}(\widehat{f})$. *Further,* $\widehat{f} < f_b$ *will hold for* ε *sufficiently large.*[38]

4. *If some subset of positive measure,* $\mathfrak{F}$, *of* **M**-*firms restructures, then the optimal monopoly price is* $\widetilde{p} \in [\widehat{p}, \overline{p}]$, *and depends on the size and location, in initial efficiency terms, of the set of firms that restructure. The marginal restructured firm supplied is,* $\widehat{F}(\widetilde{p}) \leq \widehat{f}$, *and firms in* $\mathfrak{F}$ *with* $\widehat{P}(f) \leq \widehat{p}$ *are ignored by* **G.** *If* $\widehat{F}(\widetilde{p})$ *is less than* f_b, *then* $f_b - \widehat{F}(\widetilde{p})$ *firms continue to barter at* $\widehat{q} < \widehat{p}$ *where* $\widehat{q} = B$ *solving a condition similar to that in Eq. (10).*
5. *There exists a* $f^v < f_m$ *such that, if only firms up to some* $f^* \in \left(f^v, \widehat{F}(\widetilde{p})\right)$ *restructure, then the optimal monopoly price is* $p^* = \widehat{P}(f^*)$, *the input price that eliminates the surplus of the marginal firm. If* $f^* < f^v$ *then it remains optimal to sell to* f_m *at the initial price* p.

Proof. The first assertion is obvious: raising the price reduces revenues by more than costs as manufacturers drop out of the market. The second follows from the observation that such restructuring has no noticeable impact on market demand. The third assertion is just the condition that the marginal revenue from the demand curve of the restructured industry equals the (constant) marginal cost of supplying that industry. $\widehat{f} > f_b$ can hold only when marginal revenue after restructuring at f_b exceeds the marginal cost, c, of supplying the market. Note that all barter incentives are lost in supplying these restructured firms. This condition will be true for all ε such that:

$$\frac{\varrho - \eta - \kappa}{2} \cdot \frac{2\varphi + \varepsilon\left(\frac{1-\eta-\varphi q}{q}\right)}{\left[\varphi + \varepsilon\left(\frac{1-\eta-\varphi q}{q}\right)\right]^2} > c, \tag{14}$$

as $f_b = \left(\frac{1-\eta-\varphi q}{q}\right)^2$. Direct calculation, using our parameter values, gives the lower bound of $\varepsilon \cong 0.41848$.

The fourth assertion can be seen by noting that firms that restructure move up (to lower *input* coefficients), while those that were initially more efficient but don't restructure are displaced lower in the efficiency ordering. Let f^s be the most efficient firm in $\mathfrak{F}$ (assumed to be an interval; the generalization to a union of intervals is straightforward). It then displaces in the efficiency ordering to f_s such that $\widehat{P}(f^s) = P(f_s)$. The new demand curve has a discontinuous rise in marginal revenue at f_s due to the kink where the interval of length F from $\widehat{P}(\cdot)$ is pasted to $P(\cdot)$. There are two cases to consider: (a) if $|\mathfrak{F}|$ is smaller than $f^s - f_s$, then $\widetilde{p} = p$ with f_m firms supplied on the monetized market, or $\widetilde{p} = \widehat{P}(f^s + |\mathfrak{F}|)$ with only $f^s + |\mathfrak{F}|$ so supplied, depending on which generates greater profit. (b) If

[38] $\varepsilon > 0.41848$, in our numerical example.

$|\mathfrak{F}|$ is greater than $f^s - f_s$ then $\widetilde{p} \in (p, \widehat{p})$ where the new higher marginal revenue equals c, or where the discontinuity (downward) crosses c at $f_s + |\mathfrak{F}|$.

To see assertion 5, note that there exists an f^v such that

$$\left[\widehat{P}(f^v) - c\right] f^v = \left[P(f_m) - c\right] f_m.$$

For $f^* > f^v$, the lhs of this expression grows ($\widehat{MR} > 0$), hence it pays to maintain the higher price even if selling to fewer than f_m. As marginal revenue exceeds marginal cost, f^* is supplied at the highest price maintaining that demand. For $f^* < f^v$, profits are greater from expanding the market to f_m. □

Remark 1. Although not necessary, it simplifies the argument to assume that government incentives (the parameters $\alpha, \delta, \vartheta$) are set such that $f_b > \widehat{f}$, i.e. the least efficient firm surviving on barter is less efficient than the marginal firm supplied on the market after its restructuring. Indeed, in our analytic example $f_b = 0.812$ is substantially greater than $\widehat{f} = 0.2902 > f_m = 0.205$.

These results reinforce the corollary to Proposition 1. They show that the price of energy will never fall below $\underline{p}$ unless there are extraordinarily large efficiency gains to restructuring. Thus, $\widehat{p}$ remains near or above p, rendering restructuring undesirable for all firms engaged in, and subsidized through, "barter."

3.3 Equilibrium with possible restructuring

We are now in a position to consider the equilibrium of the interaction between **G** and the continuum of nonatomic firms in **M.** We begin from an initial equilibrium, as characterized in Sect. 2 and illustrated in Figs. 3 and 5, where no manufacturing firms have yet restructured, and ask which firms would choose to do so.

Formally, there are three stages to the interaction. First, **M**-firms simultaneously and independently choose to restructure or not. Restructuring is an irreversible decision, committing the firm to a new technology and to abandoning all barter networks. In the second stage, after observing the restructuring decision of all manufacturers, **G** selects a monetized price charged to all firms on the open market, and an optimal barter price for those firms in the barter network that did not restructure. Finally, **M**-firms can either produce, acquiring inputs through purchase or barter (if they previously bartered and don't restructure), or cease production due to inability to cover costs. The choice to restructure is made knowing that **G** has a final move in which it will set a price optimally exploiting the restructuring decision. Thus firms in **M**, in choosing whether to restructure, will take into account the optimal pricing decision of **G**, which affects their viability in production. The general structure of the interaction in terms of firm 'types' is illustrated in the simplified game tree in Fig. 7.

As Proposition 2 shows, if all manufacturers refuse to restructure, the optimal response of the monopolist is to maintain the discriminating prices (p, q). However, at those prices, every firm on the monetized market has an individual

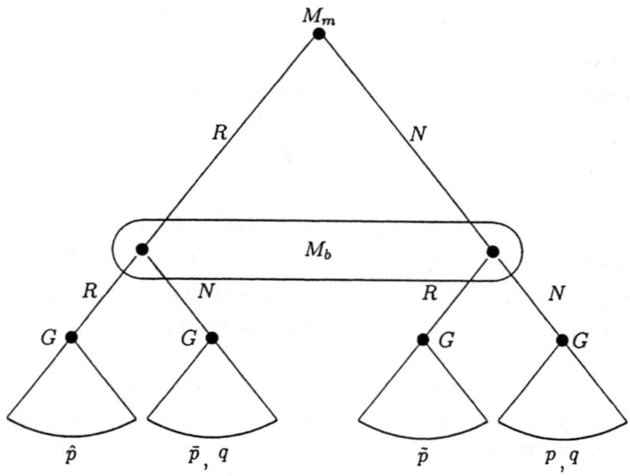

Fig. 7. Simplified restructuring game tree

incentive to restructure, although in many cases those firms engaging in barter would give up too much by restructuring, and so avoid it. This observation gives a first simple equilibrium result:

Proposition 3. *Let the initial equilibrium in the manufacturing industry be* $\{f_m, p\}$, *i.e. all active firms buy at the market price p and no firms are supported through "barter." Then all* **M**-*firms* $f \in (\tilde{f}, \hat{f}]$ *will restructure, giving equilibrium* $\{\hat{f}, \hat{p}\}$ *with* $\hat{f} > f_m$ *and* $\hat{p} < p$.

Proof. The result is obvious from Figs. 6 and 8. Part 3 of Proposition 2 gives the new monopoly optimum for **G**. Part 4 of proposition 1 then shows that all initially active firms, $f \in (\tilde{f}, f_m]$ will optimally choose to restructure, while some initially inactive firms, $f \in (f_m, \hat{f})$, can make a strict profit by restructuring and producing. The manufacturer $\hat{f}$ just breaks even when producing with energy price $\hat{p}$, and so also enters the market, while firms $f \in (\hat{f}, \bar{f}]$ remain inactive. □

If only those firms initially on the monetized energy market restructure, so that the monopoly price becomes $\overline{p}$, then every such firm loses some of the surplus that it originally had, and is worse off than if none had restructured. Hence, if manufacturing firms were able to explicitly cooperate, to coordinate their restructuring decisions, then all the firms in the monetized market would be better off by refusing (collectively) to restructure. But those who fail to restructure when others do so, unless they are safely in the "barter" network, suffer an even greater loss and run the risk of being forced to cease production, while any firm that restructures alone, when others fail to do so, reaps a windfall as productivity soars and the price of energy remains at p. Thus any firm on the monetized market has an individual incentive to restructure regardless of what the other manufacturing firms do. However, unless restructuring is phenomenally productive ($\widehat{p} < \underline{p} \Rightarrow \widehat{f} < f_b$ as in part 6 of Proposition 1), no firm in the "barter" network will have an incentive to restructure. This gives a "barter barrier" to restructuring as a subgame perfect Nash equilibrium.

Proposition 4. *Let ε be such that $\widehat{f} < f_b$. Then there exists a subgame perfect Nash equilibria of this Energy-Market Restructuring Game such that:*

1. *All firms $f \in \left(\widetilde{f}, f_m\right)$ choose to restructure, but no firms in $[0, \widetilde{f}] \cup [f_m, \overline{f}]$ choose to do so. The equilibrium is $\{f_m, f_b; \overline{p}, q\}$, where $\overline{p} = \widehat{P}(f_m)$.*
2. *There exists an open set of $(\varepsilon, \kappa, \varrho)$ such that no firm engaging in barter would choose to restructure at equilibrium: $\widehat{s_f} \le s_f$.*

Proof. The first thing to notice is that no firm $f \in [0, \widetilde{f}]$ will choose to restructure, regardless of the price **G** charges, as for them restructuring lowers the *economic* efficiency of their use of energy (Proposition 1, part 1). Further, Corollary 1 and Proposition 1, part 6 imply that no firm $f \in [f_m, \overline{f}]$ would ever choose to restructure as long as the condition on ε is met; for $f \in \left[f_m, f_b\right]$ too much is lost in giving up the subsidy, while for $f \ge f_b$ the condition on ε means restructuring fails to raise productivity sufficiently to cover the costs of production. Thus the only firms which might restructure in equilibrium are those $f \in \left(\widetilde{f}, f_m\right)$ who are active on the monetized energy market.

Next note that **G** solves an optimization problem at the final strategic stage of the game, i.e. in all proper subgames, insuring subgame perfection of any Nash equilibrium. By Proposition 2, part 2, **G** will never respond to a single firm's restructuring decision, but only to what a set of manufacturing firms of positive measure does. Proposition 2, part 5 then implies that the optimal price set by **G** is $p^* \ge \overline{p} = \widehat{P}(f_m)$ if any interval of the firms in $\left(\widetilde{f}, f_m\right)$ restructures. Thus any firm that restructures in that interval suffers a loss relative to the case where no manufacturing firm restructures: $\widehat{s_f} \le s_f$, with equality holding only at the least efficient boundary of the interval, f^*. But every firm that fails to restructure when the monetized price rises to p^* suffers an even greater loss. Indeed, since no firm on the monetized market can individually affect the price it pays, Proposition 1, part 2 shows that it will always choose to restructure: if other manufacturers restructure, it must do so to maintain profitability $\left(p^* \widehat{a_f} + \widehat{\eta} < p^* a_f + \eta\right)$, while if others don't, it reaps a windfall $\left(p\left(a_f - \widehat{a_f}\right) + (\eta - \widehat{\eta})\right)$. Thus restructuring is a dominant strategy for manufacturing firms on the monetized market; the more efficient increase their surplus, while the less efficient in $\left(\widetilde{f}, f_m\right)$ avoid ceasing operation. As a consequence of all $f \in \left(\widetilde{f}, f_m\right)$ restructuring, **G** will set a monetized market price of $p^* = \overline{p}$ (Proposition 2, part 4) as illustrated in Fig. 8. Firms in $\left(f_m, \overline{f}\right)$, including those operating on barter, will not restructure (Proposition 1, part 6), and will continue to face a "barter price," q, which

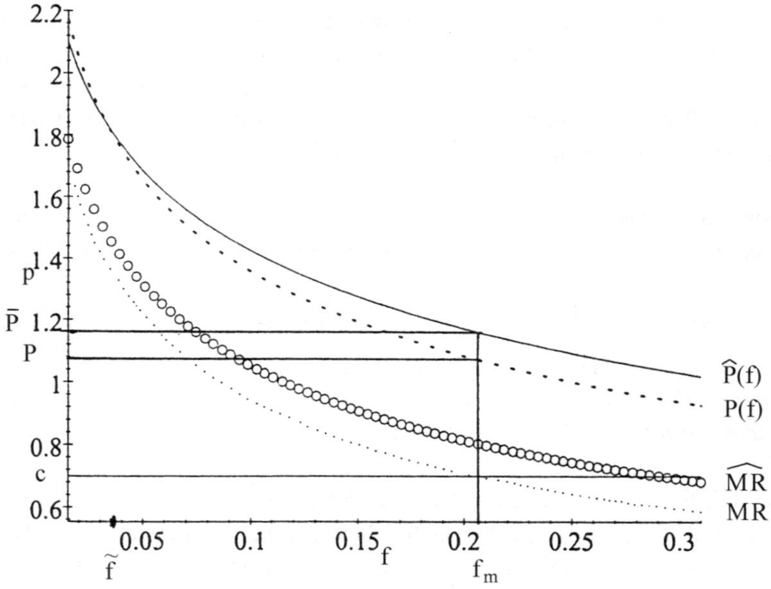

Fig. 8. Restructuring incentives on market

remains optimal for **G** as the overall quantity of energy sold on the monetized market doesn't change (see Sect. 2.2.1, especially Eq. (10)).

Part 2 is obvious from our analytic forms. The constraints on $\varepsilon, \kappa, \varrho$ are clearly open and satisfied by intervals of values: $\varepsilon \in (\underline{\varepsilon}, 1)$, where $\underline{\varepsilon}$ satisfies (14); $\varrho - 1 < \kappa$. □

Remark 2. Clearly, given that no firm on barter will restructure, all manufacturers on the monetized market would be better off *not* restructuring: $s_f > \widehat{s}_f$, $\forall f \in \left(\widetilde{f}, f_m\right)$. But they must *all* (but for a set of measure zero) avoid restructuring in order for **G** to optimally maintain the lower price $p < \overline{p}$. Thus the first stage interaction among manufacturers on the monetized market has the nature of a Prisoners' Dilemma. That is not the case for firms in the barter network as their restructuring decision, by forcing exit from the network, directly affects the "price" they face, removing the collective action problem.

Thus we see that there are equilibria in which no firm, already engaged in barter as a road to viability, would choose to abandon the barter network and restructure. A typical situation is depicted, using our example's parameter values, in Fig. 9. For these firms, restructuring and buying energy at $\widehat{p}$ gives a far smaller surplus (shaded) than that (outlined) from sticking with the barter network.

As a result of government incentives, there is just too large a surplus generated by barter to be overcome by restructuring, within the bounds we have placed on the restructuring parameters. However, if the impact of restructuring is sufficiently strong, i.e. if ϱ is large enough or ε and/or κ small enough, then firms can be enticed from barter through restructuring. In addition, if the gov-

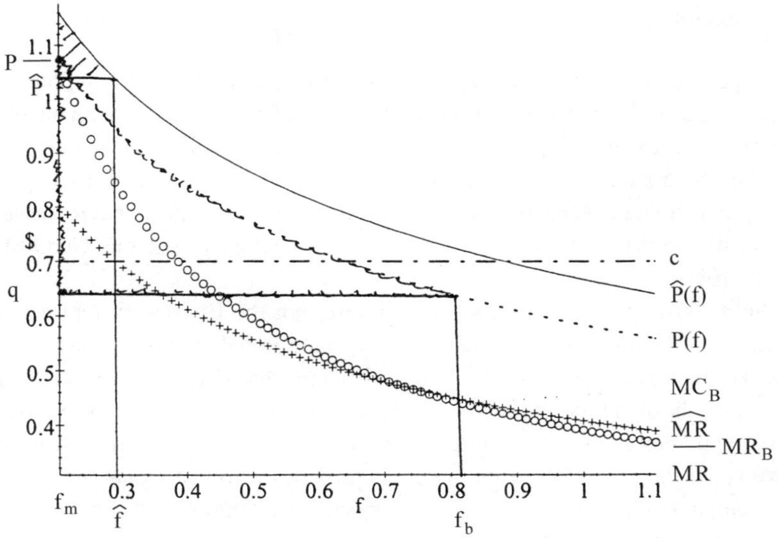

Fig. 9. Barter and restructuring

ernment removes the incentives to **G** to support barter [see Sect. 2.2.1], then the barter "price" of energy will be higher, and restructuring becomes a much more desirable option for inefficient manufacturing firms. That alone, however, is still insufficient to induce firms to leave barter networks unless restructuring is so effective that $\widehat{f} \gg f_b^0$ (i.e., the marginal firm operating on barter in the absence of government incentives). Notice also, that when bartering firms refuse to restructure, **G** can raise the price to those firms that do restructure to $\overline{p}$, reducing their incentive to do so ex-post. However, if any firm fails to restructure while others do so, leading to a price greater than p, it loses substantially more.

Under differing assumptions about manufacturers' expectations and ability to coordinate restructuring, and/or the ability of **G** to distinguish among manufacturers, there would seem to be many other equilibria also. But the result, that firms gaining from barter would refuse to restructure, seems robust.[39] Indeed, Proposition 3 shows that, without the option of virtual economy barter, all firms would choose socially efficient restructuring. When the virtual economy is available to inefficient firms, only substantial changes in government or **G**-sector policies can draw the firms out of barter networks. If the government removes its incentives for barter, and/or **G** loses the ability to discriminate among users, the incentives to restructure would become dominant for firms in barter networks. The "virtual economy" thus poses a substantial barrier to the successful transformation of the Russian economic system.

[39] It is, for example, easy to show that, if **G** can observe and respond to an individual firm's isolated restructuring by raising the price of energy to that firm, then the unique perfect equilibrium involves all manufacturing firms refusal to restructure. This might reflect a situation in which **G** is under pressure by tax authorities to increase cash collections (as in 1997–1998), and so jumps on any firm showing a discrete increase in profitability.

4 Conclusion

This paper begins an analytic exploration of the virtual economy hypothesis. It has provided a static partial-equilibrium model of a central component of that hypothesis – the transfer of value from a productive sector to loss-makers, giving them the appearance (a "virtual reality") of market viability. Thus it has begun the development of consistent micro-foundations supporting the behavior assumed in more macro-oriented analyses of the "virtual economy" such as Gaddy-Ickes (1998b, 1999).

The analysis provides a reason to suppose that the Russian virtual economy reflects a stable systemic configuration of economic behaviors, at least if agents horizons are sufficiently short.[40] It has also introduced a more formal welfare analysis of the benefits and costs of the functioning of the "virtual economy," focussing in particular on an indirect structural cost – the barrier it erects to the restructuring of L/NVA enterprises. It provides a robust example, and some more general conditions, such that involvement in a "barter" network counteracts any incentive to engage in productivity-enhancing restructuring of industrial processes. Hence "barter,"[41] which, as shown in our simple model, can be welfare enhancing given inherited structural distortions in the relevant (in the model – energy) market, can also provide a strong incentive to individual producers to avoid investment in productivity enhancing restructuring.

Thus the virtual economy poses an obstacle to the fundamental restructuring of industrial capacities that is essential for creating firms that are viable in a market economy. By substantially reducing incentives for investment in restructuring, the virtual economy provides a structural and institutional barrier to Russia's successful transition to a modern market economy. Therein lies a significant part of the explanation of the anomalies of the Russian transition discussed in the introduction.

Of course, we have only begun to scratch the surface of a very complex issue. There are other critical sectors to incorporate in a complete model of the phenomenon, including the budget sector and explicit derivation of government policy parameters as optimal decisions, a household sector active on both labor and consumers' goods markets, and the important interaction during transition with a "foreign" sector, the rest of the world. Incorporating such sectors would allow more adequately addressing the role of tax and wage arrears and offsets, other forms of involuntary credit provision, and the impact of import competition, export opportunities and exchange rate variation on the operation of the virtual economy and its interaction with industrial restructuring.

---

40 A dynamic version, explicitly considering the time preferences of agents is the subject of ongoing research.

41 That is, the whole panoply of non-monetized practices and instruments of exchange allowing idiosyncratic pricing unrelated to economic costs or market demand.

In addition, there are fascinating issues of the dynamic stability, development, and eventual decay of the virtual economy as a local equilibrium in the transition process. We expect the virtual economy to be, ultimately, a passing phenomenon, but one with a substantial half-life. It is an outgrowth of the still largely underappreciated distortions built into the social and economic fabric of Russia by central planning and other institutions of the command economy. We believe that the virtual economy is a locally rational response to this legacy. We hope to have contributed in this paper to its analysis as such.

References

Aukutsionek, S. (1994), Barter in Russian industry. *Russian Economic Barometer* 3(3): 3–13

Aukutsionek, S. (1998), Industrial Barter in Russia. *Communist Economies and Economic Transformation* 10(2): 179–188

Blanchard, O. (1977), *The Economics of Post-Communist Transition*. Clarendon Press, Oxford

Commander, S., Mumssen, C. (1998), Understanding Barter in Russia. *EBRD Working Paper #37*, December 1998

Dolgopiatova; T. (1998), *Informal Sector in the Russian Economy: Forms of Existence, Role and Scale*. IPSSA (in Russian) Moscow

Ericson, R.E. (1998), The revenge of the 'virtual economy'. *The Harriman Review*, Special Issue: 3–6

Ericson, R.E. (1999), The structural barrier to transition hidden in input-output tables of centrally planned economies. *Economic Systems* 23(3): 199–224

Gaddy, C.G., Ickes, B.W. (1998a), To restructure or not to restructure: Informal activities and enterprise behavior in transition. *WDI Working Paper #134* , February 1998

Gaddy, C., Ickes, B.W. (1998b), Russia's virtual economy. *Foreign Affairs*, September-October 1998: 53–67

Gaddy, C., Ickes, B.W. (1999), An accounting model of the virtual economy in Russia. *Post-Soviet Geography and Economics* 40(2): 79–97

Guriev, S., Pospelov, I. (1998), A model of Russia's virtual economy: Transactions costs and alternative means of payment. mimeo, CEMI, Moscow, August 1998

hendley ndley, K., Ickes, B.W., Ryterman, R. (1998), Remonetizing the Russian economy. In: Broadman, H.G. (ed.) *Russian enterprise reform: Policies to further the transition*. The World Bank, Washington, DC

Ivanova, N., Wyplosz, C. (1999), Arrears: The tide that is drowning Russia. *Russian Economic Trends* 8(1): 1–9

Karpov, P.A. (1997), On the Causes of Low Tax Collection (Arrears in the Fiscal System), General Causes of the 'Arrears Crisis' And Opportunities for the Restoration of Solvency of Russian Enterprises. *Report of Interdepartmental Balance Commission*. IBC, Moscow

McKinsey Global Institute (1999), *McKinsey Global Institute Report on Russian Economic Performance*. <http://mckinsey.com/mgi.html>

MFK Renaissance Research (1999), Russia on US$1 a day – why Mr. Primakov has not yet faced social explosion. *Economic Update*. MFK Renaissance, Moscow

Pinto nto, B., Drebentsov, V., Morozov, A. (2000), Give Growth and Macro Stability in Russia a Chance: Harden Budgets by Dismantling Nonpayments. Economics Unit, World Bank Office, Moscow

Poser, J. (1998), Monetary disruption and the emergence of barter in FSU economies. *Communist Economies and Economic Transformation* 10(2): 157–178

Russian Academy of Sciences (1997), *Guidelines of the Program for Medium-Term Social and Economic Development of Russia*. IE RAS, Moscow

Tompson, W. (1998), The Price of Everything and the Value of Nothing? Unravelling the Workings of Russia's 'Virtual Economy'. (preprocessed) Birkbeck College, University of London

Woodruff, D. (1999a), It's Value that's Virtual: Bartles, Rubles, and the Place of Gazprom in the Russian Economy. mimeo, MIT, Boston

Woodruff, D. (1999b), *Money Unmade: Barter and the Fate of Russian Capitalism.* Cornell University Press, Ithaca

Yakovlev, A. (1998), Barter and clearing schemes: How to define the basic concepts. *Russian Economic Barometer* 7(2): 39–44

Yakovlev, A. (1999), Mutual Dependence of Barter, Arrears, and Tax Evasion in Russian Economy. (preprocessed) State Higher School of Economics, Moscow

Reaction to price changes and aspiration level adjustments

Itzhak Gilboa[1], **David Schmeidler**[1,2]

[1] Tel-Aviv University, Department of Economics, Recanati School of Business, 69978 Tel Aviv, Israel (e-mail: igilboa@tau.ac.il)
[2] Ohio State University (e-mail: schmeid@tau.ac.il)

Abstract. We claim that preferences of economic agents cannot be assumed given; rather, they are partly determined by the process of trade in the market, by information about the latter and so forth. In other words, preferences determine actions which, in turn, determine preferences. Thus classical tools of analysis such as the neo-classical utility function and the demand curve should be viewed merely as first approximations, which are too simplistic for many purposes.

Changing preferences are not restricted to such phenomena as addiction, advertisement and so forth. Rather, for any product a satisficing consumer has an aspiration level, which is subject to change. The consumer's preferences, as reflected in choice behavior, will also change once the aspiration level is adjusted.

We illustrate these claims by analyzing two examples concerning consumer reaction to price increases. We analyze the effect of aspiration level adjustments on the dynamic pattern of a single consumer's demand, and show that such adjustments generate predictions which do not conform to the neo-classical theory.

1 Introduction

1.1 Main thesis

Economic theory assumes that preferences are given, and based on them market operations can be analyzed. This is a theoretically appealing approach: first identify the fundamentals and based on them study the dynamics, which will hopefully converge to some equilibrium.

In this note we question this two-stage approach. An alternative view suggests that preferences are partly determined by the market process, hence they cannot be assumed a fixed and immutable basis for the analysis of the latter. Rather,

We are grateful to Enriqueta Aragones for detailed comments on an earlier version of this note. We are also grateful to an anonymous referee for comments and suggestions.

consumer preferences are endogenous in that they are affected by the market process, which, in turn, is driven by them. Preferences determine actions, but actions also affect preferences.

1.2 Hypothesis

Specifically, we focus on one type of change of preferences: we consider a consumer who is "satisficing" rather than optimizing a neo-classical utility function. Such a consumer has an "aspiration level," which, once reached, prevents the consumer from further experimentation. We assume that the aspiration level reflects the consumer's expectations regarding the "consumer surplus"; if it is not attained, the consumer would switch to substitute products.

The key to our analysis is the way the aspiration level is updated over time. The examples analyzed here focus on the effect of past consumption. Other factors that may also effect consumer's aspirations include information about other agents' trades or trade offers, fashion, advertisement and so forth. As for past consumption, we postulate the following rule: the consumer updates her aspiration level (roughly) "towards" the actual consumer surplus she has experienced. Thus past experience changes what the consumer considers to be a "satisfactory" price.

1.3 Qualitative predictions

We start by analyzing a consumer's reaction to an increase in a product's price. Section 2 shows that following such an increase, the consumer's demand may fluctuate for a while before she becomes satisficed with a certain consumption level.

We then take the analysis one step further, and show that this hypothesis yields predictions which are at odds with the neo-classical theory. Specifically, in Sect. 3 we consider the demand for a product, whose price was increased, under two scenarios: a sharp, one-shot increase versus a gradual change. We show that our theory predicts that the two scenarios would result in different demand quantities. That is, a gradual change is predicted to result in a larger demand than a corresponding one-shot increase. This stands in contrast to the standard theory, which predicts that the demand would depend solely on the final price.

Finally, Sect. 4 concludes with several comments.

2 Non-monotonic demand adjustments

A consumer is faced with a periodic decision whether to buy a single unit of a certain good. As an example, consider a consumer's daily decision whether to get to work by driving her car or using public transportation, where the good we focus on is gasoline. Thus "buying" the good refers to using one's car, while "passing" means using public transportation. (Of course, one may imagine other consumption decisions which are more directly utility-generating than getting to work.) The decision problem is repeated in the same way, apart from the gasoline price which is subject to change. For simplicity we assume that public transportation cost is fixed, and that the consumer is informed of the gasoline price only after she decided to make a purchase, if indeed she did. The analysis does not depend on this assumption and may be modified to incorporate a consumer's ability to look ahead and imagine her well-being if indeed she decides to buy the product at the new price. Similarly, one can assume that the public transportation cost is also subject to change; however, we would like to focus on a single commodity model to facilitate the comparison with the neo-classical theory.

To model satisficing behavior, we apply case-based decision theory (CBDT). (See Gilboa and Schmeidler 1995.) However, no familiarity with CBDT is assumed here. The choices available to the consumer on each day are $\{buy, pass\}$. The consumer is assumed to have some "intrinsic value" v for driving her own car. (The precise meaning of this parameter will be discussed below.) In case of a purchase decision, the consumer experiences a "consumer surplus" of $(v - p)$ where p is the price the consumer ended up paying for gasoline. If, on the other hand, our consumer ended up using public transportation ("passing"), we assume that the corresponding "consumer surplus" is a fixed parameter w, which takes into account the presumably fixed price of that alternative.

The consumer has an "instantaneous utility" function which depends on the consumer's surplus and on an aspiration level with respect to which the utility is scaled. Denoting the aspiration level at time t by h^t, the utility function at time t from consumer surplus x is given by

$$u^t(x) = x - h^t .$$

The consumer is maximizing a function U that computes, for each possible act, a similarity-weighted sum of the utility of the results this act led to in the past. The similarity function here is rather simple: it merely reflects the time that has past since the recalled case. Specifically, an experience which dates back j periods is assumed to be "discounted" by a factor of β^j (where $\beta \in (0, 1)$). Discounting of the past attempts to capture both the probability of recall, and the intuition that "old" experiences are deemed less important or less relevant than "new" ones.

Formally, the function $U^t : \{buy, pass\} \to \Re$ depends on the entire history of choices and outcomes up to time $(t - 1)$, as well as on the parameters of the model. A concise way to describe this function is given by the following recursive folrmula. At time zero, it is identically zero. If at time $(t - 1)$ the consumer chooses the act *buy*, and finds a price p, we get

$$U^t(buy) = (v - p - h^{t-1}) + \beta U^{t-1}(buy)$$

and

$$U^t(pass) = \beta U^{t-1}(pass)\,.$$

If, on the other hand, at time $(t-1)$ she chooses *pass*, the function is given by:

$$U^t(buy) = \beta U^{t-1}(buy)$$

and

$$U^t(pass) = (w - h^{t-1}) + \beta U^{t-1}(pass)\,.$$

Thus our consumer will keep purchasing the product as long as $U^t(buy) > U^t(pass)$ and will leave the market once the reverse inequality holds. (The theory does not specify the choice in case of indifference.) Of course, a consumer who decided to "leave the market," namely not to buy the product, may later decide to "come back" and decide to purchase again.

Our next major assumption concerns the consumer's aspiration level. We assume that the aspiration level is updated over time, depending on the consumer's experiences. More specifically, suppose that our consumer experiences a "consumer surplus" of x. Basically, the aspiration level is updated to be some weighted average of its previous value and this evaluation of the new consumption experience. However, we will assume that the aspiration level tends to be somewhat below this value. That is, rather than considering the value x, the consumer's aspiration will be adjusted towards the value $(x-\delta)$ for some fixed $\delta > 0$.

The intuition behind this assumption is as follows: if the aspiration level tends to the consumer surplus precisely, in the long run the consumer obtains her aspiration level and is just barely satisficed. For such a consumer the smallest shock (such as a minuscule price increase) would render the product unsatisfactory. This does not seem to be entirely plausible. People tend to exhibit some "stickiness" or "inertia" in decisions in general, and purchase decisions in particular. A price change which is smaller than some "just noticeable difference" is unlikely to make all consumers, who are used to buy the product, turn away from it to untried alternatives.

"Inertia" can be modeled and explained in several ways. (See, for instance, Bar-Ilan and Blinder 1992 who discuss "rational inertia.") In terms of aspiration level adjustments, inertia may be viewed as a consumer's tendency to be content. That is, a decision maker who gets used to a given alternative and becomes content with it, will exhibit inertia in her decisions.

Thus we postulate a "contentment factor" $\delta > 0$ for each consumer. This number is a measure of the contentment our consumer feels with respect to a product she purchases regularly. In our model, by setting the aspiration level lower than the mere average of past consumption experiences, these experiences become slightly more than just-satisficing.

Formally, the speed of adjustment of the consumer's aspiration level is given by $\alpha \in (0,1)$, and the aspiration level at time t, after experiencing a consumer surplus x, is

$$h^t = \alpha(x-\delta)^+ + (1-\alpha)h^{t-1}$$

where $(y)^+ = \max\{y, 0\}$. Notice that the new experience – evaluated as $(x - \delta)$ – is not allowed to become negative for the aspiration level update. In particular, if the consumer decided to make a purchase and found a price p which exceeds her "intrinsic value" v, her aspiration is updated as if she faced a price v (or $(v - \delta)$). This means that the consumer will not learn to be satisficed with prices exceeding her intrinsic value: the aspiration level will not drop below zero, and any negative consumer surplus will be deemed unsatisfactory regardless of the number of times it has been experienced in the past.

Let us now assume that the sequence of prices $(p^t)_t$ is such that $p^t = p$ for all $t \geq T$ and some $T \geq 0$. Consider a consumer with $v - \delta \geq p$, that is a consumer whose intrinsic value and contentment factor allow her to be content with the price p, and assume that she has indeed been purchasing the product regularly (say, for all $t \geq T$). We then get

$$h^t \xrightarrow[t\to\infty]{} (v - p - \delta)$$

and

$$U^t(buy) \xrightarrow[t\to\infty]{} \frac{\delta}{1-\beta}, \quad U^t(pass) \xrightarrow[t\to\infty]{} 0 .$$

Notice that, as long as the price does not exceed $(v - \delta)$, the long-run U-level of our consumer does not depend on p. This follows from our supposition that the aspiration level is adjusted over time and that the consumer "gets used" to a certain price level. This is not the case when one considers "too high" prices, i.e., $p > v - \delta$. To such a price our consumer will not "get used." Hence the "intrinsic value" v can be interpreted precisely thus: it is the highest price (up to δ) to which the consumer can possibly adjust.

It should be emphasized that the "intrinsic value" in this model differs from the concept of "private value." While the latter is typically interpreted as the maximal price at which the consumer will decide to make a purchase, in our model the consumer may not buy at lower prices than v, and she may decide to buy at higher prices as well. For a price lower than v, the consumer may still be unsatisficed if she expected a higher consumer surplus. Specifically, if the aspiration level is significantly above $(v - p)$ for a long enough period, the U-value of *buy* will become negative even though $(v - p)$ may be positive. In this case the consumer will turn away from the product to some alternative. On the other hand, a price which exceeds v does not prohibit a purchase. While such a price would result in negative U values, the alternative may still be worse (U-wise). Thus the intrinsic value in our model does not tell the whole story, and in particular, it certainly does not suffice to predict the consumer's behavior. Rather, it should be thought of as the highest price – over various scenarios and consumption histories – with which the consumer can still be satisficed.

Let us consider the effect of a price increase, say from some p to a new value p', on the behavior of a consumer characterized by v, δ, α, and β. Assume that for a relatively long period (where "relatively long" is determined by α and β), the price p has prevailed and the consumer has been purchasing the product. Then we start at

$$h^t \approx v - p - \delta$$

and

$$U^t(buy) \approx \frac{\delta}{1-\beta} \quad U^t(pass) \approx 0\,.$$

The new experience yields a u-value of

$$u^t(v - p') = v - p' - h^t \approx \delta - (p' - p)$$

and

$$U^{t+1}(buy) \approx u^t(v - p') + \frac{\beta\delta}{1-\beta}\,.$$

Thus, if $p' - p > \frac{\delta}{1-\beta}$, the consumer will become dissatisfied with the product and will not purchase it in the next period. On the other hand, if the price increase is small enough (so that the reverse inequality holds), the consumer will continue to purchase the product at p'.

Let us now focus on those consumers who decide to switch to the act *pass*. They experience

$$u^{t+1}(w) = w - h^{t+1}\,.$$

We further distinguish among this subset of consumers. For some, $w - h^{t+1} > 0$, and these will be satisficed with the alternative of public transportation. The aspiration level will continue to be updated, so that for large τ we get $h^\tau \approx w - \delta$. That is, these consumers may first be quite happy with public transportation and wonder why they haven't chosen it to begin with, but over time they will get used to this wonderful alternative and be just content with it. At any rate, they will not go back to choosing *buy* (i.e., driving their own cars) unless further changes occur.

For other consumers we may have $w - h^{t+1} < 0$. These consumers have no reason to feel regret over their past choices: indeed, the alternative of public transportation turned out to be worse than using one's car at the old price of gasoline. However, prices being what they are now, they are not satisficed with either alternative. If the aspiration level remains fixed, they will alternate between *buy* and *pass* with frequencies determined by $(v - p - h^t)$, $(w - h^t)$, and β. By contrast, when the aspiration level is updated over time, each consumer will become more-or-less satisficed with at least one of the two options and will settle for either *buy* or *pass*. (See related analysis, for the case $\beta = 1$, in Gilboa and Schmeidler 1996, 1997.)

Thus the dynamic pattern we should observe is as follows: some consumers keep buying gasoline, and others switch to public transportation for ever; yet another subset alternates for a while, and eventually splits into two subsets: those who go back to driving their cars (and consuming gasoline), and those who end up using public transportation (and do not buy gasoline). In particular, a consumer's reaction to a price increase need not be monotone with respect to time.

Note that aggregate demand may or may not be a monotonically decreasing function (of time) following a price increase. If, for instance, all consumers are synchronized in their decisions, aggregating over their demand may result in a non-monotonic reaction, predicting an "overshooting" phenomenon: first demand drops sharply, then it goes up again to some intermediate level. However, if the timing of consumption decisions varies across consumers, say due to existing inventory, the aggregation of non-monotonic functions may still be monotonically decreasing.

3 Speed of price change and demanded quantity

We now wish to take the analysis one step further, and show that our model provides predictions which differ from those of the neo-classical theory. Specifically, we would like to show that in our model a gradual price increase may have a different effect on demand than a corresponding one-shot increase.

Let us assume that for a long period the price of gasoline was fixed at p_0. We would like to compare two scenarios: (i) a one-shot price increase to $p_2 > p_0$, after which the price is held fixed at p_2; and (ii) a two-stage increase: first to a price level p_1 such that $p_2 > p_1 > p_0$, and then, after a long enough period of adjustment, to p_2.

For any given price increase, it is obvious that there may be consumers for which it is small enough to keep purchasing gasoline, and others for which it is not. The main point is that those consumers who remain in the market get used to the new price (provided it does not exceed their "intrinsic value") in the long run, and after a long enough period their U-value for buying tends back to the same value $\frac{\delta}{1-\beta}$. For such consumers a similar price increase in the future will have similar effects. In other words, any given consumer will remain in the market as long as (i) the current price does not exceed her "intrinsic value"; and (ii) the price increases along the path are small enough.

Coming back to the comparison of the two scenarios above, one can find ranges of the parameters v, δ, and β for which the increase from p_0 to p_2 is "too large", while both increases from p_0 to p_1 and from the latter to p_2 are not. Consumers whose parameters are in those ranges will keep purchasing the product in scenario (i) but would refrain from doing so in (ii).

Thus the question, "How many consumers will decide to buy at price p_2?" is ill-posed. In our model, it has no unique answer since the final price p_2 simply does not contain all the relevant information. Correspondingly, one cannot assume a demand curve, which may be viewed as a collection of answers to such questions. Consumer preferences – as reflected in economic behavior – depend on the economic process and cannot be assumed given independently of it.

4 Concluding remarks

4.1 Changing preferences

The adjustment of aspiration level may be viewed as a special case of changing preferences. Indeed, the literature provides generalizations of the neo-classical theory that can deal with phenomena involving changes in tastes, such as in cases of addiction, aging, advertisement and the like. (This literature dates back to Allais (1947) and Strotz (1956), and includes more recent contributions such as Pollak (1968, 1970 and 1976) and Becker (1991a,b).) But we claim that the change of preferences is pervasive and ubiquitous enough to undermine the basic tenets of the neo-classical theory. One may incorporate the phenomena we discuss here in generalizations of the neo-classical framework, for instance by assuming that the neo-classical utility function is defined over consumption streams. But we suspect that such generalizations would result in a theory which is almost tautologically true and thus useless.

4.2 Reference theory

Kahneman and Tversky have shown in experimental works (see Kahneman and Tversky (1984)) that consumer preferences may depend on the consumer's current consumption bundle. They have also suggested a new consumer theory, according to which the consumer's "neo-classical" utility function is parametrized by this bundle (Tversky and Kahneman (1990)).

In spirit, our theory bears some resemblance to theirs. However, we allow preferences to depend on the whole history of consumption, and highlight the role of aspiration level adjustments.

4.3 The supply side

The focus of this paper is consumer's behavior and the underlying theory from which one derives the concept of a "demand curve." Assuming that consumers can be "satisficed", and that their aspiration level is subject to change, we claim that the demand curve cannot be assumed given, or independent of the market process.

While the supply side is typically assumed to involve "more rational" agents than the consumers on the demand side, there is no reason to believe that the supply curve is a fixed characteristic of the market either. First, in many markets – such as the market for used cars, real-estate and so forth – the supply is also determined by individual economic households, which are not "more neo-classical" than the buyers. Second, even when firms, rather than households, constitute most of the supply side, their behavior may follow satisficing models more accurately than profit-maximization models. Wherever there are satisficing agents involved, there is room for aspiration level update, and preferences become intertwined with the economic process they are supposed to govern.

References

Allais, M. (1947) *Economie et Interet*. Paris, Imprimerie Nationale

Bar-Ilan, A., Blinder, A.S. (1992) Consumer durables: Evidence on the optimality of usually doing nothing. *Journal of Money, Credit and Banking* 24: 258–272

Becker, G.S. (1991a) Rational addiction and the effect of price on consumption. *American Economic Review Papers and Proceedings* 81(2): 237–241

Becker, G.S. (1991b) Habits, addiction and traditions. Nancy L. Schwartz Lecture, Northwestern University

Gilboa, I., Schmeidler, D. (1995) Case-based decision theory. *The Quarterly Journal of Economics* 110: 605–639

Gilboa, I., Schmeidler, D. (1996) Case-based optimization. *Games and Economic Behavior* 15: 1–26

Gilboa, I., Schmeidler, D. (1997) Cumulative utility consumer theory. *International Economic Review* 38: 737–761

Kahneman, D., Tversky, A. (1984) Choices, values and frames. *American Psychologist* 39: 341–350

Pollak, R.A. (1968) Consistent planning. *Review of Economic Studies* 35: 201–208

Pollak, R.A. (1970) Habit formation and dynamic demand functions. *Journal of Political Economy* 78: 745–764

Pollak, R.A. (1976) Habit formation and long-run utility functions. *Journal of Economic Theory* 13: 272–297

Strotz, R.H. (1956) Myopia and inconsistency in dynamic utility maximization. *Review of Economic Studies* 23: 165–180

Tversky, A., Kahneman, D. (1990) Reference theory of choice and exchange. Working paper

References

Bargaining solutions with non-standard objectives

Peter B. Linhart

74 Tall Oaks Drive, Summit, NJ 07901, USA (e-mail: phimurray@aol.com)

Abstract. I examine the pure-strategy solutions of the sealed-bid bargaining game with incomplete information, when the buyer's and seller's objectives are other than the standard objective, namely maximization of expected profit. The motivation for this exploration lies in three problems of the standard formulation: the necessity of assuming common priors, the existence of uncountably many Nash equilibria, with no means for the players to coordinate on any one of them, and the uncertain relationship between these equilibria and observed behavior in bargaining experiments. Specifically, I consider two alternative objectives: minimization of maximum regret, and maximization of maximum profit. The solution concept here is not Nash equilibrium, but rather α-individually rational strategy bundle. For that reason, I shall, where appropriate, use the word "solution" in place of "equilibrium." Yet we find that the notion of Nash Equilibrium reappears, in a sense to be explained. In the minimax-regret case I find (in contrast to the case of expected profit) a unique solution; this solution reduces, for priors with coincident support, to the linear equilibrium of Chatterjee-Samuelson. In the maximum-profit case there are many solutions; they turn out to be slight generalizations of the one-step equilibria of Leininger-Linhart-Radner.

1 Introduction

The Bayesian-Nash equilibria of the sealed-bid bargaining game were explored in some detail in Leininger et al. (1989), and Satterthwaite and Williams (1989). These papers found two classes of pure-strategy equilibria, one in differentiable strategies, the other in step-function strategies. Each class contains nondenumerably many equilibria, whose efficiences range from zero to "second-best." The second-best, i.e. most efficient, of these equilibria (for the special

I am indebted to Roy Radner, Frank W. Sinden, and Steven R. Williams for essential discussions, and to an anonymous referee for enlightening comments.

case of uniform priors) is the linear equilibrium of Chatterjee and Samuelson (1983). In these papers, mixed-strategy equilibria were not investigated; it is not even known whether all the pure-strategy equilibria were found. Of course it was assumed that each player's objective was the maximization of expected profit. This assumption is so conventional, that it was not felt necessary to offer any justification for it.

Since the formal description (to be repeated below) of the sealed-bid bargaining game contains no means whereby the players can choose among multiple equilibria, we are left with an acute coordination problem (how do the bargainers agree on which equilibrium to play?) for which no satisfactory solution is now available. Note that this coordination problem arises even in the case of sealed-bid bargaining *with complete information.* There, any pair of matching bids constitutes an equilibrium. Of course it does not help to say that the players agree on an equilibrium by means of pre-play discussion, since such discussion now becomes a strategic part of an enlarged game. In fact, "cheap talk" can increase the range of possible equilibrium behaviors; see, for example Farrell and Gibbons (1989).

An attempt to find a way out of this impasse, by changing the assumption about the bargainers' objective functions, is made in a paper by Linhart and Radner (1989). There it is assumed that each player seeks to minimize maximum regret (where regret is defined as the difference between a player's actual profit and the profit he could have made if he had known his opponent's bid before he made his own). In that paper it was assumed that each player is quite ignorant of the other's strategy, although he has some information about the other's type.[1,2] Since each player is ignorant of the other's strategy, neither responds to the other's behavior, but only to the worst that he might do. Thus "worst" is determined by the given parameters (whether they are numbers or random variables) of the problem. Hence the notion of Nash equilibrium no longer applies; it is replaced by that of the α-individually rational strategy bundle (Ichiishi 1997). For this reason, the analysis is greatly simplified, and it becomes possible to discuss bargaining over a multiplicity of attributes, rather than just over the price of a single object. For the same reason, one can now analyze randomized bidding (for the case of a single object, with complete information). In this informational setting, even if minimax-regret strategies are not unique, there is no coordination problem. In fact, for the case of bargaining over the price of a single object, unique strategies were found.

The difficulties with the conventional model are not confined to the coordination problem. It is also usual to assume (and one is hard put to proceed with the analysis without making these assumptions) that the players' prior beliefs as to each other's type are consistent, i.e. that there exists a joint distribution of

[1] The word "type" here denotes the true value to the buyer of the object to be traded, or its true cost to the seller.

[2] A player may have some information about his opponent's bid-distribution, while remaining ignorant of his opponent's strategy. For example, the buyer may know the seller's minimum cost, and also that the seller will not bid below his cost.

their two types, from which their conditional priors as to each other's types can be derived,[3] and further that this joint distribution is common knowledge. These assumptions are in general not very plausible. In Linhart and Radner (1989), they were not needed. In the present paper, as will be seen, they can be weakened, but not entirely eliminated.

In the present paper, I return part way to the notion of Nash equilibrium; that is, each player's objective function is maximized *given only certain attributes* of the other's strategy. I do not however return to the assumption of expected-profit-maximization as an objective function. The specific alternative objectives considered are minimization of maximum regret and maximization of maximum profit. Only the pure-strategy solutions are studied.

For maximum regret minimizers, I find a unique solution; it reduces (for priors with common support) to the linear equilibrium of Chatterjee-Samuelson. For maximum-profit maximizers, I find a class of solutions that reduces (for priors with common support) to a slight generalization of the one-step equilibria of Leininger-Linhart-Radner. Interestingly, these solutions do not depend on the players' priors as to each other's types, but only on the support of these priors. It is in this sense that the assumption of a common prior becomes less restrictive.

In addition to the theoretical difficulties discussed above, there is the worrisome fact that the results of bargaining experiments, for example those reported by Radner and Schotter (1989) and by Linhart et al. (1989) do not usually correspond well to any equilibrium of the one-shot bargaining game with expected-profit objectives.[4] In fact, perhaps the most conspicuous feature of the subjects' behavior is that their bargaining strategies *are not all the same*, although these behaviors do seem to fall into a small number of types, within each of which a considerable regularity is displayed. Since the assumption of expected-profit maximization runs into difficulty both theoretically and experimentally, and since experimental behavior is various, it seems natural, in an exploratory spirit, to examine the consequences of several behavioral assumptions, for example assumptions about various objective functions, as in the present paper.

The structure of the remainder of the paper is as follows. In Sect. 2, I define the sealed-bid bargaining mechanism. In Sect. 3, I find the unique Nash equilibrium in pure strategies for a buyer and seller who are both maximum-regret minimizers. In Sect. 4, I find the one-parameter family of pure-strategy Nash equilibria for a buyer and seller who are both maximum-profit maximizers. Finally, Sect. 5 summarizes the results and contains some remarks about the axiomatics of the decision rules ascribed to the players, and about the comparison of the theoretical results with experiment.

---

[3] Of course, in the special case that the players' priors are independent, which is perhaps the case most often studied, this condition is easily satisfied.

[4] Actually, the bargaining experiments reported in these papers involve repeated transactions between partners. Hence the observed behavior may involve the (as yet unknown) equilibria of some version of the corresponding supergame, not explored here.

2 The sealed-bid bargaining model

A buyer and a seller bargain over the price of an indivisible object, whose value to the buyer (the buyer's type) is V, while its cost to the seller (the seller's type) is C. (However, if the object is not traded, the seller incurs no cost.) The buyer knows V before he makes his bid, v. Similarly, the seller knows C before he makes his bid, c. It is assumed at this point that v depends *only* on V, and c depends *only* on C. In addition, each knows a bound on the other's type. By a choice of scale and location we may take these bounds to be

$$V \leq 1, \tag{1}$$

$$C \geq 0. \tag{2}$$

At this stage, we make no assumption, beyond (1) and (2) as to the support of the players' types. Thus, for example, the support of the seller's prior as to the distribution of V could be the whole closed interval $[0, 1]$, or he could know with certainty that $V = 1$.

Trade occurs if and only if $v \geq c$; if trade occurs, the price is

$$p = \frac{1}{2}(v + c). \tag{3}$$

Thus the buyer's profit[5] is

$$\Pi_B(V, v, c) = \begin{cases} V - \frac{1}{2}(v + c), & v \geq c \\ 0, & v < c, \end{cases} \tag{4}$$

while the seller's profit is

$$\Pi_S(C, c, v) = \begin{cases} \frac{1}{2}(v + c) - C, & v \geq c \\ 0, & v < c. \end{cases} \tag{5}$$

The buyer's bid is related to his type by his *strategy*,

$$v = \beta(V), \tag{6}$$

and similarly,

$$c = \gamma(C). \tag{7}$$

I also assume that

$$v = \beta(V) \leq V, \tag{8}$$

$$c = \gamma(C) \geq C, \tag{9}$$

for all V and C, since strategies that violate (8) and (9) are dominated by strategies that do not. Finally, when the buyer knows a lower bound, $\underline{c}$ on the seller's bid, there is never any reason for him to bid below it, so we may take

[5] The buyer and seller are in symmetrical situations. Therefore, I shall sometimes confine the discussion to the buyer. The nature of this symmetry is described in Sect. 3, Eq. (22).

$$v \geq \underline{c}, \tag{10}$$

and similarly

$$c \leq \bar{v}, \tag{11}$$

where $\bar{v}$ is an upper bound on the buyer's bid.

I take an *interim* point of view. The buyer, at the time he makes his bid,

- knows V,
- has some (perhaps probabilistic) information about C. If he has some information about the seller's strategy – even information as elementary as (9) – then some (perhaps probabilistic) information about c is implied.
- chooses v to maximize his payoff, however that may be defined, conditional on V.

Although alternative payoff definitions are considered here, the notion of profit is not abandoned. Thus the payoffs discussed are:

- Expected profit, $\underset{c}{E}\ \Pi_B(V, v, c)$, to be maximized;
- Maximum profit, $\underset{c}{\text{Max}}\ \Pi_B(V, v, c)$, to be maximized;
- Maximum regret, $\underset{c}{\text{Max}}\ R_B(V, v, c)$, to be minimized (or its negative to be maximized).

Here

$$R_B(V, v, c) = \Pi_B^*(V, c) - \Pi_B(V, v, c), \tag{12}$$

where $\Pi_B^*(V, c)$ is the best the buyer could have done, had he known the seller's bid:

$$\Pi_B^*(V, c) \equiv \underset{v}{\text{Max}}\ \Pi_B(V, v, c).$$

Similar (symmetric) statements apply to the seller. Regret is by definition non-negative.

3 Nash equilibrium when both buyer and seller seek to minimize maximum regret

A natural candidate for an alternative objective would seem to be maximization of minimum profit. This objective has even been provided with an axiomatic foundation (see Gilboa and Schmeidler 1989). Unfortunately, this objective is not interesting in the present application for the reason that the minimum profit is identically zero. We consider instead the minimization of maximum regret, a notion expounded by Savage (1954), and apparently originated by Wald (1950). Such an objective will gain plausibility if it turns out that the minimax regret is not so high as to be "unacceptable."

Suppose then that both players seek to minimize maximum regret, as defined by (12). (Bargaining between two players whose objective functions differ can also be analyzed, but such cases are not considered in this paper.) Expressions for optimum profit, Π^*, will be needed.

Suppose the buyer's type is V, and the seller bids c. If $c > V$, no profitable trade is possible, and $\Pi^*(V, c) = 0$. The buyer must bid, however; any bid $v \leq V$ will suffice. Now suppose $c \leq V$; if only the buyer had known the seller's bid, he could have matched it: $v = c$. His profit would then have been maximal. From (4),

$$\Pi_B^*(V, c) = \begin{cases} V - c, & V \geq c, \\ 0, & V < c. \end{cases} \tag{13}$$

Similarly,

$$\Pi_S^*(C, v) = \begin{cases} v - C, & v \geq C \\ 0, & v < C. \end{cases} \tag{14}$$

Let the *infimum* and *supremum* of the seller's bid distribution be denoted by $\underline{c}$ and $\overline{c}$, respectively, and let $\underline{v}$ and $\overline{v}$ be similarly defined, and suppose that these four values are common knowledge. In this section and the next one, I shall assume that the seller's strategy γ is lower semi-continuous and that the buyer's strategy is upper semi-continuous; this assures that $\underline{c}$ is a *minimum* and $\overline{v}$ is a *maximum*. If this latter were not the case, then (as will be seen below) the notion of *best* response would not be well defined. Because the supports of V and C are assumed to be closed intervals,[6] Eqs. (8) and (9) imply that the extreme values $\overline{c}$ and $\underline{v}$ are also attained. Three situations are possible for the buyer, as shown in Fig. 1.

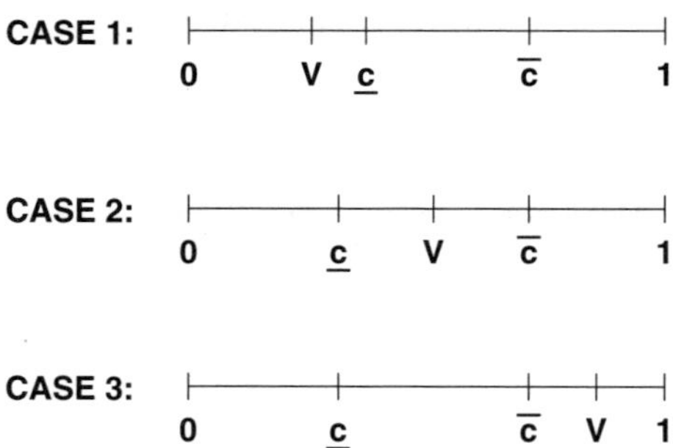

Fig. 1. Possible relationships of the buyer's type

In Case 1 of Fig. 1, $v \leq V < \underline{c} \leq c$; therefore no trade is possible. Both profit and maximum profit are zero, so $R_B = 0$.

In Cases 2 and 3, $V \geq \underline{c}$; either trade occurs, or it does not. If trade occurs,

$$R_B = \frac{1}{2}(v - c) \tag{15}$$

from (4) and (14). In this case

[6] I assume for convenience that the supports of the distributions of types are closed intervals, but this restriction is not essential.

$$\operatorname*{Max}_{c} R_B = \frac{1}{2}(v - \underline{c}). \tag{16}$$

If trade does not occur, Π_B is zero, so

$$R_B = \Pi_B^* = V - c. \tag{17}$$

Since trade has not occurred, we must have $c > v$, and of course $v \geq \underline{c}$, from (10). Thus

$$\operatorname*{Sup}_{c} R_B = V - v. \tag{18}$$

It seems at first glance that the buyer's supremum regret, as a function of his bid, must be as shown in Fig. 2.

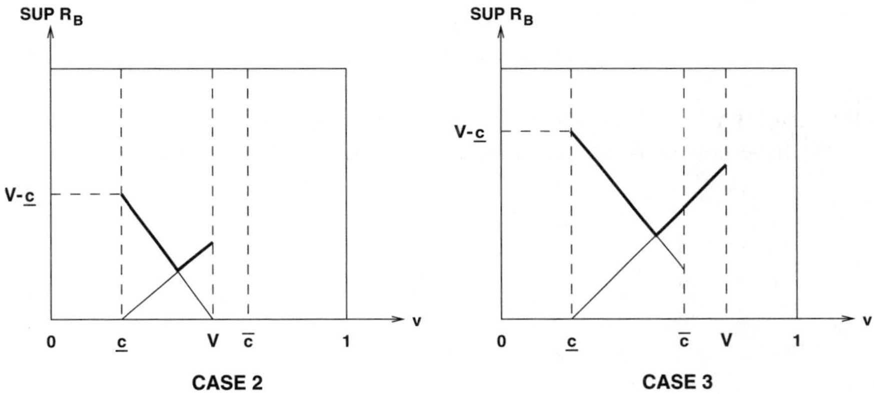

Fig. 2. Buyer's maximum regret for cases 2 and 3

In this situation, $\operatorname*{Sup}_{c} R_B$ is minimized where

$$V - v = \frac{1}{2}(v - \underline{c})$$

i.e. by the bid

$$v = \frac{2}{3}V + \frac{1}{3}\underline{c}. \tag{19}$$

But what if this value of v is above $\overline{c}$, as could occur in Case 3? For any bid above $\overline{c}$, trade *must* occur; Fig. 2 must then be modified as shown in Fig. 3. In this case, the buyer's minsup regret bid is clearly $\overline{c}$. (It will have occurred to the reader, correctly, looking at Figs. 2 and 3, that buyer bids above $\overline{c}$ will not actually be made, since they are dominated by bids at $\overline{c}$.)

There is a critical value of V — call it V^* — above which the situation is as in Fig. 3. V^* is determined by

$$\frac{2}{3}V^* + \frac{1}{3}\underline{c} = \overline{c},$$

or

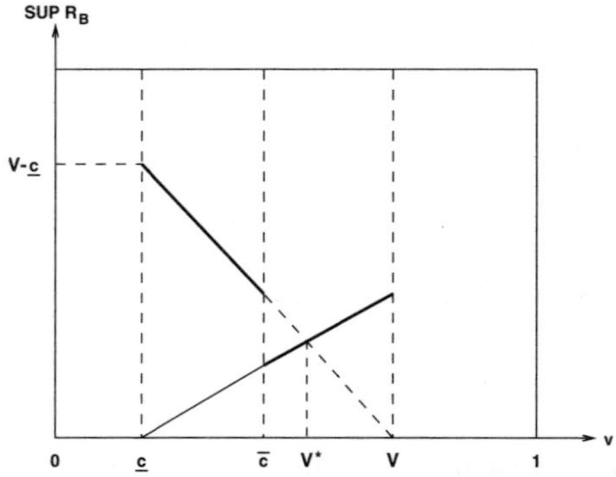

Fig. 3. Buyer's supremum regret when $V^* > \overline{c}$

$$V^* = \frac{3}{2}\overline{c} - \frac{1}{2}\underline{c}. \tag{20}$$

Of course, if $V^* > 1$, the situation $V \geq V^*$ cannot arise.

We have now constructed the buyer's minimax regret strategy. It is:

$$v \begin{cases} \leq V & \text{for} \quad V < \underline{c}, \\ = \frac{2}{3}V + \frac{1}{3}\underline{c} & \text{for} \quad \underline{c} \leq V \leq \operatorname{Min}(V^*, 1), \\ = \overline{c} & \text{for} \quad V^* < V \leq 1, \text{ if } V^* < 1. \end{cases} \tag{21}$$

This strategy is illustrated in Fig. 4; the buyer's bid is indeterminate within the shaded area.

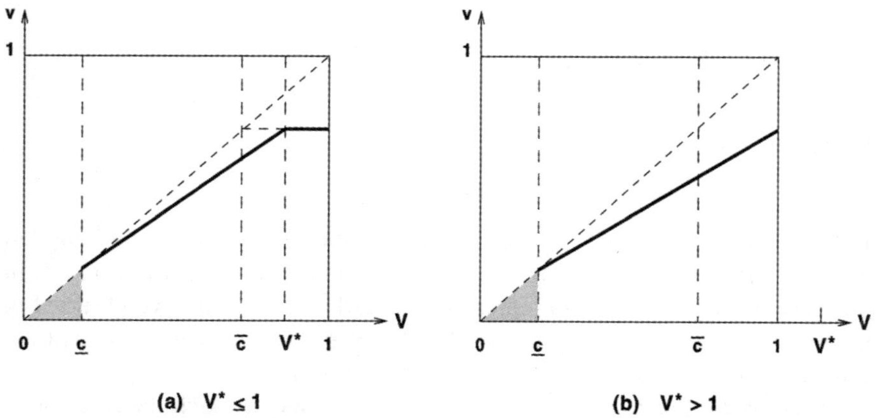

Fig. 4 a,b. Buyer's minimax regret strategy $V^* = \frac{3}{2}\overline{c} - \frac{1}{2}\underline{c}$

The seller's minimax regret strategy can be written down by applying symmetry to (21). The symmetry between buyer and seller is expressed by:

$$
\begin{aligned}
C &\sim 1 - V, \\
c &\sim 1 - v.
\end{aligned}
\tag{22}
$$

From (21) and (22), the sellers minimax regret strategy is found to be

$$
c \begin{cases} \geq C & \text{for} \quad C > \overline{v}, \\ = \frac{2}{3}C + \frac{1}{3}\overline{v} & \text{for} \quad \mathrm{Max}(C^*, 0) \leq C \leq \overline{v}, \\ = \underline{v} & \text{for} \quad 0 \leq C < C^*, \text{ if } C^* > 0, \end{cases} \tag{23}
$$

where

$$
C^* = \frac{3}{2}\underline{v} - \frac{1}{2}\overline{v}.
$$

This strategy is illustrated in Fig. 5.

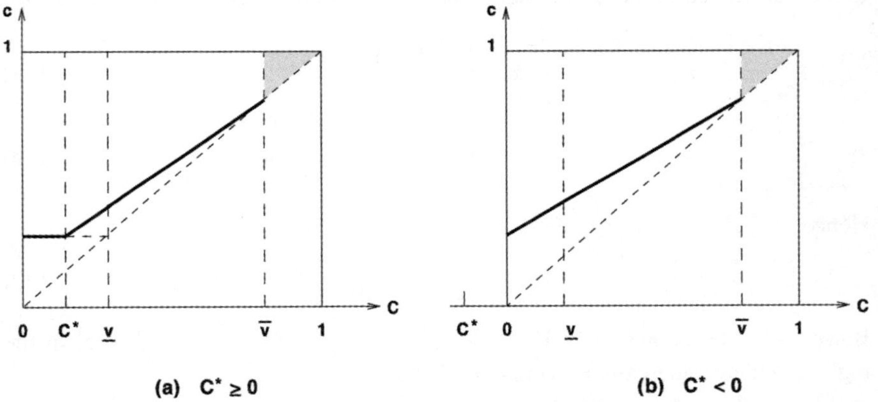

Fig. 5 a,b. Seller's minimax regret strategy $C^* = \frac{3}{2}\underline{v} - \frac{1}{2}\overline{v}$

If the players involved in Eq. (21) are the same as those involved in Eq. (23), then (21) and (23) must be consistent with each other. This condition can be used to determine $\underline{c}$ and $\overline{v}$. In this way the concept of equilibrium is reintroduced. I illustrate this by two examples: the case of priors with coincident support and the case of "complete information" (about one's opponent's type).

3.1 Priors with coincident support

Suppose $\mathrm{Supp}V = \mathrm{Supp}C = [0, 1]$.

Since $V = 0$ is possible, and $v \leq V$, we know that $\underline{v} = 0$. Similarly $\overline{c} = 1$. Thus

$$
V^* = \frac{3}{2} - \frac{1}{2}\underline{c} \tag{24}
$$

$$
C^* = -\frac{1}{2}\overline{v}. \tag{25}
$$

Since, by definition, $\underline{c} \leq \overline{c}$, we know that $\underline{c} \leq 1$,

$$\underline{c} \leq v \leq V \leq 1.$$

Hence,

$$V^* \geq 1. \tag{26}$$

Similarly,

$$\overline{v} \geq c \geq C \geq 0,$$

whence

$$C^* \leq 0. \tag{27}$$

Thus we are in the case of Figs. 4b and 5b. Evaluating (21) at $V = 1$ and (23) at $C = 0$ for this case, we find (since both strategies are monotone nondecreasing)

$$\overline{v} = \frac{2}{3} + \frac{1}{3}\underline{c} \tag{28}$$

$$\underline{c} = \frac{1}{3}\overline{v}. \tag{29}$$

Hence,

$$\overline{v} = \frac{3}{4}, \quad \underline{c} = \frac{1}{4}. \tag{30}$$

If we make the choices $v = V$ for $V < \underline{c}$, and $c = C$ for $C > \overline{c}$ (i.e. in the regions where trade cannot occur), we have the strategies

$$v = \beta(V) = \begin{cases} V, & V \leq \frac{1}{4} \\ \frac{2}{3}V + \frac{1}{12}, & \frac{1}{4} \leq V \leq 1 \end{cases} \tag{31}$$

$$c = \gamma(C) = \begin{cases} \frac{2}{3}C + \frac{1}{4}, & 0 \leq C \leq \frac{3}{4}, \\ C, & \frac{3}{4} \leq C \leq 1. \end{cases} \tag{32}$$

(It is easily checked that for these strategies $V^* > 1$, $C^* < 0$.) Equations (31) and (32) describe the Chatterjee-Samuelson linear equilibrium for coincident uniform priors on [0, 1], when both players are expected-profit maximizers. In the present minimax-regret context, however:

- this equilibrium is unique (except for the inessential indeterminacy when $V \leq 1/4$ or $C \geq 3/4$),
- and it obtains for *any* priors such that

$$\mathrm{Supp}V = \mathrm{Supp}C = [0, 1].$$

We may now ask: How well has the buyer succeeded in minimizing his maximum regret by using the strategy (31)? His minsup regret is, by construction, the same whether trade occurs or not, and is given by (18):

$$\min_{v} \sup_{c} R_B = V - v = \frac{1}{3}V - \frac{1}{12}. \tag{33}$$

For the buyer's *worst* response to the seller's most damaging move ($v = \underline{c} = \frac{1}{4}$, $C = \epsilon$, $c = \frac{1}{4} + \frac{2}{3}\epsilon$), there is no trade and we have

$$\max_{v} \sup_{c} R_B = V - \frac{1}{4}. \tag{34}$$

Thus the strategy (31) has reduced maximum regret by two-thirds. Of course, similar considerations apply to the seller.

3.2 Complete information

In this case, a strategy is just a bid. Each player, knowing the other's bid, can maximize his profit, and reduce his regret (trivially equals maximum regret) to zero, just by matching that bid. We now derive this obvious result, in order to verify that the present formalism works in this case.

Suppose then that

$$V = 1, \quad C = 0, \tag{35}$$

and both players know it.

Since v can depend only on V, and c only on C,

$$\begin{aligned} \underline{c} &= \overline{c} = \hat{c}, \text{ say}, \\ \underline{v} &= \overline{v} = \hat{v}, \text{ say}. \end{aligned} \tag{36}$$

Thus

$$\begin{aligned} V^* &= \frac{3}{2}\hat{c} - \frac{1}{2}\hat{c} = \hat{c} \leq 1, \\ C^* &= \frac{3}{2}\hat{v} - \frac{1}{2}\hat{v} = \hat{v} \geq 0. \end{aligned}$$

The situation of Figs. 4a and 5a obtains. Therefore

$$\hat{c} = \hat{v} = b, \quad \text{say, the common bid.} \tag{37}$$

The bids are otherwise undetermined. That is, any pair of matching bids constitutes an equilibrium, just as with the profit (trivially equals expected profit) objective under certainty. There is an obvious coordination problem.

4 Solutions when both buyer and seller seek to maximize maximum profit

We are dealing here, perhaps, with the kind of person who invests only in the lottery with the biggest first prize, regardless of the probability of winning. We confine our attention to the example of priors with coincident support,

$$\text{Supp}V = \text{Supp}C = [0, 1]. \tag{38}$$

Referring again to the categorization of Fig. 1: In Case 1, $v < c$. There can be no trade.

$$\Pi_B = 0, \quad \underset{c}{\text{Max}}\ \Pi_B = 0, \quad \underset{v}{\text{Max}}\ \underset{c}{\text{Max}}\ \Pi_B = 0.$$

Any $v \leq V$ is sure to attain this zero profit.

In Cases 2 and 3, both v and c must lie in $[\underline{c}, V]$, and hence in $[C, V]$. Π_B is still defined by (4).

$$\underset{c}{\text{Max}}\ \Pi_B \text{ is attained at } c = \underline{c}\text{, and is } V - \frac{1}{2}(v + \underline{c}),$$

and

$$\underset{v}{\text{Max}}\ \underset{c}{\text{Max}}\ \Pi_B \text{ is attained at } v = c = \underline{c}\text{, and is } V - \underline{c}.$$

Thus the buyer's best response is

$$v \begin{cases} \leq V & \text{for } 0 \leq V < \underline{c} \\ = \underline{c} & \text{for } \underline{c} \leq V \leq 1. \end{cases} \tag{39}$$

Symmetrically, the seller's best response is

$$c \begin{cases} = \overline{v} & \text{for } 0 \leq C < \overline{v} \\ \geq C & \text{for } \overline{v} < C \leq 1. \end{cases} \tag{40}$$

If the players involved in Eq. (39) are the same as those involved in Eq. (40), then (39) and (40) must be consistent, whence

$$\overline{v} = \underline{c} = a, \text{ say} \tag{41}$$

and the bids are not otherwise determined. These equilibrium strategies are illustrated in Fig. 6.

For the particular choices in the shaded areas

$$\begin{aligned} v = 0 \quad &\text{for} \quad 0 \leq V < a, \\ c = 1 \quad &\text{for} \quad a < C \leq 1, \end{aligned} \tag{42}$$

these equilibria are identical to the family of one-step equilibria found in Leininger-Linhart-Radner (1989) for expected-profit maximizers. For these latter, however, the arbitrariness represented by the shaded regions in Fig. 6 does

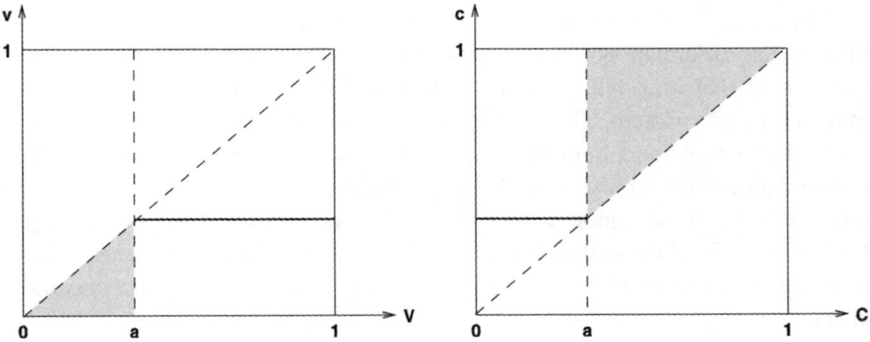

Fig. 6. Buyer's and seller's equilibrium strategies to maximize maximum profit

not exist; that is, (39) and (40) represent an equilibrium between expected-profit maximizers only when the choices (42) are made.

The values of the buyer's and seller's maximum profit for these equilibria are

$$\begin{aligned} \max_{C} \ \Pi_B &= V - a, \\ \max_{V} \ \Pi_S &= a - C, \end{aligned} \tag{43}$$

where $C \leq a \leq V$. In view of the coordination problem, we cannot say that the players have been effective in their objective of maximizing maximum profit.

5 Concluding remarks

5.1 Summary of results

A maximum regret-minimizer is α-individually rational in that he is optimizing against the worst his opponent can do (to increase regret), rather than against whatever his opponent actually does. However, in the present context, the worst that his opponent can do depends on the extreme possible values of this opponent's bid, and these extreme values are in turn partially determined by the opponent's strategy. Moreover, the extreme values of the first player's bids are determined by his responsive strategy. Thus each player is optimizing against certain implications of the other's strategy, and we may, with this qualification, speak of a Nash Equilibrium.

I have shown that there is a unique equilibrium between a buyer and a seller both of whom seek to minimize maximum regret. Hence there is no coordination problem. The form of this equilibrium depends only on the *support* of the bargainers' priors. Hence the problem of assuming priors that are common knowledge is alleviated. For the case of priors with common support, the minimax-regret equilibrium is identical to the "second-best" expected-profit equilibrium of Chatterjee and Samuelson; however the latter applies only for uniform priors. The magnitude of the minimax regret is one-third that of worst-case regret.

I have also applied the formalism to find minimax-regret equilibria in the case of complete information. These are the same as the expected-profit equilibria; any pair of matching bids constitutes an equilibrium. For these equilibria, the maximum regret is zero. The coordination problem still exists.

Between bargainers both of whom seek to maximize maximum profit, there is a one-parameter family of Nash equilibria; these are identical, except for an indeterminacy in the region of no trade, to the one-step equilibria of Leininger-Linhart-Radner. The coordination problem still exists, and the mechanism therefore cannot be said to be effective in enabling either player to maximize maximum profit.

5.2 Undesirable properties of these alternative objectives

A clear description of the properties possessed and not possessed by various rules for decision-making under uncertainty is given in Milnor (1954). The minimax-regret rule fails to have the property Milnor calls "row-adjunction," which is equivalent to what Arrow (1951), in a social-choice context, calls "independence of irrelevant alternatives." It is argued in Linhart and Radner (1989) that, in the context of sealed-bid bargaining, this failure is not serious; that is, no *plausible* change in the allowed ranges of the players' bids changes the optimum bids within the ranges assumed here.

The maximax profit objective is a special case of the Hurwicz (1951) rule which maximizes a linear combination of minimum and maximum profit. The Hurwicz rule fails to have the property Milnor calls "convexity." That is, a maximax strategy that randomly mixes two equally "good" bids may be worse than either of them. I have not considered mixed strategies in this paper, but for the maximax-profit problem considered here, no pair of equally good bids exists.

(The Hurwicz rule also fails to have the property Milnor calls "row linearity." However, there is no obvious reason why this property should be required in the present context.)

5.3 Relationship to experiment

The reappearance of the Chatterjee-Samuelson linear equilibrium, when the players' objectives are changed from maximization of expected profit to minimization of maximum regret, suggests a certain naturalness or robustness about this equilibrium. This suggestion is reinforced by three further considerations:

i) Linear behavior may be relatively easy for bargainers to understand and implement.
ii) This equilibrium is the most efficient of the incomplete-information equilibria for expected-profit maximizers who hold uniform priors on $[0, 1]$.
iii) This equilibrium is independent of the form of the priors, as long as their supports are coincident, for maximum-regret minimizers.

Despite all this, the experimental results do not unambiguously show (in the repeated game) the Chatterjee-Samuelson equilibrium behavior (of the one-shot game).

On the other hand, these experimental results do often[7] show behavior qualitatively like a particular case of the maximax-profit equilibria of Eqs. (39) and (40), namely

$$v = \begin{cases} V & \text{for} \quad 0 \leq V < a \\ a & \text{for} \quad a \leq V \leq 1, \end{cases} \tag{44}$$

$$c = \begin{cases} a & \text{for} \quad 0 \leq C \leq a \\ 1 & \text{for} \quad a \leq C \leq 1. \end{cases} \tag{45}$$

References

Arrow, K.J. (1951) *Social Choice and Individual Values*. 2nd Edn. Yale University Press, New Haven, CT

Chatterjee, K., Samuelson, W. (1983) Bargaining under incomplete information. *Operations Research* 31: 835–851

Farrell, J., Gibbons, R. (1989) Cheap talk can matter in bargaining. *Journal of Economic Theory* 48: 221–237

Gilboa, I., Schmeidler, D. (1989) Maxmin expected utility with a non-unique prior. *Journal of Mathematical Economic* 18: 141–153

Hurwicz, L. (1951) Some specification problems and applications to economic methods (Abstract). *Econometrica* 19: 343–344

Ichiishi, T. (1997) *Microeconomic Theory*. Blackwell, Cambridge, MA

Leininger, W., Linhart, P.B., Radner, R. (1989) Equilibria of the sealed-bid mechanism for bargaining with incomplete information. *Journal of Economic Theory* 48: 63–106

Linhart, P.B., Radner, R. (1989) Minimax-regret strategies for bargaining over several variables. *Journal of Economic Theory* 48: 152–178

Linhart, P.B., Radner, R., Schotter, A. (1989) *Behavior and Efficiency in the Sealed-Bid Mechanism*. mimeo. New York University

Milnor, J. (1954) Games against nature. In: Thrall, R.M., Coombs, C.H., Davis, R.L. (eds) *Decision Processes*. Wiley, New York, pp. 49–59

Radner, R., Schotter, A. (1989) The sealed-bid mechanism: An experimental study. *Journal of Economic Theory* 48: 179–220

Satterthwaite, M.A., Williams, S.R. (1989) Bilateral trade with the sealed-bid double auction: Existence and efficiency. *Journal of Economic Theory* 48: 107–133

Savage, L.J. (1954) *The Foundations of Statistics*. Wiley, New York

Wald, A. (1950) *Statistical Decision Functions*. Wiley, New York

[7] But not always.

Investment and concern for relative position

Harold L. Cole[1,2], **George J. Mailath**[3] **Andrew Postlewaite**[3]

[1] Research Department, Federal Reserve Bank of Minneapolis, 250 Marquette Ave., Minneapolis, MN 55480, USA

[2] Department of Economics, Bunche Hall 9377, UCLA, Los Angeles, CA 90095-1477, USA (e-mail: hlcole@econ.ucla.edu)

[3] Department of Economics, 3718 Locust Walk, University of Pennsylvania, Philadelphia, PA 19104-6297, USA (e-mail: {gmailath; apostlew}@econ.sas.upenn.edu)

Abstract. Economists typically analyze individuals' market behavior in isolation from their nonmarket decisions. While this research strategy has generally been successful, it can lead to systematic errors when agents' nonmarket behavior affects their market choices. In this paper we analyze how individuals' investment behavior changes as a result of nonmarket behavior. Specifically, we analyze a model in which individuals must decide how to allocate their initial endowment between two random investments, where the returns are perfectly correlated across individuals for the first investment but independent across individuals for the second. We consider an environment in which men and women match, with wealthier individuals more successful in matching. We show how individuals' concern about relative wealth can affect their investment decisions, and we provide conditions under which individuals bias their investments either toward or away from the investment with correlated returns. A modification of the model is used to explain why agents' investments might exhibit a home country bias.

1 Introduction

The analysis of markets and consumer behavior in markets has been a central concern – perhaps *the* central concern – of economists since Adam Smith. While economists well understand that there are many important aspects of peoples' lives that are determined outside those markets, they investigate market behavior in the hope and belief that individuals' behavior in those markets can be studied, understood, or predicted isolated from the nonmarket behavior of those individuals. This separation of human activity into market and nonmarket components has, by and large, been hugely successful. The focus on market behavior has resulted in parsimonious general models of individual decision making that

Support from the NSF is gratefully acknowledged.

are applicable to a broad range of problems, rather than idiosyncratic, problem specific models.

While there are sound reasons underlying the modelling choice that segregates market from nonmarket behavior, that separation potentially comes at a large cost if individuals' decisions outside markets truly affect their attitudes and choices in markets. In earlier work, Cole et al. (1992), we demonstrated how a particular decision that was not mediated through markets, matching between men and women, could affect market behavior.[1] In particular, we showed that if matching between men and women is positively assortative in wealth, matching considerations give people an incentive to save more than they would in the absence of matching concerns.

In this paper we investigate how nonmarket concerns, such as matching, can affect not only the level of investments that people make, but also the composition of their investments. Our interest is in how, in a given society, a particular agent's asset allocation decision is influenced by the asset allocations of others in that society. We are particularly interested in whether nonmarket activities might provide agents with an incentive to allocate assets in a manner similar to that of other agents in the society.

We analyze a model in which individuals allocate their initial endowment between two random investments, where the returns are perfectly correlated across individuals for the first investment but independent across individuals for the second. This standard portfolio choice problem is augmented with a matching/marriage decision following the realization of the agents' investments. It is assumed that following matching, consumption is joint, so that, all else equal, both men and women prefer wealthy partners to poor ones. The addition of a matching decision introduces a tournament aspect to the investment decision. The consumption of an agent depends not only on the realization of that agent's portfolio, but also on the wealth of that agent's partner in the subsequent matching. But an agent's ability to attract a wealthy partner depends not only on his or her own wealth, but also on the wealth of the "competition," the other agents of the same sex.

Hence, the addition of a matching decision to an otherwise standard portfolio choice problem adds an important general equilibrium component to the problem. In the absence of the nonmarket decision, each agent could make his or her investment decisions in isolation, since other agents's decisions have no effect on the agent's ultimate consumption; the addition of the particular nonmarket decision will generally make the agent's investment choice depend on other agents' choices. We show that the inclusion of the matching decision causes agents to care about the extent to which their wealth is correlated to that of other agents, and will provide conditions under which agents want to increase and decrease, relative to the standard model, that correlation.

[1] There is a substantial body of literature analyzing the interaction between market resource allocation mechanisms and nonmarket resource allocation mechanisms. See, e.g., Ichiishi (1993) and the references therein.

The next section contains our formal model and results. In Sect. 3, we apply the model to a specific question of independent interest, why agents may fail to adequately diversify their investments. We use a variant of the model from Sect. 2 to show that if some agents in a group are exogenously constrained so as to prevent them from optimally diversifying, concern for relative rank will induce all agents to inadequately diversify, even though they may not be constrained. We conclude in Sect. 4 with a discussion and interpretation of our results, and a discussion of related literature.

2 The investment model

There is a continuum of men and a continuum of women, each uniformly distributed on $[0, 1]$.[2] Male $i \in [0, 1]$ is endowed with $e(i)$ units of the male good, where $e : [0, 1] \rightarrow \Re_+$ is strictly increasing. In addition to this good, there is a nonconsumable capital good and a produced female consumption good. For simplicity, we assume that only females have the capital good, and hence the ability to produce the female consumption good. Females are *ex ante* identical, and each female is endowed with one unit of the capital good, which she can invest in either of two investment projects. There is a common project for which the random rate of return is identical across females and is denoted by a. The second project is a private value project on which the rate of return is individual specific and will be denoted b_i; we assume a and b_i take on values between zero and one. We also assume that a and each b_i are independently distributed, with the distribution functions over the first and second investments given by H and F respectively, and the density functions denoted h and f. The wealth of female agent i is given by $y_i = x_i a + (1 - x_i)b_i$, where x_i denotes the fraction of her capital invested in the common project. The female agents make their investment decisions prior to the realization of the rates of return on the two projects.

Females' preferences are given by $E\{u(\tilde{c}) + \hat{w}(\tilde{e})\}$, where $\tilde{c}$ denotes the (random) consumption level of the female good and $\tilde{e}$ denotes the (random) consumption of the male good. Since consumption of the male good is joint, it is determined by the identity of the male that the female matches with. We denote by w the von Neumann utility of matching with male j, that is, $w(j) = \hat{w}(e(j))$. It is important to keep in mind that since the utility function over male mates w is the composition of the endowment function e and the utility function over male good $\hat{w}$, even if the utility function over the male good is concave, the endowment function e may be such that the composition is either convex or concave (or neither). Males preferences are increasing in the consumption of both the male good (which is predetermined) and the female good. As will become clear, it is unnecessary to be more specific about male preferences.

The sequence of events is as follows. First, each female chooses an allocation of her capital between the two investment projects. After the returns of the

[2] The assumption that there is a continuum of men and a continuum of women is not innocuous. Making the number of agents finite would introduce subtleties absent from the continuum model; this is discussed in the last Section.

projects are realized, males and females match. After matching, agents jointly consume the goods available to the pair. We assume that there is no commitment technology for enforcing agreements, which rules out any sort of insurance market among the females. Hence the only decisions that the agents make are their matching decisions and the females' investment decisions. Since all males value female wealth, and all females value male wealth (as measured by e), the only stable matching (in the sense of Roth and Sotomayer 1990) is positively assortative in wealth. This allows us to restrict attention to positively assortative matchings, without specifying the matching process.

We restrict attention to symmetric equilibria, which substantially simplifies the analysis since if all females make identical investment decisions, we can assume that the distribution of females' wealth depends only on this common decision and the realized aggregate rate of return, a. It is relatively straightforward to determine the equilibrium matching outcome in this case. Since matching is positively assortative in wealth, a portfolio allocation $x \in [0, 1]$ is *a symmetric equilibrium* if each female finds it optimal to choose that portfolio allocation when all other females do so. Note that, apart from $x_i = x = 1$, the probability that female i assigns to another female having the same final wealth as her is zero, irrespective of her portfolio decision. Thus, positive assortative matching on wealth determines her utility for all portfolio decisions. If $x_i = x = 1$ then all females are only investing in the common project, and in that case we assume each female is randomly matched with a male.

A common investment level x for all women results in a determinate distribution of female wealth and hence a determinate matching conditional on an individual female's wealth. An equilibrium is characterized by a common level x that maximizes each woman's expected utility given this matching relation.

First we calculate the distribution of female wealth that will result from a common division of capital between the two projects. This distribution will determine the probability distribution over matches that results from an arbitrary female's investment decision.

Assume that $x_{i'} = x$ for all $i' \neq i$. For a given realization a, female wealth within the population is distributed on $[xa, xa + (1 - x)]$ with a fraction $F\left((y - xa) / (1 - x)\right)$ having wealth less than or equal to y. Since the rank, $\tilde{s}_i$, of female i with wealth $\tilde{y}_i$ is the fraction of females with wealth less than or equal to $\tilde{y}_i$,

$$\tilde{s}_i = F\left((\tilde{y}_i - xa) / (1 - x)\right).$$

The probability, *conditional on a*, of her rank being less than or equal to $s_i < 1$ is given by[3]

[3] The second equality does not hold for $s_i = 1$, since it is possible that $(\tilde{y}_i - xa) / (1 - x) > 1$. While F is only one-to-one on $[0, 1]$, it is easy to see that the second equality does hold for $s_i = 0$.

$$\begin{aligned}\Pr\{\tilde{s}_i \leq s_i|a\} &= \Pr\left\{F\left((\tilde{y}_i - xa)/(1-x)\right) \leq s_i|a\right\} \\ &= \Pr\left\{(\tilde{y}_i - xa)/(1-x) \leq F^{-1}(s_i)\,|a\right\} \\ &= \Pr\left\{\tilde{y}_i - xa \leq (1-x)F^{-1}(s_i)\,|a\right\}.\end{aligned}$$

Female i is investing x_i in the common project, so $\tilde{y}_i = x_i a + (1-x_i)\,b_i$, and we have

$$\begin{aligned}\Pr\{\tilde{s}_i \leq s_i|a\} &= \Pr\left\{x_i a + (1-x_i)\,b_i - xa \leq (1-x)F^{-1}(s_i)\,|a\right\} \\ &= \Pr\left\{b_i \leq \frac{(1-x)F^{-1}(s_i) + (x-x_i)\,a}{(1-x_i)}\middle|\, a\right\} \\ &= F\left[\frac{(1-x)F^{-1}(s_i) + (x-x_i)a}{1-x_i}\right].\end{aligned}$$

Taking expectations over the returns of the common project (which is realized *after* female i chooses x_i) yields the probability distribution function over female i's rank contingent on her choice of x_i alone, denoted $G(s_i; x_i)$,

$$G(s_i; x_i) = \int_0^1 F\left[\frac{(1-x)F^{-1}(s_i) + (x-x_i)a}{1-x_i}\right] h(a)da.$$

A female agent's rank in the output distribution determines her equilibrium match, and so her consumption of the male good, specifically, female i of rank s_i is matched with male s_i and so receives utility $w(s_i)$. We now explicitly define the symmetric equilibrium portfolio decision.

Definition 1. *A portfolio allocation x is a symmetric equilibrium if, for all i, $x_i = x$ solves*

$$\max \iint u(x_i a + (1-x_i)b_i)h(a)f(b_i)dadb_i + \int w(s_i)G(ds_i; x_i).$$

Consider for a moment the special case where both u and w are linear. In this case, females are both risk neutral and "rank neutral," that is, females care only about the expected rank in the wealth distribution. However, since rank is not a linear function of wealth, maximizing the expected value of one's wealth rank is not the same as maximizing expected wealth. This implies that there is a tradeoff between expected consumption and expected wealth rank. Our first observation is that if the distributions are symmetric, a female's expected wealth rank is independent of her portfolio choice.

Lemma 1. *Suppose the distributions of the returns on the projects are symmetric (i.e., $F(x) = 1 - F(1-x)$ and $H(x) = 1 - H(1-x)$ for all $x \in [0,1]$). Then a female's expected rank equals $\frac{1}{2}$, independent of her portfolio choice x_i.*

Proof. First, note that $F^{-1}(s) + F^{-1}(1-s) = 1$. Now,

$$
\begin{aligned}
G(1-s_i;x_i) &= \int_0^1 F\left[\frac{(1-x)F^{-1}(1-s_i)+(x-x_i)a}{1-x_i}\right]h(a)da \\
&= \int_0^1 F\left[\frac{(1-x)(1-F^{-1}(s_i))+(x-x_i)a}{1-x_i}\right]h(a)da \\
&= \int_0^1 \left\{1-F\left[1-\frac{(1-x)(1-F^{-1}(s_i))+(x-x_i)a}{1-x_i}\right]\right\}h(a)da \\
&= \int_0^1 \left\{1-F\left[\frac{(1-x)F^{-1}(s_i)+(x-x_i)(1-a)}{1-x_i}\right]\right\}h(a)da \\
&= 1-G(s_i;x_i),
\end{aligned}
$$

where the last equality holds because a and $1-a$ are identically distributed (i.e., $h(a)=h(1-a)$). Since $G(s_i;x_i)$ is symmetric, $\int s_i G(ds_i;x_i)=\frac{1}{2}$. □

The first order condition associated with a female agent's problem is

$$
\iint u'(x_i a+(1-x_i)b_i)(a-b_i)h(a)f(b_i)dadb_i+\frac{\partial}{\partial x_i}\int w(s_i)G(ds_i;x_i)=0.
$$

Standard optimal portfolio arguments, which ignore matching effects, would imply that the first term in the above expression is equal to zero. To see how concerns about relative wealth can alter investment decisions, consider the following approximation to the second term:

$$
\begin{aligned}
\frac{\partial}{\partial x_i}\int w(s_i)G(ds_i;x_i) \;\approx\;& w'\left(\frac{1}{2}\right)\frac{\partial}{\partial x_i}\int\left(s_i-\frac{1}{2}\right)G(ds_i;x_i) \\
&+\frac{1}{2}w''\left(\frac{1}{2}\right)\frac{\partial}{\partial x_i}\int\left(s_i-\frac{1}{2}\right)^2 G(ds_i;x_i).
\end{aligned}
$$

This expression separates the second term into an expected rank component, and a variance of rank component.

If female i invests x_i in the first project, the support of the distribution of her possible output conditional on the realized value of a is $[x_i a, x_i a+(1-x_i)]$. If all other females invest x in the first project, the support of the ex post distribution of female output conditional on a is $[xa, xa+(1-x)]$. It follows therefore that if $x_i > x$, the support of female i's conditional distribution of output lies strictly inside the support for the aggregate distribution for all $a \leq 1$. Similarly, if $x_i < x$ and $a \leq 1$, then while the expected level of female i's output is still the same, the upper and lower supports of her conditional distribution exceeds those of the aggregate distribution. Thus, while female i cannot affect her expected wealth rank because of the assumed symmetry, she may reduce the variance of rank by investing more heavily in the common project.

In the following example we illustrate how concerns over the variance of one's wealth rank can alter equilibrium outcomes. In the equilibrium of the example we consider, when agents have concave preferences over their rank they invest less in projects whose returns are idiosyncratic and more in projects whose returns are correlated with the returns of other agents than they would if these concerns were absent. If their preferences over their wealth rank are convex then the reverse is true.

Example. Assume that $u(c) = D_1 c - c^2$, $w(j) = d_1 j - dj^2$, and that D_1 and d_1 are both positive. The functions u and w will be increasing in the relevant range as long as $D_1 \geq 2$ and $d_1 \geq 2d$ (since $c, j \in [0,1]$). We also assume that each b_i is uniformly distributed on $[0,1]$. We will assume that a is symmetrically distributed on $[0,1]$, so that $\mathscr{E} a = \frac{1}{2}$. Given our quadratic preference specification only the first two moments of the distribution over y_i and s_i matter. Since both a and b_i are symmetrically distributed, then as shown above, the expected value of a female's status level is independent of her investment portfolio decision. As we will show below, the variance of a female agent's status is not independent of her investment decision. Similarly, since $\mathscr{E} y_i = x_i a + (1 - x_i) b_i = \frac{1}{2}$, female i can only affect the variance of her output, but not its expected value.

The variance of y_i, and hence of consumption, is given by

$$\mathscr{E}\left\{\left(x_i a + (1 - x_i) b_i - \frac{1}{2}\right)^2\right\} = x_i^2 \sigma_a^2 + (1 - x_i)^2 \sigma_b^2.$$

The choice of x_i that minimizes the variance of y_i thus solves

$$x_i \sigma_a^2 - (1 - x_i)\sigma_b^2 = 0,$$

which implies

$$x_i = \frac{\sigma_b^2}{\sigma_a^2 + \sigma_b^2} \equiv x^*. \tag{1}$$

The consumption variance minimizing portfolio allocation, x^*, will play an important role in what follows.

The remainder of this section proves the following proposition. A symmetric equilibrium is *interior* if the equilibrium portfolio allocation has strictly positive weight on both the common project and the private value project.

Proposition 1. *Suppose $u(c) = D_1 c - c^2$, $w(j) = d_1 j - dj^2$, with $D_1 \geq 2$, $d_1 \geq \max\{0, 2d\}$. Assume the common project return distribution is symmetric and that the private project returns are uniformly distributed on $[0,1]$. If a symmetric equilibrium exists, it is unique. If a symmetric interior equilibrium exists, then $4dx^* \leq (1 - x^*)^2$ and the fraction in the common project is given by*

$$x^- \equiv \frac{1 + x^* - \sqrt{(1 - x^*)^2 - 4dx^*}}{2},$$

which is a strictly increasing function of d and equals x^* when $d = 0$. Thus, if females are rank risk averse ($d > 0$), they invest more than x^* in the common project, while if they are rank risk loving ($d < 0$), they invest less than x^* in the common project.

For $-1 \leq d \leq 0$, a symmetric interior equilibrium exists if $4dx^* \leq (1 - x^*)^2$ and $\left(1 - x^-\right)^2 \geq -d$.

For $d \geq 0$, a symmetric interior equilibrium exists if $4dx^* \leq (1 - x^*)^2$ and $\left(1 - x^-\right)^2 \geq 2dx^*$.

For $d \leq -1$, a symmetric equilibrium exists and it is the boundary equilibrium at $x = 0$.

For $2dx^* \geq (1 - x^*)^2$, a symmetric equilibrium exists and it is the boundary equilibrium at $x = 1$.

Since females cannot affect either the expected value of their consumption or the expected value of their rank (Lemma 1), we can ignore this component in their payoff. The relevant part of the expected payoff of female agent i then has two parts: the variance of consumption and the variance of rank, which we denote by $A(x_i; x)$ and $B(x_i; x)$, respectively. The variance of consumption is

$$A(x_i; x) = \mathscr{E}(x_i a + (1 - x_i)b_i - 1/2)^2 = x_i^2 \sigma_a^2 + (1 - x_i)^2 \sigma_b^2.$$

Lemma 2. *The variance of rank is given by*

$$B(x_i; x) = \begin{cases} \dfrac{(x_i - x)^2 \sigma_a^2 + (1 - x_i)^2 \sigma_b^2}{(1 - x)^2}, & \text{if} \quad x_i \geq x, \\[2ex] \dfrac{1}{4} - \dfrac{(1 - x)}{6(1 - x_i)}, & \text{if} \quad x_i < x. \end{cases}$$

Proof. Consider first $x_i \geq x$. In this case, the support of female i's wealth is contained within the support of the aggregate distribution of female wealth. Conditional on a, the rank of female i is given by $\{(x_i - x)a + (1 - x_i)b_i\}/(1 - x)$ for all a and b_i. The variance of the rank is then (recall that a and b_i are independent)

$$\mathscr{E}\left\{\left[\frac{(x_i - x)a + (1 - x_i)b_i}{1 - x} - \frac{1}{2}\right]^2\right\} = \frac{(x_i - x)^2 \sigma_a^2 + (1 - x_i)^2 \sigma_b^2}{(1 - x)^2}. \tag{2}$$

Consider now $x_i < x$. Now, the distribution of possible output levels, conditional on a, does not lie within the support of the aggregate output distribution, and the ranks 0 and 1 occur with positive probability. Denoting female i's rank by $s_i(b_i; a)$, we have

$$s_i(b_i; a) = \begin{cases} 0, & \text{if } b_i \leq (x - x_i)a/(1 - x_i), \\[1ex] \dfrac{(x_i - x)a + (1 - x_i)b_i}{(1 - x)} & \text{if } (x - x_i)a/(1 - x_i) < b_i \\ & \quad < [(x - x_i)a + (1 - x)]/(1 - x_i), \\[1ex] 1, & \text{if } [(x - x_i)a + (1 - x)]/(1 - x_i) \leq b_i. \end{cases}$$

Thus, with probability $(x - x_i)a/(1 - x_i)$, female i has wealth rank 0, with probability $(x - x_i)(1 - a)/(1 - x_i)$, rank 1, and with the residual probability, $(1 - x)/(1 - x_i)$, her rank is uniformly distributed between 0 and 1. The variance of her rank is $\mathscr{E}\left\{(s_i(b_i; a) - \frac{1}{2})^2\right\} = \mathscr{E}_a \mathscr{E}_b\left[(s_i(b_i; a) - \frac{1}{2})^2 | a\right]$. We first evaluate the expectation conditional on a:

$$
\begin{aligned}
\mathscr{E}_b\left[\left(s_i(b_i;a)-\frac{1}{2}\right)^2|a\right] &= \frac{1}{4}\times \Pr\{s_i=0\}+\frac{1}{4}\times \Pr\{s_i=1\} \\
&\quad +\mathscr{E}_b\left[\left(s_i(b_i;a)-\frac{1}{2}\right)^2\middle| a, s_i\in(0,1)\right] \\
&\quad \times \Pr(s_i\in(0,1)) \\
&= \frac{(x-x_i)}{4(1-x_i)}+\int_{s^{-1}(0)}^{s^{-1}(1)}\left(s_i(b_i;a)-\frac{1}{2}\right)^2 db_i \\
&= \frac{(x-x_i)}{4(1-x_i)}+\int_0^1\left(s_i-\frac{1}{2}\right)^2\left(\frac{ds_i}{db_i}\right)^{-1} ds_i \\
&= \frac{(x-x_i)}{4(1-x_i)}+\frac{(1-x)}{(1-x_i)}\int_0^1\left(s_i-\frac{1}{2}\right)^2 ds_i \\
&= \frac{(x-x_i)}{4(1-x_i)}+\frac{(1-x)}{12(1-x_i)}=\frac{1}{4}-\frac{(1-x)}{6(1-x_i)}. \quad (3)
\end{aligned}
$$

Since this is independent of a, this is also the unconditional variance of rank for $x_i \leq x$. □

The problem of female agent i can be written as

$$\min_{x_i}\left[A(x_i;x)+dB(x_i;x)\right].$$

While $A(x_i;x)$ is obviously convex in x_i, $B(x_i;x)$ is more complicated (particularly for $x_i < x$), and may not be continuously differentiable in x_i at x.

In the following, we first consider the right and left derivatives of the female's objective function. A necessary condition for an interior equilibria at x is that the left derivative of the agent's objective function is nonpositive and the right derivative is nonnegative at $x_i = x$. We show that in this case, the two derivatives are equal and so equal zero, allowing us to solve for an interior equilibrium allocation when it exists. We then examine the relevant second order terms to establish conditions under which an interior equilibrium exists. Finally, we examine the conditions under which boundary equilibria might exist.

The derivative of $A(x_i;x)+ dB(x_i;x)$ with respect to x_i for $x_i \geq x$ is

$$2\left[x_i+\frac{d(x_i-x)}{(1-x)^2}\right]\sigma_a^2-2\left[1+\frac{d}{(1-x)^2}\right](1-x_i)\sigma_b^2.$$

This is proportional to

$$2\left[x_i+\frac{d(x_i-x)}{(1-x)^2}\right](1-x^*)-2\left[1+\frac{d}{(1-x)^2}\right](1-x_i)x^*. \quad (4)$$

The derivative is nonnegative at $x_i = x$ only if

$$x-x^*-\frac{dx^*}{1-x}\geq 0. \quad (5)$$

The derivative of a female's objective function when $x_i < x$ is nonpositive only if

$$2\left[x_i(\sigma_a^2+\sigma_b^2)-\sigma_b^2\right]+\frac{d(1-x)}{6(1-x_i)^2}\leq 0,$$

which, dividing by $(\sigma_a^2+\sigma_b^2)2$, and making use of the fact that $\sigma_b^2 = 1/12$, yields

$$(x_i-x^*)-\frac{dx^*(1-x)}{(1-x_i)^2}\leq 0. \tag{6}$$

Evaluating at $x_i = x$,

$$x-x^*-\frac{dx^*}{1-x}\leq 0. \tag{7}$$

Since (5) and (7) must hold simultaneously for x to be an interior equilibrium, the right and left hand derivatives are both equal to zero. This gives us a simple quadratic in x, which has two solutions

$$x^+\equiv\frac{1+x^*+\sqrt{(1-x^*)^2-4dx^*}}{2},$$

and

$$x^-\equiv\frac{1+x^*-\sqrt{(1-x^*)^2-4dx^*}}{2}. \tag{8}$$

For the roots to be real, we need (as claimed)

$$4dx^*\leq(1-x^*)^2. \tag{9}$$

If $d < 0$, only x^- is admissible, because x^+ is strictly larger than one. While both roots are feasible for some values of $d \geq 0$, we show below that only x^- is consistent with the second order conditions. Note that x^- is increasing in d; if $d = 0$, then $x^- = x^*$, while if $d > 0$, $x^- > x^*$ and if $d < 0$, $x^- < x^*$.

Additionally, for x^- to be between zero and one,

$$1+x^*-\sqrt{(1-x^*)^2-4dx^*}\leq 2,$$

which is implied by $x^* < 1$.

In order to verify that $x_i = x^-$ is a solution to the female i's problem it is sufficient to show that her objective function is convex (recall that we have written her problem as a minimization problem). We find sufficient conditions for the derivatives in (4) and (6) to be both nondecreasing in x_i. The derivative of the expression in (4) with respect to x_i is nonnegative if

$$1+\frac{d}{(1-x)^2}\geq 0,$$

which, evaluated at $x = x^-$, is $\left(1-x^-\right)^2 \geq -d$. It is straightforward to verify that this holds with equality at $d = -1$ and is violated for all $d < -1$.

The derivative of the left hand side of (6) with respect to x_i is nonnegative if

$$1 - \frac{2d(1-x)x^*}{(1-x_i)^2} \geq 0. \tag{10}$$

This condition is always satisfied if $d < 0$. If $d \geq 0$, a necessary and sufficient condition for (10) to hold for all $x_i \leq x$ is that it hold at $x_i = x$:

$$1 - \frac{2dx^*}{(1-x)^2} \geq 0. \tag{11}$$

Evaluating at $x = x^-$ yields $\left(1 - x^-\right)^2 \geq 2dx^*$.

We now show why, for the case $d \geq 0$, the root x^+ is not a symmetric equilibrium. Evaluating (11) at $x = x^+$ and simplifying yields the inequality

$$\left(1 - x^*\right)^2 - 4dx^* \geq 2\left(1 - x^*\right)\sqrt{(1-x^*)^2 - 4dx^*} + 4dx^*,$$

which in turn requires

$$\sqrt{(1-x^*)^2 - 4dx^*} \geq 2\left(1 - x^*\right),$$

or

$$-4dx^* \geq 3\left(1 - x^*\right)^2,$$

which is impossible. But this implies that the female's objective function when $x = x^+$ is not quasiconvex in a neighborhood of $x_i = x = x^+$.

We turn now to the possibility of boundary equilibria. We consider first the case where $d > 0$. There cannot be a boundary equilibrium at $x = 0$, because inequality (5) would need to hold at $x = 0$, which is impossible when $d > 0$. If $x = 1$, and female i sets $x_i = 1$, then all females have the same output. In this case the value of her objective function is $\sigma_a^2 + d/12$, since the male match quality is uniformly distributed on the unit interval and hence has variance $1/12$. If on the other hand, a female deviates by setting $x_i < 1$, then she receives the best match if $b_i > a$ or the worst match $b_i < a$. Since the event $a = b$ is a probability zero event, and a and b are symmetrically distributed around $\frac{1}{2}$, she will receive rank 1 or 0 with probability $\frac{1}{2}$. This implies that if a female sets $x_i < 1$, then the best she can do is set $x_i = x^*$, in which case the value of her objective function is $(x^*)^2\,\sigma_a^2 + (1-x^*)^2\sigma_b^2 + d/4$. Thus, for there to be a boundary equilibrium at $x = 1$,we must have

$$\left(x^*\right)^2\sigma_a^2 + \left(1 - x^*\right)^2\sigma_b^2 + d/4 \geq \sigma_a^2 + d/12,$$

or, rearranging,

$$d/6 \geq (1 - \left(x^*\right)^2)\sigma_a^2 - \left(1 - x^*\right)^2\sigma_b^2.$$

But substituting for $\sigma_b^2 = \frac{1}{12}$ on the left hand side and dividing by $\left(\sigma_a^2 + \sigma_b^2\right)$ yields

$$\begin{aligned} 2dx^* &\geq \left(1 - \left(x^*\right)^2\right)\left(1 - x^*\right) - \left(1 - x^*\right)^2 x^* \\ &= \left(1 - x^*\right)^2, \end{aligned}$$

or

$$d \geq \frac{(1-x^*)^2}{2x^*} > 0. \tag{12}$$

It is worth noting that if $2dx^* < (1-x^*)^2 < 4dx^*$, then no symmetric equilibrium exists (since both (9) and (12) are violated).

Consider now $d < 0$. From (12), $x = 1$ cannot be a boundary equilibrium. The other possible boundary equilibrium is at $x = 0$. In this case, the distribution of aggregate output is uniform on the unit interval, and hence a female's relative wealth rank is equal to her output. In this case her objective function is given by (again from the expressions of $A(x_i;x)$ and $B(x_i;x)$)

$$(1+d)\left[x_i^2\sigma_a^2 + (1-x_i)^2\sigma_b^2\right].$$

This objective function is minimized at $x_i = 0$ if and only if $d \leq -1$; otherwise $x_i = x^*$, and there cannot be a boundary equilibria at $x_i = x = 0$.

3 Multiple common projects

As we discussed above, the model illustrates how a concern for relative position can lead agents to bias their decisions either toward or away from the average investment strategy of their reference group. We now consider an interesting application of this observation. Economists have for some time puzzled that individuals inadequately hedge their investments across countries (see, e.g. Lewis (1999)). The analysis of our model suggests a possible explanation. We show that if some agents are constrained to bias their portfolio (for example, rules that restrict institutions to invest only in home-country companies), then this will induce all other agents to also bias their portfolio in order to minimize the variance of their rank with respect to the constrained group.

To illustrate this point, we consider in this section a modification of the model above. We consider the case in which there are two common projects (which we could interpret as domestic and foreign market portfolios), with each project's returns distributed symmetrically and independently on the unit interval. All other details of the model are unchanged.

Suppose females are rank risk averse. We first argue that in any symmetric equilibrium, the portfolio allocation between the two common projects must minimize the variance of the common project portfolio returns. This implies that pure herding cannot explain portfolio bias. We then show that if some fraction of the population is forced to bias their portfolio, then this can induce the other agents to bias their portfolio in a similar direction.

Proposition 2. *Assume the common project returns are symmetrically and independently distributed on* $[0,1]$, *and that the private project returns are uniformly distributed on* $[0,1]$. *Suppose females are rank risk averse and that* $\left(x^1, x^2, 1-x^1-x^2\right)$ *is a symmetric equilibrium portfolio. Then,* $x^1/\left(x^1+x^2\right)$ *is the share in the first common project that minimizes the variance of returns from the common project portfolio.*

Proof. Suppose all females other than i choose portfolio $\left(x^1, x^2, 1-x^1-x^2\right)$. Define $x \equiv x^1+x^2$ and $\gamma \equiv x^1/x$. Since a female's optimal portfolio optimally allocates the investment in common projects between the two common projects, it is enough to argue that, for $\gamma_i \neq \gamma$, the rank of female i under portfolio $(\gamma_i x, (1-\gamma_i)x, 1-x)$ is a mean preserving spread of her rank under portfolio $(\gamma x, (1-\gamma)x, 1-x)$.

We first describe the distribution of female i's rank for arbitrary γ_i. These calculations are very similar to those for the case of a single common project. For given realizations of $a^1$and a^2, female wealth within the population is distributed on $[\gamma x a^1+(1-\gamma)xa^2, \gamma x a^1+(1-\gamma)xa^2+(1-x)]$ with a fraction $F((y-\gamma x a^1-(1-\gamma)xa^2)/(1-x))$ having wealth less than or equal to y. Since the rank, $\tilde{s}_i$, of female i with wealth $\tilde{y}_i$ is the fraction of females with wealth less than or equal to $\tilde{y}_i$,

$$\tilde{s}_i = F\left(\left(\tilde{y}_i - \gamma x a^1 - (1-\gamma)xa^2\right)/(1-x)\right).$$

The probability, *conditional on* a^1 *and* a^2, of her rank being less than or equal to $s_i < 1$ is given by (since $F^{-1}(x) = x$ for $x \in [0,1]$)

$$\begin{aligned}
\Pr\{\tilde{s}_i \le s_i | a\} &= \Pr\left\{\tilde{y}_i - \gamma x a^1 - (1-\gamma)xa^2 \le (1-x)s_i | a^1, a^2\right\} \\
&= \Pr\left\{\tilde{y}_i - \gamma x\left(a^1-a^2\right) - xa^2 \le (1-x)s_i | a^1, a^2\right\}.
\end{aligned}$$

Since female i is also investing x in the common projects, $\tilde{y}_i = \gamma_i x\left(a^1-a^2\right) + xa^2 + (1-x)b_i$, and we have

$$\begin{aligned}
\Pr\{\tilde{s}_i \le s_i | a\} &= \Pr\{\gamma_i x(a^1-a^2) + (1-x)b_i - \gamma x(a^1-a^2) \\
&\qquad \le (1-x)s_i | a^1, a^2\} \\
&= \Pr\left\{ b_i \le s_i + \frac{(\gamma-\gamma_i)x\left(a^1-a^2\right)}{(1-x)} \middle| a^1, a^2 \right\} \\
&= F\left[s_i + \frac{(\gamma-\gamma_i)x\left(a^1-a^2\right)}{(1-x)}\right].
\end{aligned}$$

Taking expectations over the returns of the common projects yields the probability distribution function over female i's rank contingent on her choice of γ_i alone, denoted $G(s_i;\gamma_i)$,

$$G(s_i;\gamma_i) = \mathcal{E}_{a^1,a^2} F\left[s_i + \frac{(\gamma-\gamma_i)x\left(a^1-a^2\right)}{(1-x)}\right].$$

The uniformity of F and the symmetry of the distributions of a^1 and a^2 imply that G is also symmetric:

$$
\begin{aligned}
G(s_i;\gamma_i) &= \mathscr{E}_{a^1,a^2}\left\{1-F\left[1-s_i-\frac{(\gamma-\gamma_i)x\left(a^1-a^2\right)}{(1-x)}\right]\right\}\\
&= \mathscr{E}_{a^1,a^2}\left\{1-F\left[1-s_i+\frac{(\gamma-\gamma_i)x\left(a^1-a^2\right)}{(1-x)}\right]\right\}\\
&= 1-G(1-s_i;\gamma_i).
\end{aligned}
$$

Not surprisingly, if $\gamma_i = \gamma$, the distribution of rank is uniform on $[0,1]$. We want to show that when $\gamma_i \neq \gamma$, the distribution of rank is a mean preserving spread of the uniform distribution. Since $G(\cdot;\gamma_i)$ is symmetric, we need only show that for any $s_i \in (0,1)$, the density of $G(\cdot;\gamma_i)$ never exceeds 1, and that it is strictly less than 1 on a positive measure set of s_i.

Let $z = a^1 - a^2$; we denote the density of z by k. The random variable z is distributed symmetrically on $[-1,1]$. Suppose $\zeta \equiv (\gamma-\gamma_i)x/(1-x) > 0$. Since z is symmetrically distributed around 0, the following analysis also covers the possibility $\zeta < 0$. Fix s_i. We consider first the case $s_i < \zeta$ and $1 - s_i < \zeta$. The first inequality implies that for low realizations of z, $s_i + \zeta z < 0$, while the second inequality implies that for large realizations of z, $s_i + \zeta z > 1$. Thus,

$$
\begin{aligned}
G(s_i;\gamma_i) &= \int_{-1}^{-s_i/\zeta} F(s_i+\zeta z)k(z)\,dz + \int_{-s_i/\zeta}^{(1-s_i)/\zeta} F(s_i+\zeta z)k(z)\,dz\\
&\quad + \int_{(1-s_i)/\zeta}^{1} F(s_i+\zeta z)k(z)\,dz\\
&= \int_{-s_i/\zeta}^{(1-s_i)/\zeta} (s_i+\zeta z)k(z)\,dz + \int_{(1-s_i)/\zeta}^{1} k(z)\,dz,
\end{aligned}
$$

since $F(s_i+\zeta z) = 0$ for $s_i + \zeta z \leq 0$ and $F(s_i+\zeta z) = 1$ for $s_i + \zeta z \geq 1$. The density of G is then (using Leibniz's rule)

$$
g(s_i;\gamma_i) = \int_{-s_i/\zeta}^{(1-s_i)/\zeta} k(z)\,dz.
$$

The other cases are handled analogously, so that we have

$$
g(s_i;\gamma_i) = \begin{cases}
\displaystyle\int_{-s_i/\zeta}^{(1-s_i)/\zeta} k(z)\,dz, & \text{if } s_i < \zeta \text{ and } 1-s_i < \zeta,\\
\displaystyle\int_{-1}^{(1-s_i)/\zeta} k(z)\,dz, & \text{if } s_i \geq \zeta \text{ and } 1-s_i < \zeta,\\
\displaystyle\int_{-s_i/\zeta}^{1} k(z)\,dz, & \text{if } s_i < \zeta \text{ and } 1-s_i \geq \zeta,\\
1, & \text{if } s_i \geq \zeta \text{ and } 1-s_i \geq \zeta.
\end{cases}
$$

Note that $g(s_i;\gamma_i) < 1$ in all cases except for the last. □

This result implies that the rank variance minimizing value of γ_i equals γ. However, to the extent that this differs from the consumption variance minimizing level of γ_i, the optimal choice will involve trading off these costs. Since at the rank (consumption) variance minimizing value, the first-order effect of shifting γ_i from this value is zero, the optimal choice will lie strictly between the rank and consumption variance minimizing values. Since this is true for all of the females, it implies that the only equilibrium value of γ is the consumption variance minimizing value, which is $1/2$ when the projects are symmetrically, independently and identically distributed.

We next show that if some fraction of the population is constrained to invest more than 1/2 of the resources that they devote to investing in the common projects in one of these projects, this induces other females to invest relatively more in this project as well.

Proposition 3. *If a fraction $\alpha > 0$ of the females is constrained to set $\gamma_i = \bar{\gamma} > 1/2$, then in the symmetric equilibrium, all other females set $\gamma_i > 1/2$.*

Suppose the females in $[0, \alpha)$ are constrained, and that they choose portfolio $(\bar{\gamma}x, (1-\bar{\gamma})x, 1-x)$. Suppose all females other than i in $[\alpha, 1]$ choose portfolio $(\gamma x, (1-\gamma)x, 1-x)$. As before, we first describe the distribution of female i's rank for arbitrary γ_i. Here there are two different distributions of female returns. However, the rank of female i will be a weighted average of her rank in each of these two populations, with the weights given by the respective fractions of the total population. Hence

$$\begin{aligned} s_i &= (1-\alpha)F\left(\left(\tilde{y}_i - \gamma x a^1 - (1-\gamma)xa^2\right)/(1-x)\right) \\ &\quad +\alpha F\left(\left(\tilde{y}_i - \bar{\gamma} x a^1 - (1-\bar{\gamma})xa^2\right)/(1-x)\right). \end{aligned}$$

This immediately implies that her expected rank is 1/2 regardless of her investment decision. This implies that the probability distribution function over female i's rank contingent on her choice of γ_i alone, which we again denote by $G(s_i;\gamma_i)$, is a weighted average of her probability distribution within each of these populations, or

$$\begin{aligned} G(s_i;\gamma_i) &= \mathscr{E}_{a^1,a^2}\left\{\alpha F\left[F^{-1}(s_i) + \frac{(\bar{\gamma}-\gamma_i)x\left(a^1-a^2\right)}{(1-x)}\right]\right. \\ &\quad \left. +(1-\alpha)F\left[F^{-1}(s_i) + \frac{(\gamma-\gamma_i)x\left(a^1-a^2\right)}{(1-x)}\right]\right\}. \end{aligned}$$

By the same logic as before, if female i sets $\gamma_i = \gamma$, the variance of her rank among the population of females $[\alpha, 1]$ is minimized, and the first-order cost of deviating is zero. Hence, if $\gamma = 1/2$, then the first-order cost of deviating in the direction of $\bar{\gamma}$ is zero both in terms of the variance of her consumption and the variance of her rank among the $[\alpha, 1]$ females. Hence it would be optimal to do so. However, if it is optimal to do for her, it is optimal for all of the females

$j \in [\alpha, 1]$. Hence, in equilibrium $\gamma > 1/2$. Moreover, since in equilibrium $\gamma_i = \gamma$, this implies that all the females in $[\alpha, 1]$ have minimized the variance of rank among the population $[\alpha, 1]$ and hence, at the margin, they are off increasing the variance of their consumption against decreasing the variance of their rank amongst the females in $[0, \alpha)$.

4 Discussion

1. In laying out the model, we mentioned that there could be subtle differences between a model with a continuum of men and a continuum of women and a model in which the number of agents were finite. In a model with a finite number of agents, there would typically be a positive distance between the wealth of any two women. Because of this, very small changes in any woman's wealth, up or down, will not affect the man with whom she was matched. Large changes, of course, will affect the wealth of her partner. Consequently, a woman will find attractive a lottery with a large probability of a sufficiently small loss and a small probability of a large gain. This phenomenon is illustrated by Robson (1996a), who shows in a biologically motivated model that finiteness can induce agents who are "fundamentally" risk neutral to choose some risky lotteries. Robson's model thus shares with our model the property that even when individuals are "fundamentally" risk neutral, their attitudes toward risk over wealth will depend on the shape of the function relating wealth to the items over which fundamental preferences are defined.[4] This also illustrates that our restriction to symmetric random variables is not without cost.

2. In addition to the work mentioned above, Robson has pursued a research agenda that is conceptually closely related to our approach. Robson (1992) lays out a model of decision making in which it is assumed that agents care not only about their wealth, but also about their relative standing in the wealth distribution (status). He assumes that individuals have identical utility functions that are concave in wealth, but convex in status. He uses this framework to show that even though an individual's utility function is concave in wealth itself, utility can nevertheless be convex in wealth over some ranges because of the indirect utility in status. He further investigates which income distributions would have the property that no individual would accept fair gambles.

As does our paper, that paper illustrates how a concern for relative standing can affect risk attitudes. However, it takes the concern for status, or relative rank, as exogenously given. The paper mentioned above, and Robson (1996b), however, endogenizes the concern. In that model males care about maximizing expected number of offspring and females match with males to maximize resources per offspring. If a male has twice the resources as a second male, he will be able to attract twice the number of females, and consequently, will have twice the expected number of offspring. Hence as in our model, males care about

[4] Robson (1996a) provides a nice discussion of this latter point.

their relative wealth position not because it is exogenously posited, but because it affects equilibrium quantities.

While there is a close relationship between our work and that of Robson, there are also several substantial differences. Robson's focus is on the risk attitudes that would likely arise from evolutionary pressures due to biology. We begin from the conventional economic assumption of risk aversion over consumption, and are interested in how the inclusion of decisions that are not mediated by markets, such as matching, can alter the attitudes toward risky gambles over wealth. Our emphasis is not on explaining which risk attitudes will be hard-wired. Instead, we ask, taking as given whatever the hard-wiring of attitudes towards risk is, how do nonmarket mediated activities affect decision making? More generally, our work is distinguished from evolutionary models in that agents are fully rational, and we study equilibrium behavior. Agents understand fully the consequences of their actions and maximize utility. A last, more minor difference between this paper and Robson's is that the emphasis here is not so much on the attitudes towards risk *per se*, but on the degree to which individuals will want their situations correlated with other agents' situations.[5]

3. A consequence of agents desiring to increase the correlation of their portfolio to that of others is that we should see more "clustering" of agents than in a model devoid of incentives to mimic. Bikhchandani et al. (1992) investigate what they term a striking regularity, localized conformity. They identify several mechanisms that have been suggested as explanations of a higher than expected degree of conformity within groups: sanctions on deviants, positive payoff externalities, conformity preference, and communication. Bikhchandani et al. (1992) present an alternative explanation – informational cascades – that they suggest explains not only conformity in groups, but also the fragility of the conformist behavior in the sense that the observed behavioral patterns can change swiftly and without obvious cause. The basic idea of informational cascades is as follows. Suppose that there is a sequence of similar agents who are making similar decisions in an uncertain common environment, and further, that the agents have independent signals about the state of the environment. When a particular individual is to make his decision, previous agents' decisions provide additional information in that they reflect the information the agents had at the time they made their decisions. Bikhchandani et. al. show that in some circumstances, agents may find it optimal to ignore their own private information and simply mimic the decisions taken by previous agents. In this event, agents will be seen making identical choices even though they have different information.[6]

When preferences over rank are concave, our model will also exhibit more conformity of behavior than would be expected if the nonmarket matching was ignored. As the example demonstrated, in this case agents invested more in projects whose returns are correlated with the returns of other agents than they

[5] Robson (1998) analyzes an evolutionary model in which there is a choice between idiosyncratic and common random variables. The choice there is driven by questions of observability of outcomes rather than competition.

[6] See also Banerjee (1992).

would if there were no ranking concerns. Further, while our model isn't dynamic, it is clear that the underlying idea behind the conformity of behavior suggests fragility: if other agents in my reference group change investment strategies for some reason, I have an incentive to follow their lead to avoid increasing my risk of rank. The driving force however, is clearly different from that underlying informational cascades. If informational cascades arise, it is because agents are asymmetrically informed, while there is no asymmetry of information in our model. The conformity of behavior in our model is driven entirely by an *induced* desire to be similar to other agents. We emphasize "induced" because there is no inherent desire to conform in the agents' "deep" preferences; those preferences depend only on consumption.[7] Any desire to conform comes entirely from the nonmarket decisions – matching – and the consumption changes that follow more or less conformity with other agents' investment decisions.

5. The role matching plays in our model is to induce naturally a concern for relative position in the wealth distribution. While matching appears to us a plausible reason that individuals would care about relative rank, it is by no means the only such reason. Technically, all that is necessary for our results is the existence of a benefit or reward that accrues to each agent strictly as a function of the rank in the wealth distribution. If there are any positive consequences that come from simply being wealthier than others in the reference group, the analysis would be essentially the same as above. One can imagine any number of things richer agents might enjoy, such as preferential treatment for oneself or one's family in restaurants, schools, hospitals, churches or synagogues, easier access to politicians or governmental officials, and so on. All that matters is that the better treatment is not paid for directly, but rather is tied to one's rank in the wealth distribution.

There is an alternative interpretation of our model and results. Suppose one took the view that evolution has hard-wired into humans a concern for rank as in Robson (1992). In our model, women get indirect utility from rank equal to the utility they would get from the wealth of the man at that rank level. If one posited that women got direct utility from rank equal to this utility, there would be no change in the analysis. The discussion would be about whether the utility function over rank was concave or convex rather than whether the male wealth function was concave or convex, but except for terminology, it would be the same.

6. The previous two discussion points suggest that there can be substantial differences in the degree of conformity of investment between different groups. As noted above, even if all agents have identical preferences over consumption, preferences over rank will differ across groups to the extent that the rewards to rank differ across those groups. In particular, if an agent's reward to rank was precisely the wealth of the person with whom that agent was subsequently matched, differences in the wealth distribution of potential mates would lead to

[7] This distinguishes the basis for conformism in our model from that in models such as Bernheim's (1994) that assume a direct taste for conformist behavior.

different induced preferences over rank. For example, if in one group the wealth distribution of potential mates was convex, and in a second, concave, we would expect to see relative high amounts of correlation among investments in the first but high amounts of idiosyncratic investments in the second. Aside from differences of concavity/convexity, if the wealth distribution of potential mates in one group is twice that of a second group, both groups will exhibit the same bias toward or against correlated investments, but the bias will be greater in the group with wealthier potential mates. These implications hold not only across groups, but within a group across time. That is, if the wealth distribution among potential mates increases across time, any bias toward or against correlation of investments will be exacerbated.

In the point above, we argued that there can be sources other than the wealth of potential mates for a concern for rank. We would expect that the differences among groups in these kinds of rewards to rank are at least as great as the differences in the distributions of wealth of potential mates across groups. Both the shape and the magnitude of the return to rank function will depend on the fine details of the social organization within groups.

7. Our focus in this paper has been the effect of nonmarket decisions on market decisions, but there is an alternative interpretation to our results. Suppose that Bruce is interested in buying a condominium in Florida when he retires, as is everyone else in his cohort. Then as an approximation, we can imagine that the condominiums will ultimately be allocated among Bruce's cohort, with the nicest going to the wealthiest, the next nicest to the next wealthiest, and so on, with poorer people ending up with less desirable condominiums. Bruce realizes that if he is at the eighty-seventh percentile in the wealth distribution now, and he invests precisely as the others in his cohort do, he will end up in the eighty-seventh percentile condominium, regardless of how well the investments do. If the investments soar, the price of condominiums will be bid up to absorb the higher returns, while with poor investment performance prices will drop.

This is of course an exaggeration since the supply of condominiums isn't perfectly inelastic and there are alternatives to condominiums in consumption, but there is an element of truth in the basic idea that the equilibrium prices of many inelastically supplied goods will be correlated to asset market performance. Hence, there will be less uncertainty in Bruce's final consumption if he holds the same asset portfolio as others in his cohort than if he were to hold different assets. If Bruce believes that the S&P 500 mutual fund he holds is overpriced, he can sell while others continue to hold. His relative wealth rank can change dramatically, up if Bruce is correct and down if he is incorrect. Even if the expected wealth change of selling the S&P mutual fund is positive, Bruce may rationally choose not to sell so as to avoid the risk he would face in relative rank.

This example is certainly not a tight argument, but is meant to illustrate a simple idea. Bruce's "deep" utility function has as an argument his consumption of goods and services. His consumption of goods and services will depend on his wealth. Bruce can then consider the reduced form utility function which is a concatenation of the mapping from wealth to consumption and the mapping from consumption to utility; this is standard fare in economics. We do have to bear in mind, however, that the concatenation of the two mappings is possible only as long as prices are fixed. This is generally an innocuous assumption when we analyze a single agent's investment decisions; he forecasts consumption prices with the plausible notion that they will be independent of his personal decisions.

It is a different matter, however, if we analyze a set of people rather than a single individual; we can't take prices as given independent of *all* the agents' choices. In this case, when an agent considers whether he should buy an asset, he considers the random amount of money that is associated with the asset and the (random) consumption that money will purchase. But the second step – determining the consumption that is associated with the asset's return – depends on the prices at that time. But, as we've argued, those prices depend on *other agents' asset choices*. In other words, there is a fundamental problem with a single agent trying to determine his optimal asset choice independently of other agents' choices.

The important point of this discussion is that what is sometimes taken as a primitive – an agent's utility function over wealth – is an "equilibrium" object. It is only in the context of an equilibrium of the full model with asset choices and contingent consumption choices after asset values are realized that there is an unambiguous utility function over wealth for an individual, and that utility function is appropriate only for that equilibrium. There may well be different equilibria of the full model, with different utility functions over wealth for that agents in different equilibria.[8]

References

Banerjee, A. (1992) A simple model of herd behavior. *Quarterly Journal of Economics* 107: 797–817

Bernheim, D. (1994) A theory of conformity. *Journal of Political Economy*: 841–877

Bikhchandani, S., Hirshleifer, D., Welch, I. (1992) A theory of fads, fashion, custom, and cultural change as informational cascades. *Journal of Political Economy* 100: 992–1026

Cole, L., Mailath, G.J., Postlewaite, A. (1992) Norms, savings behavior, and growth. *Journal of Political Economy* 100: 1092–1125

Ichiishi, T. (1993) The Cooperative Nature of the Firm. Cambridge University Press, Cambridge, U.K.

Lewis, K. (1999) Trying to explain the home bias in equities and consumption. *Journal of Economic Literature* 37: 571–608

Robson, A. (1992) Status, the distribution of wealth, private and social attitudes to risk. *Econometrica* 60: 837–858

Robson, A. (1996a) A biological basis for expected and non-expected utility. *Journal of Economic Theory* 68: 397–424

[8] We emphasize that this discussion depends on there not being complete markets. If there is a full set of contingent markets, contingent market prices will be sufficient to establish a utility function over wealth for an individual.

Robson, A. (1996b) The evolution of attitudes to risk: Lottery tickets and relative wealth. *Games and Economic Behavior* 14: 190–207

Robson, A. (1998) Naive adaptive behavior and the observability of gambles. *Games and Economic Behavior* 24: 190–207

Roth, A., Sotomayer, Oliveira, M.A. (1990) Two-Sided Matching. Cambridge University Press, Cambridge

Coordination of economic activity: An example

Stanley Reiter

Center for Mathematical Studies in Economics and Management Science, Northwestern University, Evanston, IL 60208-2014, USA (e-mail: s-reiter@kellogg.nwu.edu)

1 Introduction

In this paper we consider issues of organization of economic activity, especially coordination of productive activity. We begin with a classic question; "Which economic activities are (or should be) coordinated by markets, and which by other means?" "Other means" usually refers to administrative or bureaucratic mechanisms; sometimes the word "hierarchies" is used. This paper presents a formal model focused on productive activities, in which this question can be asked. The paper also presents an example – a specialization of the model – in which efficient coordination means just-in-time production. The example has two cases. In Case 1 it is shown that the market mechanism cannot achieve efficient coordination, even though there are market equilibria. There are alternative mechanisms, especially one called a direct mechanism, that does achieve efficient coordination. In Case 2 both types of mechanism achieve efficient coordination, but the market mechanism has higher informational costs. The two cases are the same except in one respect. Therefore the different outcomes in the two cases cannot be due to properties that are the same in both cases.

It is a widely held view that a need for coordination of the activities of economic agents exists when different agents have different information, a condition that arises, at least in the production sector, from division of labor and specialization. When agents have private information incentives exist to use it to their advantage. The analysis of the example assumes that the agents will act as the mechanism prescribes, and not in their own self-interest, if those two behaviors are in conflict. If the market mechanism operated by selfless agents cannot bring about efficient coordination, then the market mechanism operating with rational agents acting on their private information in their own self-interest cannot bring

I am indebted to Leo Hurwicz and members of the Decentralization Conference, April 1999, New York University, New York, NY for helpful comments.

about efficient coordination. Thus, the result in Case 1 of the example serves as an impossibility result – a benchmark for mechanism design when incentives are taken into account.[1]

Questions about how economic activity should be coordinated have usually been addressed in the context of 'theory of the firm.' But that seems to us not a useful setting in which to study choice among coordinating mechanisms. A mechanism of coordination that is used within a firm may also be used across firms. One can observe a variety of coordinating mechanisms each commonly and persistently used in the economy, especially in the production sector, between, across and within firms. This phenomenon is not likely to be understood by way of theories in which the only coordinating mechanisms are firms and markets. The concept of 'firm' currently prevalent is essentially legal; a firm is seen as a collection of assets with an owner, an agent who has the legal right to control the use of the assets, and the right to the residual income. A firm that has more than one person in it generally has a mechanism for coordinating its internal activities, and generally a firm is a participant in external mechanisms that coordinate its actions with the actions of other economic units. A given firm can change its internal coordination mechanisms without changing its identity as a firm; the mechanisms that coordinate a firm's actions with those of others might also change without changing the identities of the firms involved.

A manufacturer of tractors, General Tractors (GT) requires a transmission for each tractor it produces. The transmissions are supplied by another firm, GG, that makes them. It is important to coordinate the delivery of transmissions with the production schedule of tractors. At the same time another producer of tractors, UT, has an internal unit, UG, that produces transmissions. The same coordination problem exists inside UT between its tractor division and its transmissions division as exists between GT and its supplier. It may happen that the same coordinating mechanism is used in both cases, for the same reasons.

It is not infrequent that a firm will use another firm as a supplier of components, then at a later time set up an internal unit for the same purpose, and at a still later time shut down or sell the internal unit, returning again to using an outside supplier, all with essentially the same coordination mechanism. In such a case the coordination mechanism stays the same, but the firm structure changes. It is therefore likely that the problem of understanding which coordination mechanism is or should be used is different from understanding which firms do or should form.[2] Because our focus is on understanding choice among coordina-

[1] Whether a given performance objective or goal is achievable when behavior is assumed to be selfless has a certain logical priority over considerations of incentives. For example, one might think up powerful incentive schemes to induce individuals with private knowledge to cooperate to design a certain machine. But if the desired machine is a perpetual motion device, it would be better for the designer of incentive schemes to know that in advance, because the task is impossible.

[2] It is well-known that a single multi-divisional firm can sometimes use a market mechanism to coordinate production across divisions using internal markets with transfer prices. However, these internal markets often differ in essential respects from real markets, and lack a crucial property of 'market' as defined in this paper.

tion mechanisms, it seems best to approach that problem directly, without asking whether it is within or across firms.

It may be the case that the transmission's design is unique to the GT tractor, different from the transmissions used by other tractor manufacturers. When the design of the transmission is uniquely specific to the GT tractors, there cannot be competitive market, or perhaps any market, where that transmission is routinely bought and sold.[3] It is common practice in this situation that the transaction between the transmission supplier and the tractor maker is coordinated by direct exchange of information and negotiation between the two parties. But it is also possible to use direct contact and negotiation between GT and GG to coordinate their actions even when the transmissions are standardized and there is a market for them. In that case there is the possibility of using either coordination mechanism.

The view of the market as a mechanism for coordinating economic activity is both old and familiar, beginning with Adam Smith. The fundamental modern formal expression of this view is in the general equilibrium model. There conditions for the existence of competitive equilibrium are established, as are conditions for the first welfare theorem. These results concern static competitive equilibrium. Specifically, they deal with allocations and prices that are verified to be competitive equilibria. But these results are not sufficient to ensure that efficient coordination of economic activity results from the market mechanism. In the Example presented below general competitive equilibrium exists, and the first welfare theorem holds, but the market mechanism does not produce efficient coordination of production. To understand and justify our interpretation of this result it is useful to state some perhaps obvious things.

First, coordination refers to a relation between actions of economic agents. Thus, each of, say, two agents can take one of several actions, determining an array of individual actions taken. The array is coordinated if and only if it satisfies some given condition, expressing the idea that the two actions match. In the case of the competitive market mechanism, the action of a producer is determined by the rule that it maximizes profit over the set of actions available to that producer, given the prices of commodities; the action of a consumer is determined by the rule that it maximizes the consumer's utility subject to his budget constraint given the prices and initial endowment; the prices are determined by the requirement that excess demand at those prices is non-positive. Coordination means that the actions of all agents are feasible and jointly consistent.

In general, the action of each agent is determined by a behavior rule that is part of the coordinating mechanism. The joint action is coordinated if it satisfies a given requirement.

---

[3] While there cannot be a market for 'GT transmissions' because they do not fit the tractors made by other manufacturers, there could be a market for the manufacturing capacity of suppliers of transmissions. GT, UT and other users of transmissions can be viewed as buying the use of the machines and workers in GG when they buy transmissions. However, this 'product' and market can be very complex, because of scheduling problems internal to the supplier, in this case the transmission manufacturing entity (see Reiter 1965).

Second, a fully specified coordinating mechanism must produce a specific action outcome. If the mechanism is not fully specified, in which case it can result in several possible actions for some or all agents, then it must be the case that any selection of the action of each player must be an array that is coordinated.

As a motivating example consider the situation of two musicians who are to perform a certain duet together. For simplicity we suppose that they must start playing simultaneously. This is the meaning of coordination in this example. If the coordinating mechanism was such that it allowed each player to start at any time within a two second interval, then the mechanism would not be fully specified. The players could start at the same time, in which case their actions would be coordinated, or they could not, in which case the actions are not coordinated. A coordinating mechanism that resulted in this performance would not be an acceptable mechanism. This suggests that the appropriate requirement for coordination is that *every* array of actions of agents that is a result of the mechanism constitute a coordinated array.

The literature that seems closest to the problem posed here is in its earlier manifestations one that considered two organizations of production in firms; one in which two production units formed one vertically integrated firm; the other in which the two production units formed two firms, one buying inputs from the other in an intervening market (see Grossman and Hart 1986). More recently another alternative has been introduced into the theoretical literature. A firm requiring inputs from another, its supplier, can enter into an on-going relationship with one or more firms to supply it with inputs. These relationships can be contractual or not, but they are the result of direct contacts between the manufacturer and the potential suppliers. Thus, there may be three alternative modes of organization to consider. When the third alternative is present the issues of whether a firm should or should not own a supplier, or whether a supplier should own a firm it supplies remain, but a broader range of questions having to do with the arrangements between the supplied firms and the supplying firms also arises. In this literature the analysis of investment and incentives is extended to the multi-firm network setting under broader assumptions about uncertainty and other matters (Kranton and Minehart 1999, who give extensive references to the literature we have been alluding to).

A formal model in which the Question we started with can be asked must include what is meant by: 'economic activity;'

- coordination;
- coordination mechanisms, including:
- markets;
- other mechanism – not markets.

The environment of production provides a setting in which specific coordination problems arise naturally, because specialization entails dispersion of information among agents. Therefore we begin by defining a production environment. The model used for this purpose is a modification of a standard model of technology used, for instance, in general equilibrium models. *Production units*, each run by a *manager*, are introduced, and the *action* of a manager is defined. A criterion for *desired joint action* is introduced. *Coordinated action* means actions of individual producers that combine to make up a desired joint action.

The *information structure* is defined, specifying what each manager knows directly about the technology and the parameters characterizing other aspects of the environment.

Coordination mechanism is defined. It is a representation of a distributed computation through which each manager computes his action, thereby determining the joint action. Different coordination mechanisms using the same basic information correspond to different distributed algorithms and may involve different communication channels.

Following that we present the *criteria for comparing* coordination mechanisms.

We then turn to our Example. In the Example there are two stages of production, and there are two slightly different conditions of demand for final products. In one demand regime users of final products regard units of product delivered at any time within a given week as equivalent (perfect substitutes). In the other regime, users regard units delivered early in the week as different from those delivered late in the week (not perfect substitutes). The technology of production is the same in each case. Two modes of coordinating the intermediate stages of production are considered: a mechanism using a market channel, and a mechanism using a direct channel. We discuss these mechanisms more explicitly in Section 2. In the example, under the first demand regime the market mechanism cannot achieve efficient coordination of production, while the mechanism using a direct channel can achieve efficient coordination. Under the second demand regime both mechanisms achieve efficient coordination.

The production setting used here resembles the setting used by Grossman and Hart (1986) to analyze the formation of firms. While the settings are superficially similar, the questions asked, and the assumptions made, are different. Grossman and Hart are interested in incentive effects associated with the ownership of assets in an environment in which certain actions are not contractible. They derived conclusions about which firms should or will form, but, except for general comments, do not concern themselves with how the actions internal to a firm will or should be coordinated. On the other hand, we ask how actions between the two production units should or will be coordinated without asking whether they are sub-units of a single firm, or two separate firms, assuming away incentive issues.

1.1 Production technology

A *commodity* is an equivalence class of 'objects' having specified characteristics including location in time and space. There is a finite number l of commodities. The *commodity space* X, is a subset of the Euclidean space R^l that is closed under addition. Thus, the amount of a commodity can be a real number, if it is divisible, or an integer, if it is not.

A *production technology* is knowledge of how to transform commodities. It is modeled as a set T of *processess* ; each process represents a technically possible transformation of commodities.

An example of a process might be a collection of (linear or nonlinear) activities, say, an activity 1 that has as its output commodity 1, and as inputs commodities 3 and 4 and also another activity 2 that has as its output commodity 2 with 3 and 4 as inputs. The state of this process would be $\lambda = \lambda(1) + \lambda(2)$, where $\lambda(i)$ is the level of activity i, $i = 1, 2$.

Generally a process ρ has a set S of *states*. Each state of a process determines a point – a *commodity bundle*, or *input-output vector* – in the commodity space. Thus, a process ρ is characterized by an ordered pair, (S_ρ, f_ρ), where f_ρ is a function mapping S_ρ into X. Each process has a state, 0, that represents not using that process; the corresponding point in the commodity space is the vector 0.

In the previous example ρ is the process consisting of activities 1 and 2, and f_ρ is the function that maps the state λ into the commodity space vector $\lambda(1)\,a + \lambda(2)\,b$, where a and b are the commodity space vectors characterizing activities 1 and 2 respectively. The model also admits more subtle technologies, one of which is illustrated in the Example discussed in Section 3.

Production is carried out in production units. A *production unit* consists of a collection of processes – a subset of T – together with a manager, who is in charge of the unit. A manager can be in charge of at most one production unit. The task of a manager is to choose the state of each process in his unit.

Suppose there is a finite number of production units, $\{1, \cdots, N\}$ and correspondingly a finite number of managers, $\{M_1, \cdots, M_N\}$. Formally, there is a correspondence that associates with each production unit the set of processes in that production unit, and therefore, also associates with the manager of production unit i the set T_i of processes in T that she is in charge of. This set can be identified with that manager.

A given process can be used by different production units. For example, there can be several units that use the same process to make steel blanks from which a certain kind of gear is made. Because the same process in different production units can be in different states, those 'copies' of the process must be distinguished from one another. This can be done formally by labeling the process with the name of the unit, or its manager, who is uniquely associated with that unit. If the process ρ is in production unit j and also in j' then we write ρ^j and $\rho^{j'}$ where $\rho^j = \rho^{j'} = \rho$. For $i \in \{1, \cdots, N\}$ write T_i for the set of processes in production unit i, $T_i = \{\rho^i_{1_i}, \cdots, \rho^i_{n_i}\}$. Denote the state of process $\rho^i_{j_i}$ by $s^i_{\rho_{j_i}}$. Correspondingly, the function $f^i_{\rho_{j_i}}$, which is the function mapping the state of the copy of process ρ in production unit i, gives the commodity vector corresponding to the state of that process in production unit i. A *profile of states* s is an array consisting of the states of processes in the sets $T_1, T_2, \cdots, T_N$, in order within each set. Let S denote the set of profiles of states, and, under the assumption that for each i, T_i consists of just one process, define the function $T : S \to X$ by $T(s) = H\left(f_{\rho_1}^1\left(s_{\rho_1}^1\right), \cdots, f_{\rho_N}^N\left(s_{\rho_N}^N\right)\right)$. When there are no externalities in production, the function H is the sum of its arguments. The value $T(s)$ is the net input -output vector associated with the profile s, and $T(s)$ is the set of technologically feasible net input-output vectors in the commodity space. Other feasibility constraints, such as the availability of resources, determine a subset consisting of technologically feasible commodity bundles that also satisfy the restrictions on use of resources. Correspondingly there is a subset of attainable profiles of states, denoted S^A. The set $T\left(S^A\right)$ is the production set in the commodity space.

Because we are interested in mechanisms for coordinating the actions of the group of managers, the simplest case to consider is that in which the technology of each production unit consists of exactly one process, in which case no problem of coordination internal to production units arises. One consequence of the assumption that each manager is in charge of a single process is that when a process appears in two different production units, then the units have identical technologies.

The purpose of production is to satisfy some outside requirements, such as demands of economic agents outside the particular sector of production under consideration. We model these demands or requirements in terms of parameters that characterize them, such as parameters of utility or demand functions of consumers or the demands of other producers who are not operating the given technology T. Let Θ denote the parameter space. An environment is a pair (T, θ), where T is the given, known technology and $\theta \in \Theta$ is a possible parameter value characterizing demand. We assume here that the technology is fixed and known, but that the outside environment is not known – only the set of possible outside environments is known. (It can be the case that the technology itself depends on parameters and that the organizational design must be determined knowing only the set of possible values of those parameters as well, rather than a particular value.)

2 Efficient production

A *performance criterion* is a function $g : S \times \Theta \to R$. This function expresses the goals of production in the way that a designer's utility function would express the designer's goals. For each value of θ, the function g induces a partial ordering of S such that states higher in the ordering are closer to the goal. That is, a higher value of $g$associated with a state in a given environment means that the state results in a better production outcome in terms of the criterion g. In this way goals such as "productive efficiency", or Pareto optimality, or "corporate profitability", or "meeting specified demands" can be represented. More specifically, for $\theta \in \Theta$, $s \in S^A$ let $v_{\max} = \max_{s \in S^A} g(s, \theta)$. Under conventional assumptions on the constraints that determine feasibility $v_{\max}$ exists. Then, the set of g-efficient profiles is

$$\mathrm{E}(\theta) = \left\{ s \in S^A : g(s,\theta) \geq v_{\max} \right\}.$$

Whenever $\mathrm{E}(\theta)$ happens to be a singleton, its element represents the desired joint action of the managers.

2.1 Information

The *initial information* of a manager consists of:

- knowledge of the processes assigned to her; thus, the manager assigned process ρ knows (S_ρ, f_ρ);
- a subset Θ_j for manager for manager j, possibly empty, consisting of the parameters $\theta \in \Theta$ that j can observe directly.

In addition to initial information a manager may acquire information through communication. Each manager can send and receive messages to or from other managers, using communication channels. We consider two types of channels, called *direct channels* and *market channels*, respectively. Channels are directed; the channel used by manager A to send a message to manager B is different from the one used by B to send a message to A.

A direct channel carries addressed messages from one specific agent to another.[4] The sender and receiver are known to one another in the sense that for each message, the sender knows who the receiver is and vice versa. As with any communication channel, sender and receiver share the language in which messages are expressed. The structure and content of messages is otherwise restricted only by channel capacity. An agent who communicates with several other agents via direct channels can use her knowledge of who is at the other end to send a different message to each of the other agents. She can receive different messages from each of them.

The concept of a market channel requires some discussion. The term "market" is ubiquitous in economics. It has many different meanings. One can speak of the wheat market in Chicago, or the real estate market in Chicago, or the advertising market in Chicago, though these are very different things. If the term 'market' can be used in a way that suggests that it applies to any situation in which two or more economic agents exchange something, or agree on a joint economic action, then the question we started with, 'Which economic activities are, or should be, coordinated by markets and which by something else?' has only one possible answer. For this question to make sense, we need a class of things, which we may call *coordination mechanism s*, with (at least) two elements, one of which is called "market" and the other isn't. Before introducing coordination mechanisms formally we explain the motivation for the formal concepts introduced in the next section.

It seems desirable to require that a coordination mechanism called the market mechanism should cover the case of a competitive market mechanism as

[4] Marschak and Reichelstein (1995, 1998) have studied communication where messages are addressed to specified agents.

it appears in general equilibrium models, such as the classical Arrow-Debreu model. It seems slightly ironic that there is no formal entity called "market" in that model; there is only "commodity", "price" and the actions of agents. This suggests that all communication among agents in a market mechanism should be via messages restricted to the commodities in the given list of commodities and their prices.

The most familiar formal specification of a competitive market is the one in terms of the Walrasian auctioneer. It is also suggestive to think about examples of markets, such as the local supermarket for groceries, or a hardware store, or some types of farmer's market or flea market. The supermarket stands ready to sell a variety of commodities to buyers, and buys what it has to sell from sellers. A buyer who goes to the supermarket can expect to buy what he wants, if he is willing to pay the posted market price. A seller who supplies the supermarket can offer to the buying agency of the supermarket what he wants to sell at a given price. There is no direct communication between those who buy from the supermarket and those who sell to the supermarket. The price at which goods are offered to buyers is the same for all buyers. Similarly, in a competitive situation, the price paid for a given product is the same to all sellers of that product. Furthermore, the supermarket cannot tell any buyer what to buy at the posted prices, nor can it instruct a seller what to sell. However, a supermarket or hardware store provides economic services that are not just informational. Conceptually we can separate these functions from the purely informational function of acting as a communication link between buyers and sellers, concentrating our attention on only the latter function.

With these suggestive remarks in mind we give the following concept of "market channel", a concept that combines the device of the Walrasian auctioneer with the informational role of the supermarket.

A market is personified as an agent, called the *market agent*. *Messages* flow only between individual managers and the market agent. The form of messages is prescribed. In the case of a perfectly competitive market a message from a manager to the market agent is a supply or demand function, while a message from the market agent to a manager is a vector of prices, the same for each manager.[5] This is a static formulation. If, as is the case in our Example, several time periods are involved, the market is viewed as finding a multi-period equilibrium at the beginning of the relevant time period, as in Debreu's model (1959).

In some institutional situations that we would naturally think of as markets, buyer and seller do meet directly. For example, in a farmers' market or a flea market this is usually the case. The basic distinction we draw here is whether or not there is bargaining between buyer and seller. In our local farmers' market, where buyer and seller meet, the prices of the items for sale are posted. If a price is changed in the course of a market day, the new price is posted. This market can be described as one in which the seller – the farmer – is represented by an agent

[5] To allow the market agent to send messages about quantities would in effect transform the mechanism into one of central planning.

who merely transmits information-the price of each item for sale – from seller to buyer, and also accumulates information about demand of buyers. In fact, it is often the case that the sales booth is not manned by the supplier of the items offered for sale, but by an agent who is not authorized to change the posted prices in response to individual buyers. Furthermore, the identity of buyers or sellers is not used in determining the market agent's response to messages received.

In the case of a competitive market, as modeled here, the market agent's message is obtained by aggregating the messages of managers to obtain the aggregate demand correspondence, and finding a price (if there is one) such that the aggregate excess demand at that price is or contains zero,. If so, that price is the message sent from the market agent to all managers, i.e., posted.

There is another aspect of markets that should be addressed, namely its scope. Consider a somewhat idealized flea market in which the items offered for sale at each booth are unique to that booth. In other words, the commodity vector is partitioned into sub-vectors each associated with a subset of sellers, in this case a unique seller. While buyers (and possibly also sellers) might consider the entire vector of prices in calculating their decisions to supply or demand commodities, in this situation it may be the case that there is a different market agent for each segment of the market corresponding to the partition of the commodity vector into its components – in the simplified flea market, a single market agent for each booth. The case where the sub-vectors of the commodity vector corresponding to different 'local' markets can overlap is more complicated; we do not treat it here.

We can also consider cases where the market is not perfectly competitive, but still a market, i.e., it is still the case that communication between buyers and sellers is mediated in a way that does not constitute direct personalized communication between an individual buyer and an individual seller. For example, a market agent might communicate to each seller the demand function for that seller's product as a function of the prices of the products of certain other sellers, without naming the buyers, or permitting the offered terms of sale to be different for different buyers. This would fit the case of non-discriminating duopolists, for example.

When the interaction between agents is *direct*, as in bilateral bargaining, we do not speak of a market between them. Thus, a farmers' market, or flea market in which the price of an item for sale is not posted, but can change from one buyer to another is not a market channel.

2.2 Coordination mechanisms

As we have said, the task of a manager is to choose the state of her process. The group of managers compute their decisions about actions in a joint distributed computation, each using his initial information, including the results of observation, and the information obtained as a result of communication. The joint computation, including the algorithm that it uses and the assignment of resources used to carry out the computation, constitute the coordination mechanism.

The algorithm used to compute the desired actions is represented by an F-network, as in Mount and Reiter (2001). An F-network consists of a directed graph and a set F of elementary functions. Functions in F can be 'located' at the vertices or nodes of the graph. Certain vertices are input nodes, at which information from outside the graph may be fed into the computation. Computation proceeds by having the function located at a particular vertex calculate its value at the input it receives from preceding vertices or from outside the network. Each evaluation of an elementary function takes a unit of time. The output of computation appears at the output vertices of the network after a certain time.

It was noted above that the assignment of processes to managers determines a partition of the set of (possibly replicated) processes. Therefore, certain sub-nets of the F -network that expresses the algorithm can be associated with the manager whose actions are being computed. Furthermore, because the network's inputs are determined by the initial information, and the structure of initial information is also associated with the managers, the connections between sub-networks associated with different managers consist exclusively of communication channels. To facilitate exposition, suppose there are two managers who have been assigned processes, correspondingly there are two sub-nets N_1, N_2, that compute the states of the two processes involved, N_1 associated with manager 1 and $N_2$with manager 2. The (directed) arcs of the graph G that connect the graph G_1 of N_1 with the graph G_2 of , N_2 carry communications between the two managers. These arcs are direct channels.

Alternatively, if a market agent were introduced between the two managers, two things would be different.

First, all communication between the managers would take place through the market agent. In the case of a competitive market, messages from managers to the market agent would be about commodity vectors, e.g., supply or demand functions, and messages from the market agent would be prices. That is, communication between the managers would be via a market channel.

Second, the nets N_1, N_2 would be replaced by nets that compute the messages required by the market channel, but the class F of elementary operations would have to be the same as in the case of an F-network with direct channels. When there is a competitive market agent between the two managers, each manager would compute her excess demand by maximizing her profit taking the prices transmitted by the market agent parametrically. Her action would be a state of her process that would result in a commodity vector yielding the maximum possible profit to her production unit, given all the data and the prices.

In a market with other structure, the behavior of the managers would be determined by the equilibria of the game that models the market. In either case, the task of manager i, which is to compute her action from the inputs to her sub-network, is represented by sub-network N_i. The inputs are the variables whose values come into the sub-network either from the environment or via communication lines into the sub-network.

The use of a competitive market channel usually, but not necessarily, entails the assumption that there are many production units using the same process, with a different manager in charge of each unit. When several managers are in charge of replicas of a given process, or set of processes, we say they are the same *type*. In that case, all managers of the same type carry out the same computation. On the other hand when the channels between sub-networks corresponding to different managers are direct channels, then the algorithm embodied in the network specifies the computations to be carried out by each manager, which might be different for each manager. Generally these computations will be different from those required when the channel is a market channel.

An *information technology* consists of the set of F-networks available, the restrictions on observation as expressed above, and the channels available for communication. In operating an F-network a manager can use *agents* who, under her supervision, carry out the elementary steps of the computation specified by the network. The manager herself may be one of those agents. Each agent works for only one manager. An agent supervised by a given manager is subject to the same constraints on initial information as her manager. Thus, the vertices of the graph of the network are assigned to agents under certain restrictions described below in the subsection 'Costs of information processing and efficient assignments'. A network whose vertices are assigned to agents is called an F-network. The simplest case is that in which all computations of a manager are carried out by that manager.

A coordination mechanism is an assigned F-network.

For a given technology T and a given class of environmental parameters Θ, a coordination mechanism – an assigned F-network – computes the actions of each manager. Specification of the F-network includes specification of the messages sent between managers, depending of course on the parameter θ. Manager M may receive a message from another manager at any stage of computation, depending on the algorithm expressed by her F-network. For a given coordination mechanism, the network is given. We may therefore describe the message received by manager M from other managers by the notation $m^{-\mathrm{M}} = m^{-\mathrm{M}}\left(\theta^{-\mathrm{M}}\right)$, where $\theta^{-\mathrm{M}}$ refers to the components of observed by the managers other than M, reflecting dependence of their messages on the parameters they observe. The notation refers to the entire ordered array of messages received by M in the course of the computation. Thus, for fixed T and Θ, the computation of manager M can be represented by the mapping $\xi^{M}\left(m^{-M},\theta^{M}\right)$. In general ξ^{M} is not single-valued. In that case in order for the coordination mechanism to be well-defined, i.e., to determine a particular action of manager M, it is necessary that she be able to choose an element of $\xi^{M}\left(m^{-M},\theta^{M}\right)$ arbitrarily. This must be the case for every manager. Thus, if the coordination mechanism is to result in outcomes that are g-efficient, then every manager must be able to choose an arbitrary element of the set of actions determined for him by his computation. To express this we say that a coordination mechanism C, consisting of an assigned F-network, is **g-satisfactory** if and only if for every $\theta \in \Theta$, for every $i = 1,\cdots,n$ and for every state $s^{M_i} \in \xi^{M_i}\left(m^{-M_i},\theta^{M_i}\right)$, the profile $s = \left(s^{M_1},\cdots,s^{M_n}\right)$ is in $E\left(\theta\right)$.

2.3 Comparison of coordination mechanisms

Given an environment, (T, Θ), a performance criterion, g, a set of production units, and an information technology, the question we started with, namely, "Which activities should be coordinated by market mechanisms and which by administrative organizations?", becomes, "Which managers should communicate via direct channels, and which by market channels?" To make this a well-posed question we must specify the criteria by which alternative organizations are to be compared.

If a coordination mechanism, C, is applied to an environment (T, Θ) the mechanism determines the actions of the managers, including the observations, the communications and the computations that are carried out in arriving at those actions. Generally, resources are used in observing, communicating and computing. resources include those used to set up and to operate the facilities needed to carry out the information processing. resources used in information processing are not available for use in production.[6] Ideally all this could be described for each mechanism by a mapping from (T, Θ) to the commodity space, where the image of each point in (T, Θ) is the net input-output vector in the commodity space resulting from the use of the mechanism.[7]. Thus, C determines a function from $(T, \Theta) \quad X$ that describes the performance of the mechanism C in that environment. Choice among alternative mechanisms amounts to choice from the set of functions that describe the performance of alternative mechanisms in a given environment. However, we are not yet able to deal adequately with criteria for comparing alternative mechanisms at this level of generality. Instead we require that the mechanism compute actions that maximize the performance criterion g and among those mechanisms look for ones that are efficient in the space of the cost determinants. This amounts to a lexicographic principle according to which we first require g-efficiency and second, given that the mechanism is g-efficiency that it be *cost-efficient* in the set of all g-efficient mechanisms (ref. Hurwicz xx p. 299).

2.4 Cost of information processing and efficient assignments

As noted above, we use the F-network model to represent algorithms for computing a function. In the present context the function to be computed is one whose domain is the totality of initial information, i.e., (T, Θ) and whose range is the set $E(\theta)$ of actions that maximize g when the parameter is θ. The execution of the algorithm requires that the modules of the network be assigned to agents, who carry out the elementary operations specified by the modules. For a given algorithm, different assignments of modules to agents can result in different performance, as we see below.

---

[6] The costs associated with incentive payments, or institutions for monitoring behavior would also be taken into account, as would the incentive effects on outcomes resulting from private information.

[7] In a more general model the set X would be the set of allocations.

An agent is characterized by the set of elementary operations he can carry out, by the input variables he can observe directly and by the property that he can do at most one elementary operation at a time. That is, an agent must operate sequentially. Of course, a network of agents can operate in parallel, doing several things at a time, depending on the algorithm – the underlying F-network – and the capabilities of the agents. We may assume without loss of generality that the given F-network is acyclic; we do not assume here that it is a tree.[8] This is to avoid being forced to duplicate modules in situations where it is possible to use the result of a computational step in several successor steps.

Different assignments of modules to agents can result in different performance. For instance, the time (the number of sequential computational steps) needed to evaluate the function being computed, and the patterns of communication and retrievals from memory depend on the assignment of modules to agents. If the computations can be spread out among many agents, the time required may be reduced by doing more of them in parallel. But distributing the computation might entail more communication among agents, which might offset or even reverse the advantage of parallel operation. Furthermore, using more agents, who are typically paid employees, usually entails higher cost. In these circumstances it is of interest to assign the modules of the network so that the computation is carried out efficiently. The determinants of cost considered here are:

(i) the length of time required to complete the computation, called *delay* ;
(ii) the amount of communication required between agents supervised by different managers, measured by the number of *crosslinks* in the assigned graph;
(iii) the amount of communication required between agents supervised by the same manager; measured by the number of *selflinks* in the assigned graph;
(iv) the total number of agents used.

The relation between minimizing cost as a function of these factors and efficiency of assignments is treated in the Appendix. It is shown that to characterize efficient assignments it suffices to study efficiency in the space of crosslinks and delay as a function of the number of agents.

To sum up, the comparison between alternative coordination mechanisms in a given class of environments may involve using different algorithms in different mechanisms, but the basic computational resources available for use in executing those algorithms is the same for each coordination mechanism, namely, the set of elementary operations in F.

We turn next to our example.

2.5 Example

This example has two parts. The first is a case in which the coordination of production specified by the performance criterion cannot be achieved using a

[8] It is shown in Mount and Reiter (2001) that a modular network with loops can be replaced by an equivalent network without loops, and indeed by an equivalent tree, using the same elementary operations together with projections.

market channel, while it can be achieved using a direct channel. Therefore, according to our lexicographic criterion for comparing coordination mechanisms, the first step is decisive; there is no need to go on to a comparison of informational costs.

The second part is a variation of the first in which the desired coordination can be achieved using either a market channel or a direct channel, hence bringing the comparison of costs of the two mechanisms into play.

2.6 Technology

Suppose the technology T consists of two processes, P_1, P_2 each with two states, s_1^i, s_2^i, $i = 1, 2$. In state s_1^1 P_1 produces one unit of good W(hite) with one unit of input B(lue) and uses the services of one unit of facility F_1 for half a week. In state s_2^1 P_1 produces one unit of G(reen) from one unit of R(ed), using the same facility for half a week.

For example, the facility F_1 consists of machines for manufacturing tractors. There are two types of tractor, a large heavy tractor that requires a heavy duty gear-train, and a smaller light tractor that uses a light duty gear train. To set up the machinery to produce a heavy tractor requires a period of time, and once the machinery is so configured it is not possible to produce light tractors until the machinery is reconfigured for that purpose.

In state s_1^2 P_2 produces one unit of B(lue) from a unit of raw material, using the services of one unit of facility F_2 for half a week, and in state s_2^2 P_2 produces one unit of R(ed) from raw material, using one unit of facility F_2 for half a week. To avoid cluttering up the calculations without adding generality, we assume that the raw material is free. There is one unit of each facility available. W and G are final products; B and R are intermediate products. There are two production units, one operating P_1 and the other P_2.

This technology operates in time. We assume that the unit of time is a half-week. Each process can operate in each half-week, and correspondingly, commodities are dated, the date being the half-week in which they become available. For purposes of exposition fix a time t_0 and consider the periods shown in Fig. 1. These are $\left(t_0 - \frac{1}{2}, t_0\right), \left(t_0, t_0 + \frac{1}{2}\right), \left(t_0 + \frac{1}{2}, t_0 + 1\right)$ which we relabel $v = 1, v = 2, v = 3$, respectively. Then a typical commodity vector has the form $(W(2), W(3), G(2), G(3), B(1), B(2), R(1), R(2))$. The commodity space is further restricted by requiring the amount of each commodity to be a nonnegative integer. (Thus, we abuse the notation by using the same symbol for the name of the commodity and its quantity, and rely on the context to make clear which is intended). When a market channel is used, prices are introduced; the price vector corresponding to the commodity subspace is $(\omega(2), \omega(3), \gamma(2), \gamma(3), p(1), p(2), q(1), q(2))$.

The space of attainable states is

$$S^A(t_0) = \left\{s_j^i(v), i, j \in \{1,2\}, v \in \{1,2,3\}\right\} \quad .$$

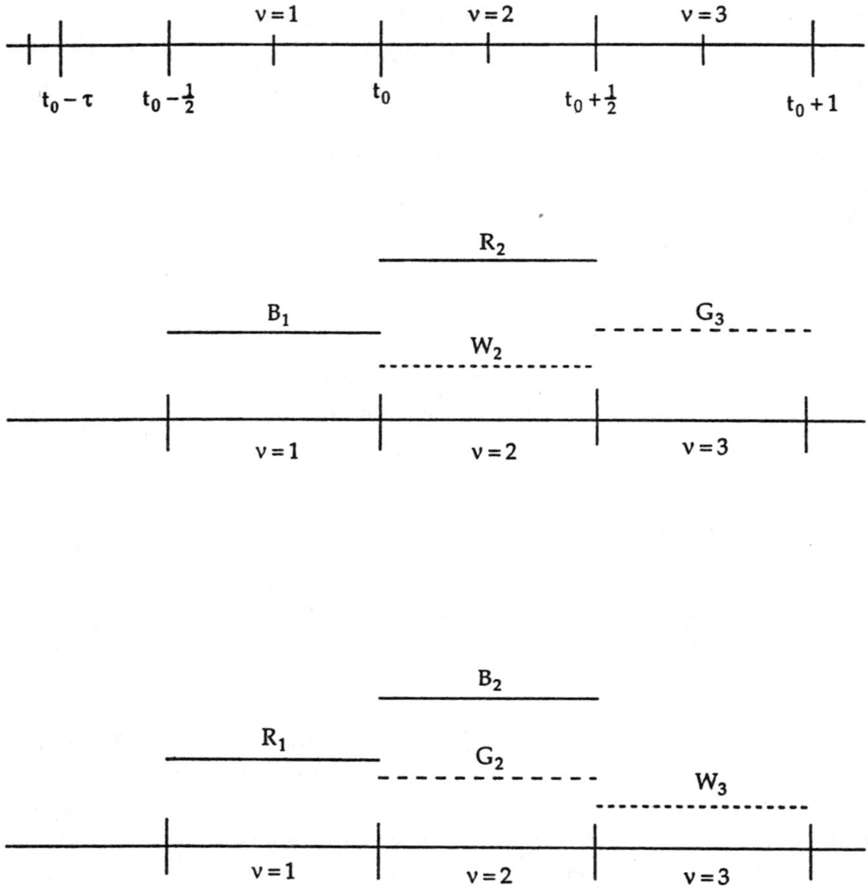

Fig. 1. Two just-in-time production plans

A profile of states for the time period under consideration has the form $s\,(t_0) = \left(s^1\,(1)\,, s^1\,(2)\,, s^1\,(3)\,, s^2\,(1)\,, s^2\,(2)\,, s^2\,(3)\right)$, where $s^i\,(v) \in \left\{s_j^1,\ i,j = 1,2\right\}$.

We suppose that there is a representative end user who receives the final products. The end user can absorb at most two units of product in a given week. He pays $\omega\,(2)$ for a unit of $W\,(2)$ delivered at time $t_0 + {}^1\!/\!_2$ and $\omega\,(3)$ for a unit of $W\,(3)$ delivered at time $t_0 + 1$. The end user can refuse delivery of items he didn't order and pay nothing. Because only one unit of each commodity is possible, when the final commodities have prices, the payments $\omega\,(j)$, and $\gamma\,(j)$ $j = 2, 3$ coincide with those prices.

We distinguish two cases, each leading to a different conclusion.

Case 1. The end user does not distinguish time periods shorter than a week. In this case periods 2 and 3 together make up one time period in which the end user does not distinguish $W\,(2)$ from $W\,(3)$ nor $G\,(2)$ from $G\,(3)$ The effect of this will be to require $\omega\,(2) = \omega\,(3)$ and $\gamma\,(2) = \gamma\,(3)$.

Case 2. The end user recognizes half-weeks, and thus distinguishes $W(2)$ from $W(3)$ and $G(2)$ from $G(3)$ (The effect will be to allow $\omega(2) \neq \omega(3)$ or $\gamma(2) \neq \gamma(3)$).

In Case 1 the demand parameters are $\Theta = \{\theta_1, \theta_2, \theta_3\}$. Buyers of W (resp. G) do not distinguish between units of W (resp. G) delivered at any time within the week for which they are desired. Demand for W and G is determined for each week independently. and the demand for week (t,t+1) beginning at t is known at time $t - \tau$, $\tau \geq \frac{1}{2}$.

Demand for final products delivered in any period is shown in Table 1 in terms of θ.

Table 1.

$\theta(t) = \theta_1$	1 unit each of W and G in week (t,t+1)
$\theta(t) = \theta_2$	2 units of W and 0 units of G in week (t,t+1)
$\theta(t) = \theta_3$	0 units of W and 2 units of G in week (t,t+1)

In Case 2 the demand parameters are as shown in Table 2.

We focus on the actions of a manager M_1 of process P_1 and a manager M_2 of process P_2. We can think of these managers as representatives of managers of their types.

Recall from the specification of the technology that to produce one unit of W in week (t,t+1) requires either one unit of B delivered by time t, in which case one unit of W can be produced in the interval (t,t+1/2), or one unit of B delivered by time t + 1/2) in which case one unit of W can be produced in the interval (t + 1/2,t). Similarly for G and R. Satisfaction of demand in the time period indexed by t_0 is expressed by the condition that

$$\begin{aligned} W^d(t_0) &= W^s(2) + W^s(3) \\ G^d(t_0) &= G^s(2) + G^s(3) \end{aligned}$$

where the superscript "d" indicates a quantity required or demanded and "s" indicates a quantity supplied. Demand quantities for the periods corresponding to t_0 are the functions shown in Table 1 in Case 1 and Table 2 in Case 2. Supplies are the functions of $s(t_0)$ defined above.

To avoid an unnecessarily tedious exposition of the performance criterion g and an equally tedious analysis of the example, we take note of two points:

- If inventories can be kept, then any pattern of demand can be met, provided initial inventories are suitable;
- If carrying inventories is costly, and if every admissible pattern of demand can be met without inventories, then no production plan that involves carrying inventories can be g-efficient.

The three patterns of demand shown in Table 1 can be met by M_1 the manager of the producer using process P_1 by choosing:

Table 2.

$\theta(t) = \theta_{11}$	1 unit of W and 0 units of G in period (t,t+1/2), or 0 units of W and 1 unit of G in period (t+1/2,t+1).
$\theta(t) = \theta_{12}$	0 unit of W and 1 units of G in period (t,t+1/2), or 1 units of W and 0 unit of G in period (t+1/2,t+1).
$\theta(t) = \theta_2$	2 units of W and 0 units of G in week (t,t+1)
$\theta(t) = \theta_3$	0 units of W and 2 units of G in week (t,t+1)

$\theta(t) = \theta_1$:	$s^1(2) = s_1^1; s^1(3) = s_2^1$, *or* $s^1(2) = s_2^1; s^1(3) = s_1^1$
$\theta(t) = \theta_2$	$s^1(2) = s_1^1; s^1(3) = s_1^1$
$\theta(t) = \theta_3$	$s^1(2) = s_2^1; s^1(3) = s_2^1$

provided that the inputs are available in time. This can be assured by the following rule for the producer using P_2:

If $s^1(2) = s_1^1$, *then* $s^2(1) = s_1^2$
If $s^1(2) = s_2^1$, *then* $s^2(1) = s_2^2$
If $s^1(3) = s_1^1$, *then* $s^2(2) = s_1^2$
If $s^1(3) = s_2^1$, *then* $s^2(2) = s_2^2$

These are the desired actions derived from the performance criterion g implied by the two simplifying points made above; that is, these actions maximize g on the feasible set.

We turn now to comparison of the coordination mechanisms under consideration. and compare two mechanisms, D and M for coordinating the actions of the managers of the two processes. The first mechanism, uses a direct channel between the two managers; the second, uses a market channel between the two managers.

We assume that transmission over each channel is instantaneous and costless. This simplification avoids having to keep track of transmission delays and the accounting that goes with them. With this simplification, we shall see that in Case 1 the comparison of mechanisms reduces to verifying that the mechanism using a direct channel is efficient and that the market mechanism is not. Therefore the need to compare information processing costs does not arise. In Case 2, both mechanisms are g-efficient therefore the need to compare information processing costs does arise.

2.7 $\mathscr{D}$ Direct channels

At time $t_0 - \tau$ manager M_1 learns the demand for the final products in period t_0. With that information M_1 can decide on her actions $s^1(2), s^1(3)$

thereby determining $W^s(2), W^s(3), G^s(2), G^s(3)$, and therefore also determining the input requirements $B^d(2), B^d(3), R^d(2), R^d(3)$ Availability of a direct channel whose capacity is sufficient to carry four one digit numbers allows M_1 $W^s(2), W^s(3), G^s(2), G^s(3)$ $W^s(2), W^s(3), G^s(2), G^s(3)$to communicate these requirements directly to M_2 , who can then determine his actions $s^2(1), s^2(2)$ and, if necessary, communicate them to M_1 .

The availability of a direct channel allows the managers to achieve just-in-time delivery of intermediate products, and therefore to meet demand without carrying inventories of intermediate or final products, thus attaining the maximum value $\nu_{\max}$ of g.

2.8 $\mathscr{M}$. Market channels

Under this mode of organization transactions between the managers of processes of type $P_1$and those of type P_2 are mediated by a competitive market. (We do not model the transactions between producers of the final products and consumers of them explicitly, but these could also be mediated by a competitive market.) Using competitive market channels as the coordinating mechanism prescribes the behavior of the managers; each manager of a process must determine her action as the solution of a profit maximization problem.

Consider first the profit $\pi^{M_1} = \pi^1$ of the manager of process P_1 when the coordination mechanism is the market mechanism.

$$\pi^1 = \omega(2)W(2) + \omega(3)W(3) + \gamma(2)G(2) + \gamma(3)G(3) \\ -(p(1)B(1) + p(2)B(2) + q(1)R(1) + q(2)R(2)).$$

To derive the demand for $B(1), B(2), R(1), R(2)$ we maximize π^1 subject to the technological constraints

$$W(2) = B(1); W(3) = B(2); G(2) = R(1); G(3) = R(2),$$

$$W(j)G(j) = 0 = B(i)R(i),\ j = 2, 3; i = 1, 2, \text{ and}$$

$$W(j), G(j), B(i), R(i) \in \{0, 1\}\ \textit{for}\ i \in \{1, 2\}, j \in \{2, 3\}.$$

In addition there is the resource constraint

$$0 \leq W(2) + W(3) + G(2) + G(3) \leq 2.$$

Using the technological constraints we can write the profit function in the form

$$\pi^1 = (\omega(2) - p(1))B(1) + (\omega(3) - p(2))B(2) \\ +(\gamma(2) - q(1))R(1) + ((\gamma(3) - q(2))R(2)) \qquad (*)$$

with the constraints

$$0 \leq B(1) + B(2) + R(1) + R(2) \leq 2,$$

and

$$B(j)R(j) = 0,\ \textit{for}\ j = 1, 2,\ \textit{and}\ B(j), R(j) \in \{0, 1\}. \qquad (**)$$

The technological and resource constraints define the feasible set in the four-dimensional subspace whose coordinates are$B(1), B(2), R(1), R(2)$ This set consists of the origin and the eight points whose coordinates have exactly one coordinate different from 0, and the four points that have exactly two coordinates different from 0.

We assume that demand is not satiated. Then the points having only one coordinate different from 0 are not g-efficient. Then we can confine attention to the four points that have two coordinates different from 0, and, of course, those coordinates are each equal to 1.

Because of (**) two of the coordinates in the demand vector for inputs $(B(1), B(2), R(1), R(2))$ must be zero. Therefore we can abbreviate the notation, letting (B, R) represent demand for a unit of B in the first period and a unit of R in the second and (R, B) represents demand for a unit of R in the first period and a unit of B in the second, and so on. The demand correspondence for inputs of a manager of type 1 is shown in the next table as a function of certain intervals of prices.

Table 3.

	$\omega - p(2) > \gamma - q(2)$	$\omega - p(2) < \gamma - q(2)$	$\omega - p(2) = \gamma - q(2)$
$\omega - p(1) > \gamma - q(1)$	(B, B)	(B, R)	(B, R), (B, B)
$\omega - p(1) < \gamma - q(1)$	(R, B)	(R, R)	(R, R), (R, B)
$\omega - p(1) = \gamma - q(1)$	(R, B), (B, B)	(R, R), (R, B)	(R, R), (R, B) (B, R), (B, B)

Recalling that the prices $p(i), q(i)$ are net of the cost of the input to process P_2, which we assumed to be zero, the profit function of the second type of manager is

$$\pi^2 = p(1)B(1) + p(2)B(2) + q(1)R(1) + q(2)R(2).$$

The constraints are the same as those displayed for process P_1 above. Then supply correspondence for the manager of process P_2 is shown in Table 4.

Table 4.

	$p(2) > q(2)$	$p(2) < q(2)$	$p(2) = q(2)$
$p(1) > q(1)$	(B, B)	(B, R)	$(B, R), (B, B)$
$p(1) < q(1)$	(R, B)	(R, R)	$(R, R), (R, B)$
$p(1) = q(1)$	$(R, B), (B, B)$	$(R, R), (B, R)$	$(R, R), (R, B)$ $(B, R), (B, B)$

For the coordination mechanism using the market channel to be g-efficient, it must have a (g-efficient) equilibrium for every state of demand θ.

For the sake of the argument suppose π^2 is maximized at the point ($B(1)$, $B(2)$, $R(1)$, $R(2)$) = $(1,0,0,1)$, which we also write (B,R) ,indicating that a unit of B is produces in the period $\upsilon = 1$, and a unit of R is produced in the period $\upsilon = 2$. Then the profit of M_2 at (B,R) is

$$\pi^2 (B, R) = p(1) + q(2).$$

If this maximizes π^2 on the feasible set, then the following three inequalities must hold.

$$\begin{aligned} p(1) + q(2) &\geq p(1) + p(2) \\ p(1) + q(2) &\geq q(1) + p(2) \\ p(1) + q(2) &\geq q(1) + q(2) \end{aligned}$$

It follows that

$$p(1) \geq q(1) \tag{1a}$$

$$q(2) \geq p(2) \tag{1b}$$

$$p(1) + q(2) \geq q(1) + q(2) \geq q(1) + p(2) \tag{1c}$$

If (B, R) is to be an equilibrium, it must also maximize π^1 on the feasible set. In Case 1 $\omega(2) = \omega(3) =_{def} \omega$, and $\gamma(2) = \gamma(3) =_{def} \gamma$. If (B,R) maximizes π^1 on the feasible set, then the following three inequalities must hold.

$$\begin{aligned} \omega + \gamma - (p(1) + q(2)) &\geq 2\omega - (p(1) + p(2)) \\ \omega + \gamma - (p(1) + q(2)) &\geq 2\gamma - (q(1) + q(2)) \\ \omega + \gamma - (p(1) + q(2)) &\geq \gamma + \omega - (p(1) + p(2)) \end{aligned}$$

which can be written

$$\gamma - (p(1) + q(2)) \geq \omega - (p(1) + p(2)) \tag{2a}$$

$$\omega - (p(1) + q(2)) \geq \gamma - (q(1) + q(2)) \tag{2b}$$

$$-(p(1) + q(2)) \geq -(q(1) + p(2)) \tag{2c}$$

Thus, inequalities (1a)–(1c) and (2a)–(2c) must hold. Together they imply

$$p(1) + q(2) = q(1) + q(2) = q(1) + p(2)$$

and hence

$$p(1) = q(1), \quad p(2) = q(2)$$

Then it follows from (2a) that

$$\omega = \gamma.$$

Substituting in the expression for π^1 gives

$$\pi^1 = (\omega - p(1))(B(1) + R(1)) + (\omega - p(2))(B(2) + R(2))$$

Thus, π^1 takes the same value$2\omega - (p(1) + p(2))$ at each of the four nonzero feasible actions, i.e., those that produce (1,0,0,1) , (0,1,1,0) , (1,1,0,0) and (0,0,1,1) in the subspace with coordinates $B(1), B(2), R(1), R(2)$.

Turning now to π^2 after substitution

$$\pi^2 = p(1)(B(1) + R(1)) + p(2)(B(2) + R(2)).$$

This function takes the same value at every non-zero feasible action of M_2. Because not every pair consisting of a feasible action of M_1 and a feasible action of M_2 is g-efficient it follows that the mechanism using a market channel does not assure g-efficient performance in Case 1.

Note that there are competitive equilibria in this example. The price vector

$$\begin{aligned}&(p(1), p(2), q(1), q(2), \gamma(1), \gamma(2), \omega(1), \omega(2))\\&= (p(1), p(2), p(1), p(2), \gamma(1), \gamma(2), \gamma(1), \gamma(2))\end{aligned}$$

and either of the two commodity vectors

$$\begin{aligned}&(W(1), W(2), G(1), G(2), B(1), B(2), R(1), R(2))\\&= (1, 0, 0, 1, 1, 0, 0, 1).\end{aligned}$$

or

$$\begin{aligned}&(W(1), W(2), G(1), G(2), B(1), B(2), R(1), R(2))\\&= (0, 1, 1, 0, 0, 1, 1, 0).\end{aligned}$$

form competitive equilibria. In each case the markets for final goods and for intermediate goods clear. Both equilibria are efficient.

However, if manager M_1 chooses (1,0,0,1) while M_2 chooses (0,1,1,0), the market for final goods clears, but the market for intermediate goods does not. Similarly if the managers choose (0,1,1,0) and (1,0,0,1) respectively. In neither of theses cases do we have a competitive equilibrium. Therefore the hypothesis of the first welfare theorem is not satisfied, and hence the theorem is vacuously true.

In Case 2 the profit function of M_2 remains the same as in Case 1. Hence equations (1a)–(1c) remain valid. However, it is not required that $\omega(2) = \omega(3)$ or that $\gamma(2) = \gamma(3)$; in general neither of these equalities will hold. The profit function of M_1 in Case 2 is

$$\begin{aligned}&(\omega(2) - p(1))B(1) + (\omega(3) - p(2))B(2) +\\&(\gamma(2) - q(1))R(1) + (\gamma(3) - q(2))R(2)\end{aligned}$$

which is to be maximized subject to the constraints

$$\begin{aligned}&B(1)R(1) = 0 = B(2)R(2)\\&0 \leq B(1) + R(1) + B(2) + R(2) \leq 2\end{aligned}$$

where all variables are nonnegative integers.

In this case for each of the four possible states of final demand there is a competitive equilibrium with a unique associated production plan for each production unit. For example, the price vector

$$(\omega(2), \omega(3), \gamma(2), \gamma(3), p(1), p(1), p(2), q(1), q(2))$$
$$= (8, 4, 5, 6, 3, 2, 1, 3)$$

is part of the competitive equilibrium that leads to the commodity vector

$$(1, 0, 0, 1, 1, 0, 0, 1) \quad .$$

The price vector

$$(\omega(2), \omega(3), \gamma(2), \gamma(3), p(1), p(1), p(2), q(1), q(2))$$
$$= (8, 7, 4, 4, 3, 3, 1, 2)$$

is part of a competitive equilibrium with commodity vector

$$(1, 1, 0, 0, 1, 1, 0, 0,) .$$

To summarize, in Case 1, because each producer of a given type has no information on which to distinguish among profit maximizing production plans, each could choose any of them. Thus, there is no assurance of efficient equilibrium. Even when there are several producers of each type, and the number of producers of each type is the same, and even if all producers of a given type choose the same production plan, equilibrium would not be assured. This is, of course, the case when there is just one producer of each type. Thus, the mechanism using a market channel cannot be guaranteed to achieve just-in-time production, and consequently cannot coordinate production without inventories. This result may be anticipated whenever the supply and demand correspondences are not single-valued at equilibrium. This in itself might not be considered too serious a difficulty.[9] except for the fact that in this case the multiplicity of values arises not from linearity in the technology, but from relations of timing. These are likely to be prevalent in the economy, and that prevalence indicates that the example is more typical than its simplified form might suggest. The practices associated with just-in-time production in the automobile industry provide a good example. There are many other important examples that attest to the prevalence in the economy of coordination mechanisms that use direct channels. Because the market mechanism cannot ensure just in time production, the criteria specified for comparing mechanisms tell us that informational costs, or informational efficiency properties, do not come into play.

In contrast, in Case 2 the market mechanism is in the class of g-efficient mechanisms. Therefore, comparison of the cost or informational efficiency properties of the two mechanisms is in order.

---

[9] When multiple maximizers of profit arise because of linearity in the underlying technology, the slightest displacement from linearity would result in unique maximizers. But linearity itself is a kind of razor's edge phenomenon.

2.9 Comparison of the informational properties of $\mathcal{M}$ and $\mathcal{D}$ in Case 2

To compare the informational cost or efficiency of the two mechanisms requires that we construct the two networks that represent the computations to be carried out. For this we must specify the class F of elementary functions. For our example it is natural to consider the binary operations of arithmetic, together with the two unary functions, the identity, Id and the sign function, sgn. Thus, the networks used are (2,1)-networks, where $F = \{add, subt, mult, Id, sgn\}$.

To begin with we consider the informational tasks under the assumption that the relevant networks are given, and that the communication channels exist.

In the direct mechanism the computational task of a manager of type M_1 is to observe the demand vector for final products, and having done so, to select from the four feasible plans a production plan that meets the demand. The computation involved is to choose a vector $(W(2), W(3), G(2), G(3))$,
to translate that choice into demand for inputs

$$(B^d(1), B^d(2), R^d(1), R^d(2))$$

evaluating a (vector) identity function at the given demand point and sending the result to the other manager. This computation has no delay, and requires at most four crosslinks, i.e., there are four one dimensional direct channels over which these messages are transmitted.

The task of M_2 is also to evaluate identity functions at the points communicated to her by M_1. Because communication is assumed to be instantaneous and computation of the identity function is also without delay, this computation is without delay.

In the mechanism M, a manager of type M_1 must find a profit maximizing production plan, and hence her demand for the intermediate products, given all the prices. From equation (*) we see that finding the profit maximizing demands for intermediate products reduces to the following computation. M_1 must first compute the four differences

$$\begin{aligned}\omega(2) - p(1) &= a\\ \omega(3) - p(2) &= b\\ \gamma(2) - q(1) &= c\\ \gamma(3) - q(2) &= d.\end{aligned}$$

In addition, M_1 must compute the signs of the expressions

$$\begin{aligned}&a + d - b + c\\ &d - b\\ &a - c\\ &a + b - c + d\end{aligned}$$

That is, in addition to computing four differences, M_1 must compute two sums and make the comparisons indicated among the eight resulting quantities. Verifying that the maximum profit is nonnegative follows from the signs of the differences and sums. Using (2,1) -networks it follows that if the manager carries out the computation alone, the delay would be eleven units of time, with an additional agent 6 units of time, and with 3 additional agents, the minimum attainable delay of 3 units of time. The calculation of M_2 is similar.

The calculation of the market agent, M_0 is to receive the excess demands of M_1 and, and to select the eight prices to make excess demand equal to zero. When, as is usually the case, there are replications of the producers, M_0 must first aggregate excess demand, which involves executing $2(N-1)$ adds when there are N managers of each type. Finally, the prices must be communicated from the market agent to all the managers. This could be done by broadcast channels, in effect posting the prices.

It is clear from these comparisons that in this example, the direct mechanism is informationally more efficient than the market mechanism. This seems to be in conflict with the conventional wisdom that market mechanisms are informationally more efficient than alternatives.

However, the calculation we made is based on the assumption that the communication channels exist. In the case of a direct mechanism each direct channel must be created. In industrial practice this usually involves activities of a purchasing agent, or team of them, for the producing unit that is buying, and a salesperson, or team of them, for the producing unit that is selling. Typically each side invests resources to create and maintain a long term relationship. Negotiation between the two units often takes place repeatedly, even when a long term relationship is established between them, because contracts are usually for a specified period of time. Thus although once a direct channel is established the cost of using it may be very small, the cost of setting it up and maintaining it can be significant.

Market channels exist in different institutional forms, including organized markets, like the Chicago Board of Trade, or in more decentralized manifestations, like the existence of intermediaries such as brokers or supply companies, which combine informational functions with other service functions. An organized market may be costly to set up, but the costs of creating the market are usually borne by the market intermediaries, and not directly by the buyers and sellers. Buyers and sellers typically pay for each use of a market channel.

As remarked above, it sometimes happens that two producing units, one a supplier to the other, are in the same firm. It is often remarked that the firm could if it wished introduce an internal market channel between the units. It would be interesting to know how frequently coordination of the two units is done by market channels. When the two units are in the same firm it is likely that the cost of setting up and maintaining a direct channel between them is relatively small, while the cost of creating a genuine market channel is relatively large. Furthermore, to create and maintain an internal market may be more difficult in light of incentive issues when the channel is internal to a single firm. It should also be noted that the use of internal transfer prices is in itself not sufficient to constitute an internal market. A mechanism that looks like a competitive market can be modified so that it becomes a central planning mechanism that uses prices and competitive behavior rules. The modification needed is to allow the market agent to communicate prices and quantities to each producing unit directly. In Case 1 that extension of the market agent's function would allow him to select one of the equilibria from the excess demand correspondence and communicate each manager's part of that equilibrium to that manager, in effect communicating the production plan. In the example direct mechanism would bring about efficient coordination more cheaply. Thus, if the example were typical, except for incentive reasons, we should not expect to observe price coordinated central mechanisms in such cases. Indeed, casual observation suggests that we do not see such mechanisms very often. Usually incentive schemes are tacked on to direct coordination mechanisms is such cases. However, if the computations required to operate the direct mechanism were sufficiently more complex than the calculations involved in figuring out profit maximizing actions, the comparison might go the other way.

References

Debreu, G. (1959) *Theory of Value*. Wiley, New York

Grossman, S.J., Hart, O.D. (1986) The costs and benefits of ownership: A theory of vertical and lateral integration. *The Journal of Political Economy* 94(4): 691–719

Hurwicz, L. (1972) On Informationally Decentralized Systems. In : McGuire, C.B., Radner, R. (eds.) *Decision and Organization. (Studies in Mathematical Economics and Managerial Economics.)* North Holland Elsevier, New York

Kranton, R., Minehart, D. (1999) Vertical Integration, Networks, and Markets. Preprint, University of Maryland

Marschak, T., Reichelstein, S. (1995) Communication Requirements for Individual Agents in Networks and Hierarchies. In: Ledyard, J. (ed.) *The Economics of Informational Decentralization: Complexity Efficiency and Stability*. Kluwer

Marschak, T., Reichelstein, S. (1998) Network Mechanisms, Information Efficiency and Hierarchies. *Journal of Economic Theory* 106–141

Mount, K., Reiter, S. (1990) A model of computing with human agents. CMSEMS Discussion Paper No. 890, June

Mount, K., Reiter, S. (2001) *Computational Complexity in Economic Behavior and Organiozation*. Cambridge University Press, New York

Reiter, S. (1995) Coordination and the structure of firms. CMSEMS Discussion Paper No. 1121

Transversals, systems of distinct representatives, mechanism design, and matching

Leonid Hurwicz[1], **Stanley Reiter**[2]

[1] Department of Economics, University of Minnesota, Minneapolis, MN 55455, USA (e-mail: hurwicz@tc.umn.edu)

[2] Center for Mathematical Studies in Economics and Management Sciences, Northwestern University, Evanston, IL 60208–2014, USA (e-mail: s-reiter@kellogg.nwu.edu)

Abstract. A transversal generated by a system of distinct representatives (SDR) for a collection of sets consists of an element from each set (its representative) such that the representative uniquely identifies the set it belongs to. Theorem 1 gives a necessary and sufficient condition that an arbitrary collection, finite or infinite, of sets, finite or infinite, have an SDR. The proof is direct, short. A Corollary to Theorem 1 shows explicitly the application to matching problems.

In the context of designing decentralized economic mechanisms, it turned out to be important to know when one can construct an SDR for a collection of sets that cover the parameter space characterizing a finite number of economic agents. The condition of Theorem 1 is readily verifiable in that economic context.

Theorems 2–5 give different characterizations of situations in which the collection of sets is a partition. This is of interest because partitions have special properties of informational efficiency.

1 Introduction

A class of sets is said to be *representable* if there is a function that assigns to each set in the class an element of that set in such a way that no two sets are assigned the same element. Such a representation is called a *system of distinct representatives* (SDR). In this paper we present necessary and sufficient conditions for the existence of an SDR covering cases in which both the class of sets and the sets in the class may be infinite.

Our interest in systems of distinct representatives arises from mechanism design, more specifically, from our construction of an algorithmic procedure for designing decentralized mechanisms to realize a given goal function. Ordinarily to come up with a mechanism that solves a given design problem requires the

This research was supported by NSF Grant No. IRI-902070

designer to have some insight into the problem – an idea for a mechanism that will meet the given requirements. And ordinarily the designer must then show that her mechanism does in fact work. An algorithmic procedure for constructing mechanisms relieves the designer of both of these burdens. Following the steps of the algorithm results in a mechanism that is guaranteed to work. The algorithm for constructing mechanisms makes use of systems of distinct representatives. This is discussed in more detail after the concepts and technical machinery have been introduced. The algorithmic construction is presented immediately following Theorem 1. The construction relies on both the result stated in Theorem 1, and part of its proof.

Research on mechanism design divides into two main branches. One branch focuses on *incentive* effects arising from distributed or asymmetric information, ignoring issues of *informational* feasibility or efficiency, while the other focuses on the problem of informationally efficient coordination arising from distributed or asymmetric information, while ignoring incentive issues. There are a few papers that address both issues together (Hurwicz 1976; Reichelstein 1984; Reichelstein and Reiter 1988). Our algorithm focuses on constructing decentralized mechanisms with desirable informational properties that realize a given goal function, ignoring incentive issues.

Roy Radner's work on mechanism design contains important contributions to this branch of mechanism design theory, notably his work on Team Theory, (Radner 1972a–c; Marschak and Radner 1972 and our joint work with Roy on the B-process.[1]

Denote by a collection of subsets K of a set W. (Thus, the K's are subsets of W but elements, sometimes called members, of C.) A collection C has an SDR (is representable) if there is a function Λ that assigns to each set K in C an element of K, so that $\Lambda(K) \in K$, and Λ satisfies the condition that if $K' \neq K''$ then $\Lambda(K') \neq \Lambda(K'')$.

Not every class of sets is representable, as the following example shows. Let the underlying set W consist of two elements, a and b. Let the collection C consist of three sets, $K_1 = \{a\}, K_2 = \{b\}, K_3 = \{a, b\}$. Clearly the collection C is not representable because it is impossible to have three different representatives drawn from a set containing only two elements.

P. Hall (1935) gave a necessary and sufficient condition that a class be representable when the class contains a finite number of finite sets. Hall's condition is that each union of n elements of C contain at least n elements of W. In the above example, Hall's condition is violated because the union of the three sets has only two elements.

The following example shows that Hall's 'counting' (cardinality) argument fails when the collection C of sets is infinite (even just denumerably infinite).

Let the underlying set W be the set $N = \{1, 2, \ldots, \text{ad inf}\}$ of natural numbers. Let the collection C consist of the singleton sets, $\{n\}_{n=1,2,\ldots}$ together with the

[1] The B-process (Hurwicz et al. 1975) is a decentralized stochastic mechanism that realizes the Walras correspondence in classical and non-classical environments – environments that can include indivisibilities and non-convexities, but not externalities.

set N itself, i.e., $C = \{N, \{1\}, \{2\}, \ldots, \text{ad inf}\}$. Then the cardinality of C and N are the same, but it is clear that there can be no SDR, because each singleton $\{n\}$ must be represented by its sole element n; thus all the elements of N are used up representing the singletons and there is no distinct element of N left to represent N itself. This is a (well-known) counterexample to an analogue, based on cardinality, of Hall's theorem for the case of an infinite collection of sets. Note that not all of the sets in C are finite.

An SDR for a family of sets is closely related to the concept of a transversal. If Λ is an SDR for C, then the set $\Lambda(C)$ is a *transversal* for C. Mirsky[2] (1971) comments,

> "In the transfinite form of Hall's theorem (referring to Everett and Whaples theorem mentioned below), we operate with families of finite sets. This restriction is extremely irksome as it greatly narrows the field of possible applications of Hall's theorem, but it is not easy to see how it might be relaxed."

Mirsky goes on to present a theorem of Rado and Jung, discussed in Rado (1967) which allows an infinite number of sets, just one of which is infinite, but requires a condition to exclude the counterexample mentioned above.

M. Hall (1948) showed that Hall's condition holds for an infinite collection of finite sets. Everett and Whaples (1949) also generalized Hall's theorem to the case when the collection of sets may be infinite, but the member sets (the K's) are all finite. Their approach involves representing the collection C of sets as an indexed family, so that each member of the collection might be counted more than once. The cardinality of the index set is not restricted. Their proof is by transfinite induction, and relies on the finiteness of the sets in C to provide the bound needed for Zorn's lemma. Folkman (1968) studied the case of infinite families with finitely many infinite sets, as did Brualdi and Scrimger (1968). The problem can also be formulated as the "marriage problem" in societies consisting of men and women, and studied in the setting of bipartite graphs (see details on p. 297ff.). Damerell and Milner (1974) gave a criterion for deciding whether a countable family of sets has a transversal; an alternative criterion was given by Podewski and Steffens (1976) and Nash-Williams (1978). Shelah (1973) provided an inductive criterion which together with the other results resolved the issue for the case of countable collections of countable sets. Aharoni et al. (1983), working in the setting of bipartite graphs (matching theory) gave necessary and sufficient conditions that an infinite collection of infinite sets have a transversal.

P. Hall's criterion for the finite case involves a property of subcollections of the given family of sets, namely, that the union of every subcollection have as many elements as there are sets in the subcollection. Hall's proof of sufficiency uses an inductive argument. The generalization presented in Aharoni et al. (1983) follows the pattern of Hall's argument in both respects. Their result is that a society has a solution to the marriage problem if and only if it does not

[2] This concept of a transversal is less restrictive than some used in other parts of mathematics, e.g., the concept of a transversal to the sets making up a (differentiable) foliation.

contain any one of a certain set of structures in its subsocieties. Their proof is by transfinite induction.

In Theorem 1 we provide a necessary and sufficient condition that an arbitrary (finite or infinite) collection C of (finite or infinite) subsets of a set W have an SDR. The Corollary to Theorem 1 covers the case of an indexed family of sets, a case that more naturally accommodates matching problems. The condition requires the existence of a correspondence U (whose range is C and whose domain is the union of the members of C, denoted by Θ) that (i) *generates* C, in the sense that for each $\theta \in \Theta$, $U(\theta) \in C$, and for each element K in C there is an element $\theta \in \Theta$ such that $U(\theta) = K$, and (ii) is *self-belonging*, i.e., $\theta \in U(\theta)$. The proof of Theorem 1 is direct, brief and does not involve transfinite induction. It does use the (equivalent) Axiom of Choice.

In the first of the examples above (pp. 290–291), our condition is violated because there is no self-belonging correspondence defined on the two-element union $\{a, b\}$ of the members of $C = \{K_1, K_2, K_3\}$ that generates all three sets. The second example (p. 291) does not contradict Theorem 1, because the collection $C = \{N, \{1\}, \{2\}, \ldots, \text{ad inf}\}$ cannot be generated by a self-belonging correspondence whose domain is N, (which is the union of the members of C).

Because our criterion is equivalent to the existence of a transversal for a family of sets, and so is the criterion given in Aharoni et al. (1983), the two criteria are logically equivalent. However, they may not be equally useful in application. In our work on the design of decentralized economic mechanisms it turned out to be important to know when it is possible to construct an SDR for a covering C of a given underlying set W. In models of a decentralized economy of N agents, C is a covering of $W = \Theta$, $\Theta = \Theta^1 \times \cdots \times \Theta^N$, and the elements of Θ^i are vectors of parameters characterizing the i-th agent. Hence $W = \Theta$ is called the *parameter space*. The problem of designing decentralized mechanisms involves a given goal function $F : \Theta \longrightarrow Z$, where Z is the space of outcomes or actions. The problem is to design decentralized mechanisms that for each $\theta \in \Theta$ produce the outcome prescribed by the goal function for that environment θ. We have developed an algorithmic[3] procedure that constructs decentralized mechanisms (with desirable informational properties) for a given goal function. The procedure involves two stages. The first, called the *Rectangles Method* (RM), constructs a covering of the contour sets of the goal function F and therefore also a covering of the space Θ, by product sets, called *rectangles*.

[3] Two comments on our use of the term "algorithmic". The procedure is well-defined, but at certain steps it may involve solving nonlinear equations. In cases where there is an algorithm for solving those equations, our procedure is literally algorithmic. But there can be cases where there is no such algorithm. In such a case it is not uncommon in computer science to assume an "oracle", who provides the required solution. With the oracle, it is customary to call the entire procedure "algorithmic".

Second, in computer science it is customary to distinguish two types of algorithms, deterministic and nondeterministic. A deterministic algorithm produces a specified output from given inputs. In other words, a deterministic algorithm computes a function. A nondeterministic algorithm also computes an output from given inputs, but the output can be any member of a specified set. This is relevant to our model, because the mechanisms involve correspondences, such as the message correspondence, rather than functions.

The second stage, called the *Transversals Method* (TM), involves constructing a transversal for the covering C. In the RM construction the covering C is generated by a correspondence $U : \Theta \twoheadrightarrow \Theta$. In many cases of interest, the set $W = \Theta$ is infinite and the covering C is an infinite collection of infinite sets.[4]

The case where the covering is a partition is of particular interest in the analysis of information efficiency of mechanisms, and it is helpful to know which correspondences generate partitions. When the covering is a partition, the algorithmic procedure is deterministic[5]; when there are overlaps, it is non-deterministic.

There are examples in which the (even unique) informationally efficient mechanisms have coverings that are not partitions.

A characterization of partitions in terms of SDR's is provided in Theorem 2. We define a property of correspondences, called *block symmetry*, and show in Theorem 3 that the covering C generated by a self-belonging correspondence U is a partition if and only if U is block symmetric. Block symmetry is a strengthening of the property of symmetry of a relation. Symmetry of the generating (self-belonging) correspondence is not sufficient to ensure that the covering generated be a partition.

In Definition 6 we introduce the concept of redundant sets in a covering and the related concept of irreducibility of a covering. These concepts are of interest in connection with informational efficiency. A member set that can be eliminated while the remaining sets still constitute a covering is called *redundant*. A covering is irreducible if it contains no redundant sets. Clearly a covering that is a partition has no redundant sets and hence is irreducible. Theorem 4 characterizes partitions in terms of symmetry of the generating correspondence and irreducibility of the covering it generates. Theorem 5 summarizes the equivalencies of the combinations of conditions in Theorems 2, 3 and 4.

Returning to the concept of reducibility of coverings, it is clear that every finite covering contains an irreducible subcovering–one with no redundant sets. Dugundji (1966, p. 161) has given an example of an infinite covering of the nonnegative real line that does not have an irreducible subcovering. However, that example is a nested family of sets in which each set in the covering is a subset of other sets. A family of sets constructed by the RM procedure cannot have sets that are subsets of others in the family. Therefore Dugundji's example does not settle the question whether an infinite collection of sets constructed by RM has an irreducible subcovering. At this point the question whether infinite RM coverings have irreducible subcoverings is open (see p. 302ff.).

2 Preliminaries

Remark 1. Let C be a collection of (non-empty) subsets of some set W.

$$\text{Let } \Theta = \Theta(C) = \bigcup_{K \in C} K .$$

[4] A more detailed description of the algorithmic procedure is given below (p. 295ff.).

[5] See footnote 3 above.

Then C is a covering of Θ.

Definition 1. *A system of distinct representatives (SDR) for a collection C of subsets is a function such that*

$$\forall K \in C \quad \Lambda(K) \in K \tag{i}$$

$$(K, K' \in C,\ K \neq K') \rightarrow \Lambda(K) \neq \Lambda(K') \tag{ii}$$

Definition 2. *A collection C of subsets of W is said to be generated by a correspondence if and only if there exists a correspondence $U : \Theta \twoheadrightarrow \Theta$ such that*

(1) for every $K \in C$, there is $\theta \in \Theta$ such that $K = U(\theta)$, and
(2) for every $\theta \in \Theta$, $U(\theta) \in C$.[6]

Definition 3. *A correspondence $V : A \twoheadrightarrow B$ is called self-belonging if and only if $\forall a \in A$, $a \in V(a)$.*

Distinct representatives for an arbitrary collection of subsets

Theorem 1. *Let C be an arbitrary collection of subsets of a set W. (By Remark 1, C is a covering of Θ.) C has an SDR if and only if C is generated by a self-belonging correspondence $U : \Theta \twoheadrightarrow \Theta$.*

Proof. To prove sufficiency, suppose C is generated by a self-belonging correspondence $U : \Theta \twoheadrightarrow \Theta$. Then for each $K \in C$ there exists $\theta_K \in K$ such that $U(\theta_K) = K$. Define $\Lambda : C \longrightarrow \Theta$ by $\Lambda(K) = \theta_K$. This establishes *(i)* of Definition 1. To establish *(ii)*, suppose $\Lambda(K) = \theta_K = \theta_{K'} = \Lambda(K')$. It follows from $\theta_K = \theta_{K'}$ that $U(\theta_K) = U(\theta_{K'})$. Thus $K = K'$.

To prove necessity, suppose C has an SDR $\Lambda : C \longrightarrow \Theta$. Then by *(i)* of Definition 1, for every $K \in C$, $\Lambda(K) \in K$. We define the generating correspondence $U : \Theta \twoheadrightarrow \Theta$ in two steps. First, for $\theta \in \Lambda(C)$, let $U_1 : \Lambda(C) \twoheadrightarrow \Theta$ be given by $U_1(\theta) = K$ if and only if $\Lambda(K) = \theta$. Second, for $\theta \in \Theta \backslash \Lambda(C)$ define $U_2 : \Theta \backslash \Lambda(C) \twoheadrightarrow \Theta$ as follows. First, for all $\theta \in \Theta$, let $C_\theta = \{K \in C | \theta \in K\}$. Note that C_θ is not empty, because C is a covering of Θ. Let $U_2(\theta) = K$ for some arbitrary $K \in C_\theta$. Now, define the correspondence U by

$$U(\theta) = \begin{cases} U_1(\theta) & \text{if } \theta \in \Lambda(C) \\ U_2(\theta) & \text{if } \theta \in \Theta \backslash \Lambda(C) \end{cases}$$

Thus, U is a self-belonging correspondence that generates C. The Axiom of Choice is used in both parts of this proof.

The question of existence of an SDR for certain coverings arises naturally in designing decentralized procedures–mechanisms– to meet ('realize') a given optimality criterion.

[6] Hence for every $\theta \in \Theta$, $U(\theta) \neq \emptyset$.

The mechanisms we consider are those *whose solution outcomes*, represented by elements z of the 'outcome space' Z, *however arrived at*, are optimal. The criterion of optimality is a goal function $F : \Theta \longrightarrow Z$, where $\Theta = \Theta^1 \times \cdots \times \Theta^N$; agent i is characterized by a parameter point $\theta^i \in \Theta^i$, known only to that agent, where Θ^i is the individual parameter space of agent i. In an economically important class of cases the spaces Θ and Z are Euclidean, and in simpler subcases the goal function F is real-valued. More generally it is a vector-valued correspondence.

The verification procedure is indirect. It involves an auxiliary space M, called the *message space*.[7] The procedure is decentralized in the sense that each agent's role requires only the knowledge of its own parameter value, and not those of others.

A mechanism consists of three basic elements: a message space M, a binary verification relation ρ, relating Θ and M[8], and the outcome function $h : M \longrightarrow Z$ specifying the outcome (action) z appropriate for a given message m. The verification relation ρ can be represented by a correspondence $\mu : \Theta \twoheadrightarrow M$, such that $m \in \mu(\theta)$ if and only if $m\rho\theta$. We say the mechanism (M, ρ, θ) 'realizes' the goal function F if $F = h \circ \mu$ where the correspondence μ represents the relation ρ. We call the mechanism 'decentralized' if there exist N individual correspondences μ^i such that $m\rho\theta$ is equivalent to $m \in \mu^i\left(\theta^i\right)$, $i = 1, \ldots, N$, and $\theta = \left(\theta^1, \ldots, \theta^N\right)$. When the mechanism is decentralized, the set $U_m = \{\theta \in \Theta : m \in \mu(\theta)\}$ is the Cartesian product of N sets $U_m^i = \left\{\theta^i \in \Theta^i : m \in \mu^i\left(\theta^i\right)\right\}$, $i = 1, \ldots, N$, where each U_m^i is a subset of Θ^i.[9]

If a mechanism realizes F, the sets U_m must cover the parameter space Θ. Hence to construct a decentralized mechanism that realizes F we must find a *covering* of Θ through a process such that the equilibrium relation ρ is verified at a given message m by having each agent i separately check that θ^i satisfies the relation $m\rho^i\theta^i$, i.e., that $m \in \mu^i\left(\theta^i\right)$. If all these relations are satisfied, the proposed m qualifies as an equilibrium message, and the outcome function prescribes the corresponding optimal action $z = h(m)$.

To carry out this program we proceed in two stages, RM and TM.

Stage 1. The method of rectangles (abbreviated RM). We construct a covering of the parameter space Θ by what we call the method of rectangles, abbreviated RM; we do this by associating with each $\theta \in \Theta$ a 'rectangular'[10] contour-contained (abbreviated F-c-c)[11] subset $V(\theta) \subseteq \Theta$ containing the point θ. This construction produces a covering of Θ that is generated by a self-belonging correspondence.[12]

[7] In economic market models, prices are elements of such an auxiliary space. It is auxiliary in the sense that it helps to determine the relationship between the outcomes and the agents' characteristics represented by their parameter values.

[8] "$m\rho\theta$" is read as "m is an equilibrium message for θ".

[9] In particular, when $N = 2$ and each U_m^i is an interval on the real axis, the set U_m is a rectangle.

[10] I.e., there exist N correspondences V^i on Θ^i, such that for each $\theta \in \Theta$, we have $V(\theta) = V^1\left(\theta^1\right) \times \cdots \times V^N\left(\theta^N\right)$.

[11] I.e., for each $\theta \in \Theta$, $V(\theta)$ is a subset of the contour set $F^{-1}(F(\theta))$.

[12] It also has the properties (rectangularity and contour-containment) needed to make the resulting mechanism decentralized and one that realizes F.

Stage 2. The method of transversals (abbreviated TM). It follows from Theorem 1 that the covering $C = \{K \subseteq \Theta : K = V(\theta),\ \theta \in \Theta\}$ has an SDR, i.e., a function $\Lambda : C \longrightarrow \Theta$ with the properties specified by Definition 1. However, in describing the process of mechanism construction, we find it convenient to use a 'special' SDR, say Λ^*, satisfying (in addition to the properties required by Definition 1) the condition

$$V\left(\Lambda^*(K)\right) = K \qquad (*)$$

The first part of the proof of Theorem 1 shows that such special SDR's exist if the hypothesis of Theorem 1 is satisfied, i.e., if the covering C is generated by a self-belonging correspondence. If the covering is a partition, then $(*)$ is automatically satisfied by any SDR Λ. In general, Λ^* is not unique.

Let $T^* = \Lambda^*(C)$ be a ('special') transversal corresponding to the ('special') SDR Λ^*. This transversal can be used to construct a mechanism $\pi = (M, \mu, h)$ that realizes the goal function F. This is done by the following steps.

(i) We first use the transversal as the message space of the mechanism, i.e., we set $M = T^*$.[13] (One can also use as M a set in 1–1 correspondence with T^*.)

(ii) We define the equilibrium correspondence μ from Θ to M by the equivalence

$$m \in \mu(\theta) \text{ if and only if } m = \Lambda^*\left(V(\theta)\right) \text{ for some } \Lambda^* \text{ satisfying } (*),$$

where V is the self-belonging F-c-c correspondence on Θ that generates C.

(iii) We define the outcome function $h : M \longrightarrow Z$ by the relation

$$h(m) = F(m) \text{ for all } m \in M\,.$$

The mechanism $\pi = (M, \mu, h)$ so constructed can be shown (*using the assumption that the covering it is based on is F-c-c*) to realize the given goal function F. I.e., given any $\theta \in \Theta$, there exists a message m such that $m \in \mu(\theta)$; and for any $m \in M, z \in Z$, and $\theta \in \Theta$, if $m \in \mu(\theta)$ and $z = h(m)$ then $z = F(\theta)$.

Notice that this construction does not depend on how the covering and the transversal are obtained. If the covering has the F-c-c property, and a transversal, then the mechanism constructed from that transversal realizes the goal function F.

This mechanism is decentralized when the correspondence V is rectangular, i.e., when $V(\theta)$ is the Cartesian product of subsets $V^i(\theta)$ of the individual parameter spaces Θ^i, $i = 1, \ldots, N$, which is the case in the RM construction. In the case of a covering that is not obtained by RM, the mechanism is decentralized when the sets of the covering are rectangular.

[13] Typically the message space M provided by the transversal T^* is 'smaller' than the parameter space Θ; e.g., in cases where they each have dimension, T^* often has smaller dimension than Θ. Hence the use of such a message space increases the informational efficiency of the mechanism.

3 Families of sets

Matching problems such as the marriage problem (see p. 291) are classical applications of Hall's Theorem. Matching problems also arise in economics (see, for instance, Gale and Shapley 1962; Kelso and Crawford 1982; Roth 1984; Roth and Sotomayor 1990).

It is not clear that, in the formulation presented so far, Theorem 1 applies to matching problems. A formulation in which matching problems, such as those in economic settings, can naturally be stated involves a generalization of the framework used in Theorem 1. We present the definitions and a Corollary to Theorem 1 applicable to matching problems.

The marriage problem is a well-known example of a matching problem. In one version the marriage problem consists of a set of men, a set of women together with a specification of the women who are possible marriage partners for a given man, the requirement that each man marry a woman who is a possible marriage partner, and that no person be married to more than one partner. It is also required that all men be married, but not that all women be married. The problem is: Does there exist an assignment of women to men that meets these requirements in which all men are married? The Corollary to Theorem 1 gives necessary and sufficient conditions for the existence of such a solution. The proof of the Corollary "constructs", – using the Axiom of Choice – a solution.

Definition 4. *A family of sets is a set I (the index set) and a correspondence $i \longmapsto K_i$, where for each $i \in I$, K_i is a subset of an underlying set W. We write $\mathscr{K} = \{K_i | i \in I\}$. In the case where I is the set of natural numbers $\mathscr{K}$ is a sequence of subsets of W.*

Definition 1.1. *An SDR for a family of sets $\mathscr{K}$ is a (single valued) function $\Lambda : \mathscr{K} \longrightarrow \bigcup_{i \in I} K_i$ such that*

i) $\forall i \in I \ \Lambda(K_i) \in K_i$
ii) $i, j \in I$, $i \neq j$, *implies* $\Lambda(K_i) \neq \Lambda(K_j)$.

Definition 2.1.

a) A family of sets $\mathscr{K} = \{K_i | i \in I\}$ is generated by a correspondence if and only if there is a correspondence $\mathscr{U} : \bigcup_{i \in I} K_i \longrightarrow I \times W$ such that
   i) for each $w \in \bigcup_{i \in I} K_i$, $\mathscr{U}(w) \in \mathscr{K}$,
   ii) for each $K_i \in \mathscr{K}$ there exists $w_i \in \bigcup_{i \in I} K_i$ such that $K_i = \mathscr{U}(w_i)$.
b) A correspondence $\mathscr{U} : \bigcup_{i \in I} K_i \twoheadrightarrow I \times W$ is self-belonging if and only if for each $w \in \bigcup_{i \in I} K_i$, $w \in \mathscr{U}(w)$.

Stating the marriage problem formally, let I be the set of men; let W be the set of women. For each $i \in I$ let K_i be the set of women who are possible marriage partners for Mr. i. The family of sets $\mathscr{K} = \{K_i | i \in I\}$ is thereby defined. A solution of the marriage problem is given by an SDR, Λ, for $\mathscr{K}$. Thus, the marriage problem has a solution if and only if the family $\mathscr{K}$ has a transversal, $\Lambda(\mathscr{K})$; if $w \in \Lambda(K_i)$, then woman w will be married to man i.

Corollary to Theorem 1. *Let Θ be a family of subsets of W. K has an SDR , Θ, if and only if Θ is generated by a self-belonging correspondence Θ.*

The proof of the Corollary parallels the proof of Theorem 1.

Proof.($\Leftarrow$) Suppose $\mathscr{K}$ is generated by a self-belonging correspondence $\mathscr{U}$. For each $i \in I$ and K_i, there exists $w_k \in \bigcup_{i \in I} K_i$ such that $\mathscr{U}(w_k) = K_i$. Because $\mathscr{U}$ is self-belonging $w_k \in K_i$. Now, for $K_i \in \bigcup_{j \in I} K_j$, define $\Lambda(K_i) = w_{k_i}$. Therefore $\Lambda : \bigcup_{i \in I} K_i \longrightarrow I \times W$. This establishes *i)* of Definition 1.1. Next we establish *ii)* of Definition 1.1.

Suppose $\Lambda(K_l) = w_{K_l} = w_{K_j'} = \Lambda(K_j')$. Then, $\mathscr{U}(w_{K_l}) = K_l$ and $\mathscr{U}(w_{K_j}) = K_j'$. It follows that $K_l = K_j'$.

($\Leftarrow$) We turn now to the converse. Suppose $\mathscr{K}$ has an SDR, Λ. Then for every $K_i \in \mathscr{K}$, $\Lambda(K_i) \in K_i$. Define $\mathscr{U} : \bigcup_{i \in I} K_i \longrightarrow \mathscr{K}$, by

$$\mathscr{U}_1 : \Lambda(\mathscr{K}) \longrightarrow \mathscr{K}$$
$$\mathscr{U}_2 : \bigcup_{i \in I} K_i \backslash \Lambda(\mathscr{K}) \longrightarrow \mathscr{K}$$

where, $\mathscr{U}_1$ is given by $\mathscr{U}_1(w_i) = K_i$ if and only if $\Lambda(K_i) = w_i$. To define $\mathscr{U}_2$, let $w \in \bigcup_{i \in I} K_i \backslash \Lambda(\mathscr{K})$. Let $\mathscr{K}_w = \{K_i \in \mathscr{K} | w \in K_i; i \in I\}$. Then, let $\mathscr{U}_2(w) = K_j$ for some arbitrary j such that $K_j \in \mathscr{K}_w$. Define $\mathscr{U}$ by

$$\mathscr{U}(w) = \begin{cases} \mathscr{U}_1 & \text{if } w \in \Lambda(\mathscr{K}) \\ \mathscr{U}_2 & \text{if } w \in \bigcup_{i \in I} K_i \backslash \Lambda(\mathscr{K}) \end{cases}$$

The correspondence $\mathscr{U}(\bullet)$ is self-belonging and generates $\mathscr{K}$. (End of proof.)

4 Characterizations of partitions

In this section we consider coverings C of Θ generated by a self-belonging correspondence $U : \Theta \longrightarrow \Theta$. As indicated above (pp. 292–293), in the process of constructing economic mechanisms – especially its second phase (TM or a counterpart) –, there are significant advantages in dealing with partitions, i.e., with coverings of Θ that are free of overlaps. We therefore seek conditions ensuring that the covering generated by U is a partition.

For example, correspondence that are associated with decentralized mechanisms in some cases generate partitions but – in others – coverings with overlaps. Overlaps can also arise in other settings. For example, in the marriage problem the covering would typically have overlaps – a woman might be an eligible partner for more than one man.

If the covering generated by the correspondence U is a parttion, the U has the property of *symmetry*:

$$\theta' \in U(\theta) \quad \text{if and only if} \quad \theta \in U(\theta'). \qquad (*)$$

But symmetry of the correspondence U is not in general[14] sufficient to ensure that the covering it generates is a partition.

If a collection of sets C is a covering of Θ, and is a partition, is it generated by a correspondence, $U : \Theta \twoheadrightarrow \Theta$? Clearly, yes, but what conditions must U satisfy if C is a partition? It is obvious that if C is a partition then it has an SDR. Is there any special property that an SDR for a partition has? Theorems 2, 3 and 4 provide answers to these questions. For the record,

Definition 4. *A collection C of sets (equivalently a covering C of Θ) is a partition, if and only if, for $K, K' \in C$, either $K \cap K' = \emptyset$, or, $K = K'$.*

The following characterization of partitions in terms of SDR is straightforward to prove.

Theorem 2. *A covering C of Θ is a partition if and only if every function $\Lambda : C \longrightarrow \Theta$ that satisfies*

$$\forall K \in C,\ \Lambda(K) \in K\,, \tag{A}$$

is an SDR for C.

Proof. (Necessity). Suppose C is a partition, and suppose $\Lambda : C \longrightarrow \Theta$ satisfies (A). We show that $K, K' \in C$, $K \neq K'$ implies $\Lambda(K) \neq \Lambda(K')$. Suppose $K, K' \in C$, and $K \neq K'$. Since C is a partition, $K \cap K' = \emptyset$. Since Λ satisfies (A), $\Lambda(K) \in K$, and $\Lambda(K') \in K'$. Hence, $\Lambda(K) \neq \Lambda(K')$. Thus, $\Lambda(\bullet)$ is an SDR for C.
(Sufficiency) Suppose that every function $\Lambda : C \longrightarrow \Theta$ that satisfies (A) is an SDR for C. Because the sets $K \in C$ are not empty there are many such functions. We choose one such function, $\bar{\Lambda}$, if necessary using the Axiom of Choice. Thus, $\bar{\Lambda}$ is an SDR for C.

If C is a partition, there is nothing to prove. So suppose C is not a partition. Then there exist two sets K' and K'' in C such that

$$K' \cap K'' \neq \emptyset\,, \tag{a}$$

$$K' \neq K''\,. \tag{b}$$

By *(a)*, there is a point $\theta' \in \Theta$, such that $\theta' \in K'$ and $\theta' \in K''$. Now define the function $\Lambda' : C \longrightarrow \Theta$ by

$$\Lambda'(K) = \bar{\Lambda}(K),\ \text{ for all } K \in C \backslash \{K', K''\}\,,$$

and

$$\Lambda'(K') = \Lambda'(K'') = \theta' \tag{$*$}$$

Then, for all $K \in C$, $\Lambda'(K) \in K$. Therefore (1) is satisfied. But, by *(b)*, $K' \neq K''$, and by $(*)$, $\Lambda'(K') = \Lambda'(K'')$. Therefore, Λ' is not an SDR for C.
This completes the proof.

[14] We have shown elsewhere that when the covering is generated by the so-called *reflexive* rectangles method of mechanism construction, then the symmetry of U is sufficient.

We next give a characterization of partitions in terms of the generating correspondence. First, we define a property that we show is a property of correspondences that generate partitions.

Definition 5. *Let $\bar{\theta}, \theta', \theta''$ denote points of Θ. A correspondence $U : \Theta \longrightarrow \Theta$, is block symmetric if and only if*

$$\left[\theta' \in U(\bar{\theta}) \text{ and } \theta'' \in U(\bar{\theta})\right] \Longrightarrow \left[\theta' \in U(\theta'') \text{ and } \theta'' \in U(\theta')\right] \tag{B}$$

We show below that block symmetry is a strengthening of the concept of symmetry of relations. The term 'block symmetric' is used because, when (B) is satisfied, there is a permutation of the elements of Θ such that the graph of U consists of blocks, ('squares') with the 'northeast' and 'southwest' vertices on the diagonal of $\Theta \times \Theta$.

Theorem 3. *A covering C of Θ is a partition if and only if C is generated by a block symmetric, self-belonging correspondence $U : \Theta \twoheadrightarrow \Theta$.*

Proof. (Necessity). Suppose C is a partition of Θ. Then C has an SDR. To see this, define $\Lambda(K)$ to be any element in K. Because C is a partition, $K \neq K'$ implies $\Lambda(K) \neq \Lambda(K')$.

Because C has an SDR, it follows from Theorem 1, that C is generated by a self-belonging correspondence $U : \Theta \longrightarrow \Theta$. It remains to show that U is block symmetric.

Let $\bar{\theta}, \theta', \theta''$ be elements of Θ satisfying the hypothesis of (B), i.e., let

$$\theta' \in U(\bar{\theta}) \text{ and } \theta'' \in U(\bar{\theta}) . \tag{i}$$

To prove (B) we show that

$$\theta' \in U(\theta''), \text{ and } \theta'' \in U(\theta') . \tag{ii}$$

The relations (i) and the self-belonging property of U yield

$$\theta' \in U(\bar{\theta}) \cap U(\theta') \tag{iii.a}$$

and

$$\theta'' \in U(\bar{\theta}) \cap U(\theta'') . \tag{iii.b}$$

Since C is generated by U, there exist $\bar{K}, K', K'' \in C$ such that

$$\bar{K} = U(\bar{\theta}), \quad K' = U(\theta'), \quad K'' = U(\theta'') \tag{iv}$$

Since C is a partition,

$$\begin{aligned} &\bar{K} \cap K' = \emptyset, \text{ or } \bar{K} = K' \\ &\bar{K} \cap K'' = \emptyset, \text{ or } \bar{K} = K'' \end{aligned} \tag{v}$$

But the relations (iii.a) and (iii.b) rule out the emptiness of the intersections $\bar{K} \cap K'$ and $\bar{K} \cap K''$. Hence $\bar{K} = K'$ and $\bar{K} = K''$. By (iv), this yields

$$U(\bar{\theta}) = U(\theta')$$

and

$$U(\bar{\theta}) = U(\theta'')$$

Using each of these relations in (i) yields the corresponding relation in (ii), and hence U is block symmetric.

This concludes the proof of necessity.

(Sufficiency) Suppose that C is generated by a block symmetric, self-belonging correspondence $U : \Theta \longrightarrow \Theta$. We show that C is a partition, i.e., that for every $K, K' \in C$ either $K \cap K' = \emptyset$, or $K = K'$.

Let K and K' be elements of C. If $K \cap K' = \emptyset$ there is nothing to prove. So, suppose there is $\tilde{\theta} \in K \cap K'$. Then, since C is generated by U, there are elements, $\hat{\theta}$ and $\hat{\hat{\theta}}$ in Θ such that $K = U\left(\hat{\theta}\right)$, and $K' = U\left(\hat{\hat{\theta}}\right)$. Thus,

$$\tilde{\theta} \in U\left(\hat{\theta}\right) \text{ and } \tilde{\theta} \in U\left(\hat{\hat{\theta}}\right).$$

It follows from (B) and $\tilde{\theta} \in U\left(\bar{\theta}\right)$ that

$$\forall \theta \in U\left(\hat{\theta}\right), \ \theta \in U\left(\tilde{\theta}\right).$$

Therefore,

$$U\left(\hat{\theta}\right) \subseteq U\left(\tilde{\theta}\right).$$

Now, since $\hat{\theta} \in U\left(\tilde{\theta}\right)$, because $\hat{\theta} \in U\left(\hat{\theta}\right)$, by self-belonging, and $U\left(\hat{\theta}\right) \subseteq U\left(\tilde{\theta}\right)$ as just shown, it follows from (B) of Definition 5 (with $\hat{\theta}$ here corresponding to θ' in (B), θ to θ'', and $\tilde{\theta}$ to $\bar{\theta}$ in (B)) that

$$\forall \theta \in U\left(\tilde{\theta}\right), \ \theta \in U\left(\hat{\theta}\right).$$

Thus,

$$U\left(\hat{\theta}\right) \supseteq U\left(\tilde{\theta}\right).$$

Therefore

$$U\left(\hat{\theta}\right) = U\left(\tilde{\theta}\right).$$

The same argument applied to $U\left(\hat{\hat{\theta}}\right)$ and $U\left(\tilde{\theta}\right)$ shows that

$$U\left(\hat{\hat{\theta}}\right) = U\left(\tilde{\theta}\right).$$

Therefore,

$$K = U\left(\hat{\theta}\right) = U\left(\hat{\hat{\theta}}\right) = K'.$$

This concludes the proof.

Remark 2. Block symmetry of a correspondence is a strengthening of the usual notion of symmetry of a relation applied to the graph of the correspondence. Symmetry may be defined by the condition

$$\theta' \in U(\bar{\theta}) \Rightarrow \bar{\theta} \in U(\theta') . \tag{S}$$

To see that (B) implies (S), suppose U is block symmetric. Suppose $\theta' \in U(\bar{\theta})$. We show that $\bar{\theta} \in U(\theta')$. The hypotheses of (B) in the definition of block symmetry are satisfied for $\theta', \theta'', \bar{\theta}$, where $\theta'' = \bar{\theta}$. Therefore, $\theta'' = \bar{\theta} \in U(\theta')$.

The following example shows that symmetry of the generating (self-belonging) correspondence is not sufficient for the covering it generates to be a partition.

Example 3. Let $\Theta = \{a, b, c\}$, and let $U(a) = \{a, b, c\}$, $U(b) = \{a, b\}$, $U(c) = \{a, c\}$. Then U is self-belonging and symmetric, but the covering it generates is not a partition. However, in this example the covering is reducible in the sense of the following definition.

Definition 6. *An element of a covering C of Θ is redundant if eliminating that element from C still leaves a covering of Θ. A covering is irreducible*[15] *if it has no redundant elements; otherwise it is reducible.*

If C is a finite covering, then it has an irreducible subcovering, which might be C itself. If C is not irreducible then it has a redundant element. When C is finite, successive elimination of redundant elements must eventually result in an irreducible subcovering. This is not true when C is infinite, as is shown by Dugundji's example (1966, p. 161).

The covering C in Example 3 can be reduced in two different ways. First to the covering $C' = \{\{a, b, c\}\}$, which is generated by the (constant) correspondence $U'(\theta) = \{a, b, c\}$, for $\theta \in \{a, b, c\}$, and, second, to the covering $C'' = \{\{a, b\}, \{b, c\}\}$, which is generated by the correspondence $U''(a) = U''(b) = \{a, b\}$ and $U''(c) = \{b, c\}$. Both C' and C'' are irreducible, and U' is symmetric, while U'' is not. Of course, C' is a partition and C'' is not.

While symmetry is not enough to guarantee that the covering generated by a self-belonging correspondence be a partition, it is the case that if the covering is irreducible, then symmetry ensures that it is a partition. The converse also holds.

Theorem 4. *Let C be a covering of Θ. C is a partition if and only if (i) C is generated by a self-belonging, symmetric correspondence $U : \Theta \twoheadrightarrow \Theta$, and (ii) C is irreducible.*

Proof. ($\Leftarrow$) Suppose (i) and (ii) hold. We show that U is block symmetric, and hence, by Theorem 3, that C is a partition. To show that U is block symmetric we must show that U satisfies

$$\left[\theta' \in U(\bar{\theta}) \text{ and } \theta'' \in U(\bar{\theta})\right] \Rightarrow \left[\theta' \in U(\theta'') \text{ and } \theta'' \in U(\theta')\right] \tag{B}$$

So, suppose that $\bar{\theta}$ is an arbitrary point of Θ,and consider $U(\bar{\theta})$. Let

[15] The term "irreducible" applied to a covering was introduced by Dugundji (1966) p. 160.

$$E(\bar{\theta}) = \left\{\theta \in U(\bar{\theta}) : U(\theta) = U(\bar{\theta})\right\}$$

and

$$D(\bar{\theta}) = \left\{\theta \in U(\bar{\theta}) : U(\theta) \neq U(\bar{\theta})\right\}$$

Note that $U(\bar{\theta}) = E(\bar{\theta}) \cup D(\bar{\theta})$, and $E(\bar{\theta}) \cap D(\bar{\theta}) = \emptyset$.

Either $D = \emptyset$, or $D \neq \emptyset$.

Suppose $D \neq \emptyset$. We shall show that $D \neq \emptyset$ leads to the conclusion that the set $K = U(\bar{\theta})$ is redundant, thereby contradicting (ii).

Consider $\bar{\bar{\theta}} \in U(\bar{\theta})$. Either $\bar{\bar{\theta}} \in E(\bar{\theta})$, or $\bar{\bar{\theta}} \in D(\bar{\theta})$. If $\bar{\bar{\theta}} \in D(\bar{\theta})$, then $\bar{\bar{\theta}} \in \bigcup_{\theta \in D(\bar{\theta})} U(\theta)$.

Now suppose that $\bar{\bar{\theta}} \in E(\bar{\theta})$. Then $U\left(\bar{\bar{\theta}}\right) = U(\bar{\theta})$. Let $\hat{\theta} \in U\left(\bar{\bar{\theta}}\right)$. If for all $\bar{\bar{\theta}} \in E(\bar{\theta})$, and all $\hat{\theta} \in U\left(\bar{\bar{\theta}}\right)$ $\hat{\theta} \in E(\bar{\theta})$, then $D(\bar{\theta}) = \emptyset$. So we may suppose that $\hat{\theta} \in D(\bar{\theta})$. Since, by symmetry, $\bar{\bar{\theta}} \in U(\hat{\theta})$, it follows that $\bar{\bar{\theta}} \in \bigcup_{\theta \in D(\bar{\theta})} U(\theta)$. Since $\bar{\bar{\theta}}$ is an arbitrary point of $U(\bar{\theta})$, we have shown that $U(\bar{\theta}) \subseteq \bigcup_{\theta \in D(\bar{\theta})} U(\theta)$. In order to conclude that $K = U(\bar{\theta})$ is redundant, we must show that not every set $U(\theta)$, for $\theta \in D(\bar{\theta})$, is equal to $U(\bar{\theta})$. But this follows immediately from the definition of $D(\bar{\theta})$.

Thus, we have shown that if $D(\bar{\theta}) \neq \emptyset$, then $U(\bar{\theta})$ is redundant, contradicting (ii). Therefore, we may conclude that $D(\bar{\theta}) = \emptyset$.

It then follows from the hypotheses of (B), i.e., that $\theta' \in U(\bar{\theta})$, and $\theta'' \in U(\bar{\theta})$, that $\theta' \in U(\theta'')$ and $\theta'' \in U(\theta')$, since it follows from $D(\bar{\theta}) = \emptyset$, that for every $\theta \in U(\bar{\theta})$, $U(\theta) = U(\bar{\theta})$, and hence $U(\theta') = U(\bar{\theta}) = U(\theta'')$. Thus, (B) is satisfied. Hence U is block symmetric, and by Theorem 3, C is a partition.
($\Leftarrow$) Suppose C is a partition. A covering C is a partition if and only if it is generated by a block symmetric, self-belonging correspondence $U : \Theta \longrightarrow \Theta$. Since block symmetry implies symmetry, U is symmetric. Finally, if C is a partition, then it is irreducible. This establishes (i) and (ii).

Theorems 2, 3 and 4 may be summarized in Theorem 5.

Theorem 5. *The following four propositions are equivalent:*

1) *A covering C is a partition;*
2) *Every function $\Lambda : C \longrightarrow \Theta$ that satisfies condition (A) is an SDR for C;*
3) *C is generated by a block symmetric, self-belonging correspondence U : $\Theta \twoheadrightarrow \Theta$;*
4) *C is an irreducible covering generated by a symmetric, self-belonging correspondence $U : \Theta \twoheadrightarrow \Theta$.*

References

1. Aharoni, R., Nash-Williams, C. St. J.A., Shelah S. (1983) A general criterion for the existence of transversals. Proceedings London Mathematical Society, **47**: 43–68
2. Berge, C. (1963) Topological Spaces. Macmillan, New York

3. Brualdi, R.A., Scrimgen, E.B. (1968) Exchange systems, matchings and transversals. Journal of Combinatorial Theory **5**: 242–257
4. Damerell, R.M., Milner, E.C. (1974) Necessary and sufficient conditions for transversals of countable set systems. Journal of Combinatorial Theory Series A **17**: 350–379
5. Dugundji, J. (1966) Topology. Allyn and Bacon, Inc., Boston
6. Everett, C.J., Whaples, G. (1949) Representations of sequences of sets. American Journal of Mathematics **71**: 287–293
7. Folkman, K.J. (1968) Transversals of Infinite Families With Finitely Many Infinite Members. RAND Corp. memorandum, RM – 5676 – PR
8. Gale, D., Shapley, L. (1962) College Admissions and the Stability of Marriage. American Mathematical Monthly **69**: 9–15
9. Hall, M., Jr. (1948) Distinct representatives of subsets. Bulletin American Mathematics Society **54**: 922–926
10. Hall, P. (1935) On representatives of subsets. Journal of London Mathematic Society **10**: 26–30
11. Hurwicz, L. (1976) Mathematical Models in Economics. Papers and Proceedings of a U.S. – U.S.S.R. Seminar, Moscow
12. Hurwicz, L., Radner, R., Reiter S. (1975) A stochastic decentralized allocation process: Part I. Econometrica **43**(2): 187–221
13. Hurwicz, L., Radner, R., Reiter S. (1975) A stochastic decentralized resource allocation process: Part II. Econometrica **43**(3): 363–393
14. Hurwicz, L., Reiter S. (1990) Constructing Decentralized Mechanisms by the Method of Rectangles. Decentralization Conference, Northwestern University
15. Hurwicz, L., Reiter S. (1993) Designing Mechanisms by the 'Method of Rectangles'. Decentralization Conference, University of California, Berkeley
16. Kelso, A.S., Jr., Crawford, V.P. (1982) Job matching, coalition formation, and gross substitutes. Econometrica **50**: 1483–1504
17. Mirsky, L. (1971) Transversal Theory. Science and Engineering **75**, Academic Press, New York and London
18. Nash-Williams, C. St. J.A. (1978) Another criterion for marriage in denumerable societies. Annals Discrete Mathematics **3**: 165–179
19. Podewski, K.P., Steffens, K. (1976) Injective choice functions for countable families. Journals of Combination Theory Series B **21**: 40–46
20. Radner, R. (1972a) Normative theories of organization: an introduction. In: McGuire, C.C., Radner, R. (eds.) Decision and Organization. North Holland / American Elsevier, pp. 177–188
21. Radner, R. (1972b) Teams. In: McGuire, C.C., Radner, R. (eds.) Decision and Organization. North Holland / American Elsevier, pp. 189–216
22. Radner, R. (1972c) Allocation of a scarce resource under uncertainty: an example of a team. In: McGuire, C.C., Radner, R. (eds.) Decision and Organization. North Holland / American Elsevier, pp. 217–236
23. Reichelstein, S. (1984) Incentive compatibility and informational requirements. Journal of Economic Theory **32**: 384–390
24. Reichelstein, S., Reiter, S. (1988) Game forms with minimal message spaces. Econometrica **56**(3): 661–692
25. Rado, R. (1967) Note on the transfinite case of Hall's theorem on representatives. Journal of London Mathematic Society **42**: 321–324
26. Roth, A.E. (1984) The evolution of the labor market for medical interns and residents: A case study in game theory. Journal of Political Economy **92**: 991–1016
27. Roth, A.E., Sotomayor, M. (1990) Two-sided matching: A study in game-theoretic modeling and analysis. Cambridge University Press, Cambridge
28. Shelah, S. (1973) Notes on partition calculus. In: Hajinal, A., Rado, R., Sos, V.T. (eds.) Infinite and Finite Sets. (Colloq. Math. Soc. Janos Bolyai) **10**: 1257–1276

Roy Radner and incentive theory

Eric S. Maskin

Institute for Advanced Study and
Princeton University, Princeton, NJ 08540, USA (e-mail: maskin@ias.edu)

1 Introduction

How to provide agents with sufficient motivation to do what society – or its proxy in the guise of a center or social planner – wants them to do is the subject of incentive theory. The theory has normative force whenever, metaphorically speaking, the invisible hand of the market fails to provide such motivation automatically. Market failure can come about either because markets are imperfect in some way or because they do not exist at all. Indeed, a leading example of a non-market environment is the internal organization of a large corporation. Alfred Chandler (1977) made just this point when he gave his study of the modern American enterprise the title *The Visible Hand*.

The study of these large enterprises – which itself is an enterprise that is currently blossoming – has drawn on incentive theory in a fundamental way. And it is not surprising that Roy Radner – who had a long-standing fascination and more than casual personal acquaintance with large organizations – should have been inspired to make important contributions to this theory.

In this essay, I shall provide an outline of some of the major results in incentive theory with particular attention to Radner's work on the subject.

2 A simple model of a team

Let me begin with one of the first formal attempts to model organizations, viz, team theory, whose creation is due to Marschak and Radner (1972). Let Θ be the set of possible states of the world, and for each $\theta \in \Theta$, let $p(\theta)$ be the prior probability of θ. There are n agents, indexed by $i = 1, \ldots, n$. Each agent i has an action space A_i and a private signal space S_i. Both of these may in part be

A preliminary version of this paper was presented at a symposium in honor of Roy Radner at Cornell University, June 1992. I thank the NSF for research support and a referee for helpful comments.

exogenous and in part the choice of the team (or team "designer"). S_i can be thought of as a partition of Θ. That is, each signal $s_i \in S_i$ corresponds to a subset of Θ. Given the vector of signals $s = (s_1, ..., s_n)$, let $\pi(\theta \mid s)$ be the distribution of θ (derived from $p(\theta)$ using Bayes' rule) conditional on s. In addition to the n agents, the center (or CEO, social planner, etc.), whom we shall designate as agent 0, may be an active participant, in which case he has an action space A_0 (for simplicity, let us assume, however, that he observes no private signals, so that we can dispense with S_0).

The team is interested in implementing a *collective choice rule*, that is, a rule that specifies all agents' actions as a function of the available information s. Thus a collective choice rule f is a mapping

$$f : S_1 \times ... \times S_n \to A_0 \times ... \times A_n.$$

Much of team theory concerns the question of what constitutes the best way for agents to communicate with one another in order to implement the desired collective choice rule, assuming that communication is costly. A common simplifying assumption in this theory is that all agents and the center share the same objectives. Incentive theory, however, gains much of its interest from the presumption the agents have *different* preferences. Let us suppose that agent i's preferences can be represented by the (von Neumann-Morgenstern) utility function

$$u_i(a, \theta),$$

where $a = (a_0, ..., a_n)$. The fact agent i's payoff depends on other agents' actions embodies the idea that there may be externalities to actions. Similarly, the center has utility function

$$u_0(a, \theta),$$

which, if the center is just a surrogate for the group of agents as a whole, may take the form

$$\sum_{i=1}^{n} \lambda_i u_i(a, \theta).$$

Here λ_i is the "welfare weight" for agent i. Usually, in both team and incentive theory, the function f is chosen to maximize the expectation of u_0, i.e.,

$$f(s) \in \arg\max_{a} \sum_{\theta \in \Theta} u_0(a, \theta)\pi(\theta \mid s). \tag{1}$$

3 Adverse selection

For the time being, let us drop the actions $a_1, ..., a_n$ (but not a_0). Then the incentive problem is how to ensure that the center's action a_0 properly reflects agents' information s (in the sense of satisfying (1)), in view of the fact that the signals are private information. Models like this, where the major substantive difficulty is the private nature of information, are often called problems of *adverse selection* (or hidden information).

The solution to an adverse selection problem is normally formulated as an *incentive mechanism* (also variously called a "game form," "outcome function," "contract," or "constitution"). Suppose that each agent i is allocated a "message" space M_i. A message $m_i \in M_i$ can be thought of as agent i's announcement about his signal s_i (but this interpretation is not necessary). Then an incentive mechanism g is a function

$$g : M_1 \times ... \times M_n \to A_0.$$

We interpret this mechanism as specifying that the center will take action $g(m) \in A_0$ if the messages are $m = (m_1, ..., m_n)$. Thus $g(m)$ is called the *outcome* of the mechanism. For each vector of signals s, there will be a corresponding equilibrium (perhaps more than one) of the incentive mechanism (where each agent i evaluates the outcome $g(m)$ using his utility function u_i). Of course, exactly what an equilibrium is will depend on the solution concept that pertains. For a given solution concept, let $E_g(s)$ be the equilibrium outcome (for simplicity, we suppose that the equilibrium outcome is unique). If, for all s,

$$f(s) = E_g(s), \tag{2}$$

we say that g *implements* f (or that f is implemented by g) with respect to the solution concept. Much of the incentive literature consists of characterizing which social choice rules are implementable in this sense, with respect to particular solution concepts.

4 Adverse selection with dominant strategies

By far the simplest (and strongest) solution concept is equilibrium in dominant strategies. Agent i with signal s_i has a *dominant strategy* $m_i(s_i)$ for mechanism g if $m_i(s_i)$ solves

$$\max_{m_i} \sum_{\theta} u_i(g(m_i, m_{-i}), \theta)\pi_i(\theta \mid s_i) \quad \text{for all } m_{-i},$$

where $\pi_i(\theta \mid s_i)$ is the distribution of θ conditional on s_i and m_{-i} is the vector of other agents' messages.

Having a dominant strategy makes life easy for agent i because it obviates the need for him to form beliefs about what other players know and how they behave. Clearly, requiring that an equilibrium be independent of beliefs is demanding. Nevertheless, Groves (1973) showed that, in a special but important case of the Marschak-Radner framework, there is a large class of collective choice rules that are implementable. Specifically, suppose that the center's action a_0 takes the form

$$a_0 = (x, y_1, ..., y_n),$$

where x can be interpreted as the choice of a public good and the y_i's (which are scalars) are transfers of a private good (or money). Assume, moreover, that each agent i's utility takes the form

$$u_i(a_0, \theta) = v_i(x, s_i) + y_i. \tag{3}$$

That is, utility is *quasi-linear*. Then, as Groves demonstrated, any $f(s) = (x(s), y_1(s), ..., y_n(s))$ for which

$$x(s) \in \arg\max_x \sum_{i=1}^{n} v_i(x, s_i) \quad \text{for all } s \tag{4}$$

is implementable in dominant strategies provided that each $y_i(s)$ takes the form

$$y_i(s) \equiv \sum_{j \neq i} v_j(x(s), s_j) + k_i(s_{-i}), \tag{5}$$

where s_{-i} is the vector of signals excluding that of agent i and $k_i(\cdot)$ is an arbitrary function of s_{-i}. (Notice that (4) is the requirement that the public good be chosen to maximize social surplus.)

To see this, suppose that agents are confronted with a mechanism in which each agent i is asked to report a signal value $\hat{s}_i \in S_i$, and the outcome, given reports $\hat{s} = (\hat{s}_1, ..., \hat{s}_n)$, is $(x(\hat{s}), y_1(\hat{s}), ..., y_n(\hat{s}))$, where $x(\cdot)$ and $(y_1(\cdot), ..., y_n(\cdot))$ satisfy (4) and (5) respectively. Then, given (3), agent i's maximization problem is

$$\max_{\hat{s}_i} \left[v_i(x(\hat{s}_i, \hat{s}_{-i}), s_i) + \sum_{j \neq i} v_j(x(\hat{s}_i, \hat{s}_{-i}), \hat{s}_j) + k_i(\hat{s}_{-i}) \right]. \tag{6}$$

By varying $\hat{s}_i$, agent i can vary $x(\hat{s}_i, \hat{s}_{-i})$. But, by definition of $x(s)$,

$$x(s_i, \hat{s}_{-i}) = \arg\max_x \left[v_i(x, s_i) + \sum_{j \neq i} v_j(x, \hat{s}_j) \right].$$

Hence $\hat{s}_i = s_i$ solves (6). That is, it is a dominant strategy for agent i to tell the truth, establishing that $(x(s), y_1(s), ..., y_n(s))$ is implementable.

Green and Laffont (1979) showed, in fact, that any implementable social choice rule satisfying (4) *must* satisfy (5). To understand why this is so,[1] notice first that if mechanism $g : M_1 \times ... \times M_n \to A_0$ implements a collective choice rule f in dominant strategies and if, for all i and all s_i, $m_i(s_i)$ is agent i's dominant strategy when his signal is s_i, then g^* where

$$g^*(s_1, ..., s_n) \equiv g(m_1(s_1), ..., m_n(s_n))$$

also implements f.[2] Observe that g^* is a "direct revelation" mechanism in the sense that strategies consist of announcing a signal, and it is a dominant strategy

[1] The following argument is drawn from Laffont and Maskin (1980).

[2] Actually, it is conceivable that, in going from g to g^*, we might introduce additional, non-optimal equilibria. Although this is potentially a serious problem, we shall ignore it here (but see Dasgupta et al. (1979)).

for agents to announce signals truthfully. Thus, it suffices to restrict attention to direct revelation mechanisms when searching for mechanisms that implement a collective choice rule. Now, suppose that $f(s) = (x(s), y_1(s), ..., y_n(s))$ satisfies (4) and is implementable in dominant strategies. Suppose that, for all i, S_i is an open interval of real numbers, $v_i(\cdot,\cdot)$ is a twice differentiable function of x and s_i (with $\frac{\partial v_i}{\partial x} > 0$, $\frac{\partial^2 v_i}{\partial x^2} < 0$, and $\frac{\partial^2 v_i}{\partial x \partial s_i} > 0$), and $x(\cdot)$ and $y_i(\cdot)$ are differentiable functions of s_i. Since we can restrict attention to direct revelation mechanisms, the fact that f is implementable implies that, for all s_i and s_{-i},

$$s_i \in \arg\max_{\hat{s}_i} \left[v_i(x(\hat{s}_i, s_{-i}), s_i) + y_i(\hat{s}_i, s_{-i}) \right].$$

Hence

$$\frac{\partial v_i}{\partial x} \left(x(s_i, s_{-i}), s_i \right) \frac{\partial x}{\partial s_i}(s_i, s_{-i}) + \frac{\partial y_i}{\partial s_i}(s_i, s_{-i}) = 0. \tag{7}$$

Now from the above analysis, we know that one solution to the differential equation (7) is $y_i(s) = \sum_{j \neq i} v_j(x(s), s_j)$. Moreover, from the theory of differential equations, we know that all solutions differ by a constant $k_i(s_{-i})$. Hence, we can conclude that (5) holds.

The form (3) embodies the assumption of *private values:* agent i's payoff depends on θ only through his signal s_i, i.e., in particular, his payoff does not depend on s_{-i}. If we relax this assumption and allow s_{-i} to affect v_i, we are in the realm of *common values*. Radner and Williams (1988) showed that $f(s) = (x(s), y_1(s), ..., y_n(s))$ can be implemented in dominant strategies even when there are common values, if v_i takes the form

$$v_i(x, s) = w_i(x, s_i) + z_i(s). \tag{8}$$

To see this, observe that when (8) holds and agent i is confronted with the direct revelation mechanism $(x(\hat{s}), y_1(\hat{s}), ..., \hat{y}_n(\hat{s}))$ satisfying (4) and

$$y_\ell(\hat{s}) = \sum_{j \neq \ell} w_j \left(x(\hat{s}_j, \hat{s}_{-j}), \hat{s}_j \right) + k_\ell \left(\hat{s}_{-\ell} \right) \quad \text{for all } \ell,$$

his maximization problem is

$$\max_{\hat{s}_i} \left[w_i(x(\hat{s}_i, \hat{s}_{-i}), s_i) + z_i(s_i, s_{-i}) + \sum_{j \neq i} w_j(x(\hat{s}_i, \hat{s}_{-i}), \hat{s}_j) + k_i(\hat{s}_{-i}) \right]. \tag{9}$$

But because $z_i(s_i, s_{-i})$ does not depend on $\hat{s}_i$, $\hat{s}_i = s_i$ solves (9), establishing that it is a dominant strategy for i to tell the truth.

Radner and Williams went a step further, in fact, and showed that, with common values, (8) *must* hold for a collective choice rule $f(s) = (x(s), y_1(s), ..., y_n(s))$ satisfying (4) to be implementable. To see this, let us make the same differentiability assumptions as before (with the additional assumption that $\frac{\partial^2 v_j}{\partial x \partial s_i} \geq 0$ for $j \neq i$). Suppose that f is implementable by direct revelation mechanism $(x(\hat{s}), y_1(\hat{s}), ..., y_n(\hat{s}))$. Then, analogous to (7), we obtain the following first-order condition for agent i:

$$\frac{\partial v_i}{\partial x}\left(x(s_i,\hat{s}_{-i}),s_i,s_{-i}\right)\frac{\partial x}{\partial s_i}(s_i,\hat{s}_{-i})+\frac{\partial y_i}{\partial s_i}(s_i,\hat{s}_{-i}) \qquad (10)$$
$$=0 \quad \text{for all } s_i, s_{-i}, \quad \text{and } \hat{s}_{-i}.$$

Because $\frac{\partial^2 v_i}{\partial x \partial s_i} > 0$, $\frac{\partial^2 v_i}{\partial x^2} < 0$, and $\frac{\partial^2 v_j}{\partial x \partial s_i} \geq 0$, we have $\frac{\partial x}{\partial s_i} > 0$.[3] Hence if, given s_i and $\hat{s}_{-i}$, (10) is to hold for all s_{-i}, we must have $\frac{\partial^2 v_i}{\partial x \partial s_{-i}} = 0$. Hence, v_i must be additively separable between x and s_{-i}, i.e., it takes the form (8).

5 Adverse selection: Other solution concepts

The positive results for dominant strategies in the case of quasi-linear preferences do not readily generalize to significantly broader environments, as the results of Gibbard (1973), Hurwicz (1972), and Satterthwaite (1975) make clear. Accordingly, a large literature has developed in which various species of Nash equilibrium (see Moore 1992 for a recent survey) or Bayesian equilibrium (see Palfrey 1992) are appealed to instead.

One principle that this literature makes clear is that typically the more that Nash or Bayesian equilibrium is refined – i.e., the more restrictive the definition of equilibrium – the *bigger* the class of implementable collective choice rules becomes. At first this principle may seem at odds with the foregoing discussion. After all, it was precisely because insufficiently many collective choice rules were implementable in dominant strategies that the solution concept was relaxed. The paradox is resolved, however, when one notices that, in order to satisfy equation (2), not only must there be an equilibrium (a requirement which is hard to satisfy when dominant strategy equilibrium is the solution concept) but there must be no equilibrium outcomes *other* than $f(s)$ (a requirement which is more problematic for Nash and Bayesian equilibrium). By refining the Nash and Bayesian concepts (for which the existence of equilibrium is usually not a problem), there is, therefore, hope of eliminating the unwanted equilibria.

6 Moral hazard

We temporarily left actions $(a_1,\ldots,a_n)$ out of the model above in order to concentrate on pure adverse selection, but we can readily restore them to that model if these actions are *perfectly observable* to the center. Indeed, in that case we can regard $(a_1,\ldots,a_n)$ as part of the center's choice a_0, since he can simply "order"

[3] To see this, note that the first-order condition determining $x(s)$ is $\sum_{j=1}^{n}\frac{\partial v_j}{\partial x}(x(s),s) = 0$. Differentiating this identity with respect to s_i, we obtain

$$\sum_{j=1}^{n}\frac{\partial^2 v_j}{\partial x^2}\frac{\partial x}{\partial s_i}+\sum_{j=1}^{n}\frac{\partial^2 v_j}{\partial x \partial s_i}=0,$$

from which the conclusion follows.

agents to choose the desired actions. The more difficult problem arises when the a_i's are only imperfectly observable – the case of *moral hazard.*

Assume, therefore, that the center cannot observe $(a_1, ..., a_n)$ but only a noisy signal $z \in Z$. Let $q(z \mid a_1, ..., a_n)$ be the distribution of z conditional on $(a_1, ..., a_n)$. We will think of the center as choosing a_0 contingent on the realization of z. Hence, it will be convenient to suppose that the agents first (and simultaneously) choose their actions, and that then, after z is realized, the center chooses a_0. Because I wish to focus on the case of "pure" moral hazard, I will drop the signals $s = (s_1, ..., s_n)$. Hence, for $i = 0, 1, ..., n$, we can write agent i's utility as

$$\phi_i(a_0(\cdot), a_1, ..., a_n) = \sum_{z \in Z} u_i(a_0(z), a_1, ..., a_n) q(z \mid a_1, ..., a_n).$$

7 The principal-agent relationship

Suppose that $n = 1$ (so that there is just one agent) and that the center's payoff depends on a_1 only through z:

$$\phi_0(a_0(\cdot), a_1) = \sum_{z \in Z} r_0(a_0(z), z) q(z \mid a_1),$$

where $r_0(\cdot, \cdot)$ is a function of a_0 and z. Assume, finally, that A_0 consists of the real numbers and that A_1 is a set of nonnegative numbers (we can think of a_0 as a monetary transfer and a_1 as an effort level). Then we are in the standard principal-agent framework (the center is the principal).

Let us first consider the case in which the principal's and agent's payoffs are *linear* in a_0. Specifically suppose that

$$r_0(a_0, z) = z - a_0$$

and

$$u_1(a_0, a_1) = a_0 - \tfrac{1}{8} a_1,$$

where z is the output produced by the agent (and which accrues to the principal), and $a_1 \in \{0, 1\}$ (i.e., the agent can either "work" and set $a_1 = 1$, or "shirk" and set $a_1 = 0$). Let us suppose that if the agent works, there is an equal chance of high ($z = 2$) or low ($z = 0$) output. But if he shirks, output is low for sure. That is,

$$\Pr\{z = 2 \mid a_1 = 1\} = \Pr\{z = 0 \mid a_1 = 1\} = \frac{1}{2} \text{ and } \Pr\{z = 0 \mid a_1 = 0\} = 1.$$

Because expected net surplus from the agent's working $\left(\frac{1}{2} \cdot 2 - \frac{1}{8}\right)$ is positive, it is efficient for the agent to work (i.e., set $a_1 = 1$). Thus, because payoffs are linear in a_0, the Pareto frontier (the locus of Pareto optimal payoffs) is the straight line $v_0 + v_1 = \frac{7}{8}$, where v_0 and v_1 are the principal's and agent's payoffs, respectively. Now for the agent to be induced to work, his monetary payments when output is high ($a_0(2)$) or low ($a_0(0)$) must be such that

$$\frac{1}{2}a_0(2) + \frac{1}{2}a_0(0) - \frac{1}{8} \geq a_0(0). \tag{11}$$

Hence, in particular, the principal and agent can sustain the expected payoffs $\left(\frac{1}{2}, \frac{3}{8}\right)$ on the Pareto frontier by agreeing on monetary payments $a_0(2) = \frac{3}{4}$ and $a_0(0) = \frac{1}{4}$.

Next, suppose instead that the Pareto frontier is *nonlinear*. Specifically, assume that

$$\begin{aligned} r_0(a_0, z) &= z - a_0 \\ u_1(a_0, a_1) &= a_0 - \tfrac{1}{4}a_0^2 - \tfrac{1}{8}a_1, \end{aligned}$$

but that the model is otherwise the same as before. Notice that the agent is now risk-averse with respect to his monetary payment.

Observe that if $a_1 = 0$ (i.e., the agent shirks), then either the principal's or the agent's payoff must be non-positive. Hence, assuming that a player has the option not to participate if his payoff is negative, it remains efficient for the agent to work, i.e., to choose $a_1 = 1$. To derive the Pareto frontier, take $v_0 \equiv r_0(a_0, 1) = 1 - a_0$ and $v_1 \equiv u_1(a_0, 1) = a_0 - \frac{1}{4}a_0^2 - \frac{1}{8}$. Replacing a_0 by $1 - v_0$ (using the first equation) in the second equation, we obtain

$$v_1 = \frac{7}{8} - v_0 - \frac{1}{4}(1 - v_0)^2.$$

Because this curve is strictly concave, convex combination of points on the frontier lie strictly below. This implies that points on the frontier can no longer be sustained since in order to induce the agent to work it must be the case that $a_0(2) > a_0(0)$; i.e., the agent's payoff is a convex combination of two different points.

Suppose, however, that this principal-agent model is repeated infinitely many times and that players maximize their discounted sum of payoffs using discount factor δ. Then, the principal maximizes

$$E\sum_{t=0}^{\infty} \delta^t (z^t - a_0^t)$$

and the agent maximizes

$$E\sum_{t=0}^{\infty} \delta^t \left(a_0^t - (a_0^t)^2 - \frac{1}{8}a_1^t\right),$$

where, for each t, z^t is the period-t realization of z and a_0^t and a_1^t are the choices of a_0 and a_1 in period t.

Even in the repeated game, Pareto optimal points are unattainable as equilibria. To see this, note that if (v_0, v_1) are the average payoffs[4] of a Pareto optimal

[4] If $\left(v_0', v_1'\right)$ are a pair of total payoffs in the repeated game, then the corresponding average payoffs (v_0, v_1) are those that would on average have to accure every period to sum to $\left(v_0', v_1'\right)$, i.e.,

$$\left(v_0', v_1'\right) = \frac{(v_0, v_1)}{1 - \delta}.$$

perfect Bayesian equilibrium of the repeated game, then

$$(v_0, v_1) = (1-\delta)\left(v_0^1, v_1^1\right) + \delta\left(\frac{1}{2}(v_0(2), v_1(2)) + \frac{1}{2}(v_0(0), v_1(0))\right), \tag{12}$$

where (v_0^1, v_1^1) are the first period equilibrium payoffs and, for $z = 0, 2, (v_0(z), v_1(z))$ are the average continuation equilibrium payoffs (i.e., the average equilibrium payoffs starting in period 2) following the realization of output z in the first period. Now if (v_0, v_1) correspond to a Pareto optimum, then from (12), so must $\left(v_0^1, v_1^1\right)$and $\frac{1}{2}(v_0(2), v_1(2)) + \frac{1}{2}(v_0(0), v_1(0))$. But since Pareto optimality requires that the agent be induced to work in the first period, we must have $v_1(2) > v_1(0)$. Moreover, because the Pareto frontier is strictly concave, this implies that $\frac{1}{2}(v_0(2), v_1(2)) + \frac{1}{2}(v_0(0), v_1(0))$ cannot be Pareto optimal, and so neither can (v_0, v_1).

Nevertheless, as Radner (1981) and (1985) showed, any point in the *interior* of the utility possibility set (the UPS is the set of payoffs that are feasible—including those obtained by randomization—in the one-shot model), no matter how close to the Pareto frontier, can be attained as the average payoffs of a perfect Bayesian equilibrium (PBE) of the repeated game, provided that δ is near enough 1. To see this, choose small $\varepsilon > 0$ and consider the interior point $\left(\frac{1}{2} - \varepsilon, \frac{5}{16} - \varepsilon\right)$ near the Pareto optimal point $\left(\frac{1}{2}, \frac{5}{16}\right)$. Let B be the ball of radius ε around the point $\left(\frac{1}{2} - \varepsilon, \frac{5}{16} - \varepsilon\right)$. I will argue that, for δ near enough 1, any point (v_0, v_1) in B can be "decomposed" in the sense that there exist a_0^1 and

$$(v_0(2), v_1(2)), (v_0(0), v_1(0)) \in B, \tag{13}$$

such that

$$\begin{aligned}(v_0, v_1) &= (1-\delta)\left(1 - a_0^1, a_0^1 - \frac{1}{4}\left(a_0^1\right)^2 - \frac{1}{8}\right) \\ &\quad + \delta\left(\frac{1}{2}(v_0(2), v_1(2)) + \frac{1}{2}(v_0(0), v_1(0))\right)\end{aligned} \tag{14}$$

and

$$\begin{aligned}(1-\delta)&\left(a_0^1 - \frac{1}{4}\left(a_0^1\right)^2 - \frac{1}{8}\right) + \delta\left(\frac{1}{2}v_1(2) + \frac{1}{2}v_1(0)\right) \\ &\geq (1-\delta)\left(a_0^1 - \frac{1}{4}\left(a_0^1\right)^2\right) + \delta v_1(0).\end{aligned} \tag{15}$$

Establishing that, for given δ, all points in B can be decomposed according to (13)-(15) allows us to conclude that all points in B correspond to PBE's for discount factor δ. Indeed, we can iteratively *construct* the PBE corresponding to (v_0, v_1). Specifically, choose $a_0 = a_0^1$ and $a_1 = 1$ as the first-period actions. Let $(v_0(2), v_1(2))$ and $(v_0(0), v_1(0))$ be the continuation payoffs after high and low output respectively. Because (15) holds, the agent does not have the incentive to deviate from working. Hence, the first-period behavior is consistent with equilibrium. But from (13), both $(v_0(2), v_1(2))$ and $(v_0(0), v_1(0))$ can be decomposed à la (13)-(15). These decompositions will determine the equilibrium second-period behavior following high and low output. Continuing in the same way, we can derive the equilibrium behavior for all subsequent periods, thereby completing the construction.

It remains, therefore, only to show that we can actually perform the decomposition. Consider the point $\left(\frac{1}{2}, \frac{5}{16} - \varepsilon\right)$ in B. Let

$$a_0^1 = 2 - \frac{\sqrt{9 + 16\varepsilon}}{2} \tag{16}$$

and

$$(v_0(2), v_1(2)) = \left(\left(\frac{3}{2} - \delta - \frac{(1-\delta)\sqrt{9+16\varepsilon}}{2}\right)/\delta, \frac{5}{16} - \varepsilon + \frac{1-\delta}{8\delta}\right) \tag{17}$$

$$(v_0(0), v_1(0)) = \left(\left(\frac{3}{2} - \delta - \frac{(1-\delta)\sqrt{9+16\varepsilon}}{2}\right)/\delta, \frac{5}{16} - \varepsilon - \frac{1-\delta}{8\delta}\right). \tag{18}$$

Simple substitution verifies that (14) and (15) hold when the values given by (16)-(18) are used. As for (13), note that, because B is a ball, the vertical distance from the point $p = \left(\left(\frac{3}{2} - \delta - \frac{(1-\delta)\sqrt{9+16\varepsilon}}{2}\right)/\delta, \frac{5}{16} - \varepsilon\right)$ to B's boundary is on the order of the *square root* of the horizontal distance x from p to $\left(\frac{1}{2}, \frac{5}{16} - \varepsilon\right)$, if x is small (see Fig. 1). But $x = \frac{1-\delta}{2\delta}\left(\sqrt{9+16\varepsilon} - 3\right)$ and so, as δ tends to 1, x does indeed become small. Furthermore, the vertical distance from $(v_0(2), v_1(2))$ or $(v_0(0), v_1(0))$ to p is $\frac{1-\delta}{8\delta}$, which (for δ near 1) is of the same order as x, and hence less than $\sqrt{x}$. Hence for δ near 1, $(v_0(2), v_1(2))$ and $(v_0(0), v_1(0))$ lie in B.

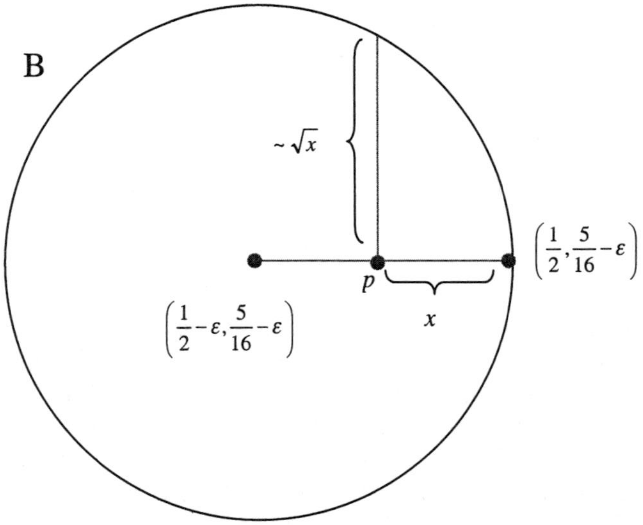

Fig. 1. Decomposition of $\left(\frac{1}{2}, \frac{5}{16} - \epsilon\right)$

We have shown, therefore, that $\left(\frac{1}{2}, \frac{5}{16} - \varepsilon\right)$ can indeed be decomposed for δ near 1. The argument is similar for the other points of B. Hence repetition permits points that are nearly efficient to be attained as equilibria.

To summarize, for the agent to be induced to work in a one-shot principal-agent relationship, his monetary payment contingent on output must be variable. This variability has no adverse consequences if the agent is risk-neutral, but interferes with Pareto optimality if he is risk-averse. Once the relationship is repeated, the agent's monetary payment no longer need be made variable; the agent can be "punished" or "rewarded" through variations in his continuation payoff. Furthermore, if δ is near 1, not much variation in these payoffs is required to provide adequate incentive —so the equilibrium shortfall from Pareto optimality is correspondingly small. That is, repetition allows us to exploit the fact that the Pareto frontier is *locally* linear.

8 Partnerships

Next let $n = 2$ but eliminate agent 0 (the center), so that we are now in a partnership (double moral hazard) framework, i.e., neither agent can observe the other's action. In this setting, an efficient outcome may be impossible to implement even if the Pareto frontier is linear. Specifically, consider the following model based on an example in Fudenberg et al. (1994). Suppose that each player's action a_i can equal w ("work") or s ("shirk"). Working imposes a disutility of 3, whereas shirking is costless. There are two possible output levels, $z = 0$ and $z = 12$. If both players work, the probability that $z = 12$ is $\frac{2}{3}$; if only one works the probability is $\frac{1}{3}$; and if neither works it is 0. Output is divisible and can be allocated in any way between the two agents. Agent i's utility is

$$z_i - d_i(a_i),$$

where z_i is his share of total output and $d_i(a_i)$ is his disutility from action a_i (i.e., either 0 or 3).

It is easy to verify that it is efficient for both agents to work and that the Pareto frontier is the straight line $v_1 + v_2 = 2$. Despite the linear preferences, however, no point on the frontier is implementable. To see this, note that to induce player i to work (given that the other player is working), his shares – $z_i(12)$ and $z_i(0)$ – of the output when $z = 12$ and $z = 0$ must satisfy

$$\frac{2}{3}z_i(12) + \frac{1}{3}z_i(0) - 3 \geq \frac{1}{3}z_i(12) + \frac{2}{3}z_i(0).$$

Hence

$$z_i(12) - z_i(0) \geq 9 \qquad i = 1, 2. \tag{19}$$

Adding the two inequalities (19) together, we obtain

$$12 \geq 18,$$

a contradiction. Thus efficiency is not implementable.

Informally, to induce an agent to work, the difference between the outputs allocated to him in the high and low states must be sufficiently big (9, to be precise, and therefore 18 if we add the two agents' differences together). But the difference between high and low total output is only 12. So to get both agents to work, output has to be "thrown away" in the low state, i.e., output must be reduced to -6, which is inefficient. An alternative to throwing away output is to resurrect the center (agent 0). Imagine that this agent chips in two units of output in the high state and takes away 4 in the low state. Then, agents 1 and 2 can be induced to work without any expected efficiency loss (the center breaks even on average: $\frac{2}{3}2 - \frac{1}{3}4 = 0$). This is basically Holmström's (1982) interpretation of the Alchian and Demsetz (1972) rationale for separation of ownership and management in corporations: the owner can serve as a "budget-breaker" in setting up an efficient incentive scheme for managers.

In studying the principal-agent model above, we noted that the value of repeating the game was to exploit the fact that a concave frontier is still locally linear. In our partnership example, however, efficiency is not implementable even when the frontier is linear. Consequently, it should not be surprising that repetition does not help to restore efficiency. Indeed, the partnership example is closely related to one used by Radner et al. (1986) to illustrate the potential inefficiency of repeated game equilibria when there is double moral hazard.

The inefficiency in our partnership example, however, turns out to depend crucially on the fact that there are only two possible observable outcomes (this is true as well of the Radner-Myerson-Maskin example). Indeed let us now modify the model so that there are three possible output levels, $z = 12, 8, 0$. If both agents work, the probability distribution over these levels is $\left(\frac{1}{3}, \frac{1}{2}, \frac{1}{6}\right)$. If agent 1 shirks and 2 works, the distribution is $\left(\frac{1}{3}, 0, \frac{2}{3}\right)$. If 1 works and 2 shirks, it is $\left(0, \frac{1}{2}, \frac{1}{2}\right)$, and if both shirk it is $(0, 0, 1)$.

Once again, it is efficient for both agents to work, and the Pareto frontier is described by $v_1 + v_2 = 2$. In this case, however, it is possible to implement any point on the frontier. Specifically, suppose we let $z_2(12) = 12$, $z_1(8) = 8$, and set all the other allocations equal to zero. That is, we give agent 2 all the output when $z = 12$ and agent 1 all the output when $z = 8$. It is straightforward to verify that (w, w), i.e. both agents working, is an equilibrium:

$$\frac{1}{3}0 + \frac{1}{2}8 + \frac{1}{6}0 - 3 \geq \frac{1}{3}0 + \frac{2}{3}0 \tag{20}$$

and

$$\frac{1}{3}12 + \frac{1}{2}0 + \frac{1}{6}0 - 3 \geq \frac{1}{2}0 + \frac{1}{2}0. \tag{21}$$

Intuitively, it makes sense to allocate agent 1 all the output when $z = 8$: if he had shirked, such an output level would not have been possible; and so the allocation serves as an effective inducement for his working; similarly, assigning agent 2 all the output when $z = 12$ is a good way to reward *him* for working.

Mathematically, the virtue of having sufficiently many output levels (in this case, 3) is that we can satisfy incentive constraints (20) and (21) together with the efficiency conditions

$$\begin{aligned} z_1(0) + z_2(0) &= 0 \\ z_1(8) + z_2(8) &= 8 \\ z_1(12) + z_2(12) &= 12 \end{aligned}$$

simultaneously. More generally, Radner and Williams (1988) and Legros (1988) showed that, as long as agents utilities are linear in output, then for generic partnership games where the number of output levels is at least $m_1 + m_2 - 1$ (where m_i is the number of actions in A_i), efficiency is implementable. As Fudenberg et al. (1994) showed, a similar result obtains for a repeated partnership (with δ near 1) without the hypothesis that the Pareto frontier is linear.

9 Conclusion

Roy Radner once expressed the wish that a book as elegant as Debreu's (1957) analysis of competitive markets might one day be written about nonmarket institutions (specifically, the large firm). His own work on teams and incentives (not to mention his many contributions to our understanding of information, and organizational structure) constitutes a good start toward making that wish come true.

References

Abreu, D., Pearce, D., Stacchetti, E. (1986) Optimal cartel equilibria with imperfect monitoring. *Journal of Economic Theory* 39: 251–269

Alchian, A., Demsetz, H. (1972) Production, information costs and economic organization. *American Economic Review* 62: 777–795

Chandler, A. (1977) *The Visible Hand: The Managerial Revolution in American Business.* Harvard University Press, Cambridge

Dasgupta, P., Hammond, P., Maskin, E. (1979) The implementation of social choice rules: Some general results on incentive compatibility. *Review of Economic Studies* 46: 185–216

Fudenberg, D., Levine, D., Maskin, E. (1994) The folk theorem with imperfect public information. *Econometrica* 62: 997–1039

Gibbard, A. (1973) Manipulation of voting schemes: A general result. *Econometrica* 41: 587–601

Green, J., Laffont, J.-J. (1979) *Incentives in Public Decision-Making*. North-Holland, Amsterdam

Groves, T. (1973) Incentives in teams. *Econometrica* 41: 617–631

Holmström, B. (1982) Moral hazard in teams. *Bell Journal of Economics* 13: 324–340

Hurwicz, L. (1972) On informationally decentralized systems. In: McGuire, C.B., Radner, R. (eds.) *Decision and Organization*. North-Holland, Amsterdam

Laffont, J.-J., Maskin, E. (1980) A differential approach to dominant strategy mechanisms. *Econometrica* 48: 1507–1520

Laffont, J.-J., Maskin, E. (1982) The theory of incentives: An overview. In: Hildenbrand, W. (ed.) *Advances in Economic Theory*. Cambridge University Press, Cambridge

Legros, P. (1988) Sustainability in partnerships. Mimeo, California Institute of Technology

Marschak, J., Radner, R. (1972) *Economic Theory of Teams*. Yale University Press, New Haven

Moore, J. (1992) Implementation in Environments with Complete Information. In: J.-J. Laffont (ed.) *Advances in Economic Theory*. Cambridge University Press, Cambridge

Palfrey, T. (1992) Implementation in Bayesian Equilibrium: the Multiple Equilibrium Problem in Mechanism Design. In: J.-J. Laffont (ed.) *Advances in Economic Theory*. Cambridge University Press, Cambridge

Radner, R. (1981) Monitoring cooperatirve agreements in a repeated principal-agent relationship. *Econometrica* 49: 1127–1148

Radner, R. (1985) Repeated principal agent games with discounting. *Econometrica* 53: 1173–1198
Radner, R., Myerson, R., Maskin, E. (1986) An example of a repeated partnership game with discounting and with uniformly inefficient equilibria. *Review of Economic Studies* 53: 59–70
Radner, R., Williams, S. (1988) Informational externalities and the scope of efficient dominant strategy mechanisms. Mimeo
Rubinstein, A., Yaari, M. (1983) Repeated insurance contracts and moral hazard. *Journal of Economic Theory* 30: 74–97
Satterthwaite, M. (1975) Strategy-proofness and arrow's conditions: Existence and correspondence theorems for voting procedures and social welfare functions. *Journal of Economic Theory* 10: 187–217
Williams, S., Radner, R. (1988) Efficiency in partnership when the joint output is uncertain. Mimeo

Sufficient conditions for Nash implementation

Steven R. Williams

Department of Economics, The University of Illinois, Champaign, IL 61820, USA
(e-mail: swillia3@uiuc.edu)

Abstract. Given an objective for a group of three or more agents that satisfies monotonicity and no veto power, Maskin (1977) proposes a two-step procedure for constructing a game that implements the objective in Nash equilibrium. The first step specifies the strategy set of the game and three properties of the game rule that are together sufficient to insure Nash implementation of the objective. The second step is the explicit construction of a game that has these properties. An example is presented here that shows that the constructed game of the second step need not have one of the three properties of the first step, and it does in fact not Nash implement the objective in the example. The problem is attributable to restricted preferences. A solution proposed here is to appropriately expand the domain of definition of the objective. This insures that the constructed game has the properties of the game in Maskin's first step, and it therefore Nash implements the original objective.

1 Introduction

Given an objective for a group of three or more agents that satisfies *monotonicity* and *no veto power*, Maskin (1977)[1] presents a two-step procedure for constructing a game that implements the objective in Nash equilibrium. The first step defines the strategy set of a game and three properties of the game rule. Maskin's Theorem 4 proves that a game with these properties implements the given objective in Nash equilibrium. The second step is Maskin's Theorem 5, which explicitly constructs a game that satisfies the hypotheses of his Theorem 4.

This research was partially supported by National Science Foundation Grant No. IST-8308283. I thank Leonid Hurwicz for his encouragement and his assistance in developing the example that is presented in Section 3. I also thank Tatsuyoshi Saijo and a referee of this paper for their comments. Finally, I thank Tom Marschak and Tatsuro Ichiishi for their patience and their suggestions as I prepared this paper for publication.

[1] This paper has been published in a revised form as Maskin (1999).

The two theorems together form a constructive proof that monotonicity and no veto power are sufficient conditions in the case of at least three agents for Nash implementation of an objective.

I show in this paper that the game constructed in Maskin's Theorem 5 does not necessarily have one of the three properties that are required by his Theorem 4. An example is presented in which the game constructed in Maskin's Theorem 5 in fact fails to Nash implement a given objective to which it should apply. One way in which this problem is addressed in the literature is by enlarging the strategy set of the game in Maskin's Theorem 4. This, however, has led to some rather odd games for demonstrating Nash implementation. The failure of Maskin's game to necessarily satisfy all three of the properties required for his Theorem 4 can be attributed to restricted preferences. The solution proposed here is to suitably expand the domain of definition of the objective. The main ideas of Maskin's Theorem 5 then guide the construction of a game that has all of the properties required by his Theorem 4, and so it Nash implements the extended objective. It therefore also Nash implements the original objective. This completes a proof that monotonicity and no veto power are sufficient conditions for Nash implementation of an objective in the case of at least three agents.[2]

History. I wrote this paper in the spring of 1984 while working as a postdoctoral fellow at the Institute for Mathematics and Its Applications in Minneapolis. Leonid Hurwicz organized the program of the institute that year and the topic (not surprisingly) was mechanism design. A major subject of interest was the relatively new problem of incorporating incentives into the design of mechanisms. Given the limits that had been demonstrated by Gibbard (1972), Satterthwaite (1975), and others on the objectives that can be accomplished using the dominant strategy solution concept, the possibility of implementing objectives in Nash equilibrium was of particular interest. The problem of Nash implementation had been recently formulated and addressed in Maskin (1977).

In Williams (1984a, 1986), I merged Maskin's theory of Nash implementation with the theory of mechanisms as formulated by Hurwicz (1960, 1972). This second line of research has mostly focused on the ways in which agents can economize in communication in achieving a common objective. The emphasis has been upon the design of the *message space* (or language) for communication, with less emphasis upon the incentives of the agents in selecting their messages. By combining the two approaches, I showed how a message space that is sufficiently rich to *realize* (or compute) a given objective can be used to construct a mechanism that Nash implements the objective. This addressed a shortcoming of the game that Maskin outlined in his Theorem 4, namely that each agent is required to announce his preferences and the preferences of all other agents. Such announcements are unrealistic in most economic settings, where economizing on communication is in fact an important feature of the mechanism.[3] I showed how

[2] As discussed below, this statement assumes that the objective satisfies surjectivity and that the set of alternatives satisfies property (7).

[3] A commonly cited example is Hayek's contention that the competitive mechanism is informationally efficient relative to centralized economic systems. Informational efficiency here refers to

any economizing on communication in the message space that is used to realize an objective translates into a savings on communication in the strategy space of the game that Nash implements the objective.[4]

This result is proven by first constructing a message process that realizes the objective and then following the outline of Maskin's construction in his Theorems 4 and 5, substituting the messages for preference announcements. I discovered several flaws in Maskin's construction as I tried to use it in my proof. First, *surjectivity* of the objective[5] and *finiteness* of the set of alternatives are assumptions that Maskin used in his proof of his Theorem 5 without explicitly stating them as assumptions. Surjectivity seems innocuous because one can always restrict attention to those alternatives that are actually assigned. The designation of the set of alternatives, however, plays a key role in determining whether or not the objective is monotonic. An objective can be monotonic when some large set is considered as the set of alternatives but not when some smaller set is used. I avoid this issue in Williams (1984a, 1986) and in this paper by simply adding surjectivity as a hypothesis. The finiteness assumption was at odds with the goal of my research, for economizing on communication is most interesting when the set of alternatives and the preferences over that set can be rich. I added a very general mapping condition (stated as (7) below) on the set of alternatives to avoid assuming that it is finite.

Even in the case considered by Maskin, however, in which the set of alternatives is finite and the objective satisfies surjectivity, problems remained with the logical correctness of the proof of his Theorem 4. In Williams (1984a, 1986), I added an assumption on the cardinality of the preimage of any alternative, which appears as (8) below. Roughly, condition (8) requires that each alternative is assigned to at least three distinct profiles of the agents' preferences. This is a sufficient condition that insures that the game constructed in Maskin's Theorem 4 has all of the properties required by his Theorem 5. It therefore Nash implements the objective. Leo Hurwicz encouraged me to make my criticism of Maskin's proof more concrete by demonstrating an objective that Maskin's game fails to implement in Nash equilibrium. He and I began by considering majority rule with $n \geq 3$ agents when preferences are restricted in a particular way. This objective satisfies monotonicity, no veto power, and surjectivity, and the set of alternatives in the example is finite. Leo had to leave for an appointment and

communication among consumers and firms using prices and proposed trades, which is parsimonious in comparison to all that consumers know concerning their preferences and all that firms know concerning their production processes. Much of Hurwicz's work on mechanism design was motivated by the goal of formalizing this insight.

[4] In Maskin's defense, his game is universal in the sense that it shows how to Nash implement any objective that can be implemented in this sense; economizing on communication typically involves exploiting features of the particular objective, which was true of my paper. As he noted at the time, his game represents an *a priori* upper bound on the communication requirements of Nash implementation.

[5] That is, every social alternative is assigned to some profile of agents' preferences. Otherwise, Maskin's game need not satisfy hypothesis (5) of Theorem 1 below.

so I completed the proof that game constructed in Maskin's Theorem 5 does not implement this objective in Nash equilibrium.

The contributions of this paper. The example appears below in Section 3. It is then shown in Section 4 that the additional assumption (8) on the objective, while sufficient to complete Maskin's argument, is not in fact needed to prove the sufficiency of no veto power and monotonicity for Nash implementation in the case of $n \geq 3$ agents. With no veto power and at least three agents, (8) holds if preferences are unrestricted. A failure of (8) is thus attributable to restricted preferences. Zorn's Lemma is applied to prove that any objective satisfying monotonicity and no veto power can be extended over a larger domain of preferences so that the extension retains these two properties but also satisfies (8). Maskin's method then defines a game that Nash implements this extended objective, which also implements the original objective when restricted to the original set of environments. Property (8) is thus not needed for Nash implementation.

The paper that follows made two contributions. First, by identifying some flaws in Maskin's proof, it contributed to making the theory of Nash implementation mathematically rigorous, clear, and accessible.[6] The problem of Nash implementation is fundamental and it has a precise mathematical formulation. It therefore warrants a careful and complete analysis. The paper that follows complemented Maskin (1977) and advanced the research program that was posed by this seminal work. The scrutiny of Maskin's paper that follows below reflects the esteem that I have for this work and the intellectual stimulation that I received from it: lesser work is not worthy of such a careful examination. I must also add that I have grown to appreciate the scope and the difficulty of Maskin's paper as I revised this paper, which concerns only one of his results.

Second, the use of Zorn's Lemma to expand the domain of an objective is a useful technique for addressing problems that arise due to restricted preferences. The literature on Nash implementation has mostly avoided assumptions such as (8) by instead expanding the size of the strategy space. Maskin's construction had each agent announce a profile of preferences for all of the agents along with an alternative that is assigned by the objective to that profile. He deemed this appropriate for a general game for Nash implementation in that it reflects the fact that Nash equilibrium is commonly motivated by assuming that the agents have complete information concerning each other's preferences. This intuition vanishes as additional information is announced by each agent, especially if that information has no meaning in context of the model (e.g., the announcement of an integer by each agent in addition to a profile of preferences and an alter-

[6] In particular, Williams (1984a and b) were the starting point for Saijo (1988), which is a notable paper for at least two reasons. First, it contains one of the first proofs that monotonicity and no veto power are sufficient for Nash implementation when there are at least three agents that was both published and logically complete. Saijo used neither assumption (8) of the paper below nor surjectivity of the objective in his proof. Second, his proof does not follow the outline of Maskin's construction, and it therefore represents an alternative approach. In particular, it uses a smaller strategy set for each agent than Maskin's construction. It thereby reveals that complete reporting of every agent's preferences by each agent is never necessary for Nash implementation (as has sometimes been suggested in the literature).

native, which has been common in the literature).[7] The games that have been constructed over the years to solve Nash implementation problems became increasingly unrealistic as the strategy sets of the agents were enlarged more and more to facilitate the construction. A virtue of the construction in the final section of this paper is that it uses the original strategy space of Maskin (1977), with the caveat that agents may now announce preference profiles that are inadmissable in the original problem. Zorn's Lemma may thus prove useful as a tool for avoiding the odd strategy spaces that have sometimes been concocted to solve implementation problems when preferences are restricted.

2 Notation and fundamentals

There are $n \geq 3$ agents. For each $1 \leq j \leq n$, E_j is a nonempty set whose elements describe the possible characteristics of the jth agent. The product $E = \prod_{i=1}^{n} E_i$ is the *set of environments*. Let $e = (e_i)_{1 \leq i \leq n}$ be an arbitrary element of E. The set A is the *set of alternatives*. To avoid the trivial case, A is assumed to have more than one element. For every $1 \leq j \leq n$, each $e_j \in E_j$ defines a complete preordering on A.[8] This represents agent j's preferences over A when his characteristics are determined by e_j. No assumption is imposed concerning the size of the set of preorderings that is obtained as e_j varies over E_j. The notation $a(>, e_j)b$ means that agent j with characteristics e_j prefers alternative a to alternative b and $a(\geq, e_j)b$ means that this agent either prefers a to b or is indifferent between them. $L(a, e_j)$ is the *lower contour set* of $a \in A$ when preferences are determined by e_j:

$$L(a, e_j) = \{b \in A | a(\geq, e_j)b\}.$$

The alternative $a \in A$ is a *top-ranked alternative* for agent j with characteristics e_j if $L(a, e_j) = A$.

A *game* is a pair (S, g) consisting of a product $S = \prod_{i=1}^{n} S_i$ and a mapping $g{:}\prod_{i=1}^{n} S_i \to A$. The product S is the *strategy set* of the game and S_j is *agent j's strategy set*. The mapping g is the *game rule*. A *Nash equilibrium* of (S, g) for the environment e is a point $s^* = (s_i^*)_{1 \leq i \leq n} \in S$ such that

$$\{a \in A | a = g(s_j, s_{-j}^*), s_j \in S_j\} \subset L(g(s^*), e_j)$$

for each agent j. Here, (s_j, s_{-j}^*) denotes the element of S obtained by starting with s^* and changing the jth component from s_j^* to s_j.

An *objective* is any correspondence F from E to A whose value at any environment is a nonempty subset of A. F is *surjective* if there exists for any $a \in A$ an environment e such that $a \in F(e)$. Let $\tau : E \to S$ denote the

[7] This is true even of the game that Saijo (1988) constructs in his alternative to Maskin's proof: each agent i in his game announces preferences for himself and those of agent $i + 1$, along with an alternative and an integer.

[8] See, for instance, Debreu (1959, p. 8).

correspondence whose value at e is the set of all Nash equilibria for e. The game (S, g) *implements* F in Nash equilibrium if

$$g \circ \tau(e) = F(e)$$

for every $e \in E$.

Turning next to the sufficient conditions for Nash implementation, the objective F is *monotonic* if for any $e, e' \in E$ and $a \in F(e)$,

$$L(a, e_j) \subset L(a, e_j') \text{ for each value of } j \Rightarrow a \in F(e'). \tag{1}$$

Statement (1) depends upon which set A is designated as the set of alternatives because A has a role in determining the lower contour sets. The objective F satisfies *no veto power* if for all $a \in A$ and $e \in E$,

$$L(a, e_j) = A \text{ for all but at most one value of } j \Rightarrow a \in F(e).$$

A discussion of each of these properties can be found in Maskin (1985).

As discussed in the Introduction, Maskin's construction of a game that Nash implements an objective is in two steps: step 1 establishes a set of conditions on a game (S, g) that are sufficient to insure that it Nash implements a given objective, and step 2 explicitly constructs a game with these properties. Step 1 is provided by the following theorem. The outline (2)–(5) below for the desired game was originally proposed by Karl Vind (Groves (1979, p. 44)).

Theorem 1 (Maskin 1977, Theorem 4). *For $n \geq 3$, let $F : \prod_{i=1}^{n} E_i \to A$ be an objective that satisfies monotonicity and no veto power. Suppose that a game (S, g) exists with the following four properties.*

1. Each agent j's strategy set is

$$S_j \equiv \{(e, a) \in E \times A | a \in F(e)\}. \tag{2}$$

2. The game rule g has the following three properties at $s = (s_i)_{1 \leq i \leq n} \in S$:

$$\text{if each } s_i = (e, a), \text{ then } g(s) = a; \tag{3}$$

$$\text{if } s_\ell = (e, a) \text{ for all } \ell \neq j, \text{ then } g(\cdot, s_{-j}) \text{ maps } S_j \text{ onto } L(a, e_j); \tag{4}$$

$$\text{if } s_\ell \neq s_j \text{ and } k \neq \ell, j, \text{ then } g(\cdot, s_{-k}) \text{ maps } S_k \text{ onto } A. \tag{5}$$

The game (S, g) implements F in Nash equilibrium.

The proof below follows the argument in Maskin (1977). I include it here so that the role of each of the properties (3)–(5) of (S, g) in the Nash implementation of F is clear to the reader.

Proof. Let $\tau : E \to S$ be the Nash equilibrium correspondence for (S, g) and let $a \in F(e^*)$. Properties (3)–(4) imply that the strategy profile $s = (s_i)_{1 \leq i \leq n}$ such that $s_i = (e^*, a)$ for each agent i is a Nash equilibrium for the environment e^*. Therefore,

$$F(e^*) \subset g \circ \tau \left(e^*\right).$$

It remains to be shown that $g(s) \in F(e^*)$ if $s \in \tau(e^*)$. The argument is made in two cases. Suppose first that each $s_i = (e, a)$. Assumption (4) implies that each agent j can implement any element of $L(a, e_j)$ by varying his strategy. The assumption that $s \in \tau(e^*)$ implies

$$L(a, e_j) \subset L(a, e_j^*)$$

for each agent j. Definition (2) of S implies $a \in F(e)$, and so monotonicity implies $g(s) = a \in F(e^*)$.

Alternatively, suppose that $s_\ell \neq s_j$ for some l, j. Property (5) implies

$$g(S_k, s_{-k}) = A \tag{6}$$

for all $k \neq j, l$. Either (i) $s_l \neq s_k$ or (ii) $s_j \neq s_k$ for at least one value of $k \neq j, l$. If (i) holds, then (5) implies $g(S_j, s_{-j}) = A$; if (ii) holds, then (5) implies $g(S_l, s_{-l}) = A$. In either case, (6) holds for at least $n - 1$ values of k. The assumption that s is a Nash equilibrium for e^* implies

$$A = g(S_k, s_{-k}) \subset L(g(s), e_k^*)$$

for all $n - 1$ of these agents, from which $g(s) \in F(e^*)$ follows by no veto power. □

Step 2 for constructing a game that Nash implements F is stated here as a special case of Theorem 3 of Williams (1986), as applied to a revelation mechanism for realizing F. Let $F^{-1}(a) \equiv \{e | a \in F(e)\}$.

Theorem 2 (Williams 1986, Theorem 3). *Let* $F : \prod_{i=1}^n E_i \to A$ *be surjective, where* $n \geq 3$. *If* F *has the following properties, then there exists a game* (S, g) *that implements* F *in Nash equilibrium:*

1. *F is monotonic;*
2. *F satisfies no veto power;*
3. *There exists a mapping P_A from A^n to A such that for $(a_i^*)_{1 \leq i \leq n} \in A^n$ and for each value of j,*

$$P_A(\cdot, a_{-j}^*) : A \to A \text{ is surjective.} \tag{7}$$

4. *for any $a \in A$,*

$$\left|F^{-1}(a)\right| \geq 2 \text{ if } n \geq 4 \text{ and } \left|F^{-1}(a)\right| \geq 3 \text{ if } n = 3. \tag{8}$$

Theorem 2 is proven by constructing a game (S, g) that satisfies the hypotheses of Theorem 1 above, which then implies the desired result. The construction follows the method invented by Maskin (1977) in his proof of his Theorem 5, with modifications to avoid the assumption that A is finite and corrections for errors. The strategy set S is defined by (2), and (3) specifies $g(s)$ whenever each agent selects the same strategy. The game rule g is defined in Williams (1986, eq. (19)) as follows to insure that (5) holds:

$$\textit{if } s_j = (e^*, a^*),\ s_\ell = (e, a) \text{ for } \ell \neq j, \text{ and } s_j \neq s_l, \text{ then} \quad (9)$$

$$g(s) = \begin{cases} a^* \text{ if } a^* \in L(a, e_j) \\ a \text{ otherwise} \end{cases}. \quad (10)$$

The construction is completed in Williams (1986, eq. (21)) by defining $g(s)$ as follows at profiles s that cannot be reached by first having every agent select the same strategy and then having a single agent deviate: letting $a^{(j)}$ denote the alternative selected by the jth agent in such a strategy profile s,

$$g(s) = P_A(a^{(1)}, \ldots, a^{(n)}). \quad (11)$$

As noted above, Maskin (1977) assumes that A is a finite set,

$$A = \{a_0, \ldots, a_{m-1}\}. \quad (12)$$

For any choice of $e_j \in E_j$ and $a_t \in A$, the set $L(a_t, e_j)$ is also finite and can be represented as[9]

$$L(a_t, e_j) = \{a_{0,e_j}, \ldots, a_{m(a,e_j)-1,e_j}\}, \quad (13)$$

where $m(a_t, e_j) \equiv |L(a_t, e_j)|$. Let $\delta(j)$ denote the index of the alternative in the jth agent's strategy.[10] Maskin (1977, eq. (7)) defines g as follows when (9) holds:[11]

$$\begin{aligned} \textit{if } s_j &= (e^*, a_{\delta(j)}),\ s_\ell = (e, a_t) \text{ for } \ell \neq j, \text{ and } s_j \neq s_l, \text{ then} \\ g(s) &= a_{k,e_j} \in L(a_t, e_j), \text{ where } k = \delta(j) + t \pmod{m(a_t, e_j)}. \end{aligned} \quad (14)$$

Either (10) or (14) insures that g satisfies property (4) of Theorem 1. While more complicated than (10), (14) is used in Section 3 for the legitimacy of the example. Using (10) instead would not, however, correct the problem that the example illustrates.

For the strategies profiles to which (11) applies, Maskin (1977, eq. (8)) uses addition modulo m as his mapping P_A:

---

[9] I surpress the dependence of the numbering in (13) upon the subscript t of a_t in order to keep the notation as simple as possible. This will not be an issue in the remainder of the paper.

[10] The distinction made here is between a superscript (j) that indexes the alternative announced by agent j and a subscript $\delta(j)$ that indicates the alternative in A that he announces: agent j announces the alternative $a^{(j)}$, which is the element $a_{\delta(j)}$ in eq. (12) for A.

[11] There is a misprint in some versions of Maskin (1977). The formula for $g(\bar{s}_1, \ldots \bar{s}_n)$ in his (7) should be $g(\bar{s}_1, \ldots, \bar{s}_n) = b([r+s]|m(a(r), \bar{R}_i); a, \bar{R}_i)$. It is clear that this is intended by comparing (7) to hypothesis (4) of his Theorem 4 (p. 19).

$$g(s) = a_k \text{ where } k = \sum_{j=1}^{n} \delta(j) \pmod{m}. \tag{15}$$

Assumption 3 in the above theorem simply assumes that a mapping P_A with the needed property exists, whatever the cardinality of the set A.[12]

The only property of the game (S, g) that is not immediate is (5), which asserts that if two agents select distinct strategies, then any third agent can implement any alternative by varying his strategy. Surjectivity of F and (8) were added in Williams (1986) specifically to address this point. Surjectivity implies that every alternative may be announced by each agent j, which insures that S_j is sufficiently large so that $P_A(S_j, s_{-j}) = A$ is possible. Condition (8) on the cardinality of $F^{-1}(a)$ is the focus of this paper.[13] Without this assumption, the game rule that is constructed in Maskin (1977, Theorem 5) or Williams (1986, Theorem 3) does not necessarily satisfy property (5). This is addressed in Williams (1986, p. 150), and it is illustrated by the example that follows in Section 3 below.

To clarify the problem, consider first the special case of $n = 3$ agents. Suppose that

$$s_1 = (e', a') \neq s_2 = (e'', a'') \tag{16}$$

as in (5) and let $s_3 = (e''', a''')$. Formula (11) defines

$$g(s_1, s_2, s_3) = P_A(a', a'', a'''), \tag{17}$$

whenever s_1, s_2 and s_3 are distinct. If (17) held for all s_3, then (7) insures that (5) holds. Defining g in this way, however, may conflict with defining g so that (4) holds. At issue is $g(s_1, s_2, s_3)$ for $s_3 = s_1$ or $s_3 = s_2$, in which case (17) cannot be applied blindly. The game rule g may thus fail to satisfy (5), for $g(s_1, s_2, S_3)$ may not include $P_A(a', a'', a')$ and $P_A(a', a'', a'')$.

To understand how (8) resolves this problem, assume first that $s_3 = s_1 = (e', a')$. Property (8) guarantees that there exists at least three environments e such that $a' \in F(e)$. Consequently, such an environment e can be chosen so that e, e', and e'' are distinct. Equation (17) applies to compute $g(s_1, s_2, s_3)$ for s_1 and s_2 as above and $s_3^* = (e, a')$:

$$g(s_1, s_2, s_3^*) = P_A(a', a'', a') \in g(s_1, s_2, S_3),$$

as desired for the sake of (5). A similar argument shows that $P_A(a', a'', a'') \in g(s_1, s_2, S_3)$.

In the case of $n \geq 4$ agents, Formula (11) defines

---

[12] Assumption 3 is satisfied whenever A can be given the structure of a group (e.g., when A is finite, countable, or even a Banach space). It can also hold when A does not have an obvious group structure. While I am not aware of results that show that this property holds for an arbitrary set A, I also know of no examples in which it does not hold.

[13] In Williams (1984a, Theorem 7), it is shown that (8) can be replaced in Theorem 2 with the assumption that for any $a \in A$ and $e_j \in E_j$ the set

$$\{b \in A | b(>, e_j)a\}$$

is either empty or contains at least three elements.

$$g(s) = P_A(a^{(1)}, \ldots, a^{(n)}) \tag{18}$$

whenever s cannot be obtained by starting at a diagonal element of S at which each agent announces the same pair (e, a) and then having a single agent deviate. In (18), $a^{(i)}$ denotes the alternative announced by the ith agent. Again, suppose that s_1 and s_2 satisfy (16) and fix the values of $s_4, \ldots, s_n$. If either

$$s_1 = s_4 = \ldots = s_n \tag{19}$$

or

$$s_2 = s_4 = \ldots = s_n \tag{20}$$

does not hold, then (18) defines $g(s)$ for all s_3 and (7) insures that

$$g(s_1, s_2, S_3, s_4, \ldots, s_n) = A. \tag{21}$$

If (19) holds, then (7) does not imply (21) because (18) does not define g at $s_3 = s_1$. At issue is whether or not

$$P_A\left(a', a'', a', \ldots, a'\right) \in g(s_1, s_2, S_3, s_4, \ldots, s_n). \tag{22}$$

Property (8) insures that there exists at least two environments e such that $a' \in F(e)$. Select one that is distinct from e'. Setting $s_3^* = (e, a')$, the strategy profile $(s_1, s_2, s_3^*, s_1, \ldots, s_1)$ can be reached only by having at least two agents deviate from a diagonal element of S. Formula (18) defines

$$g(s_1, s_2, s_3^*, s_4, \ldots, s_n) = P_A\left(a', a'', a', \ldots, a'\right),$$

which verifies (22). A similar argument addresses the case in which (20) holds, which completes the argument that (21) holds when $n \geq 4$.

3 The example

The construction in Theorem 5 of Maskin (1977) is applied in this section to an objective that satisfies all of the hypotheses of Theorem 2 except (8). The constructed game neither satisfies (5) nor implements the objective in Nash equilibrium.

There are three agents and two alternatives – $A = \{a_0, a_1\}$. For $j = 2, 3$, $E_j = \{>, <\}$, where " $>$ " means a_0 is strictly preferred to a_1 and " $<$ " means a_1 is strictly preferred to a_0. E_1 contains a single element – $E_1 = \{>\}$.

The objective F is determined by majority rule. For $e = (e_1, e_2, e_3) \in \prod_{i=1}^{3} E_i$,

$$F(e) = \begin{cases} a_1 & \textit{if } e_2, e_3 =< \\ a_0 & \textit{otherwise} \end{cases}.$$

It is easy to verify that F satisfies both monotonicity and no veto power, and F is clearly surjective. F does not satisfy (8) since $F^{-1}(a_1)$ is a singleton.

Maskin's game has $\prod_{i=1}^{3} S_i$ as its strategy space, where

$$S_i = \{(e, a) \,|a \in F(e)\}.$$

The game rule g is defined as follows at $s = (s_1, s_2, s_3)$:

$$\text{if } s_1 = s_2 = s_3 = (e, a_t), \text{ then } g(s) = a_t; \tag{23}$$

$$\begin{aligned} \text{if } s_i &= s_j = (e, a_t) \neq s_k = (e^*, a_u), \quad \text{then} \\ g(s) &= \begin{cases} a_t & \text{if } L(a_t, e_k) = \{a_t\} \\ a_{t+u(\text{mod } 2)} & \text{if } L(a_t, e_k) = A \end{cases} ; \end{aligned} \tag{24}$$

$$\begin{aligned} &\text{if } s_i = (e, a_t), s_j = (\overline{e}, a_v), \quad \text{and } s_k = (e^*, a_u), \text{ where} \\ &s_i \neq s_j,\ s_j \neq s_k, \text{ and } s_k \neq s_i, \text{ then } g(s) = a_{t+u+v(\text{mod } 2)}. \end{aligned} \tag{25}$$

Formulas (24), and (25) apply (14) and (15) of Section 2 to this example. Formula (14) does not unambiguously determine (24) as it is stated above, for (14) depends upon the numbering of the elements of $L(a_t, e_k)$ when $L(a_t, e_k) = \{a_t, a_u\}$. Formula (24) is obtained when the most natural numbering is imposed upon $\{a_t, a_u\}$: a_0 is the zero element, and a_1 is the first element. If a_1 is counted as the zero element and a_0 as the first element, then (14) replaces (24) with

$$g(s) = \begin{cases} a_t & \text{if } L(a_t, e_k) = \{a_t\} \\ a_{1+t+u(\text{mod } 2)} & \text{if } L(a_t, e_k) = A \end{cases} . \tag{26}$$

The analysis below uses (24) rather than (26). This issue will be addressed after the example is completed.

Let $\bar{s}$ denote the profile of strategies

$$\bar{s}_1 = \bar{s}_3 = (>, <, <, a_1), \ \bar{s}_2 = (>, >, >, a_0).$$

Because $L(<, a_1) = A$, (24) implies that $g(\bar{s}) = a_{1+0(\text{mod } 2)} = a_1$. It is shown below that $\bar{s}$ is a Nash equilibrium for $e = (>, <, >)$. Because $F(>, <, >) = a_0$, it follows that the game rule defined by (23), (24), and (25) does not implement F in Nash equilibrium.

Table 1 lists the alternatives that agent 1 implements by varying his strategy while the second and third agents' strategies remain fixed at $\bar{s}_2$ and $\bar{s}_3$, respectively. Similarly, Table 2 lists the alternatives that the third agent implements by varying his strategy while $\bar{s}_1$ and $\bar{s}_2$ remain fixed. The "rule for computing g" in these tables refers to which of (23), (24), or (25) determines the value of g.

It is now shown that $\bar{s}$ is a Nash equilibrium for $e = (>, <, >)$. Because $g(\bar{s}) = a_1$ and agent 2 prefers a_1 to a_0 in the environment $(>, <, >)$, $\bar{s}_2$ is a best response for agent 2 to $\bar{s}_1$ and $\bar{s}_3$. Agent 1 prefers a_0 to a_1, but Table 1 shows that he cannot implement a_0 by varying his strategy away from $\bar{s}_1$. Therefore, $\bar{s}_1$ is a best response for agent 1 to $\bar{s}_2$ and $\bar{s}_3$. Similarly, Table 2 shows that $\bar{s}_3$ is a best response for agent 3 to $\bar{s}_1$ and $\bar{s}_2$, which completes the example.

Several criticisms might be aimed at this example. Consider the use of (24) rather than (26) to define g. If (26) is used to define g, then $\bar{s}$ will no longer be a

Table 1. The alternatives that agent 1 can implement by varying his strategy away from $\bar{s}_1$ when $s_2 = \bar{s}_2$ and $s_3 = \bar{s}_3$

Agent 1 s_1	Agent 2 $\bar{s}_2$	Agent 3 $\bar{s}_3$	Rule for computing g	Value of g
$>, <, <, a_1$	$>, >, >, a_0$	$>, <, <, a_1$	(24)	a_1
$>, >, >, a_0$	$>, >, >, a_0$	$>, <, <, a_1$	(24)	a_1
Any other value for s_1	$>, >, >, a_0$	$>, <, <, a_1$	(25)	a_1

Table 2. The alternatives that agent 3 can implement by varying his strategy away from $\bar{s}_3$ when $s_1 = \bar{s}_1$ and $s_2 = \bar{s}_2$

Agent 1 $\bar{s}_1$	Agent 2 $\bar{s}_2$	Agent 3 s_3	Rule for Computing g	Value of g
$>, <, <, a_1$	$>, >, >, a_0$	$>, <, <, a_1$	(24)	a_1
$>, <, <, a_1$	$>, >, >, a_0$	$>, >, >, a_0$	(24)	a_1
$>, <, <, a_1$	$>, >, >, a_0$	Any other value for s_3	(25)	a_1

Nash equilibrium for $(>, <, >)$. Problems might arise elsewhere in this example if (26) is used instead of (24), but it is conceivable that defining g in this manner might insure that the game implements F in Nash equilibrium. It is also possible that (24) and (26) might be used in combination to define g, with the choice of formula dependent upon the profile of strategies. The point of the example, however, is to illustrate a flaw in Maskin's argument. In a given example, it may indeed be possible to define a game rule on the strategy space (2) that Nash implements the objective. Maskin's 1977 argument, however, fails to prove this.

The example might also be criticized because E_1 is a singleton. Maskin's result assumes that there are at least three agents and a problem in which E_1 is a singleton seems close to the two agent case. In response to this criticism, recall from the Introduction that no veto power together with $n \geq 3$ implies that (8) holds if preferences are unrestricted. A counterexample to Maskin's construction thus requires restricted preferences, as in the example. It is also true that the difficulty that Maskin overlooks is present in problems with more agents, more alternatives, and a richer class of environments. It does not hinge upon features of the above example. Such richer problems are unsuitable as examples because of their complexity; for purposes of illustration, elementary examples such as the one above are appropriate.

As a final note, a game exists that implements the objective F in Nash equilibrium. Extend the set $E_1 = \{>\}$ to the larger set $E_1^{'} = \{>, <\}$ and let $E' = E_1^{'} \times E_2 \times E_3$. Define $F' : E' \to A$ by majority rule, so that $F' = F$ when restricted to E. The objective F' satisfies (8) in addition to monotonicity and no veto power. Apply Maskin's construction to define a game (S', g') that Nash implements F'. The strategy set of each agent j in this new game provides him with four strategies that he does not have in the above game, namely,

$$(<, >, >, a_0), (<, <, >, a_1), (<, >, <, a_1), \text{ and } (<, <, <, a_1).$$

Formulas (3), (14) and (15) define the game rule g' on this larger strategy set. Nash implementation of F' implies

$$g' \circ \tau(e) = F'(e) = F(e)$$

for every $e \in E$, where $\tau : E \to S'$ is the Nash equilibrium correspondence of (S', g') on E'. The extended game (S', g') thus implements the original objective F in Nash equilibrium. In particular, (S', g') addresses the particular issue posed in the preceding example by allowing agent 1 to implement a_0 by selecting $s_1^* = (<, <, <, a_1)$ when agents 2 and 3 select $\bar{s}_2$ and $\bar{s}_3$: because $s_1^* \neq \bar{s}_2, \bar{s}_3$, and $\bar{s}_2 \neq \bar{s}_3$, (25) applies to define

$$g'(s_1^*, \bar{s}_2, \bar{s}_3) = a_{1+0+1(\text{mod } 2)} = a_0.$$

The strategy profile $(\bar{s}_1, \bar{s}_2, \bar{s}_3)$ is therefore not a Nash equilibrium for the environment $(>, <, >)$ in the larger game (S', g').

4 Hypotheses (8) can be omitted

It is shown in this section that (8) can be dropped as a hypothesis for Theorem 2. The approach is motivated by the discussion at the end of the last section. Let F be an objective on $E = \prod_{i=1}^{n} E_i$ that satisfies monotonicity and no veto power but not (8). Assuming for the moment that each E_i has at least two elements, it must be true for some $a \in A$ that at least one agent j *never* has a as a top-ranked alternative, no matter what value in E_j determines his characteristics. If this were false, i.e., if for any $a \in A$ and any $1 \leq j \leq n$, there exists $e_j \in E_j$ such that a is a top-ranked alternative relative to the preferences determined by e_j, then no veto power implies that F satisfies (8).[14]

This suggests the following approach. Given an objective that satisfies monotonicity and no veto power but not (8), extend its domain to a larger set of environments so that the extension satisfies monotonicity, no veto power and (8). The preceding discussion indicates that there are certain preference orderings that should be added to each E_j. The challenge is to prove that a suitable extension of F to a larger class of environments actually exists. Once this extension has been

[14] No veto power in fact implies $\left|F^{-1}(a)\right| \geq n$ for every $a \in A$ if (i) $\left|E_j\right| > 1$ for each agent j, and (ii) there exists for each j an element $e_j^{'} \in E_j$ such that $L(a, e_j^{'}) = A$. Letting $e_j \in E_j$ be distinct from $e_j^{'}$, this is proven by applying no veto power to show that

$$a \in F(e_1^{'}, \ldots, e_{j-1}^{'}, e_j, e_{j+1}^{'}, \ldots, e_n^{'})$$

for each value of j. The degenerate case in which $\left|E_j\right| = 1$ for some j is treated separately in the discussion that follows.

obtained, Theorem 2 applies to the extended objective if the original objective satisfies surjectivity. The original objective is implemented in Nash equilibrium when the agents that are characterized by the original set of environments play the game that is constructed to Nash implement the extended objective. This is how a game is devised at the end of Section 3 to show that the objective in the example can be implemented in Nash equilibrium.

Carrying out this argument requires an assumption about the original set of environments $E = \prod_{i=1}^{n} E_i$. Assume that there exists a set $\tilde{E} = \prod_{i=1}^{n} \tilde{E}_i$ with the following properties for each value of j:

1. $E_j \subset \tilde{E}_j$;
2. each element $\tilde{e}_j \in \tilde{E}_j$ determines a complete preordering on A;
3. $\tilde{E}_j$ contains at least two elements;
4. for any $a \in A$, there exists $\tilde{e}_j \in \tilde{E}_j$ such that $L(a, \tilde{e}_j) = A$.

I state this as a hypothesis because an element of E_j may contain other information besides the preordering that it determines on A.[15] Given $F{:}E \to A$ and a set E' such that $E \subset E' \subset \tilde{E}$, an *extension of* F *to* E' is any objective from E' to A that equals F at every environment in E.

The argument is divided into three steps. Assume that $F{:}E \to A$ satisfies monotonicity and no veto power but not (8) and let E' be an arbitrary subset of $\tilde{E}$ containing E. Theorem 3 states necessary and sufficient conditions on F and E' for the existence of an extension of F to E' that satisfies monotonicity and no veto power. This result is then used to prove Theorem 4, which states the existence of a subset $E^* \subset \tilde{E}$ and an extension F^* of F to E^* that satisfies monotonicity, no veto power, and (8). As the preceding discussion explains, Theorem 4 then implies that (8) can be omitted as a hypothesis in Theorem 2.

The proof of Theorem 3 is simplified with a few observations. Suppose $e \in E'$ and $e^* \in E$ satisfy

$$L(a, e_j) \subset L(a, e_j^*) \textit{ for each agent } j\textit{, but } a \notin F(e^*). \tag{27}$$

Statement (27) implies that $a \notin F'(e)$ if the extension F' is monotonic. Define the correspondence $\rho{:}\tilde{E} \to A$ as

$$\rho(e) \equiv \{a \in A | \exists\ e^* \in E \textit{ that satisfies } (27)\}.$$

The set $\rho(e)$ may be empty. The monotonicity of F on E implies that this is the case for $e \in E$. If F' is an extension of F to E' satisfying monotonicity,

[15] I have in mind such examples as the knowledge of consumers of their initial endowments and the information held by firms concerning their production technologies. Such information is distinct from their preferences over allocations and production plans. If each $e_j \in E_j$ only determines preferences on A and contains no other information, then the existence of $\tilde{E}$ is obvious. This is also true if the information that is given by each e_j can be represented as an ordered pair whose first component determines a preordering on A and whose second component represents the rest of the information contained in e_j. If information is encoded into the elements of each E_j in some more complicated fashion, then the existence of $\tilde{E}$ is not obvious.

then $F'(e) \subset A \backslash \rho(e)$ for all $e \in E' \backslash E$. A monotonic extension F' of F to E' is constructed in the proof of Theorem 3. The preceding remarks suggests defining

$$F'(e) \equiv A \backslash \rho(e) \tag{28}$$

for every $e \in E'$, where $F'(e) = F(e)$ for $e \in E$ because $\rho(e)$ is empty at such environments. Equation (28) defines an extension of F from E to E' if and only if $\rho(e)$ is a proper subset of A for every $e \in E' \backslash E$. This motivates the following theorem.

Theorem 3. *Let F be an objective from E to A that satisfies monotonicity and no veto power. Let E' be a subset of $\tilde{E}$ containing E. There exists an extension F' of F to E' that satisfies monotonicity and no veto power if and only if $\rho(e)$ is a proper subset of A for every $e \in E' \backslash E$.*

Proof. Necessity follows immediately from the discussion that precedes the statement of this theorem. Turning to sufficiency, (28) defines an extension F' of F to E' if $\rho(e) \neq A$ for all $e \in E' \backslash E$. It will be shown by contradiction that F' satisfies both monotonicity and no veto power.

Starting with monotonicity, let $e', e'' \in E'$ and let $a \in F'(e')$ satisfy $L(a, e_j') \subset L(a, e_j'')$ for each value of j. Assume that $a \notin F'(e'')$. There exists $e \in E$ such that

$$L(a, e_j'') \subset L(a, e_j) \textit{ for each } j, \textit{but } a \notin F(e).$$

Since $L(a, e_j') \subset L(a, e_j'')$ for each value of j, it follows that

$$L(a, e_j') \subset L(a, e_j) \textit{ for each } j, \textit{ but } a \notin F(e). \tag{29}$$

Statement (29) implies $a \in \rho\left(e'\right)$, which contradicts $a \in F'(e')$. Monotonicity of F' is thus verified.

Turning next to no veto power, let $e' \in E'$ and $a \in A$ satisfy $L(a, e_j') = A$ for all but at most one value of j. Assume that $a \notin F'(e')$. As argued above, there exists $e \in E$ such that

$$L(a, e_j') \subset L(a, e_j) \textit{ for each } j, \textit{ but } a \notin F(e). \tag{30}$$

Statement (30) implies that $L(a, e_j) = A$ for all but at most one value of j. Since $e \in E$ and F satisfies no veto power, it follows that $a \in F(e)$. This contradicts (30), and so F' satisfies no veto power. □

The discussion at the beginning of this section indicates that if F does not satisfy (8), then certain environments should be added to E. This suggests a method for extending F so that it satisfies (8). If F does not satisfy (8) and each E_j contains at least two elements, then there exists an alternative a and a value of j such that a is not a top-ranked alternative for any of the preference preorderings that are determined by the elements of E_j. Choose $e_j'' \in \tilde{E}_j$ such that a is a top-ranked alternative relative to the preference preordering that is determined by e_j'', and define E'' as

$$E'' = \prod_{i=1}^{n} E_i'', \ \text{where} \begin{cases} E_i'' \equiv E_i \ \text{if} \ i \neq j \\ E_j'' = E_j \cup \{e_j''\} \end{cases} .$$

Theorem 3 implies that there exists an extension of F to E'' that satisfies both monotonicity and no veto power. If F'' does not satisfy (8), then repeat this procedure using F'' and E'' instead of F and E. If A is finite, then in a finite number steps an extension of F is obtained that satisfies monotonicity, no veto power, and (8). The proof of Theorem 4 generalizes this construction, using Zorn's Lemma[16] to insure the success of this approach when the cardinality of A is arbitrary.

Theorem 4. *Let F be an objective from E to A. If F satisfies monotonicity and no veto power, then there exists a subset $E^* = \prod_{i=1}^{n} E_i^*$ of $\tilde{E}$ that contains E and an extension F^* of F to E^* that satisfies monotonicity, no veto power, and (8).*

Proof. Let $\mathscr{E}$ denote the set of all subsets $E' \subset \tilde{E}$ such that:

1. $E' = \prod_{i=1}^{n} E_i'$, where $E_j \subset E_j'$ for each value of j;
2. there exists an extension F' of F to E' that satisfies monotonicity and no veto power.

The set $\mathscr{E}$ is nonempty because it contains E.

Zorn's Lemma is applied below to prove the existence of $E^* \in \mathscr{E}$ that is *maximal* in the sense that it is not a proper subset of any other element of $\mathscr{E}$. The proof is then completed by showing that the extension F^* of F to E^* must satisfy (8). It must first be shown that $\mathscr{E}$ satisfies the hypothesis of Zorn's Lemma. Let $\mathscr{N}$ be any subset of $\mathscr{E}$ that is linearly ordered by the inclusion relation, i.e., if $E', E'' \in \mathscr{N}$, then $E' \subset E''$ or $E'' \subset E'$. It must be shown that $\mathscr{N}$ has an upper bound in $\mathscr{E}$. Define N as

$$N \equiv \bigcup_{E' \in \mathscr{N}} E'. \tag{31}$$

This set is an upper bound for $\mathscr{N}$ and so it remains to be shown that $N \in \mathscr{E}$. It has the structure of a Cartesian product: representing $E' \in \mathscr{N}$ as $E' = \prod_{i=1}^{n} E_i'$, then

$$N = \prod_{i=1}^{n} \left(\bigcup_{E' \in \mathscr{N}} E_i' \right)$$

because $\mathscr{N}$ is linearly ordered. The set N thus satisfies property 1 above.

Turning to property 2, Theorem 3 implies that it is sufficient to show that $\rho(e) \neq A$ for $e \in N \backslash E$. By the definition of N in (31), $e \in N \backslash E$ must be in $E' \backslash E$ for some $E' \in \mathscr{N}$. By property 2, there exists an extension of F to E'

---

[16] See Kelley (1955, p. 33).

that satisfies monotonicity and no veto power. Theorem 3 then implies that $\rho(e) \neq A$, which completes the argument that $N \in \mathscr{E}$.

Zorn's Lemma therefore asserts the existence of a maximal element $E^* = \prod_{i=1}^{n} E_i^*$ in $\mathscr{E}$. Let F^* denote an extension of F to E^* that satisfies monotonicity and no veto power. It remains to be shown that F^* satisfies (8). The proof is by contradiction. If F^* does not satisfy (8), then one of the following statements must be true of some agent j:

1. there exists $a \in A$ such that

$$L(a, e_j^*) \neq A \tag{32}$$

for all $e_j^* \in E_j^*$; or
2. E_j^* consists of a single element e_j^*.

Case 2 is treated separately at the end of the proof. In case 1, apply the procedure outlined immediately before the statement of this theorem. Choose an element $e_j^{**} \in \tilde{E}_j$ such that $L(a, e_j^{**}) = A$. Define the set E^{**} as

$$E^{**} \equiv \prod_{i=1}^{n} E_i^{**}, \; where \; \begin{cases} E_i^{**} \equiv E_i^* \; if \; i \neq j \\ E_j^{**} = E_j^* \cup \{e_j^{**}\} \end{cases}. \tag{33}$$

It is shown below that an extension F^{**} of F to E^{**} exists that satisfies monotonicity and no veto power. Therefore, $E^{**} \in \mathscr{E}$, which contradicts the maximality of E^* in $\mathscr{E}$.

Theorem 3 implies that it is sufficient to show that $\rho(e) \neq A$ for every $e \in E^{**} \backslash E$. This is true for all $e \in E^* \backslash E$ because there exists an extension of F to E^*. Assume therefore that $e \in E^{**} \backslash E^*$. The argument is completed by showing that the value of a satisfying (32) cannot be in $\rho(e)$. If $a \in \rho(e)$, then there exists $e' \in E$ such that

$$L(a, e_j) \subset L(a, e_j^{'}) \; for \; each \; value \; of \; j, \; but \; a \notin F(e'). \tag{34}$$

Since $e \in E^{**} \backslash E^*$, (33) implies that $e_j = e_j^{**}$. Because $L(a, e_j^{**}) = A$, by (34) it must also be true that $L(a, e_j^{'}) = A$. The values a and j were selected, however, because $L(a, e_j^*) \neq A$ for all $e_j^* \in E^* \supset E$. This contradiction implies that $a \notin \rho(e)$.

Finally, consider case 2 in which $E_j^* = \{e_j^*\}$ for some j. Select any $e_j^{**} \in \tilde{E}_j \backslash E_j^*$ and define E^{**} as in (33). It is shown below that for $e_{-j}^* \in \prod_{i \neq j} E_i^*$,

$$a \in F^* \left((e_j^*, e_{-j}^*) \right) \Rightarrow a \notin \rho \left((e_j^{**}, e_{-j}^*) \right). \tag{35}$$

The existence of an extension of F to E^* implies that $\rho(e) \neq A$ for all $e \in E^*$. Statement (35) then implies that $\rho(e) \neq A$ for all $e \in E^{**}$, and hence Theorem 3 implies the existence of an extension of F from E to E^{**} satisfying monotonicity and no veto power. This contradicts the maximality of E^* and completes the proof. If $a \in \rho \left((e_j^{**}, e_{-j}^*) \right)$, then there exists $e \in E$ such that

$$L(a, e_j^{**}) \subset L(a, e_j) \text{ and } L(a, e_i^*) \subset L(a, e_i) \text{ for } i \neq j, \text{but } a \notin F(e).$$

Because $E_j \subset E_j^*$, it follows that $e_j = e_j^*$. Consequently,

$$L(a, e_j^*) \subset L(a, e_j) \text{ and } L(a, e_i^*) \subset L(a, e_i) \text{ for } i \neq j, \text{but } a \notin F(e). \tag{36}$$

It is assumed that $a \in F^*\left(\left(e_j^*, e_{-j}^*\right)\right)$, however, and so (36) contradicts the monotonicity of F^* on E^*. □

References

Debreu, G. (1959) *Theory of Value.* Yale University Press, New Haven

Gibbard, A. (1972) Manipulation of voting schemes: A general result. *Econometrica* 41: 587–601

Groves, T. (1979) Efficient collective choice with compensation. In: Laffont, J.-J. (ed.) *Aggregation and Revelation of Preferences.* North-Holland, Amsterdam

Kelly, J. (1955) *General Topology.* Springer, Berlin Heidelberg New York

Hurwicz, L. (1960) Optimality and informational efficiency in resource allocation processes. In: Arrow, K.J., Karlin, S., Suppes, P. (eds.) *Mathematical Methods in the Social Sciences. 1959.* Stanford University Press, Stanford

Hurwicz, L. (1972) On informationally decentralized systems. In: McGuire, C.B., Radner, R. (eds.) *Decision and Organization.* North Holland, Amsterdam

Maskin, E. (1977) Nash equilibrium and welfare optimality. mimeo

Maskin, E. (1985) The theory of implementation in Nash equilibrium: a survey. In: Hurwicz, L., Schmeidler, D., Sonnenschein, H. (eds.) *Social Goals and Social Organization, Essays in Memory of Elisha A. Pazner*, pp. 173–204 . Cambridge University Press, Cambridge

Maskin, E. (1999) Nash equilibrium and welfare optimality. *Review of Economic Studies* 66: 23–38

Saijo, T. (1988) Strategy space reduction in Maskin's theorem: Sufficient conditions for Nash implementation. *Econometrica* 56: 693–700

Satterthwaite, M.A. (1975) Strategy proofness and Arrow's conditions: Existence and correspondence theorems for voting procedures and social welfare functions. *Journal of Economic Theory* 10: 187–217

Williams, S.R. (1984a) Realization and Nash implementation: Two aspects of mechanism design. Institute for Mathematics and its Applications preprint, University of Minnesota

Williams, S. R. (1984b) Sufficient conditions for Nash implementation. Institute for Mathematics and its Applications preprint, University of Minnesota

Williams, S. R. (1986) Realization and Nash implementation: Two aspects of mechanism design. *Econometrica* 54: 139–151

Majority rule with dollar voting

James S. Jordan

G13 Kern Building, University Park, PA 16803, USA (e-mail: jxj13@psu.edu)

Abstract. Consider a majority game in which each player's voting strength is equal to the player's payoff. In this game, wealth is the only source of power, and any coalition with more than half the wealth can take everything. Only extreme concentrations of wealth, in which one player owns everything or two players each own half the total wealth are undominated, and thus constitute the core. However, the stable set (von Neumann-Morgenstern solution) is significantly larger. Allocations in which one player has half the wealth, or which divide the total wealth equally among a number of players equal to a power of two, constitute the unique stable set. The stable set thus provides a formal model of an endogenous balance of power.

1 Introduction

Majority rule, as a coalitional game, is represented by a characteristic function that gives the value unity to each coalition with more than half the votes, and gives the value zero to every other coalition. The characteristic function is based on the exogenous specification of the voting power of each player. More generally, any characteristic function for a coalitional game embodies an exogenous specification of the power of each coalition. When the voting power of each player depends on the outcome of the game, it is no longer possible to represent the game by a characteristic function. The present paper is devoted to the extreme case in which the voting power of each player is equal to the player's payoff. Even though there is no characteristic function for this game, the concepts of *core* and *stable set* can be defined with reference to a dominance relation alone.

An outcome of a majority game with fixed voting power is a distribution of spoils that respects the specified power of each player. Under dollar voting, an

The author is grateful to the referee for numerous useful suggestions.

outcome is itself an endogenous balance of power. Not surprisingly, the cores and stable sets in the two cases are quite different. For the conventional majority game, the core is empty and there is a multiplicity of stable sets. Under dollar voting, the core is nonempty, albeit small, and the more interesting stable set is unique.

We can introduce these concepts with a somewhat informal discussion of the three-person case. There is a fixed amount of wealth, normalized to unity, to be allocated among three players. First consider the traditional majority game, in which each person has one vote, so any coalition of two players can dictate an allocation. This is summarized by the characteristic function

$$v(\{1,2\}) = v(\{2,3\}) = v(\{1,3\}) = v(\{1,2,3\}) = 1,$$

$$v(\{1\}) = v(\{2\}) = v(\{3\}) = v(\emptyset) = 0,$$

which specifies the amount of wealth each coalition can collectively obtain for itself. The core is then defined as the set of allocations $w = (w_1, w_2, w_3)$ satisfying, for every coalition C,

$$\Sigma_{i \in C} w_i \geq v(C).$$

Hence a core allocation must satisfy $(w_1+w_2)+(w_2+w_3)+(w_1+w_3) \geq 3$, which contradicts the feasibility constraint that $w_1+w_2+w_3 = 1$. Thus the core is empty.

The coalitional power represented by the characteristic function can equivalently but more directly be described by a *dominance relation*. Say that an allocation w' *dominates* w if

$$\#\{i : w'_i > w_i\} = 2.$$

That is, w' dominates w if the set of players who prefer w' have sufficient power to enforce their preference. The core is then defined as the set of undominated allocations. Again, the core is empty, because every allocation admits reallocations in which two players share the spoils from dispossessing the third.

The dominance relation, like the characteristic function, provides no information about the process of coalition formation. The fact that the allocation $w' = (\frac{1}{2}, \frac{1}{2}, 0)$ dominates the allocation $w = (\frac{1}{3}, \frac{1}{3}, \frac{1}{3})$, for example, means only that if the allocation w were somehow to be attained, players 1 and 2 would have both the motive and the ability to force a reallocation to w'. There are also many other allocations that dominate w, and the dominance relation does not specify which coalition would form or which reallocation a particular coalition would favor. In contrast, a noncooperative game includes much more detail about the specific actions each player can take and, in extensive form, about the order in which players can act. In particular, a noncooperative game restricts communication among the players to the messages explicitly specified in the description of the game. A noncooperative game thus describes both an economic environment and a mechanism for choosing allocations. The three-player majority game specified by the dominance relation describes only an economic environment in which any two players have the power to reallocate wealth. Indeed, the absence of a specified decision mechanism suggests that "voting power" in this game should be interpreted as technological rather than political. Any coalition of two players is physically strong enough to dispossess the third. The absence of a fully specified noncooperative game form prevents strategic analysis at the level of detail encompassed in Nash equilibrium and its refinements. However, if communication among players cannot be restricted, a noncooperative game form can be subverted by collusion among the players. Moreover, a noncooperative game form also assumes that players will refrain from using force to overturn the allocation generated by the outcome function. Thus a noncooperative game form entails the use of external enforcement power both to restrict communication and to prevent reallocation by force. A noncooperative game form itself presumes a prior resolution of the basic conflicts in the majority game.

For this reason, it is useful to ask which allocations seem the most plausible outcomes on the basis of the dominance relation alone. The von Neumann-Morgenstern solution (1947), now more commonly known as the *stable set* (e.g., Lucas 1992 or Myerson 1991), was the first solution concept to answer this question, antedating even the core[1]. Von Neumann and Morgenstern interpret a stable set as a social expectation or "accepted standard of behavior" (von Neumann-Morgenstern 1947, p. 41). That is, a stable set is a set of allocations that the players could plausibly expect to be attained and preserved. A stable set S is defined by two conditions that capture this interpretation. First, no allocation $w \in S$ can be dominated by another allocation $w' \in S$. Otherwise, the stability of w' would entice the two players who prefer w' to enforce their preference, contradicting the stability of w. This property is called *internal stability*. Second, any allocation that is dominated only by unstable allocations is stable, which means that every unstable allocation must be dominated by a stable allocation. This property is called *external stability*.

For the three-person majority game, the set $S = \{(\frac{1}{2}, \frac{1}{2}, 0), (\frac{1}{2}, 0, \frac{1}{2}), (0, \frac{1}{2}, \frac{1}{2})\}$ is a stable set. Internal stability is immediate, since only one player can benefit from a reallocation within this three-element set. If $w \notin S$, suppose without loss of generality that $w_1 \geq w_2 \geq w_3$. Then w is dominated by the stable allocation $(0, \frac{1}{2}, \frac{1}{2})$, so external stability is also satisfied. In particular, the unstable allocation $(\frac{1}{3}, \frac{1}{3}, \frac{1}{3})$ is dominated by all three stable allocations, so the stable set does not necessarily determine which coalition would overturn an unstable allocation.

The role of expectations in preserving stable allocations can be illustrated by considering the allocation $(\frac{1}{2}, \frac{1}{2}, 0)$. At this allocation, player 3 might propose to player 2 that they collude to obtain the allocation $(0, \frac{3}{4}, \frac{1}{4})$, which they both prefer. However, player 2 would expect this reallocation to be followed by a move to the stable allocation $(\frac{1}{2}, 0, \frac{1}{2})$ by the coalition of players 1 and 3, and would therefore decline player 3's proposal. Thus, player 2 would be dissuaded by the expectation of treachery by player 3.

This stable set S is not unique. For each $0 \leq c < \frac{1}{2}$, there is a stable set of the form $\{w : w_i = c\}$, for each $i = 1, 2, 3$ (e.g., Lucas (1992, p. 556)). This illustrates an important distinction between the core and stable set. The core can

[1] The stable set is unrelated to the Kohlberg-Mertens (1986) concept of stability in noncooperative games.

be the empty set, as it is in this game, but is always a unique set. A stable set cannot be empty, because of external stability, but it can fail to be unique, and can even fail to exist (Lucas 1992, p. 565). This is due to the fact that, unlike the core, a stable set is not defined pointwise, but with reference to itself as a set. Indeed, it is a misnomer to refer to an allocation as stable or unstable, though we will continue to do so, with reference to a specific stable set, for expositional convenience.

Now suppose that the power of each coalition is determined solely by its total wealth. A characteristic function for this game cannot be defined, because power depends on the allocation itself. For example, at the allocation $(\frac{3}{4}, \frac{1}{4}, 0)$, a characteristic function v would have to satisfy $v(\{1\}) = 1$ and $v(\{2, 3\}) = 0$, while at the allocation $(\frac{1}{3}, \frac{1}{3}, \frac{1}{3})$, v would be the same as in the majority game. The dominance relation, in contrast, is easily defined. An allocation w' dominates w if

$$\sum_{\{i: w'_i > w_i\}} w_i > \frac{1}{2}.$$

That is, a coalition possessing a majority of the wealth at an allocation w can enforce its preference for the allocation w'. It is clear that the allocation $(1, 0, 0)$ and its permutations are undominated, so the core of this game is nonempty. The allocation $(\frac{1}{2}, \frac{1}{2}, 0)$ and its permutations are also undominated, and thus are also core allocations. Every other allocation is dominated, because at every other allocation, there is a coalition of one or two players who possess more than half but less than all of the wealth, and are therefore willing and able to despoil the complementary coalition.

External stability implies that the core is a subset of every stable set, so a stable set must include the allocations $(1, 0, 0)$ and $(\frac{1}{2}, \frac{1}{2}, 0)$ and their permutations. The core is internally stable in general, so if the core were also externally stable, the core would be the unique stable set. In this game, the core is not externally stable, since allocations of the form $(\frac{1}{2}, w_2, w_3)$ and their permutations are not dominated by any core allocation.

Let $\hat{S}$ denote the set consisting of the core together with all allocations of the form $(\frac{1}{2}, w_2, w_3)$ and their permutations. Then $\hat{S}$ is the unique stable set. Internal stability is evident from the fact that at an allocation $w = (\frac{1}{2}, w_2, w_3)$, any enforceable reallocation would have to be preferred by player 1 and one other player. However, the only reallocation in $\hat{S}$ that benefits player 1 is $w' = (1, 0, 0)$, which obviously is not preferred to w by either of the other players. In fact, an allocation $(\frac{1}{2}, w_2, w_3)$ is dominated only by allocations w' with $1 > w'_1 > \frac{1}{2}$, which are in turn dominated by the core allocation $(1, 0, 0)$. An argument due to Roth (1976) then shows that any stable set must contain $\hat{S}$. Let B denote the set of allocations w satisfying $1 > w_1 > \frac{1}{2}$ and their permutations. Since any stable set must contain the core, and allocations in B are dominated by core allocations, internal stability implies that any stable set must *exclude* B. Then external stability implies that any stable set must include allocations that are dominated *only* by allocations in B, so any stable set must include $\hat{S}$. If $\hat{S}$ is externally stable, it follows that $\hat{S}$ is the unique stable set. To show external stability, let $w \notin \hat{S}$. If $w \in B$, then w is dominated by a core allocation in $\hat{S}$, so let $w \notin B$. Assume without loss of generality that $w_1 \geq w_2 \geq w_3$. Since $w \notin \hat{S} \cup B$, $\frac{1}{2} > w_1$, so $(\frac{1}{2}, \frac{1}{2}, 0)$ dominates w, which proves that $\hat{S}$ is externally stable.

Since power is endogenous, an allocation in $\hat{S}$ constitutes an endogenous balance of power. For core allocations, the balance is trivial. At the allocations $(1, 0, 0)$ and $(\frac{1}{2}, \frac{1}{2}, 0)$, any coalition with sufficient power to enforce its preferences already possesses all the wealth. The balance of power at an allocation $(\frac{1}{2}, w_2, w_3)$ is more delicate. At $(\frac{1}{2}, \frac{1}{4}, \frac{1}{4})$, for example, players 1 and 2 could join to despoil player 3 and obtain the allocation $(\frac{5}{8}, \frac{3}{8}, 0)$. However, this allocation gives player 1 enough power to despoil player 2 and obtain the core allocation $(1, 0, 0)$. At an allocation $(\frac{1}{2}, w_2, w_3)$, players 2 and 3 lack the power to increase their wealth without the aid of player 1, and cannot use the aid of player 1 for fear of enabling player 1 to take everything.

The stable set remains unique in games with more than three players. The core again consists of the allocations $(1, 0, \ldots, 0)$ and $(\frac{1}{2}, \frac{1}{2}, 0, \ldots, 0)$ and their permutations. The stable set again contains the core and the allocations $(\frac{1}{2}, w_2, \ldots, w_n)$ and their permutations. However, there are additional stable allocations of the form $(2^{-j}, \ldots, 2^{-j}, 0 \ldots, 0)$ and their permutations, for each $j \leq \log_2 n$, where n is the number of players. For example, with four players, the stable set includes the allocation $w = (\frac{1}{4}, \frac{1}{4}, \frac{1}{4}, \frac{1}{4})$. Any coalition powerful enough to overturn this allocation must contain three players. To obtain a reallocation w' in the stable set, one coalition member must receive $w'_i = \frac{1}{2}$, which means the other two coalition members cannot each receive more than $\frac{1}{4}$. Hence w is not dominated by any other stable allocation, so a stable set must include w. It is straightforward to show that including w restores external stability, which also implies the uniqueness of the stable set. For general n, the proof uses an induction argument on $j \leq \log_2 n$.

Section 2 gives the formal definitions of the game and the concepts of core and stable set. Section 3 proves the main result, Theorem 2, characterizing the unique stable set. Some concluding remarks are given in Sect. 4.

2 Definitions

The set of players is the finite set $\{1, \ldots, n\}$, where $n \geq 2$. Subsets will be called *coalitions*. An *allocation* is an n-tuple $w = (w_1, \ldots, w_n)$ satisfying $w_i \geq 0$ for each i, and $\sum_i w_i = 1$. Let A denote the set of allocations. The symbols w and w' will always denote allocations. An allocation w' *dominates* an allocation w if

$$\sum_{\{i : w'_i > w_i\}} w_i > \frac{1}{2} . \qquad (D)$$

The *core* is defined as the set of undominated allocations. A set $S \subset A$ is a *stable set* if s.1) (internal stability) no allocation in S is dominated by an allocation in S; and

s.2) (external stability) every allocation not in S is dominated by an allocation in S.

Equivalently, a set $S \subset A$ is stable if

$$A \backslash S = \{w : w \text{ is dominated by some } w' \in S\}.$$

3 Results

This section characterizes the core and stable set.

Definitions. *Let* $S^* = \{w : w_i = \frac{1}{2}$ *for some* $i\}$. *For each nonnegative integer* $j \leq \log_2 n$, *define* $S_j = \{w :$ *there is some coalition* C *such that* $\#C = 2^j$ *and* $w_i = 2^{-j}$ *for each* $i \in C\}$. *Let* $\hat{S} = S^* \cup \{S_j : 0 \leq j \leq \log_2 n\}$.

The set S_0 is the set of allocations giving all the wealth to one player, and S_1 is the set of allocations giving half the wealth to each of two players. These are easily seen to be the only undominated allocations.

Theorem 1. *The core is* $S_0 \cup S_1$.

Proof. Immediate.

The stable set can be constructed using a procedure due to Roth (1976), mentioned in Sect. 1. The procedure begins with the observation that any stable set must contain the core, and then uses internal and external stability alternately in an iterative construction of sets G and B such that any stable set S must satisfy $G \subset S \subset A \backslash B$. For the game considered here, $G = A \backslash B$, and thus constitutes the unique stable set. More generally, it is often the case that G is a proper subset of $A \backslash B$. In games with an empty core, such as the three-player majority game, $G = B = \emptyset$, so the procedure is uninformative. Roth (1976) shows that the set G, which he calls the *supercore*, can be constructed for any abstract game defined by a dominance relation. The general construction uses transfinite induction, but only finite induction on the S_j's is required in the present case. Asilis and Kahn (1992) call G the "good" set, B the "bad" set, and $A \backslash (G \cup B)$ the "ugly" set.

Theorem 2. $\hat{S}$ *is the unique stable set.*

Lemma. *Let* w *satisfy* $\frac{1}{2} > w_i$ *for all* i, *and for some* i, j, $w_i > w_j > 0$. *Then there exists some coalition* C *and some* $i^o \in C$ *satisfying*

$$\sum_{i \in C} w_i > \frac{1}{2}; \text{ and} \tag{1}$$

$$\sum_{i \in C \setminus \{i^o\}} w_i < \frac{1}{2} . \tag{2}$$

Proof. Let $j \leq n$ such that $\Sigma_{i=1}^{j} w_i > \frac{1}{2}$. Assume without loss of generality that $w_1 \geq \cdots \geq w_j$. By the hypothesis of the Lemma we can also assume that $\frac{1}{2} > w_1 > w_j > 0$. Let $h = \min\{i : w_1 + \cdots + w_i \geq \frac{1}{2}\}$. If $w_1 + \cdots w_h > \frac{1}{2}$, let $C = \{1, \ldots, h\}$, otherwise let $C = \{1, \ldots, h, j\}$. Then C satisfies (1), and $i^o = 1$ satisfies (2). □

Proof of Theorem 2. External stability requires that any stable set contain the core, $S_0 \cup S_1$. Any allocation w such that $1 > w_i > \frac{1}{2}$ for some i is dominated by the core allocation $(0, \ldots, 0, 1_i, 0, \ldots, 0)$. Define $B_1 = \{w : 1 > w_i > \frac{1}{2}$ for some $i\}$. Then internal stability requires that any stable set exclude the set B_1. Now let $w \in S^*$, so that $w_i = \frac{1}{2}$ for some i. If an allocation w' dominates w, then (D) implies that $\{j : w'_j > w_j\}$ includes player i and at least one other player. Therefore $1 > w'_i > \frac{1}{2}$, so $w' \in B_1$. Thus allocations in S^* are dominated only by allocations in B_1. Since any stable set must exclude B_1, external stability requires that any stable set include S^*. Hence any stable set S must satisfy $S^* \cup S_0 \subset S \subset A \setminus B_1$.

For each $k = 1, \ldots, n$, let E_k denote the set of allocations that divide the total wealth equally among k players. In particular $E_{2^j} = S_j$ for each $0 \leq j \leq \log_2 n$. Let $E = \cup_{1 \leq k \leq n} E_k$. Let $B_2 = \{w : \frac{1}{2} > w_i$ for all $i\} \setminus E$, and let $w \in B_2$. Then w satisfies the hypothesis of the Lemma. Let C and $i^o \in C$ satisfy (1) and (2). By (2), $w_{i^o} + \Sigma_{i \notin C} w_i > \frac{1}{2}$. Let $\delta = [\Sigma_{i \notin C} w_i - (\frac{1}{2} - w_{i^o})]/(\#C - 1)$. Then $\delta > 0$, so (1) implies that w is dominated by the allocation w' defined by

$$w'_i = \begin{cases} \frac{1}{2} & \text{if } i = i^o; \\ w_i + \delta & \text{if } i \in C \text{ and } i \neq i^o; \text{ and} \\ 0 & \text{otherwise.} \end{cases}$$

Thus every allocation in B_2 is dominated by some allocation in S^*, so any stable set must exclude B_2. Hence any stable set S must satisfy $S^* \cup S_0 \subset S \subset A \setminus (B_1 \cup B_2)$.

For each integer $3 \leq \ell \leq 2 + \log_2 n$, define

$$B_\ell = \cup\{E_k : 2^{(\ell-2)} < k \leq \min\{n, 2^{(\ell-1)} - 1\}\},$$

with the convention that $B_\ell = \emptyset$ at $\ell = 2 + \log_2 n$. For example, if $n = 14$, then $B_3 = E_3$, $B_4 = E_5 \cup \cdots \cup E_7$ and $B_5 = E_9 \cup \cdots \cup E_{14}$. The allocation $w = (\frac{1}{3}, \frac{1}{3}, \frac{1}{3}, 0, \ldots, 0) \in B_3$ is dominated by the allocation $w' = (\frac{1}{2}, \frac{1}{2}, 0, \ldots, 0) \in S_1 \subset S^*$. Similarly, any allocation in B_3 is dominated by an allocation in S_1, so any stable set must exclude B_3. Now let $w \in S_2$, say $w = (\frac{1}{4}, \frac{1}{4}, \frac{1}{4}, \frac{1}{4}, 0, \ldots, 0)$. Suppose that w is dominated by some allocation w'. Then (D) implies that $\#\{i : w'_i > \frac{1}{4}\} = 3$ so $w'_i < \frac{1}{2}$ for all i. Hence $w' \in B_2 \cup B_3$. Thus allocations in S_2 are only dominated by allocations in $B_2 \cup B_3$, so external stability implies that any stable set must include S_2. More generally, suppose that for some $\ell \geq 3$, any stable set must include $S_{\ell-2}$. Every allocation in B_ℓ is dominated by some allocation in $S_{\ell-2}$, so internal stability implies that any stable set must exclude B_ℓ. Now let $w \in S_{\ell-1}$, and suppose that w is dominated by an allocation w'. By the definition of $S_{\ell-1}$ and (D), $\#\{i : w'_i > 2^{-(\ell-1)}\} > 2^{\ell-2}$, so $w' \in B_2 \cup B_\ell$. Since allocations in $S_{\ell-1}$ are only dominated by allocations in $B_2 \cup B_\ell$, any stable set must include $S_{\ell-1}$.

This induction argument proves that any stable set S must satisfy $S^* \cup S_0 \cup \cdots \cup S_k \subset S \subset A \backslash (B_1 \cup \cdots \cup B_{k+2})$, where k is the largest integer not larger than $\log_2 n$. But $S^* \cup S_0 \cup \cdots \cup S_k = \hat{S} = A \backslash (B_1 \cup \cdots \cup B_{k+2})$, so $\hat{S}$ is the only possible stable set. Since $A \backslash \hat{S} = B_1 \cup \cdots \cup B_{k+2}$ and every allocation in $B_1 \cup \cdots \cup B_{k+2}$ has been shown to be dominated by some allocation in $\hat{S}$, we have shown that $\hat{S}$ is externally stable. Since allocations in $\hat{S}$ have been shown to be undominated or dominated only by allocations in $B_1 \cup \cdots \cup B_{k+2}$, we have shown that $\hat{S}$ is internally stable, and is thus the unique stable set. □

Remark. Theorems 1 and 2 extend directly to the case in which the set of players is countably infinite, assuming that $\Sigma_{i=1}^{\infty} w_i < \infty$, so that the dominance relation is well-defined. In this case, $\hat{S} = S^* \cup (\cup_{j=1}^{\infty} S_j)$. The proof of Theorem 2 extends without modification. Note that the coalition C constructed in proving the Lemma is finite, which is used in applying the Lemma to prove Theorem 2.

4 Conclusion

In the majority game with dollar voting, wealth is the only source of power, and any coalition with more than half the wealth can take everything, costlessly and with certainty. The core reflects the extreme simplicity of this environment. Only extreme concentrations of wealth, in which one player owns everything or two players each own half, are undominated. However, the stable set yields some interesting insights into the balance of power. The unique stable set $\hat{S}$ consists of two components, S^* and $S_0 \cup \cdots \cup S_k$, where k is the largest integer such that $2^k \leq n$. The component S^* consists of allocations in which one player owns half the wealth. In this case, any majority must contain the wealthy player, but any majority that overturns the status quo will necessarily make the wealthy player powerful enough to take everything, which is sufficient to discourage majority coalitions. Thus any distribution of the remaining half of the wealth among the other players is stable. This component of the stable set solves the principal problem of monarchy: how to make the king strong enough to protect his subjects but not strong enough to oppress them.

The second component consists of allocations that divide the total wealth equally among 2^j players for any $0 \leq j \leq \log_2 n$. These allocations are more egalitarian than those in S^*, at least for large j, but they illustrate some inherent limitations of egalitarianism. First, the allocation $w^e = (\frac{1}{n}, \ldots, \frac{1}{n})$ alone is not a stable set because it lacks external stability. In particular, it does not dominate allocations in S^*. For example, at the allocation $(\frac{1}{2}, \frac{1}{8}, \frac{1}{8}, \frac{1}{8}, \frac{1}{8}) \in S^*$, the coalition $\{2, \ldots, 5\}$ lacks sufficient power to overthrow player 1 in order to establish the allocation $w^e = (\frac{1}{5}, \ldots, \frac{1}{5})$. Second, internal stability prevents the stable set from containing equal divisions among every possible number of players because w^e, for example, admits a sequence of successively dominating allocations with majorities consisting of successively smaller numbers of players. If wealth is allocated equally among a coalition of more than two players, any majority subcoalition has the incentive and ability to dispossess the minority and distribute the spoils equally among themselves. The set $S_0 \cup \cdots \cup S_k$ of equal-division allocations is internally stable because it excludes equal division among majority subcoalitions. Of course, the reduction of egalitarianism to equality among coalitions of size 2^j is a simplistic outcome of a simplistic model, but it shows that egalitarianism, as an "accepted standard of behavior," can increase rather than lessen the incentive to marginalize subgroups.

The majority game with dollar voting could be extended in several potentially useful ways. The voting strength of a coalition could be assumed to depend on both the coalition's wealth and the number of its members. Dollar voting and the traditional majority game are the two extreme cases. This class of games could be interpreted as modeling power as a technological function of capital and labor. Such technologies have already been studied in the noncooperative game theoretic literature on allocation by force (e.g., Garfinkel and Skaperdas 1996). In Jordan (1999), the dominance relation is enlarged to allow a coalition to pillage subgroups of its complement. A pillaging coalition is only required to have more wealth than its victims. More precisely, w' dominates w if

$$\sum_{\{i:w'_i>w_i\}} w_i > \sum_{\{i:w'_i<w_i\}} w_i \ . \qquad (D')$$

The core is unaffected, but the stable set is different. The set S^* is no longer internally stable because, for example, the allocation $(\frac{1}{2}, \frac{1}{3}, \frac{1}{6}) \in S^*$ is now dominated by the core allocation $(\frac{1}{2}, \frac{1}{2}, 0)$. Thus (D') allows player 2 to despoil player 3 without sharing the proceeds with player 1. The dominance relation (D) effectively requires bystanders to be paid an arbitrarily small but positive share of the spoils to withhold their protection from the victims. By allowing more potential reallocations by force, (D') describes a more complete state of anarchy. The new stable set, which again is unique, consists of allocations such as $(\frac{1}{4}, 0, \frac{1}{16}, \frac{1}{8}, \frac{1}{4}, \frac{1}{16}, \frac{1}{8}, \frac{1}{8})$, in which each player holds either nothing or some power of $\frac{1}{2}$. For fixed $n < \infty$, the stable set is finite, though still significantly larger than the core. If the power of a coalition depends on its size as well as its total wealth, the stable set can be quite different, and in some cases does not exist (Jordan 1999, Proposition 4.6), but is always at most finite for fixed $n < \infty$ (Jordan 1999, Theorem 2.9).

It remains to be seen whether the balance of power can be a fruitful solution concept in richer economic models. The ultimate object of this line of research is to understand how the rights and protections on which a market economy rests could emerge in an environment with agents motivated only by gain and constrained only by the limits of brute force. In the simple environment studied here, the core consists of the only allocations at which the few owners of wealth can defend their possessions by their own power. The "accepted standard of behavior," as defined by the unique stable set $\hat{S}$, is much larger. This offers some encouragement to extend the model to economic environments with multiple commodities, production and investment.

References

1. Asilis, C., Kahn, C. (1992) Semi-stability in game theory: A survey of ugliness. In: Dutta, B. et al. (eds.) *Game Theory and Economic Applications*. Springer, Berlin Heidelberg New York
2. Garfinkel, M., Skaperdas, S. (eds.) (1996) *The Political Economy of Conflict and Appropriation*. Cambridge University Press, Cambridge
3. Jordan, J. (1999) Pillage and Property. Mimeo
4. Kohlberg, E., Mertens, J.-F. (1986) On the strategic stability of equilibria. *Econometrica* 54: 1003–1037
5. Lucas, W. (1992) Von Neumann-Morgenstern stable sets. In: Aumann, R., Hart, S. (eds.) *Handbook of Game Theory*. Elsevier Science Publishers B.V., 543–590
6. Myerson, R. (1991) *Game Theory: Analysis of Conflict*. Harvard University Press, Cambridge
7. Roth, A. (1976) Subsolutions and the supercore of cooperative games. *Mathematics of operations research* 1: 43–49
8. Von Neumann, J., Morgenstern, O. (1947) *Theory of Games and Economic Behavior*. Wiley, New York

Mediation and the Nash bargaining solution

Charles A. Wilson

Department of Econimics, New York University, New York, NY 10003, USA
(e-mail: Charles.Wilson@nyu.edu)

Abstract. This paper analyzes a model of bargaining in which two parties use a mediator who sequentially makes random proposals until agreement by both parties is reached. I show that as the cost of delay shrinks to zero, the subgame perfect payoff converges to the asymmetric Nash bargaining solution with weights determined by the relative discount rates of the players. I also establish conditions for the uniqueness of the subgame perfect equilibrium for arbitrary discount rates.

1 Introduction

This paper analyzes a model of bargaining in which two parties use a mediator to agree upon a contract. At the outset of the game, a mediator draws a contract proposal according to an exogenous probability distribution over some feasible set of alternatives. After the proposal is announced, each player chooses to either accept or reject it. If one of the players rejects the proposal, the game proceeds to the next stage where the mediator draws another proposal using the same distribution. If the proposed contract is accepted by both players at stage t, then each player receives his corresponding discounted von Neumann-Morgenstern payoff.

The main result of the paper is that as the discount rates become arbitrarily small, the subgame perfect (SP) payoffs converge to the asymmetric Nash bargaining solution (ANBS) (Nash (1953)) with weights determined by the discount rates of the players. This result applies to any game in which the distribution of proposals has a continuous density f on a compact, convex, comprehensive support, U, that defines the utility possibility set. I also establish that for any

I thank Ariel Rubinstein for pointing me toward this problem and an anonymous referee for pointing out some ambiguities in an earlier version. Support from the C. V. Starr Center for Applied Economics at New York University is gratefully acknowledged.

pair of discount factors, the subgame perfect payoff is unique if f is a concave function on U.

The model is motivated by problems where the underlying issues are sufficiently complex that the benefits of a particular contract may not be readily apparent to a mediator. Even if the parties are willing and able to discuss their general preferences, important features of the contracts may interact in ways that make it impossible for the players to articulate reasonably complete preference orderings over the space of contracts. Under such circumstances, the mediator may be forced to "discover" a mutually acceptable proposal by trial and error. Since each contract proposal implies a payoff to each player, the space of possible contracts defines a utility possibility set in the space of payoff pairs. The model to be studied corresponds to the extreme case where the mediator learns nothing about the payoffs of other possible contracts from the players' responses to any specific contract proposal. Consequently, the payoff pair proposed by the mediator at any stage is effectively drawn from same exogenous probability distribution over the utilty possibility set.

Binmore, Rubinstein, and Wolinksy (BRW) (1986) demonstrate the convergence of the SP payoffs to the ANBS in two versions of the standard bargaining game with alternating offers (Rubinstein (1982)). The model studied here has essentially the same asymptotic properties as does BRW, but for non negligible discount rates, the properties of the SP equilibria are significantly different. Since the available proposal in any stage is determined by a exogenous random process rather than purely strategic considerations, agreement need not occur in the first stage of the process. Also, when agreement is reached, typically neither player extracts all of the surplus over their respective returns to delaying agreement for one period. One consequence of these differences is that here the SP payoff need not be unique, and in any case, generally depends on the exogenous distribution used by the mediator. As a consequence, it is not possible to translate their argument for the convergence of the SP payoff to the ANBS to the mediation game.

The analysis used here follows the basic approach used in Merlo and Wilson (MW) (1995). I first study the restricted class of stationary subgame perfect (SSP) equilibria and then extend the results to the class of all SP payoffs. An SSP strategy may be characterized by a reservation payoff level below which the player rejects the mediator's proposal, permitting a simple characterization of an SSP payoff. This characterization is used to establish the convergence of the SSP payoffs to the ANBS and to provide conditions for the uniqueness of the SP payoff. To extend these results to the set of all SP payoffs, I show that the set of SP payoffs is bounded by a pair of SSP payoffs. Consequently, if the SSP payoff is unique, then the SP payoff is as well. Similarly, if the set of SSP payoffs converges to a single point, then so does the set of SP payoffs.

The argument for the convergence of SSP payoffs to the ASNB goes as follows. The pair SSP reservation values (v_1, v_2) determine an acceptance set A of proposals in U, which combined with the density f yields the probability p that an offer is accepted by both players and the expected payoff $\bar{u}_i$ of a mutually acceptable proposal for each player i. Letting δ_i denote the rate at which payoffs are discounted when agreement is delayed, Bellman's equation requires that the reservation value for each player i be chosen so that $\delta_i v_i = p(\bar{u}_i - v_i)$. Taking the ratio of these equations, we obtain

$$\frac{\delta_2 v_2}{\delta_1 v_1} = \frac{(\bar{u}_2 - v_2)}{(\bar{u}_1 - v_1)}.$$

To establish the convergence of (v_1, v_2) to the ASNB, I show that as the discount rates converge to zero, the acceptance set A shrinks to a point. Consequently, for sufficiently small discount rates, f is approximately constant on A. But for a constant density f and small discount rates, $\frac{\bar{u}_2 - v_2}{\bar{u}_1 - v_1}$ is approximately equal to the slope of the utility possibility frontier. This equality leads to the same conditions for (v_1, v_2) that characterize the ASNB with weights δ_2 and δ_1 for players 1 and 2 respectively.

2 The game

Starting at stage 0, a mediator proposes a payoff allocation chosen according to some density function f over a *utility possibility set* $U \subset \mathbb{R}^2_+$. After the proposal is announced, player 1 chooses to either accept or reject the proposal. If he accepts, then player 2 chooses to accept or reject the proposal. If either player rejects the proposal, the game proceeds to the next stage where the mediator draws another proposal using the same probability density f and the players choose to accept or reject in the same order as before. This process continues until some proposal is accepted. If the proposed allocation (u_1, u_2) is accepted in some stage t, then the von Neumann-Morgenstern payoff is $u_i \beta_i^t$ for each player i, where $0 < \beta_i < 1$. If the players never agree, then their payoffs are both 0.

A more natural specification of the game might have the players respond simultaneously at each stage. I avoided this specification because it admits an additional stationary subgame perfect equilibrium in which both players choose a strategy that rejects every feasible proposal. From the analysis below, however, it should be apparent that any subgame perfect payoff for the game in which the players respond sequentially is also a subgame perfect payoff for the game in which they respond simultaneously. Furthermore, the set of subgame perfect payoffs does not depend on the order in which the players respond in any period. For instance, the players may respond first in alternate stages or the first responder may be chosen according some stochastic process which may even depend on the choice of the proposal.[1]

We assume that $U \equiv \left\{(u_1, u_2) \in \mathbb{R}^2_+ : g(u_1, u_2) \leq 0\right\}$ where $g : \mathbb{R}^2 \to \mathbb{R}$ is a continuous, convex, and strictly monotonic with $g(1, 0) = g(0, 1) = 0$. This implies that U is a strictly comprehensive, convex, compact set with a nonempty

[1] In fact, the game with simultaneous responses yields the same set of subgame perfect payoffs as does the game with sequential responses if, for each player i, there is some subset of proposals, which the mediator offers with positive probability, that he must accept.

interior. Payoffs are normalized so that the maximum value of both u_1 and u_2 is 1. To represent the *utility possibility frontier*, we define the concave function $\phi_2 : [0,1] \to [0,1]$ and its inverse $\phi_1 : [0,1] \to [0,1]$ by

$$g(u_1, \phi_2(u_1)) \equiv 0 \quad \text{and} \quad g(\phi_1(u_2), u_2) \equiv 0.$$

Let $\phi_2^-(u_1)$ and $\phi_2^+(u_1)$ respectively denote the left and right derivatives of ϕ_2 at u_1.

The probability density f is assumed to be continuous and strictly positive on its support U. Then, since our assumptions on g imply that U is a compact set, there is some lower bound $f_m > 0$ such that $f(u_1, u_2) > f_m$ for all $(u_1, u_2) \in U$.

A strategy for each player i may be characterized by a specification of which proposals he accepts at any stage, given the sequence of proposals and responses by the two players that has preceded it. For any subgame perfect (SP) equilibrium, define $\beta_i u_i$ to be the *SP payoff* to player i, where u_i is his expected payoff before the mediator announces his proposal.[2] A *stationary subgame perfect* (SSP) equilibrium is a SP equilibrium in which set of proposals that a player accepts is the same at each history of the game.

We begin our analysis by studying the SSP payoffs and then extend our analysis to the SP payoffs in Sect. 6. Proofs of all formal results are provided in the Appendix.

3 Necessary and sufficient conditions for SSP payoffs

For any SSP equilibrium, let v_i denote the expected discounted payoff to player i if the current proposal is rejected. Then if player 1 accepts the current proposal (u_1, u_2), the best response for player 2 is to accept the proposal if and only if $u_2 \geq v_2$. But if player 1 correctly anticipates the response of player 2, then for any proposal (u_1, u_2) with $u_2 \geq v_2$, his best response is to accept if and only if $u_1 \geq v_1$. We call v_i the *reservation value* for player i and refer to $v \equiv (v_1, v_2)$ as the *reservation value pair.*

Given a reservation value pair (v_1, v_2), we define the *acceptance set,*

$$A(v_1, v_2) \equiv \{(u_1, u_2) \in U : u_1 \geq v_1,\ u_2 \geq v_2\},$$

to be the set of proposals that are accepted by both players. As illustrated in Fig. 1, $w_1 \equiv \phi_1(v_2)$ and $w_2 \equiv \phi_2(v_1)$ are the respective maxima of the payoffs in the acceptance set for each player.

From Theorem 6 of Blackwell (1965), (v_1, v_2) is an SSP reservation value pair if and only if the following equation is satisfied for each player i,

$$v_i = \beta_i \left(\int_{A(v_1,v_2)} (u_i - v_i) f(u_1, u_2) d(u_1, u_2) + v_i \right). \tag{1}$$

[2] We discount his expected payoff so that the SSP payoff is equal to the SSP reservation rule to simplify notation.

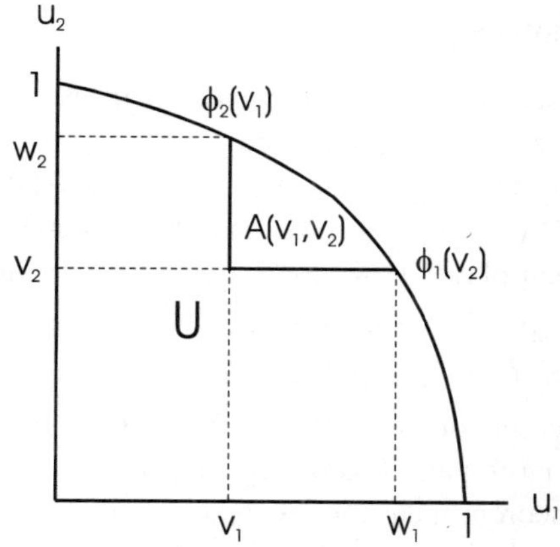

Fig. 1. The acceptance set

Equation (1) implies that each $v_i \leq \beta_i$. Therefore, since U is convex, it follows that $A(v_1, v_2)$ has positive probability for any $v_1 < 1 - \beta_2$. We conclude that any SSP reservation value pair must be strictly positive.

Let $\delta_i \equiv \frac{1-\beta_i}{\beta_i}$ denote the discount *rate* for each player i. Then, Eq. (1) may be equivalently expressed as

$$\begin{aligned} G_i(v_1, v_2) &\equiv \delta_i v_i - \int_{A(v_1,v_2)} (u_i - v_i) f(u_1, u_2) d(u_1, u_2) \\ &= 0. \end{aligned} \tag{2}$$

Notice that the optimal response of each player depends only on the value of f on $A(v_1, v_2)$. Moreover, the relative magnitude of the SSP reservation values of the two players depends only on the ratio of the differences between the reservation value and expected payoff over the acceptance set of the two players. To see this, let

$$p(v_1, v_2) \equiv \int_{A(v_1,v_2)} f(u_1, u_2) d(u_1, u_2)$$

denote the probability that the proposal is accepted and let

$$\bar{u}_i(v_1, v_2) \equiv \frac{\int_{A(v_1,v_2)} u_i f(u_1, u_2) d(u_1, u_2)}{\int_{A(v_1,v_2)} f(u_1, u_2) d(u_1, u_2)}$$

denote the expected value of an accepted proposal. Then, we may write Eq. (2) as

$$G_i(v_1, v_2) \equiv \delta_i v_i - p(v_1, v_2)(\bar{u}_i(v_1, v_2) - v_i) = 0. \tag{3}$$

Taking the ratio of Eq. (3) for the two players and suppressing the (v_1, v_2) arguments, we then obtain

$$\frac{\delta_2 v_2}{\delta_1 v_1} = \frac{\bar{u}_2 - v_2}{\bar{u}_1 - v_1}. \tag{4}$$

4 Existence and uniqueness of SSP payoffs

To establish the existence of an SSP payoff pair, we use a standard fixed point argument. Our conditions on U and f imply that $G_1(v_1, v_2)$ is continuously differentiable in both arguments, with $\frac{\partial G_1}{\partial v_1} > 0$. Also, given any $v_2 \geq 0$, $G_1(0, v_2) \leq 0$ and $G_1(1, v_2) \geq 0$. The analogous properties are satisfied for G_2. Therefore, for each player i, we may define the continuously differentiable function $v_i^* : [0,1] \to [0,1]$ to respectively satisfy

$$G_1(v_1^*(v_2), v_2) = 0 \quad \text{and} \quad G_2(v_1, v_2^*(v_1)) = 0.$$

From the characterization of an SSP payoff given in Eq. (2), it follows that (v_1, v_2) is an SSP payoff pair if and only if $(v_1, v_2) = \left(v_1^*(v_2), v_2^*(v_1)\right)$. The Brower fixed point theorem then implies the existence of an SSP equilibrium.

To investigate the uniqueness of the SSP payoffs, define $h : [0,1] \to [0,1]$ by

$$h(x) \equiv v_1^*(v_2^*(x)).$$

Then (v_1, v_2) is an SSP payoff pair if and only if $v_1 = h(v_1)$ and $v_2 = v_2^*(v_1)$. For each player i, the properties of G_i imply that $0 < v_i^*(0) < 1$ and $v_i^*(1) = 0$. Therefore, $h(0) > 0$, and $h(1) < 1$. Furthermore, since $p(v_1, v_2) > 0$ at an SSP equilibrium, it follows from Eq. (2) that $\frac{\partial G_1}{\partial v_2} > 0$ and $\frac{\partial G_2}{\partial v_1} > 0$. Then since each $\frac{\partial G_i}{\partial v_i} > 0$, implicit differentiation of (2) yields $\frac{\partial v_1^*(v_2)}{\partial v_2} < 0$ and $\frac{\partial v_2^*(v_1)}{\partial v_1} < 0$, which in turn imply that $\frac{\partial h(v_1)}{\partial v_1} \equiv \frac{\partial v_1^*(v_2)}{\partial v_2}\frac{\partial v_2^*(v_1)}{\partial v_1} > 0$. Therefore, if $\frac{\partial h(x)}{\partial x} < 1$ at each fixed point x of h, then the SSP payoff pair must be unique. However, if there is an x such that $h(x) = x$ and $\frac{\partial h(x)}{\partial x} > 1$, then there must be at least three SSP equilibria.

Without some additional restrictions on the density f, the necessary conditions for a unique SSP payoff pair may not be satisfied. Consider a game with a linear utility possibility frontier so that $\phi_1(u_1) = 1 - u_1$ and $w_2 = 1 - v_1$. To simplify the example further, suppose that the support of the distribution is concentrated on utility possibility frontier so that $u_1 + u_2 = 1$ with probability 1. Then, $\bar{u}_1(v_1, v_2) + \bar{u}_2(v_1, v_2) = 1$. Therefore, if both players have the same discount rate δ, Eq. (3) may be expressed as

$$\frac{1 - w_1}{v_1} \equiv \frac{v_2}{v_1} = \frac{\bar{u}_2 - v_2}{\bar{u}_1 - v_1} \equiv \frac{w_1 - \bar{u}_1}{\bar{u}_1 - v_1}. \tag{5}$$

If f is decreasing over $[v_1, w_1]$ so that more weight is put on proposals with u_1 near v_1, then $\frac{w_1 - \bar{u}_1}{\bar{u}_1 - v_1} > 1$. Conversely, if f is increasing over $[v_1, w_1]$, then $\frac{w_1 - \bar{u}_1}{\bar{u}_1 - v_1} < 1$. Consequently, if the probability density is bimodal so that it first decreases and then increases with u_1, there may be more than one solution to the pair of equations defined by (3).

Example 1. *Suppose the support of f is the utility possibility frontier and let $f(u_1)$ denote the probability density at each point $(u_1, \phi_1(u_1))$. If $\phi_1(u_1) = 1 - u_1$, the players have a common discount factor $\delta \in \left(0, \frac{1}{4}\right)$, and*

$$f(x) = \begin{cases} 2 - 4x & \text{for } 0 \leq x \leq \frac{1}{2} \\ 4x - 2 & \text{for } \frac{1}{2} \leq x \leq 1, \end{cases}$$

then there are three SSP equilibria.

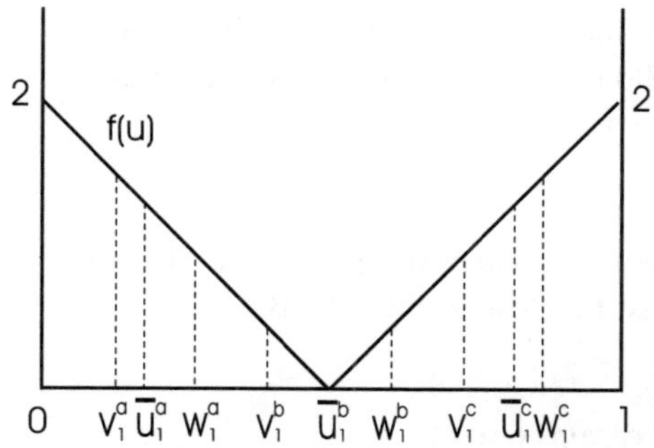

Fig. 2. Multiple SSP payoffs

The proof of this claim is in the Appendix. Figure 2 illustrates the three SSP reservation value pairs $\left(v_1^\alpha, 1 - w_1^\alpha\right)$, which are superscripted by a, b, and c respectively. For $v_1^a < w_1^a < \frac{1}{2}$, f is decreasing between v_1^a and w_1^a. Consequently, $\bar{u}_1^a - v_1^a < w_1^a - \bar{u}_1^a$, as required by Eq. (5). Similarly, for $\frac{1}{2} < v_1^c < w_1^c$, f is increasing between v_1^c and w_1^c, which implies $\bar{u}_1^c - v_1^c > w_1^c - \bar{u}_1^c$. The SSP reservation value pair $\left(v_1^b, 1 - w_1^b\right)$ is symmetric around $\bar{u}_1^b = \frac{1}{2}$.

For the general model, this type of example cannot be constructed if f is a concave function on U.

Theorem 1. *If f is concave, then there is a unique SSP payoff pair.*

5 Convergence to the asymmetric Nash bargaining solution

For any $\alpha \in [0, 1]$, the *asymmetric Nash bargaining solution* (ANBS) $\zeta(\alpha)$ is the unique element of U which maximizes $\alpha \log u_1 + (1 - \alpha) \log u_2$ subject to $g(u_1, u_2) \leq 0$. It follows from the convexity of U that $\zeta : [0, 1] \to U$ is a continuous function and, for each $\alpha \in [0, 1]$, $(z_1, z_2) \equiv \zeta(\alpha)$ is the uniquely determined by the relations,

$$-(1-\alpha) z_1 \phi_2^-(z_1) \leq \alpha z_2 \leq -(1-\alpha) z_1 \phi_2^+(z_1) \quad (6)$$

$$z_2 = \phi_2(z_1). \quad (7)$$

Also note that z_1 is nondecreasing (and z_2 nonincreasing) in α.

Our next theorem establishes that if at least one of the discount rates is sufficiently small, the pair of SSP payoffs must be be close to the ANBS, $\zeta(\frac{\delta_2}{\delta_1+\delta_2})$.

Theorem 2. *For any $\varepsilon > 0$, there is a $\delta > 0$ such that* $\min\{\delta_1, \delta_2\} < \delta$ *implies that any SSP payoff pair (u_1, u_2) satisfies* $\max\{|z_1 - u_1|, |z_2 - u_2|\} < \varepsilon$, *where* $(z_1, z_2) = \zeta\left(\frac{\delta_2}{\delta_1+\delta_2}\right)$.

The strategy of the proof is as follows. We first establish that as the discount rate of either player converges to 0, $w_i - v_i$ converges to 0 for each player i. Consequently, since f is continuous and bounded away from 0, the distribution on $A(v_1, v_2)$ becomes approximately uniform. However, if f is uniform on $A(v_1, v_2)$, then we may show that $\frac{\bar{u}_2 - v_2}{\bar{u}_1 - v_1}$ is bounded above by $-\phi_2^-(w_1)$ and below by $-\phi_2^+(v_1)$. It then follows from Eq. (4) that the relation

$$-\phi_2^+(v_1) \leq \frac{\delta_2}{\delta_1}\frac{v_2}{v_1} \leq -\phi_2^-(w_1).$$

is approximately satisfied. Then, using relations (6) and (7), we show that any SSP payoff pair must be close to the ASNB.

6 The duration of disagreement

From Theorem 2, we may establish some bounds on the duration of disagreement as δ becomes small. First note that since that (v_1, v_2) converges to the boundary of U, the acceptance set shrinks to a point. Therefore, the probability of agreement in any period converges to zero. In fact, the stopping time for agreement, τ, grows without bound with probability 1. Nevertheless, since the expected discounted SSP payoffs converge to the boundary of U, there is an upper bound on how quickly τ grows as the discount factor approaches one. In fact, if we fix the discount factor of each player i at δ_i and consider the game in which the mediator may make n sequential offers throughout each period, then Theorem 2 implies that $\lim_{n\to\infty} \frac{\tau}{n} = 0$ with probability arbitrarily close to 1. Under this interpretation, therefore, agreement occurs almost immediately as the rate at which proposals are offered grows arbitrarily large.

The argument goes as follows. Let u_i^τ denote the discounted payoff to player i that is accepted at the time of agreement τ. If the mediator can make n proposals per period, then for each player i, the effective discount factor between proposals is $\delta_i^{\frac{1}{n}}$, so that $v_i = E\left[\delta_i^{\frac{\tau+1}{n}} u_i^\tau\right]$.[3] Then, since $\left(u_1^\tau, u_2^\tau\right)$ must lie in $A(v_1, v_2)$ and (v_1, v_2) converges to the boundary of U, a straightforward argument establishes that $\lim_{n\to\infty} E\left[\delta_i^{\frac{\tau+1}{n}}\right] = 1$. But since $\delta_i^{\frac{\tau+1}{n}} < 1$, it follows that $\delta_i^{\frac{\tau+1}{n}} \to 1$ and hence $\frac{\tau+1}{n} \to 0$ with probability arbitrarily close 1 as $n \to \infty$.

7 Subgame perfect payoffs

Theorems 1 and 2 also apply to the set of SP payoffs. For each player i, let u_{i*} and u_i^* respectively denote the infinum and supremum of the set of his SP payoffs. Then we may exploit the continuity of each G_i to establish that $G_1(u_{1*}, u_2^*) = G_2(u_{1*}, u_2^*) = 0$ and $G_1\left(u_1^*, u_{2*}\right) = G_2\left(u_1^*, u_{2*}\right) = 0$, which implies the following lemma.

Lemma 1. *(u_{1*}, u_2^*) and $\left(u_1^*, u_{2*}\right)$ are SSP payoff pairs.*

From Lemma 1, it follows immediately that we may extend Theorem 1 to the set of SP payoffs.

[3] We use $\tau + 1$ rather than τ in the exponent since v_i is defined as the expected payoff to player i if he rejects the current proposal.

Theorem 3. *If f is concave, then there is a unique SP payoff pair.*

If the SSP payoff pair is not unique, then the standard bootstrapping argument generates a continuum of SP payoffs. However, since Theorem 2 requires that that each SSP payoff must be close the ASNB, it follows from Lemma 1 that each SP payoff pair must be close as well.

Theorem 4. *For any $\varepsilon > 0$, there is a $\delta > 0$ such that* $\min\{\delta_1, \delta_2\} < \delta$ *implies that any SP payoff pair* (u_1, u_2) *satisfies* $\max\{|z_1 - u_1|, |z_2 - u_2|\} < \varepsilon$, *where* $(z_1, z_2) = \zeta\left(\frac{\delta_2}{\delta_1+\delta_2}\right)$.

8 Limitations and extensions

I conclude with a discussion of possible extensions and applications of the analysis developed in this paper.

8.1 Learning

A significant limitation of this game as a model of mediation is that the probability distribution of the mediator's proposal is the same in each period. Consequently, the model implicitly forbids the mediator to "learn" in response to rejections of his previous proposals. Even if the mediator is given no strategic role, it would be of interest to examine how the behavior of the two players change when the density of proposals in future periods changes in response to rejected offers.

Although I have not worked out the details, it appears that there is a class of games with this feature for which convergence result of Theorem 4 may also apply. The critical requirement is that the "learning" along any sample path of histories eventually converges to sufficiently well behaved "nondegenerate" beliefs. Consequently, if the players wait long enough without agreeing on a proposal, they are essentially facing a fixed probability density for any proposals to be offered by the mediator in all future periods. In this case, the argument behind Theorems 2 and 4 might be applied to establish that for games starting at any history with a sufficiently long list of rejected proposals, the SP payoff must be close to ASNB when the discount factors are close to 1. Then, since the SP length of delay grows without bound as the discount factors converge to 1, it would follow that almost all SP payoffs converge to ASNB.

Clearly, there are several details that need to be carefully worked out to establish a precise statment of this result. However, the informal argument sketched above suggests to me that the convergence results do extend to the SP payoffs of games with nontrivial responses by the mediator to rejected proposals.

8.2 Models of matching

This analysis might also be applied to a class of dynamic matching models in which the players in who meet in any period have the opportuntiy to consummate their match by accepting a randomly determined payoff pair.[4] In this case the density f describes the distribution over support U of the possible values of a match to any two players in the pool.

In each period, any player in the pool has a chance of meeting another player. When two players meet, they realize some pair of payoffs in U chosen according to probability density f. If they both agree to the match, they leave the pool with their payoffs. Otherwise, they remain in the pool. Assuming that all players discount the payoff to any future match at the same rate and have the same probability of meeting in each period, the common problem they must solve in a steady state is essentially the same as the problem facing a player in the mediation game in and SSP equilibrium. So long as the steady state probability of meeting stays bounded away from zero as the common discount factor approaches 1, we should obtain convergence of the expected discounted payoffs to the ASNB.

8.3 Many players

I conclude with a brief sketch of how the convergence results of Theorem 2 for SSP payoffs may be extended to games with n players in which the acceptance of a proposal requires unanimous consent. In this case, it is straightforward to check that the analogue to Eq. (2) characterizes the SSP payoffs, which leads to the n-player analogue to Eq. (3).

$$\delta_i v_i = p(v)\,(\bar{u}_i(v) - v_i) \tag{3a}$$

where $v = (v_1, ..., v_n)$ is the vector of reservation values, $p(v)$ is the corresponding probability of agreement, and $\bar{u}_i(v)$ is the expected payoff to player i, conditional on v being acceptable to each player.

Suppose the boundary of U is the unit simplex and f is constant on U.Then, there must be a $\lambda > 0$ such that $p(v)\,(\bar{u}_i - v_i) = \frac{1}{\lambda}$ for each player i. Substitution into (3a) then leads to the analogue of Eq. (5) for each player i,

$$\frac{1}{\delta_i v_i} = \lambda. \tag{5a}$$

But Eqs. (5a) and are precisely the first order conditions for the problem of choosing $v \in U$ to maximize $\sum_{i=1}^{n} \frac{\log v_i}{\delta_i}$, which characterizes the ASNB with weights $\frac{1}{\delta_i}$ for each player i. To establish that v converges to ASNB, all that remains is to observe that Eq. (2) implies as δ_i approaches 1, $p(v)$ converges to 0 and hence v must approach the boundary of U.

For case where U is required to be only a comprehensive convex set, I have not yet worked out a proof of the convergence of SSP payoffs to ASNB. The problem is to find an analogue to Lemma A1 of the Appendix.

It should be noted that for games with more than two players, Lemma 1 fails and the convergence result stated in Theorem 4 for SP payoffs does not apply.

[4] I am grateful to Dan Levin for observing this potential application and bringing it to my attention.

In fact, we may exploit well known arguments from the bargaining literature to show that any payoff pair in $int(U)$ is an SP payoff if all of the discount factors are sufficiently close to 1.

9 Appendix

Proof of Example 1. Note first that there is a unique symmetric SSP payoff $(v_1, v_2) = (v, v)$ determined by the solution to

$$\delta v = \int_v^{1-v} (x - v) f(x) dx = 2 \int_v^{1/2} (x - v)(2 - 4x)\, dx = \frac{(1 - 2v)^3}{2}. \tag{8}$$

At this solution,

$$\frac{\partial v_1^*(v_2)}{\partial v_2} = \frac{f(1 - v_2)(1 - v_2 - v_1)}{\delta + \int_{v_1}^{1-v_2} f(x)dx} = \frac{f(v)(1 - 2v)}{\delta + \int_v^{1-v} f(x)dx} = \frac{2(1 - 2v)^2}{\delta + (1 - 2v)^2}. \tag{9}$$

From the discussion in the text, it is sufficient to show that $\frac{\partial h(v_1)}{\partial v_1} > 1$.

Using (8) to eliminate δ in (9), we obtain

$$\frac{\partial v_1^*(v_2)}{\partial v_2} = \frac{2(1 - 2v)^2}{\frac{(1-2v)^3}{2v} + (1 - 2v)^2} = 4v.$$

By symmetry, $\frac{\partial v_2^*(v_1)}{\partial v_1} = \frac{\partial v_1^*(v_2)}{\partial v_2}$. Therefore, $\frac{\partial h*(v_1)}{\partial v_1} = \frac{\partial v_1^*(v_2)}{\partial v_2}\frac{\partial v_2^*(v_1)}{\partial v_1} > 1$ if and only if $v > \frac{1}{4}$, which by Eq. (8) is true if and only if $\delta < \frac{1}{4}$. □

Proof of Theorem 1. We will show that if (v_1, v_2) is an SSP payoff pair, then $\frac{\partial h(v_1)}{\partial v_1} < 1$. From the definition of G_1, we have

$$\frac{\partial G_1(v_1, v_2)}{\partial v_2} = \int_{v_1}^{w_1} (u_1 - v_1) f(u_1, v_2) du_1$$

$$\frac{\partial G_1(v_1, v_2)}{\partial v_1} = \delta_1 + p(v_1, v_2).$$

Therefore, at any *SSP* equilibrium, we have

$$\frac{\partial v_1^*(v_2)}{\partial v_2} = -\frac{\frac{\partial G_1(v_1,v_2)}{\partial v_2}}{\frac{\partial G_1(v_1,v_2)}{\partial v_1}} = \frac{\int_{v_1}^{w_1} (u_1 - v_1) f(u_1, v_2) du_1}{\delta_1 + p(v_1, v_2)} < \frac{\int_{v_1}^{w_1} (u_1 - v_1) f(u_1, v_2) du_1}{p(v_1, v_2)}.$$

Similarly,

$$\frac{\partial v_2^*(v_1)}{\partial v_1} < \frac{\int_{v_2}^{w_2} (u_2 - v_2) f(v_1, u_2) du_2}{p(v_1, v_2)}$$

Let $a \equiv \frac{w_2 - v_2}{w_1 - v_1}$ denote the negative of the slope of the line connecting (v_1, w_2) with (w_2, v_1), and define

$$B \equiv \{(u_1, u_2) \geq (v_1, v_2) : au_1 + u_2 \leq aw_1 + v_2\}$$

as the convex hull of $\{(v_1, v_2), (v_1, w_2), (w_2, v_1)\}$. Then since $A(v_1, v_2)$ is a convex set containing these three points, it follows that $B \subset A(v_1, v_2)$, and therefore,

$$\begin{aligned} p(v_1, v_2) &= \int_{A(v_1,v_2)} f(u_1, u_2)d(u_1, u_2) \geq \int_B f(u_1, u_2)d(u_1, u_2) \\ &= \int_0^{w_1 - v_1} \left(a \int_0^x f(y + v_1, a(x-y) + v_2)dy \right) dx \end{aligned}$$

The concavity of f implies that, for $0 < x < y$,

$$f(y + v_1, a(x-y) + v_2) \geq \frac{y}{x} f(x + v_1, v_2) + \frac{x - y}{x} f(v_1, ax + v_2).$$

Therefore,

$$\begin{aligned} &\int_0^x f(y + v_1, a(x-y) + v_2)dy \\ &\geq \int_0^x \left(\frac{y}{x} f(x + v_1, v_2) + \frac{x-y}{x} f(v_1, ax + v_2) \right) dy \\ &= \frac{f(x + v_1, v_2) + f(v_1, ax + v_2)}{2} x, \end{aligned}$$

from which we obtain

$$\begin{aligned} p(v_1, v_2) &\geq a \int_0^{w_1 - v_1} \frac{f(x + v_1, v_2) + f(v_1, ax + v_2)}{2} x dx \\ &= \frac{a}{2} \int_{v_1}^{w_1} a(u_1 - v_1) f(u_1, v_2) du_1 + \frac{1}{2a} \int_{v2}^{w_2} (u_2 - v_2) f(v_1, u_2) du_2. \end{aligned}$$

Then, from the general relation, $\left(\frac{a}{2}x + \frac{1}{2a}y\right)^2 = \left(\frac{a}{2}x - \frac{1}{2a}y\right)^2 + xy \geq xy$, we obtain

$$p(v_1, v_2)^2 \geq \left(\int_{v_1}^{w_1} (u_1 - v_1) f(u_1, v_2) du_1 \right) \left(\int_{v2}^{w_2} (u_2 - v_2) f(v_1, u_2) du_2 \right).$$

We conclude that

$$\frac{\partial h(v_1)}{\partial v_1} = \frac{\partial v_1^*}{\partial v_2} \frac{\partial v_2^*}{\partial v_1} < \frac{\int_{v_1}^{w_1} (u_1 - v_1) f(u_1, v_2) du_1}{p(v_1, v_2)} \frac{\int_{v2}^{w_2} (u_2 - v_2) f(v_1, u_2) du_2}{p(v_1, v_2)} \leq 1.$$

□

The proof of Theorem 2 requires the following two lemmata.

Lemma A1. $-\phi_2^+(v_1) \leq \frac{\int_{A(v_1,v_2)} (u_2 - v_2))d(u_1, u_2)}{\int_{A(v_1,v_2)} (u_1 - v_1))d(u_1, u_2)} \leq -\phi_2^-(w_1).$

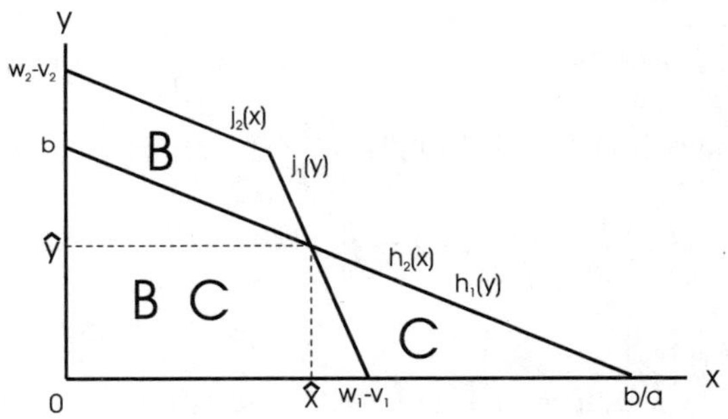

Fig. 3. Proof of Lemma A1

Proof. We will establish the first inequality of the Lemma. The argument for the second inequality is essentially the same.

Let

$$B \equiv \left\{u \in \mathbb{R}^2 : (u_1 + v_1, u_2 + v_2) \in A(v_1, v_2)\right\}$$

denote the set $A(v_1, v_2)$ with (v_1, v_2) normalized as the origin so that for each player i,

$$\int_{A(v_1,v_2)} (u_i - v_i)\, d(u_1, u_2) = \int_B u_i d(u_1, u_2). \tag{10}$$

For $a, b > 0$ let

$$C \equiv \left\{(u_1, u_2) \in \mathbb{R}_+^2 : au_1 + u_2 \leq b\right\} .$$

Fix $a \equiv -\phi_2^+(v_1) > 0$ and choose $b > 0$ so that the area of C is equal to the area of B,

$$\int_C du \equiv \int_0^{\frac{b}{a}} (b - ax)\, dx = \int_B du. \tag{11}$$

Define

$$\begin{aligned} h_2(x) &\equiv \max\{b - ax, 0\} \\ j_2(x) &\equiv \begin{cases} \phi_2(x + v_1) - v_2 & \text{for } x \in [0, w_1 - v_1] \\ 0 & \text{otherwise.} \end{cases} \end{aligned}$$

Then, since the slope of the upper boundary of C is equal to $a \equiv -\phi_2^+(v_1)$ and ϕ_2 is concave, it follows that there is an $\hat{x} > 0$ such that, for all $x \geq 0$,

$$(j_2(x) - h_2(x))\,(x - \hat{x}) \leq 0, \tag{12}$$

as illustrated in Fig. 3. (If the upper boundary of B is linear so that $C = B$, then the choice of $\hat{x}$ is arbitrary.)

By definition,

$$\int_B u_1\, d(u_1, u_2) \equiv \int_0^{w_1 - v_1} x\,(\phi_2(x + v_1) - v_2)\, dx \equiv \int_0^{\infty} x\, j_2(x)\, dx$$

and

$$\int_C u_1\, d(u_1,u_2) \equiv \int_0^{\frac{b}{a}} x\,(b-ax)\,dx \equiv \int_0^{\infty} x\, h_2(x)\, dx$$

Therefore, relations (11) and (12) imply

$$\int_B u_1\, d(u_1,u_2) - \int_C u_1\, d(u_1,u_2) = \int_0^{\infty} (x-\hat{x})\,(j_2(x)-h_2(x))\; dx \le 0.$$

Then, since,

$$\int_C u_1\, d(u_1,u_2) \equiv \int_0^{\frac{b}{a}} x\,(b-ax)\,dx = \frac{b^3}{6a^2},$$

we have

$$0 < \int_B u_1\, d(u_1,u_2) \le \frac{b^3}{6a^2}. \tag{13}$$

For player 2, we define

$$\begin{aligned} h_1(y) &\equiv \max\left\{\frac{b-y}{a}, 0\right\} \\ j_1(y) &\equiv \begin{cases} \phi_1(y+v_2)-v_1 & \text{for } y \in [0, w_2-v_2] \\ 0 & \text{otherwise.} \end{cases} \end{aligned}$$

Let $\hat{y} = b - a\hat{x}$. Then,

$$(j_1(y) - h_1(y))\,(y-\hat{y}) \ge 0$$

for all $y \ge 0$. Following the same steps as above, we obtain

$$\int_B u_2\, d(u_1,u_2) \ge \int_C u_2\, d(u_1,u_2) \equiv \int_0^{b} x\left(\frac{b-x}{a}\right) dx = \frac{b^3}{6a} > 0. \tag{14}$$

Dividing relation (14) by relation (13) yields

$$\frac{\int_B u_2 d(u_1,u_2)}{\int_B u_1 d(u_1,u_2)} \ge a \equiv -\phi_2^+(v_1)\,.$$

The desired result then follows relation (10). □

Lemma A2. *Suppose* (v_1, v_2) *is an SSP reservation value pair. Then for any* $\varepsilon > 0$, *there is a* $\delta > 0$ *such that* $\min\{\delta_1, \delta_2\} < \delta$ *implies* $\max\{w_1 - v_1, w_2 - v_2\} < \varepsilon$.

Proof. We establish the result for $\delta_1 < \delta$. The proof for $\delta_2 < \delta$ is essentially identical.

Fix $\varepsilon > 0$. Since ϕ_2 is continuous and strictly decreasing on the compact set $[0,1]$, it is uniformly continuous on $[0,1]$. Therefore, we may choose $\eta > 0$ such that $w_1 - v_1 < \eta$ implies $\phi_2(v_1) - \phi_2(w_1) \equiv w_2 - v_2 < \varepsilon$. To prove the lemma, all that remains is to show that for any $\eta > 0$, there a $\delta > 0$ such that $\delta_1 < \delta$ implies $w_1 - v_1 < \eta$.

Recall that f is bounded below by $f_m > 0$. Then, since $v_1 \leq 1$, Eq. (2) implies that

$$\begin{aligned}\delta_1 &\geq \int_{A(v_1,v_2)} (u_1 - v_1) f(u_1,u_2) d(u_1,u_2) \\ &= \int_{v_1}^{w_1} (u_1 - v_1) \left(\int_{\phi_2(w_1)}^{\phi_2(u_1)} f(u_1,u_2) du_2 \right) du_1 \\ &\geq f_m \int_{v_1}^{w_1} (u_1 - v_1)(\phi_2(u_1) - \phi_2(w_1))\, du_1 .\end{aligned}$$

Let

$$\delta \equiv f_m \int_0^{\eta} x\ (\phi_2(0) - \phi_2(\eta - x))\ dx,$$

and suppose $w_1 - v_1 \geq \eta$. We will show that $\delta_1 \geq \delta$. Since ϕ_2 is concave and strictly decreasing, it follows that

$$\begin{aligned}\int_0^{\eta} x\ (\phi_2(0) - \phi_2(\eta - x))\ dx &\leq \int_0^{\eta} x\ (\phi_2(x) - \phi_2(\eta))\ dx \\ &\leq \int_0^{w_1 - v_1} x\ (\phi_2(x) - \phi_2(w_1 - v_1))\ dx \\ &\leq \int_{v_1}^{w_1} (u_1 - v_1)\ (\phi_2(u_1) - \phi_2(w_1))\ du_1,\end{aligned}$$

and therefore

$$\delta \leq f_m \int_{v_1}^{w_1} (u_1 - v_1)\ (\phi_2(u_1) - \phi_2(w_1))\ du_1 \leq \delta_1 .$$

□

Proof of Theorem 2. Let $(z_1, z_2) \equiv \zeta(\frac{\delta_2}{\delta_1+\delta_2})$ denote the ANBS, and for $0 < \eta < 1$, let $(x_1, x_2) \equiv \zeta(\frac{\delta_2}{(1+\eta)\delta_1+\delta_2})$ and $(y_1, y_2) \equiv \zeta(\frac{\delta_2}{(1-\eta)\delta_1+\delta_2})$. Then $x_1 < z_1 < y_1$ and $y_2 < z_2 < x_2$.

Fix $\varepsilon > 0$. Since $0 < \frac{\delta_2}{(1-\eta)\delta_1+\delta_2} - \frac{\delta_2}{(1+\eta)\delta_1+\delta_2} < 2\eta$ and ζ is uniformly continuous on the compact set $[0, 1]$, we may choose $\eta > 0$ so that

$$\max\{y_1 - x_1,\ x_2 - y_2\} < \frac{\varepsilon}{2}. \tag{15}$$

Let (v_1, v_2) be an SSP reservation pair. Lemma A2 implies that we may choose $\delta > 0$ so that $\min\{\delta_1, \delta_2\} < \delta$ implies

$$\max\{w_1 - v_1,\ w_2 - v_2\} < \frac{\varepsilon}{2}. \tag{16}$$

We will show that $\delta > 0$ may also be chosen so that $\min\{\delta_1, \delta_2\} < \delta$ implies

$$v_1 \leq y_1 \quad \text{and} \quad w_1 \geq x_1, \tag{17}$$

which, by definition, also implies that

$$w_2 \geq y_2 \quad \text{and} \quad v_2 \leq x_2. \tag{18}$$

Then since any SSP payoff pair (u_1, u_2) satisfies $v_i < u_i < w_i$, it will follow from relations (15) to (18) that

$$\max\{z_1 - u_1, z_2 - u_2\} < \varepsilon$$

as desired.

Let f_H and f_L respectively denote the supremum and infinum of f over $A(v_1, v_2)$. Then, suppressing the arguments in $A(v_1, v_2)$, Eq. (2) implies

$$\delta_1 v_1 = \int_A (u_1 - v_1) f(u_1, u_2) d(u_1, u_2) \leq f_H \int_A (u_1 - v_1)\, d(u_1, u_2) \tag{19}$$

$$\delta_2 v_2 = \int_A (u_2 - v_2) f(u_1, u_2) d(u_1, u_2) \geq f_L \int_A (u_2 - v_2)\, d(u_1, u_2) \tag{20}$$

Since f is continuous and bounded below by $f_m > 0$, Lemma A2 implies that we may choose δ sufficiently small so that $1 - \eta < \frac{f_L}{f_H} < 1 + \eta$. Then, dividing relation (20) by relation (19) and using Lemma A1, we have

$$\begin{aligned} \frac{\delta_2}{\delta_1} \frac{\phi_2(v_1)}{v_1} > \frac{\delta_2 v_2}{\delta_1 v_1} &\geq \frac{f_L \int_A (u_2 - v_2)\, d(u_1, u_2)}{f_H \int_A (u_1 - v_1)\, d(u_1, u_2)} \\ &\geq -\frac{f_L}{f_H} \phi_2^+(v_1) \geq -(1 - \eta)\, \phi_2^+(v_1) \end{aligned} \tag{21}$$

and

$$\begin{aligned} \frac{\delta_2}{\delta_1} \frac{\phi_2(w_1)}{w_1} < \frac{\delta_2 w_2}{\delta_1 w_1} &\leq \frac{f_H \int_A (u_2 - v_2)\, d(u_1, u_2)}{f_L \int_A (u_1 - v_1)\, d(u_1, u_2)} \\ &\leq \frac{f_H}{f_L} \phi_2^-(w_1) \leq (1 + \eta)\, \phi_2^-(w_1). \end{aligned} \tag{22}$$

To establish that $v_1 \leq y_1$, we note that Eq. (6), the necessary condition for an ANBS, implies that $\frac{\delta_2 \phi_2(y_1)}{\delta_1 y_1} \leq -(1 - \eta)\, \phi_2^+(y_1)$. Suppose $v_1 > y_1$. Then, since ϕ_2 is concave and decreasing, we have $-\phi_2^+(v_1) \geq -\phi_2^+(y_1)$ and $\frac{\phi_2(v_1)}{v_1} < \frac{\phi_2(y_1)}{y_1}$, which implies $\frac{\delta_2 \phi_2(v_1)}{\delta_1 v_1} < -(1 - \eta)\, \phi_2^+(v_1)$, contradicting relation (21).

Similarly, Eq. (6) implies the necessary condition $\frac{\delta_2 \phi_2(x_1)}{\delta_1 x_1} \geq -(1 + \eta)\, \phi_2^-(x_1)$ which combined with relation (22) implies $w_1 \geq x_1$. □

Proof of Lemma 1. For each player i, let $A_i(v_i) \equiv \{(u_1, u_2) \in U : u_i \geq v_i\}$ denote the set of feasible payoff pairs at which player i receives at least v_i. Let $\mathscr{B}$ denote the Borel measurable subsets of U.

Regardles of the order in which he responds, the strategy of each player effectively specifies the subset of proposals that he accepts following any history up to the current stage. Consider an arbitrary history up to some stage and suppose that the strategy of player 2 is to accept proposal in the set B_2. Then the strategy of player 1 effectively determines the acceptance set at that history. Since u_2^* is the highest possible SP payoff for player 2, any SP strategy requires that he always accept any proposal (u_1, u_2) for which $u_2 > u_2^*$. Consequently, the menu of acceptance sets available to player 1 must include all Borel subsets of $A_2\left(u_2^*\right)$. In particular, player 1 may choose $A(u_{1*}, u_2^*) \equiv A_1(u_{1*}) \cap A_2(u_2^*)$. Since, in any SP equilibrium, player 1 can guarantee an expected payoff of at least u_{1*} by rejecting the current proposal, it follows that

$$\begin{aligned} u_{1*} &\geq \sup_{B \in \mathscr{B}} \left\{ \beta_1 \left(\int_B (u_1 - u_{1*}) f(u_1, u_2) d\,(u_1, u_2) + u_{1*} \right) : B \subset A_2\left(u_2^*\right) \right\} \\ &= \beta_1 \left(\int_{A(u_{1*}, u_2^*)} (u_1 - u_{1*})) f(u_1, u_2) d\,(u_1, u_2) + u_{1*} \right), \end{aligned}$$

which implies $G_1(u_{1*}, u_2^*) \geq 0$.

Similarly, since u_{1*} is the lowest possible SP payoff for player 1, he never accepts a proposal (u_1, u_2) for which $u_1 < u_{1*}$. Therefore, u_2^* satisfies

$$\begin{aligned} u_2^* &\leq \sup_{B \in \mathscr{B}} \left\{ \beta_2 \left(\int_B \left(u_2 - u_2^*\right) f(u_1, u_2) d\,(u_1, u_2) + u_2^* \right) : B \subset A_1(u_{1*}) \right\} \\ &= \beta_2 \left(\int_{A(u_{1*}, u_2^*)} \left(u_2 - u_2^*\right) f(u_1, u_2) d\,(u_1, u_2) + u_2^* \right), \end{aligned}$$

which implies $G_2(u_{1*}, u_2^*) \leq 0$. We will show that there is a $u_1 \leq u_{1*}$ and $u_2 \geq u_2^*$ such that $G_1(u_1, u_2) = G_2(u_1, u_2) = 0$. From Eq. (1), it then follows that (u_1, u_2) is an SSP reservation value pair, and therefore, that $u_1 = u_{1*}$ and $u_2 = u_2^*$.

Define $u_1^0 \equiv u_{1*}$ and $u_2^0 \equiv u_2^*$. For any integer $t > 0$, let

$$u_1^t \equiv \inf \left\{ u_1 \in \mathbb{R} : G_1(u_1, u_2^{t-1}) \geq 0 \right\}$$

and

$$u_2^t \equiv \inf \left\{ u_2 \in \mathbb{R} : G_2(u_1^{t-1}, u_2) \leq 0 \right\}.$$

Then, the inequalities above imply $u_1^1 \leq u_1^0$ and $u_2^1 \geq u_2^0$. But since $G_1(u_1, u_2)$ is nonincreasing in u_2 and $G_2(u_1, u_2)$ is nonincreasing in u_1, it then follows that $u_1^2 \leq u_1^1$ and $u_2^2 \geq u_2^1$. Proceeding by induction and using the property that $G_1(0, u_2) \leq 0$ and $G_2(u_1, 1) \geq 0$, we obtain $u_1^t \downarrow u_1 \geq 0$ and $u_2^t \uparrow u_2 \leq 1$. Also, since each G_i is continuous, it follows that for each $t > 0$, $G_1(u_1^t, u_2^{t-1}) = G_2(u_1^{t-1}, u_2^t) = 0$, and therefore that $G_1(u_1, u_2) = G_2(u_1, u_2) = 0$.

The analogous argument establishes that $\left(u_1^*, u_{2*}\right)$ is also an SSP reservation value pair. □

References

Binmore, K., Rubinstein, A., Wolinsky, A. (1986) The Nash bargaining solution in economic modelling. *Rand Journal of Economics* 17: 176–188

Blackwell, D. (1965) Discounted dynamic programming. *RAnnals of mathematical Statistics* 36: 226–235

Merlo, A., Wilson, C. (1995) A stochastic model of sequential bargaining with complete information. *Econometrica* 63: 371–399

Nash, J. (1953) Two person cooperative games. *Econometrica* 21: 128–140

Rubinstein, A. (1982) Perfect equilibrium in a bargaining model. *Econometrica* 50: 97–109

Public spending and optimal taxes without commitment

Jess Benhabib[1], **Aldo Rustichini**[2], **Andrés Velasco**[1,3]

[1] Department ov Economics, University New York, New York, NY 10003-6633, USA (e-mail: jess.benhabib@nyu.edu)

[2] Department of Economics, University of Minnesota, 271 19 Avenue South, Minneapolis, MN 55455, USA (e-mail: arust@econ.umn.edu)

[3] Kennedy School of Government, Harvard University, MA 02138, USA (e-mail: andres_velasco@harvard.edu)

Abstract. We consider a representative agent, infinite-horizon economy where production requires private and public capital. The supply of public capital is financed through distortionary taxation. The optimal (second best) tax policy of a benevolent government is time inconsistent. We therefore introduce explicitly the constraint that at no point in time the revision of the original tax plan is desirable. We completely characterize the (third best) tax plan that satisfies this constraint, and estimate the difference in tax rate between the second and third best policy for a wide range of parameters. For some of these the difference between the second and third best tax rates is large, and so are the associated rates of economic growth.

1 Introduction

The question of how much government should tax and spend is one of the key policy issues of economic development. If spending is productive and taxes are distortionary, then policymakers face a well defined trade-off. The resolution of this trade-off has implications both for the level of output and the rate of economic growth.

A good starting point is the growth model developed by Barro [1]. In that model the challenge for policy is to balance the distortions to savings decisions that arise from the taxation of capital against the benefits that arise from the provision of productive public services. Barro [1] showed that for particular specifications of preferences and technology the optimal fiscal policy in that model involves a constant tax rate, which is implementable even if government cannot commit to future taxes.

We are grateful to the C.V. Starr Center for Applied Economics at New York University for logistical support.

In more general specifications, however, a time inconsistency problem arises, with the sequences of tax rates implemented under discretion being quite different from those (the second best policy) implemented under precommitment.[1] In this paper we therefore introduce explicitly the constraint that at no point in time the revision of the original tax plan is desirable. We completely characterize the (third best) tax plan that satisfies this constraint, and estimate the difference in tax rate between the second and third best policy for a wide range of parameters.

Consider first the government's problem under precommitment. Optimal intertemporal taxation in this context has been extensively studied since the seminal works of Chamley ([6], [7]) and Judd [11].[2] In our model, the tax problem also has clear intertemporal implications. Since future taxes affect and distort savings and consumption decisions in all of the earlier periods, under precommitment optimal tax rates will (in general) not be constant: capital taxes in the earlier periods will be less distortionary than capital taxes in the future, and therefore will present a less costly trade-off in the financing of public goods.[3] This is true of in a broad class of intertemporal tax problems.[4]

Below we show that under commitment the optimal tax rates must asymptotically converge to the constant tax rate that maximizes the growth rate. This tax rate, which is independent of the capital stock because of the Barro [1] specification leading to endogenous growth, may be larger or smaller that the output-maximizing tax rate, depending on whether the elasticity of substitutionbetween

[1] Barro uses a Cobb-Douglas production function for output, with constant return to scale and private capital and public services as inputs. With this specification, the tax rate that maximizes output also maximizes the rate of return on capital, and therefore also maximizes the rate of growth. This simple setup has two implications: the optimal tax rate that maximizes the utility of the representative agent is constant, and there is no time inconsistency problem.

When we generalize the production function to a CES specification, the taxes that maximize output in each period, and which are the tax rates that would obtain in the discretionary equilibrium, are different than those which maximize the return on capital and the rate of growth. Furthermore, the optimal tax sequence under commitment is no longer constant (in particular, the initial-period tax rate is different from that of all subsequent periods), and the time-consistency problem emerges.

[2] In the models of Chamley and Judd the expenditures of government are modeled as an exogenous process. The tradeoff is between the intertemporal distortions of capital taxation and the distortions to labor supply decisions that come from labor taxes.

[3] In fact, since in the initial period capital is in fixed supply the optimal tax strategy will be to tax capital at a rate high enough that will force the public to borrow from the government a quantitity sufficient to generate interest income that will pay for all of its optimally desired expenditures. Since such a scheme with a negative net value of government bonds is highly unrealistic, it is standard in the optimal tax literature to impose bounds on the (negative) government bonds, or to limit the maximal tax rate in the first period. In the same spirit, we adopt in this paper a simplifying assumption to rule out government lending or borrowing, and we will require a balanced budget. The tradeoffs inherent in the problem of optimal capital taxation will remain, and be little affected under this assumption. The case with bonds in a model of the type considered by Chamley and Judd, but without commitment, is presented in Benhabib and Rustichini [3].

[4] In fact, Chamley and Judd obtain the remarkable result that if in the limit (as time tends to infinity), the economy converges to a stationary state, optimal capital tax rates under commitment must approach zero.

private capital and public services is above or below one. [5] Without commitment the story is very different: the government would want to reoptimize in each period and implement the tax rates that are optimal for the initial period (in our problem, these are the tax rates and associated supply of public services that maximize single-period output). Since agents would expect this and save accordingly, the outcome would be a bad (discretionary) equilibrium with low savings.[6] The inefficiency of such discretionary equilibria has led to a literature on "reputational equilibria" along the lines of trigger strategy equilibria in game theory. In models with reputational equilibria, the government must weigh the one-time benefits of deviating from the announced optimal policies against a loss of reputation that leads to a switch to policies and actions associated with the discretionary (bad) equilibrium. Many authors have shown, in a variety of contexts, that such reputational mechanisms can often sustain policies that are optimal under commitment.[7] But it is also possible –especially in a model with capital accumulation– that the one-time advantage of deviating from announced policies is so large that commitment policies are not sustainable, even if the consequence is the loss from deviating is a permanent loss of governmental reputation. Such situations lead quite naturally to the question of what the are the best sustainable or time-consistent tax policies. In this paper we fully characterize the best sustainable taxes and levels of public services in circumstances where a commitment by the government to future policies is not possible.

To characterize fully this best sustainable tax sequence we proceed in two steps. First, we must identify and characterize the worst possible equilibrium, which is the one to which the economy will revert if a deviation from the announced path takes place. It turns out that, in the extended Barro model, the worst (perfect) equilibrium is one in which, with a probability $1 - \varepsilon$ that is arbitrarily close to one, the government myopically implements the tax rate that maximizes output; since this tax rate is less than one, agents provide positive savings, and the economy grows over time. Notice that, unlike the Chari-Kehoe [8] model, this worst equilibrium is not the autarkic one in which the government attempts to tax all capital away and agents therefore save nothing. We provide below some intuition for this crucial difference between the two models.

Second, we compute the *third best* tax sequence that can be sustained by the threat of reversion to that worst equilibrium. Under some parametrizations the optimal tax rates associated with the commitment outcome cannot be sustained because the value of deviation at some future period exceeds the value of continu-

---

[5] In Benhabib and Velasco [4], a similar question is studied in the context of an open economy with international capital mobility. There it is assumed that capital taken abroad can avoid domestic taxes. Since world interest rates are fixed from the perspective of a small country, the analysis is considerably simplified. In contrast to the results of this paper, the optimal taxes under commitment, as well as those without commitment, turn out to be constant after the initial period.

[6] Results of these type are of course examples of a broader "time-consistency" problem discussed by Kydland and Prescott [12].

[7] See for example Stokey [16], Chari and Kehoe [9] or in a pure monetary context Barro and Gordon [2]. Lucas and Stokey [13] go a different route, studying how the maturity of government debt might render the commitment tax sequence time-consistent.

ation under the announced policy. We show that, in that case, the best sustainable asymptotic tax rates are constant and must lie between the output-maximizing and growth-maximizing tax rates. In particular, we show that in some very reasonably calibrated examples the optimal capital taxes under commitment can be substantially smaller than the best sustainable capital taxes.

The model presented above can be viewed within the broader context of the problem of characterizing best sustainable equilibria in dynamic games. Restricting attention to the best sustainable equilibria rather than all sustainable equilibria allows us to formulate the problem as an optimization problem subject to period-by-period incentive compatibility constraints that require the value of continuation to be larger than the value of deviation. Problems of this type have been considered by Marcet and Marimon [14] and by Benhabib and Rustichini [3]. In the optimal taxation problem considered in this paper, one further simplification arises from the Stackelberg nature of the game: the government moves first. On the other hand, additional difficulties arise from the fact that current saving decisions are complicated functions of all future tax rates.

The model also has implications for economic growth. The second best (commitment) solution would involve setting the tax rate so as to maximize the growth rate of the economy in the long run. Such a policy, however, is time inconsistent. The third best (reputational) policy involves a tax rate that is a compromise between the twin objectives of maximizing the rate of growth and maximizing the current period's level of output –and which therefore generally does not maximize the rate of growth. In short, time inconsistency leads to lower economic growth.

The next section describes the model and the equilibrium. Section 3 discusses the optimal taxes under commitment. Later sections identify and characterize the worst perfect equilibrium. The section after that sets up the problem with incentive constraints when commitment by the government to future tax rate is not possible. Section 6.3 provides some particular examples and provides a characterization of the optimal taxes without commitment. Section 7 provides a family of calibrated examples to illustrate numerically the differences between optimal taxes with and without commitment, while Sect. 8 concludes.

2 An economy with private and public services

We first describe our simple economy. There is one representative agent, who has an infinite life, and one private good, which is used both in production and in consumption. There are also public services, which are only used in production, and for which the government does not charge private agents. The government is benevolent, and can freely choose tax rates for the purpose of maximizing the utility of the representative agent. Taxes are used to finance the provision of the public capital good.

2.1 The technology

At the end of each period a certain amount of private capital, k_t, is available. Out of this a total amount $\tau_t k_t$ is then taxed away from the agent, and the rest is available for production. The output of the good is determined by a CES production function where both private capital and public services enter:

$$y_t = A\left(a(1-\tau_t)^{-\rho}k_t^{-\rho} + (1-a)g_t^{-\rho}\right)^{-\frac{1}{\rho}} \tag{2.1}$$

where g_t is the flow of public services, $\rho \in [-1, +\infty]$, $A \geq 0$. Note that the tax rate τ appears in the production function because $(1-\tau)k$ is the amount of private capital left untaxed and therefore available for production. The tax rate τ is usually assumed to range in the interval $[0, 1]$, but in some special case we may want to consider the restriction $\tau \in [\tau_L, \tau_B]$.

The provision of public services takes a very simple form. The total amount of taxes is converted one-to-one into public good, so that

$$g_t = \tau_t k_t \tag{2.2}$$

Using 2.2 in 2.1 we have

$$y_t = Ak_t\left(a(1-\tau_t)^{-\rho} + (1-a)\tau_t^{-\rho}\right)^{-\frac{1}{\rho}} \equiv Ak_t\phi(\tau_t) \tag{2.3}$$

Hence, the amount of private capital k_t affects total output in two ways: directly, and indirectly through the effect on total taxes and hence on the total amount of public services.[8]

In evaluating the return on private capital the representative agent will take the amount g_t as given, and will ignore the indirect effect. In equilibrium, however, the condition $g_t = \tau_t k_t$ can be substituted into the partial derivative of output with respect to k to obtain the marginal return that the agent is facing. If we do this we have (suppressing time subscripts for τ):

$$\frac{\partial y_t}{\partial k_t} \equiv AR(\tau) = Aa\phi(\tau)^{1+\rho}(1-\tau)^{-\rho} \tag{2.4}$$

Where clearly $R(\tau) > 0$ for every τ.[9] Note that

$$\begin{aligned} R(\tau) &= a\phi(\tau)^{1+\rho}(1-\tau)^{-\rho} \\ &\leq a\phi(\tau)^{1+\rho}(1-\tau)^{-\rho} + (1-a)\phi(\tau)^{1+\rho}\tau^{-\rho} \\ &= \frac{\partial\phi}{\partial(1-\tau)}(1-\tau) + \frac{\partial\phi}{\partial\tau}\tau = \phi(\tau) \end{aligned} \tag{2.5}$$

---

[8] Note that, because we are operating in a representative gent world, we have made no distiction between aggregate and per capita provision of public goods. In a world with many agents, on the other hand, that distinction would matter, ans would the distinction betwen rival and non-rival public services. The essentials of the analysis that follows would survive any of these extensions.

[9] If one wanted to ensure that clearly $R(\tau) > 1$ for every τ, it is possible to add a term Bk_t (where $B > 0$ is a parameter) to the production function to capture some pre-tax return on private capital. This would not affect any of the results that follow. Alternatively, one could confine the tax rate τ to a closed interval in $(0, 1)$ and make A large enough: this would also ensure the result $R(\tau) > 1$ for all allowable tax rates.

by the homogeneity of degree one of $\phi(\tau)$ in $(1-\tau)$ and τ. In particular, we have:

$$R(\tau) \leq \phi(\tau), \tag{2.6}$$

an inequality that we shall use frequently later. Note that if $\rho = 0$ we have Cobb-Douglas production, so that $R/\phi = a$.

2.2 Preferences and budget constraints

The representative agent owns the private capital stock. In each period he decides how much to consume out of the return on the private capital, minus the taxes plus a government transfer. The individual budget constraint has the form:

$$k_{t+1} = R(\tau_t)k_t + M_t - c_t = \phi(\tau_t)k_t - c_t \tag{2.7}$$

where M_t is the government transfer of the residual output after payments to capital.

The agent's utility from a consumption stream $\{c_t\}_{t\geq 0}$ is given by:

$$\sum_{t=0}^{\infty}(\frac{\sigma}{\sigma-1})c_t^{\frac{\sigma-1}{\sigma}}\beta^t \tag{2.8}$$

2.3 The competitive equilibrium for an given tax sequence

We now fix a sequence of tax rates $\tau = (\tau_0, \tau_1, \ldots)$ and compute the equilibrium of the economy for this arbitrary sequence. Details of the analysis are in the Appendix. The essential result is that for a given initial capital stock k_0 and a sequence of tax rates τ, lifetime utility for the agent can be written as a function $V(k_0, \tau)$, so that utility depends only on initial capital and the sequence of tax rates. The function is found to have the simple form

$$V(k_0, \tau) = (\frac{\sigma}{\sigma-1})(k_0)^{\frac{\sigma-1}{\sigma}}(\phi(\tau_0))^{\frac{\sigma-1}{\sigma}}h(\tau_1, \tau_2, \ldots) \tag{2.9}$$

Note that the initial capital stock k_0 and the sequence of tax rates $(\tau_0, \tau_1, \ldots)$ factor in the expression defining the value. In fact, it will be useful to isolate the term which involves only the initial and future expected tax rates:

$$H(\tau_0, \tau_1, \ldots) \equiv \phi(\tau_0)^{\left(\frac{\sigma-1}{\sigma}\right)}h(\tau_1, \ldots) \tag{2.10}$$

so that utility takes the even simpler form

$$V(k_0, \tau) = (\frac{\sigma}{\sigma-1})(k_0)^{\frac{\sigma-1}{\sigma}}H(\tau_0, \tau_1, \ldots) \tag{2.11}$$

Notice that when the terms of the sequence τ are constant over time then H has a simple form

$$H(\tau,\tau,\ldots) = \left(\phi(\tau) - (\beta R(\tau))^{\sigma}\right)^{\frac{\sigma-1}{\sigma}} \left(1 - \beta^{\sigma} R(\tau)^{\sigma-1}\right)^{-1} \tag{2.12}$$

For convenience, we assign a special symbol to the following function defined on $[0, 1]$:

$$H^*(\tau) \equiv H(\tau,\tau,\ldots). \tag{2.13}$$

This function will prove useful in the analysis that follows.

3 The optimal tax with commitment

In the previous section we have reduced the value to the agent, at the competitive equilibrium for a given sequence of tax rates, to a closed form expression in terms of the tax rates. If the government can commit to a sequence of tax rates in the first period, without possibility of revising the decision later, then the optimal sequence of tax rates is easy to determine. Existence of the optimal tax in our model is proved in the Appendix.

The trade-off between higher and lower tax rates should be clear. Since agents in the economy have no incentive to contribute to the accumulation of the public good, taxes are essential to its provision. The taxes that allow for the provision of public services, which is a complement in production, may well reduce the incentives for to private accumulation.

The details of the analysis of the optimal tax policy with commitment are in the Appendix. The main conclusion we derive there is that a necessary condition for the optimal tax sequence is that

$$\lim_{t\to\infty} R'(\tau_t) = 0 \tag{3.14}$$

That is to say, in the limit the optimal tax rate is that which maximizes the agent's perceived marginal return on investment, and therefore also maximize growth. Notice that $\widetilde{\tau}$ is henceforth defined as the tax rate that solves $R'(\widetilde{\tau}) = 0$. Under the assumed CES technology, the tax rate given by 3.14 is different from the tax rate given by $\phi'(\bar{\tau}) = 0$ which maximizes output within the period, but induces distortions to the accumulation process.

There is a clear similarity between condition 3.14 and the Chamley-Judd (see [6], [7], [11]) result that in the limit the tax rate on capital income goes to zero in optimal taxation with commitment: in both cases the tax rates in question maximize the growth rate of the economy.

In the case of Cobb-Douglas technology ($\rho = 0$) studied by Barro [1], we have an especially simple case. Since $R(\tau)/\phi(\tau) = a$, so that $\widetilde{\tau} = \bar{\tau}$. In that case, it is clear by inspection that $R'(\tau_t) = 0$ for all $t > 0$. We also have that $\phi'(\tau_0) = 0$, from maximizing $V(k_0, \tau)$. So τ_t is constant starting at time zero, and equal to the rate $\widetilde{\tau} = \bar{\tau}$. In words, the tax rate is constant and equal to the rate that simultaneously maximizes output levels and output rates of growth.

4 The model as a game

We now dispose of the assumption that the government can precommit, and study the determination of tax rates as the outcome of a game between the government and the public. To do so we must be a great deal more specific about the strategies open to both the government and the public, and about the equilibrium concept.[10]

4.1 Histories and strategies

The set of histories is the union of two distinct set of histories, one relevant for the government and the other relevant for the agents in the economy. So we let:

$$H \equiv H_G \cup H_P. \tag{4.15}$$

The histories in H_G have the form $(k_0, \tau_0, \ldots, k_{t-1}, \tau_{t-1})$; those in H_P have the form $(k_0, \tau_0, \ldots, \tau_t)$. Note that we do not report in the histories the savings of each individual, but only the aggregate savings. We call these "public histories".

A strategy for the government is a sequence $\gamma \equiv (\gamma_0, \ldots, \gamma_t, \ldots)$, where each γ_t is a function from H_G to the unit interval, describing the tax rate on capital for the period t as a function of the public history.

A strategy for the each agent in the public is a sequence $\pi^i \equiv (\pi^i_0, \ldots, \pi^i_t, \ldots)$, where each π^i_t maps the history of past tax rates and savings into future saving.

In our model the description of the strategies is simple. In fact, in this model agents are negligible, so the variables which are relevant for their decisions – namely the future tax rates and the future values of the aggregate capital– are independent from the actions of each single agent. Each agent cannot affect the value of the aggregate capital, since she is negligible, and she does not therefore have any influence on the tax rates, which depend on the aggregate savings. This implies that for a given strategy of the government the strategy of the public can be derived by solving the maximization problem of each agent. This fact is stated in the following lemma.

Lemma 1. *For each strategy of the government γ there is an induced strategy π of the public.*

Proof. Take for any t any history in H_P , and determine the pair of sequences $(k^*_s, \tau^*_{s+1})_{s \geq t}$, such that

i. the sequence of taxes is the one induced by γ and the sequence $(k^*_s)_{s \geq t}$;

[10] In setting up the model as a game we follow Chari and Kehoe [8], adjusting the structure to our situation. The main difference is that we model explicitly the strategy and the choices of the public (as they do in the section V of the paper, "Anonymous games", but not ins the main sections of the paper). The reason for this change is that we want to analyze the robustness of the equilibria in the game. To do this we need to introduce the strategies of the public explicitly. An alternative approach could be of course to consider small mistakes in the allocation rule used by the public. We chose this alternative because it is easier to use directly refinement concepts from game theory.

ii. the sequence of capital stocks is determined in each period by the maximization of the utility of each player, given the sequence $(k_s^*, \tau_{s+1}^*)_{s \geq t}$ of future aggregate capital and tax rates.

4.2 Definition of equilibrium

In our model, a *sustainable equilibrium* is defined as follows:

i. a history at t is a sequence $(\tau_0, \ldots, \tau_{t-1})$ of tax rates;
ii. a policy plan for the government is a function γ from histories into tax rates;
iii. an allocation rule is a function from histories to savings that solves the consumer's problem.

5 Perfect equilibria

We now characterize the worst perfect equilibrium in the Barro [1] model, which is the one will use as a threat in constructing the best sustainable tax sequence.

In this model there are several strategy profiles that can give rise to "bad" equilibria. By analogy with the Chari-Kehoe [8] model, one might expect the following strategies to be an equilibrium: the government sets $\tau_t = 1$ in every period, irrespective of the history. Each agent i sets the saving $k_t^i = 0$ in every period, also irrespective of the history. As the Appendix shows, this strategy profile gives rise to an equilibrium (termed Bad Equilibrium 1) that is both Nash and a sustainable equilibrium (the latter in the sense of Chari-Kehoe [8]), but it is not subgame perfect.

An alternative candidate strategy profile is the following: government chooses a tax rate equal to one in any period in which the aggregate savings are equal to zero; it chooses $\bar{\tau}$ in every period in which aggregate savings are positive; agents choose savings equal to zero in every period. As the Appendix also shows, these strategies give rise to an equilibrium (termed Bad Equilibrium 2) that is subgame perfect. However, it is not robust to small mistakes by players –that is, it is not a perfect equilibrium.

There is a third strategy profile, nevertheless, that does give rise to a perfect equilibrium. Informally, this is a situation where the government always implements the myopic output-maximizing tax rate ($\gamma_t(h_t) \equiv \bar{\tau}$ for every t and every history h_t) and the public follows the associated induced strategy, is a perfect equilibrium.

The technical definition of perfect equilibria here is complex, because there is a continuum of agents, and the action set of each has uncountable cardinality. To adapt the definition of perfect equilibria to this situation, we define a totally mixed strategy as a strategy which, with probability $\epsilon > 0$, chooses a value that is in turn drawn from a uniform distribution over the strategy space of the player (the unit interval for the government, the set of feasible savings for the agents).

Strategies are:

– the government sets the tax rate in each period to $\bar{\tau}$ with probability $1-\epsilon$. (The value of the tax rate is precisely $\bar{\tau}$, and is not affected by the ϵ);
– the public expects the tax rate $\bar{\tau}$ in each period with probability $1-\epsilon$, and with probability ϵ they expect the tax rate to be a random draw from a uniform distribution over the unit interval ; they maximize accordingly.

The ϵ *does* matter for the value of this program; so rather than a function $V(k)$ we have a function $V(k,\epsilon)$. However:

$$\lim_{\epsilon\to 0} V(k,\epsilon) = V(k) \tag{5.16}$$

for every k, even uniformly.

After any deviation, the government sets tax rate $\bar{\tau}$, also with probability $1-\epsilon$; the public saves optimally for a given sequence $\bar{\tau}$ of tax rates.

Theorem 1. *The "third best" strategies described above are a perfect equilibrium. The strategy of the government*

$$\gamma_t(h_t) \equiv \bar{\tau}$$

and the induced strategy for the public give rise to the worst Perfect Equilibrium;

Proof. For any history $h_t \in H_G$, the worst possible equilibrium depends only on the aggregate value of capital, and for any history $h_t \in H_P$ the worst possible equilibrium depends only on the aggregate capital and on the tax rate.

Notice also that the value at the worst equilibrium is increasing in the value of the aggregate capital stock. Now consider the problem of determining the tax rate, for any $\epsilon > 0$. Considering that after the period t the public and government will follow the continuation of the worst equilibrium, the government is maximizing the value of the utility of the public by choosing $\bar{\tau}$, which will give the largest value of the capital stock in the next period. Hence with probability $1-\epsilon$ the government will choose a tax rate equal to $\bar{\tau}$. □

There seems to be a considerable difference between our setup and the one of Chari-Kehoe, in view of what we have seen in this section. The single most important difference is that in Chari-Kehoe the autarchy equilibrium in which the tax rate on capital is one and private savings are zero is not only subgame perfect, but it can also easily be shown to be robust in the sense of being perfect. By contrast, in our setup an equilibrium in which the tax rate is one is not perfect –and the worst perfect equilibrium is one in which the tax rate is $\bar{\tau}$.

6 Characterizing third best tax rates

We now explicitly characterize the third best tax sequence that is supported by reputational considerations. By the definition of a perfect equilibrium, we let ε, the probability of mistakes by the government, go to zero. That means that, after deviation from the announced tax sequence, the economy reverts to a situation in which the government implements the output maximizing tax rate $\bar{\tau}$ with probability one, and the public saves accordingly.

6.1 The value of deviation

We begin by characterizing the value of deviating from the third best tax sequence. We can characterize this value before having characterized that tax sequence because, in this model, the value of deviation is independent of the path from which the government is deviating. That is not true in other models.

After the government deviates from a previously announced plan of tax rates, the sequence of events is the following. The public will believe that from that period on the government will maximize per period output –that is, will choose in each period the constant tax rate that maximizes the function $\phi()$. Appendix 9.3 shows that, if the public holds such expectations, the government's best response is to fulfill them starting the period after the deviation.

Anticipating this punishment, a government contemplating the possibility of deviating will choose the optimal deviation, which will in fact consist of maximizing output the period of deviation as well. The competitive equilibrium associated with this sequence of events is easy to characterize.

If agents expect all future values of τ to be set at $\bar{\tau}$, then it can be shown (details of this computation are in Appendix 9.3) that the closed form solution for the value of deviation is

$$V^D(k_t) = \left(\frac{\sigma}{\sigma-1}\right)(k_t)^{\frac{\sigma-1}{\sigma}} H^*(\bar{\tau}) \tag{6.17}$$

where

$$H^*(\bar{\tau}) \equiv \left(\phi(\bar{\tau}) - (\beta R(\bar{\tau}))^{\sigma}\right)^{\frac{\sigma-1}{\sigma}} \left(1-\beta^{\sigma} R(\bar{\tau})^{\sigma-1}\right)^{-1} \tag{6.18}$$

Let us point out immediately the features of this expression that we shall need in what follows, the value of deviating is independent of the current announced tax rate; results from the fact that when deviation begins, the government uses the $\bar{\tau}$ rate immediately. Second, the term $H^*(\bar{\tau})$ is a constant, and the dependence on the capital is of a very specific form –that is, it has the same functional form as utility. This will make a nice cancellation possible in the next step.

Take in fact, for a given tax plan τ, and a the capital stock k_t at period t the value to the representative agent of continuing with the plan, $V^C(k_t, \tau)$

$$V^C(k_t, \tau) = \left(\frac{\sigma}{\sigma-1}\right)(\phi(\tau_t)k_t)^{\frac{\sigma-1}{\sigma}} h(\tau_{t+1}, \tau_{t+2}, \ldots) \tag{6.19}$$

A tax plan is credible if and only if it does not give an incentive to the government to a revision in any period; that is, if and only if in each period after the first the continuation value $V^C(k_t, \tau)$ is larger than the deviation value $V^D(k_t)$.

But given the specific form of these two functions, the difference

$$V^C(k_t, \tau) - V^D(k_t) = \left(\frac{\sigma}{\sigma-1}\right) k_t^{\frac{\sigma-1}{\sigma}} \left((\phi(\tau_t))^{\frac{\sigma-1}{\sigma}} h(\tau_{t+1}, \tau_{t+2}, \ldots) - H^*(\bar{\tau})\right) \tag{6.20}$$

is non negative if and only if

$$(\phi(\tau_t))^{\frac{\sigma-1}{\sigma}} h(\tau_{t+1}, \tau_{t+2}, ...) - H^*(\bar{\tau}) \geq 0, \text{ for all } t \geq 1 \qquad (6.21)$$

The remarkable feature of 6.21 is that is does not involve the value of capital, but only of the future string of tax rates.

Before we proceed to analyze the general case, let us consider what 6.21 implies in the case of a Cobb-Douglas technology. When $\rho = 0$ then (as we have discussed above) in the optimal tax sequence for the commitment case τ_t is equal to a constant for every $t \geq 0$. So the infinitely many constraints of 6.21 reduce to a single constraint. In the general case, however, we have to take into account the entire (infinite) set.

6.2 The third best problem

If the government, at the moment of choosing a tax plan, has no commitment power over its own choices, then it has to confine the choice to the set of tax plans that in each period satisfy the constraint 6.21, which we call the *Incentive Compatibility Constraint*. Let us specify formally the problem that the government must solve. We have seen in the previous section that the value of the capital stock can be factored out in all of the constraints. So the problem

$$\max_{\tau=(\tau_0,\tau_1,...)} V(k_0, \tau) \qquad (6.22)$$

$$\text{subject to } V^C(k_t, \tau) \geq V^D(k_t) \text{ for all } t \geq 1 \qquad (6.23)$$

is equivalent to the following simple problem, which is independent of the initial capital stock:

$$\max_{\tau=(\tau_0,\tau_1,...)} \left(\frac{\sigma}{\sigma-1}\right) H(\tau_0, \tau_1, \ldots) \qquad (6.24)$$

$$\text{subject to } \left(\frac{\sigma}{\sigma-1}\right) H(\tau_t, \tau_{t+1}, \ldots) \geq \left(\frac{\sigma}{\sigma-1}\right) H^*(\tau_p) \text{ for all } t \geq 1. \qquad (6.25)$$

This problem has a Lagrangean:

$$L(\tau, \lambda) \equiv H(\tau_0, \tau_1, \ldots) + \sum_{t=1}^{\infty} \lambda_t \left[H(\tau_t, \tau_{t+1}, \ldots) - H^*(\tau_p)\right]. \qquad (6.26)$$

where the λ's are the Lagrange multipliers.

The necessary condition for the (third best) interior solutions is

$$\frac{\partial L}{\partial \tau_m} = 0 \text{ for every } m \geq 0. \qquad (6.27)$$

We now use this condition to characterize the limit tax rates in the constrained optimal (third best) problem.

6.3 Incentive compatible limit tax rates

In the commitment case, the limit tax rate is defined (as we have seen previously) by the equation:

$$R'(\tilde{\tau}) = 0. \tag{6.28}$$

The tax plan with such a limit tax rate may or may not be incentive compatible. In Sect. 4 above we saw that for a tax sequence (equivalently, tax plan) to be incentive compatible, the value of continuation along that sequence must be no smaller than the value of deviation. How does such a criterion perform in the limit case we are considering?

In fact as $t \to \infty$, the difference between the continuation value from the tax plan and the value from deviation tends to a positive multiple of

$$H^*(\tilde{\tau}) - H^*(\bar{\tau}) \tag{6.29}$$

If this difference is strictly negative then the second best (commitment) tax plan is not incentive compatible, because the incentive constraint will be violated at some date in the future. In a later section we present several examples and numerical estimates of cases in which indeed the commitment plan is not incentive compatible.

6.4 The third best tax rate

When the second best optimal tax rate is not incentive compatible in the limit, we want to characterize the limit tax rates for the optimal constrained solution. They can be determined by a very simple procedure.

First, two cases are possible: $\tilde{\tau} < \bar{\tau}$ or $\tilde{\tau} > \bar{\tau}$. We find that $\tilde{\tau} < \bar{\tau}$ if and only if $\rho < 0$. One has in fact that

$$\phi'(\tau) = \phi(\tau)^{1+\rho}[(1-a)\tau^{-(1+\rho)} - a(1-\tau)^{-(1+\rho)}];\ \bar{\tau} = \left[1 + \left(\frac{a}{1-a}\right)^{\frac{1}{1-\rho}}\right]^{-1} \tag{6.30}$$

and

$$R'(\bar{\tau}) = a\rho\phi(\bar{\tau})^{1+\rho}(1-\bar{\tau})^{-(1+\rho)} \tag{6.31}$$

so if $\rho < 0$ then $R'(\bar{\tau}) < 0$, and $\tilde{\tau} < \bar{\tau}$; the converse is true if $\rho > 0$.

We shall see that in the case in which the incentive constraints are binding, the constrained optimal tax rate τ^* is a compromise between the unconstrained tax rate and the output-maximizing rate. So the constrained tax rates are higher than the unconstrained if $\rho < 0$, and lower in the converse case. These two cases and the corresponding relations between $\tilde{\tau}, \bar{\tau}$ and τ^* are illustrated in Figs. 1 and 2. Note that the function $H^*(\tau)$ is not drawn to scale relative to $R(\tau)$ and $\phi(\tau)$: what matters and follows from the analysis is its relative position, so that τ^* is between $\bar{\tau}$ and $\tilde{\tau}$.

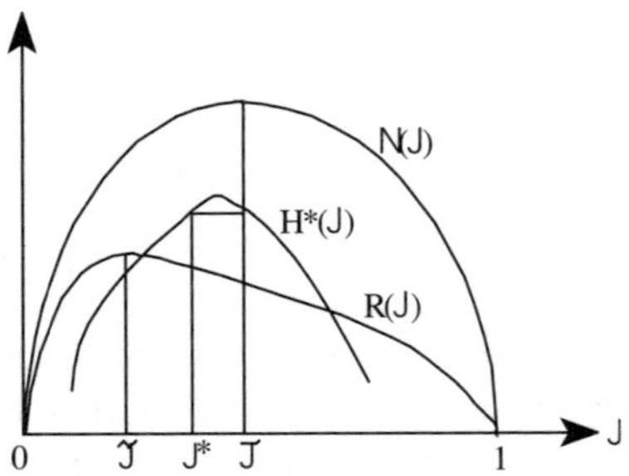

Fig. 1. $p < 0$

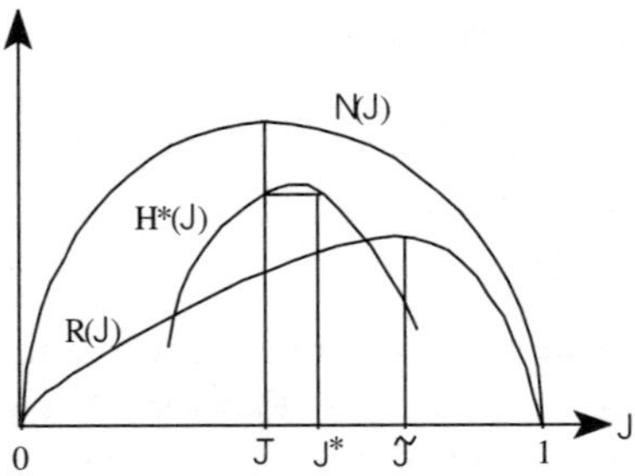

Fig. 2. $p > 0$

These two cases will turn out to be symmetric, although of course with very different implications from the point of view of economic analysis. For the sake of brevity in what follows we concentrate on the first case, where $\rho < 0$.[11]

Obviously, the interesting case is now $H^*(\tilde{\tau}) < H^*(\bar{\tau})$; *i.e.* the return after tax on capital is too high in the limit, and deviation to the output-maximizing tax becomes a dominant choice. This inequality implies that H^* is increasing in the interval $[\tilde{\tau}, \bar{\tau}]$.

Now define τ^* formally to be

$$\min\{\tau \in [\tilde{\tau}, \bar{\tau}] : H^*(\tau) = H^*(\bar{\tau})\} \tag{6.32}$$

That is to say, $\tau*$ is the lowest tax rate in between $\tilde{\tau}$ and $\bar{\tau}$ such that the value of continuation and deviation are equal.

Consider the interesting case where $\tau^* < \bar{\tau}$. Then we have immediately that

$$\frac{dH^*}{d\tau}(\tau^*) \geq 0, \text{ and } \frac{dR}{d\tau}(\tau^*) \leq 0 \leq \frac{d\phi}{d\tau}(\tau^*). \tag{6.33}$$

We now claim that at τ^* the necessary condition for optimality (in the limit) are satisfied: that is, that Lagrange multipliers exist for which τ^* satisfies the corresponding necessary conditions. The discussion of these details is technical, and can be found in the Appendix.

In the converse case of $\rho > 0$, the constrained tax rate is smaller than the limit value $\tilde{\tau}$ of the commitment solution. This difference should not hide, however, the fundamental similarity in the adjustment mechanism: in both cases the limit continuation value is too small, and the adjustment in the limit value of the tax rate makes it large enough to prevent deviation. In both cases this is achieved by increasing the limit value of output per period, at the expense of the limit value of the growth rate.

Note that, in the limit, implementing τ^* yields the same value as implementing $\bar{\tau}$ from that point on. That is to say, thereafter the value of the third-best is equal to the value of deviation associated with implementing the constant $\bar{\tau}$ forever. One might wonder, then, what is gained from implementing this third-best tax rate. Note also from Figs. 1 and 2 that there is another constant τ that lies

[11] There is a converse where all arguments that follow hold, but with reversed inequalities.

between $\overline{\tau}$ and τ^* –call it τ^H– that maximizes $H^*(\tau)$ and that would yield even higher utility from that point on. One might also wonder why it is not preferable to implement this intermediate tax rate in the limit.

The answer to both questions is the same: from the perspective of the initial planning period, it would not be optimal to implement these tax rates unless we constrain the optimization to constant sequences. Implementing $\overline{\tau}$ from the start would lower expected rates of return on investment and would deter capital accumulation. Implementing τ^H would yield a value such that the incentive compatibility constraint is not binding in the limit, so that this tax rate is implementable. We know, however, that the unconstrained optimum sequence of taxes converges to $\widetilde{\tau}$, which maximizes $R(\tau)$. Therefore, τ^H cannot be the optimal asymptotic tax rate from the perspective of the initial period. More formally, we show in the Appendix that if tax rates converge to a constant τ, the Lagrange multiplier associated with the incentive constraint must be bounded away from zero in the limit (see the condition 9.68). Since implementing τ^H in the limit yields $H\left(\tau^H\right) > H\left(\overline{\tau}\right)$, the incentive constraint is not binding and the associated Lagrange multiplier must be zero, in contradiction to the condition 9.68 given in the Appendix.

It may be useful to contrast the resolution of the incentive compatibility problem in the present model and in the analogue of the Chamley-Judd model of optimal taxation with two factors of production (see Benhabib and Rustichini 1995). The similarity is in the fact that in both models we have cases where the constrained taxes on capital are different than the unconstrained ones. The difference is in way the incentive compatibility problem is resolved. In the present model the amount of capital (on the balanced growth path) is not affected by the rate of return; similarly the value of defection is not dependent on the capital stock. All the adjustment has to take place by variations in the tax rates. In the two-factor model, the driving force of the adjustment is the following: *adjust the rate of return on capital in order to adjust the long run supply of capital, which in turn deters deviation.*

7 Second and third best: Numerical values

In this section we compute a family of calibrated examples to illustrate the divergence between the limiting optimal tax rates under commitment and the optimal tax rates that are time consistent. We also show how these tax rates change with the parameter a, which measures he relative importance of private capital in production, and how they vary with the parameter ρ, which measures the elasticity of substitution between private capital and public services. In all cases we set $A = 30$; we also choose $\sigma = 0.5$ and $\beta = 0.95$, very much standard values.

The following table illustrates the numerical results discussed above for various values of a and ρ. The first number in each cell represents the second-best tax that could be enforced under commitment, while the second number is the sustainable (third-best) taxes that are incentive constrained.

$\rho\backslash a$	0.3	0.5	0.8
−0.5	0.303, 0.408	0.146 0.394	0.015, 0.055
−0.1	0.695, 0.699	0.495, 0.498	0.196, 0.197
0.1	0.705, 0.701	0.505, 0.502	0.204, 0.203
0.5	0.804, 0.706	0.642, 0.539	0.369, 0.295
2.0	0.729, 0.646	0.654, 0.560	0.522, 0.421
10.0	0.592, 0.566	0.572, 0.545	0.539, 0.508

First we note, as expected, that tax rates are higher when the coefficient measuring the relative importance of the public good, $(1 - a)$, is higher. As we vary ρ, taxes increase as we approach and cross the Cobb-Douglas value $\rho = 0$. As we further increase ρ and approach a fixed coefficient Leontief technology, both the private and public good become increasingly essential to production and the tax rates decline again towards the 50% rate. The difference between the second best and third best tax rates declines. In the limit, as we approach the Leontief technology, the second best tax sequence becomes sustainable. For example, when $a = 0.5$ and $\rho = 100$, the incentive constraints are satisfied for the sequence of second best tax rates. Note also that at values of ρ close to 0 (the Cobb-Douglas value) the second and third tax rates are very close. As noted before, this is because for a Cobb-Douglas technology the tax rate that maximizes the rate of return R and the tax rate that maximizes output are the same: there is no time inconsistency. Any slight deviation from Cobb-Douglas does create a time inconsistency problem, however. For all parametrizations presented here, the sequence of second best (commitment) tax rates is not sustainable and differs from the best sustainable sequence.

The difference in the asymptotic second and third best tax rates are often quite significant for the parametrizations presented above. In the case of a low elasticity of substitution, for example ($\rho = 2$), the difference in the two tax rates is 10% when $a = 0.8$. The difference is also 10% when the elasticity of substitution is large ($\rho = -0.5$) and $a = 0.3$. As expected, the differences are smaller when the technology is close to Cobb-Douglas.

$\rho\backslash a$	0.3	0.5	0.8
−0.5	0.024987, 0.029590	0.011409, 0.026569	0.000746, 0.002696
−0.1	0.042377, 0.042604	0.033001, 0.033200	0.010611, 0.010666
0.1	0.043641, 0.043375	0.033669, 0.033467	0.011389, 0.013340
0.5	0.056994, 0.045232	0.045596, 0.036098	0.021966, 0.017160
2.0	0.056479, 0.043449	0.050403, 0.038151	0.035809, 0.026309
10.0	0.043116, 0.039130	0.041788, 0.037825	0.038308, 0.034224

The table above illustrates the resulting ratios of government expenditures to total output. As in the table above, the first number in each cell corresponds to the outcome under commitment, while the second number corresponds to the outcome under the sustainable (third best) tax rate. These ratios of government expenditures to total output are sensitive to the choice of the constant term A in the production function, since the tax rate τ primarily depends on the share parameter a and the elasticity parameter ρ.

The ratios average about 3% for our parametrizations. If we interpret the numbers as the share of public investment (infrastructure, etc.) in output, they are quite realistic.

8 Conclusions

We consider an economy where a benevolent government faces a trade-off between supplying productive public services and taxing private capital and thereby distorting savings and investment decisions. When the optimal path of taxes under precomittment (the second best path) turns out to be time inconsistent, reputation may enable government to sustain a third-best tax path. We fully characterize this third best policy, which asymptotically turns out to consist of a constant tax rate that lies between the precomittment (second best) and the discretionary tax rates. Simulations for plausible parameter values suggest that there may be important quantitative differences between the asymptotic second and third best tax rates.

9 Appendices

9.1 The competitive equilibrium

The first order condition of the agent gives:

$$c_{t+1} = c_t(\beta R(\tau_{t+1}))^{\sigma} \tag{9.34}$$

Iteration of the feasibility condition $k_{t+1} = \phi(\tau_t)k_t - c_t$ implies

$$c_0 + \sum_{t=1}^{T} c_t \prod_{s=1}^{t} \phi^{-1}(\tau_s) + \prod_{s=1}^{T} \phi^{-1}(\tau_s) k_{T+1} = \phi(\tau_0)k_0. \tag{9.35}$$

As is conventional we assume that

$$\lim_{T\to\infty} \prod_{s=1}^{T} \phi^{-1}(\tau_s) k_{T+1} = 0 \tag{9.36}$$

so that 9.35 becomes

$$c_0 + \sum_{t=1}^{\infty} c_t \prod_{s=1}^{t} \phi^{-1}(\tau_s) = \phi(\tau_0)k_0 \tag{9.37}$$

Iterating the first order conditions for the agent we get

$$c_t = c_0 \prod_{s=1}^{t} (\beta R(\tau_s))^{\sigma} \tag{9.38}$$

which, substituted into 9.37 gives

$$c_0 \left(1 + \sum_{t=1}^{\infty} \prod_{s=1}^{t} (\beta R(\tau_s))^{\sigma} \phi^{-1}(\tau_s) \right) = \phi(\tau_0) k_0 \tag{9.39}$$

If we now substitute the 9.38 into the expression for the utility of the agent we get that the utility from an initial capital k_0 and a tax rate sequence $\tau = (\tau_0, \tau_1, \ldots)$, denoted by $V(k_0, \tau)$, is

$$V(k_0, \tau) = (\frac{\sigma}{\sigma - 1}) c_0^{\frac{\sigma-1}{\sigma}} \left(1 + \sum_{t=1}^{\infty} \prod_{s=1}^{t} (\beta^{\sigma} (R(\tau_s))^{\sigma-1}) \right) \tag{9.40}$$

Now we can use the equation 9.39 to substitute for c_0, and obtain the value to the agent in terms of k_0 and τ only. To lighten notation, we introduce:

$$X(\tau_1, \tau_2, \ldots) \equiv \left(1 + \sum_{t=1}^{\infty} \prod_{s=1}^{t} (\beta R(\tau_s))^{\sigma} \phi^{-1}(\tau_s) \right)^{\frac{1-\sigma}{\sigma}} \tag{9.41}$$

and

$$Y(\tau_1, \tau_2, \ldots) \equiv \left(1 + \sum_{t=1}^{\infty} \prod_{s=1}^{t} (\beta^{\sigma} (R(\tau_s))^{\sigma-1}) \right) \tag{9.42}$$

so that we define

$$h(\tau_1, \tau_2, \ldots) \equiv X(\tau_1, \tau_2, \ldots) Y(\tau_1, \tau_2, \ldots) \tag{9.43}$$

Now we can write

$$V(k_0, \tau) = (\frac{\sigma}{\sigma - 1}) (k_0)^{\frac{\sigma-1}{\sigma}} (\phi(\tau_0))^{\frac{\sigma-1}{\sigma}} h(\tau_1, \tau_2, \ldots). \tag{9.44}$$

as we have in the text.

9.2 The optimal tax with commitment

Here we derive the first order conditions for the optimization. The derivative with respect to the tax rate τ_m of the two terms X and Y are as follows.

$$\begin{aligned} \frac{\partial X}{\partial \tau_m} &= \left(\frac{1-\sigma}{\sigma} \right) X^{\frac{1-2\sigma}{1-\sigma}} \sum_{t=m}^{\infty} \left(\prod_{s=1, s \neq m}^{t} (\beta R(\tau_s))^{\sigma} \phi^{-1}(\tau_s) \right) \\ &\times \left(\beta \frac{\sigma \phi(\tau_m) (R(\tau_m))^{\sigma-1} R'(\tau_m) - \phi'(\tau_m) (R(\tau_m)^{\sigma})}{(\phi(\tau_m))^2} \right) \end{aligned} \tag{9.45}$$

or

$$\frac{\partial X}{\partial \tau_m} = \left(\frac{1-\sigma}{\sigma}\right) X^{\frac{1-2\sigma}{1-\sigma}} \sum_{t=m}^{\infty} \left(\prod_{s=1}^{t} (\beta R(\tau_s))^{\sigma} \phi^{-1}(\tau_s) \right) \left(\sigma \frac{R'(\tau_m)}{R(\tau_m)} - \frac{\phi'(\tau_m)}{\phi(\tau_m)} \right) \tag{9.46}$$

For the Y term we get

$$\frac{\partial Y}{\partial \tau_m} = \sum_{t=m}^{\infty} \prod_{s=1, s\neq m}^{t} (\beta^{\sigma} R(\tau_s)^{\sigma-1})(\sigma - 1)(R(\tau_m)^{\sigma-2} R'(\tau_m) \tag{9.47}$$

or

$$\frac{\partial Y}{\partial \tau_m} = \sum_{t=m}^{\infty} \prod_{s=1}^{t} (\beta^{\sigma} R(\tau_s)^{\sigma-1})(\sigma - 1) \left(\frac{R'(\tau_m)}{R(\tau_m)} \right) \tag{9.48}$$

We can now substitute in the equation giving the value to the agent, to get:

$$\begin{aligned} \frac{\partial V(k_0, \tau)}{\partial \tau_m} = {} & (\frac{\sigma}{\sigma - 1}) (\phi(\tau_0) k_0)^{\frac{\sigma-1}{\sigma}} \\ & \times \left(Y \left(\frac{1-\sigma}{\sigma}\right) X^{\frac{1-2\sigma}{1-\sigma}} \sum_{t=m}^{\infty} \left(\prod_{s=1}^{t} (\beta R(\tau_s))^{\sigma} \phi^{-1}(\tau_s) \right) \right. \\ & \left. \times \left(\sigma \frac{R'(\tau_m)}{R(\tau_m)} - \frac{\phi'(\tau_m)}{\phi(\tau_m)} \right) \right) \\ & + (\frac{\sigma}{\sigma - 1}) (\phi(\tau_0) k_0)^{\frac{\sigma-1}{\sigma}} \left(X \sum_{t=m}^{\infty} \prod_{s=1}^{t} (\beta^{\sigma} R(\tau_s)^{\sigma-1})(\sigma - 1) \frac{R'(\tau_m)}{R(\tau_m)} \right) \end{aligned} \tag{9.49}$$

Now we assume that $\beta^{\sigma} R(\tau_s)^{\sigma} \phi^{-1}(\tau_s) < 1$ (it can be shown this condition is necessary for the value of the program to be bounded and for an optimum to exist). Therefore,

$$\lim_{m \to \infty} \sum_{t=m}^{\infty} \left(\prod_{s=1}^{t} (\beta R(\tau_s))^{\sigma} \phi^{-1}(\tau_s) \right) = 0 \tag{9.50}$$

so that

$$\begin{aligned} \lim_{m \to \infty} \frac{\partial V(k_0, \tau)}{\partial \tau_m} = {} & \left((\frac{\sigma}{\sigma - 1}) (\phi(\tau_0) k_0)^{\frac{\sigma-1}{\sigma}} \right) \\ & \times \left(X \sum_{t=m}^{\infty} \prod_{s=1}^{t} (\beta^{\sigma} R(\tau_s)^{\sigma-1})(\sigma - 1) \frac{R'(\tau_m)}{R(\tau_m)} \right) \end{aligned} \tag{9.51}$$

This, together with the optimality condition

$$\frac{\partial V(k_0, \tau)}{\partial \tau_m} = 0 \tag{9.52}$$

implies that

$$\lim_{m \to \infty} R'(\tau_m) = 0, \tag{9.53}$$

as claimed.

9.3 Bad equilibria in the Barro model

This section of the Appendix considers alternative "bad" equilibria in the Barro model.

Bad equilibrium 1

Consider the following strategy profile. The strategies are: the government sets $\tau_t = 1$ in every period, irrespective of the history. Each agent i sets the saving $k_t^i = 0$ in every period, also irrespective of the history.

This is a Nash equilibrium: if the government chooses $\tau_t = 1$ in every period, then each agent will save zero, and if each agent saves zero then the government may as well tax the entire savings.

This is also a sustainable equilibrium in the sense of Chari and Kehoe [8]. The policy plan of the government is to set the tax rate equal to one after any history of tax rates, and the allocation rule for the public is to have zero savings in every period, also after every history of taxes. In this case (differently from the case of Nash equilibrium above) we have to check that policy plan and allocation rule are optimal after any history of taxes. So consider the case where $\tau_t \neq 1$. The public still expects future tax rates to be equal to one, so it will not save even after a deviation by the government to tax rates less than one. And, once again, if each agent saves zero then the government may as well tax the entire savings.

The equilibrium, however, is not subgame perfect. Consider the history where at period t the agents have saved in aggregate a positive amount (this is an off-equilibrium path, of course). Now apply the one-period-deviation principle. The government has the following problem: choose the best tax rate, considering that in the next periods (and forever) agents will save zero and the government will set the tax rate to one in future periods. The best choice is to set the tax rate to maximize present output, and that tax rate is less than one. We conclude these strategies do not give rise to a subgame perfect equilibrium.

Bad equilibrium 2

Now suppose the government chooses a tax rate equal to one in any period in which the aggregate savings are equal to zero; it chooses $\bar{\tau}$, the output-maximizing rate, in every period in which aggregate savings are positive. The agents choose savings equal to zero in every period, independently of the history of taxes, and of the value of aggregate savings they observe.

This is a subgame perfect equilibrium, and the equilibrium outcome path has zero savings and zero output in every period. To check that this is indeed a subgame perfect equilibrium, consider first any history that a single agent i is facing. The strategy we have described prescribes zero savings for her. We have to prove that this is indeed optimal for her. Consider what tax rates she is expecting. She knows that all the other agents will save zero, so that the aggregate savings rate will be zero in all future periods, and therefore (according to the postulated strategy) the tax rate of the government will be equal to one. So a deviation to positive savings by her alone will still yield zero aggregate savings –in which case the government will still choose a tax rate equal to one, and her income in the next period will still be zero. Hence, a deviation is not profitable.

The check for the optimality of government behavior is similar to the previous case. Take any history the government is facing. When aggregate savings are zero, a one-period deviation to a tax rate less than one will not give any public good, and will leave the payoff unchanged. When aggregate savings are positive, the best choice is $\bar{\tau}$. This is because the government knows that in future periods the savings will again be zero (this is what the strategy prescribes for the public), so the continuation value is constant, and independent of his choice of tax rate today. So the government wants to maximize consumption today; given that the public will save zero, this is equivalent to maximizing output, so the government will choose $\bar{\tau}$. We conclude these strategies do indeed give rise to a subgame perfect equilibrium.

However, this equilibrium is not perfect. To prove this claim, suppose there is a sequence of ϵ, tending to zero, where for each ϵ the strategy for the public is zero savings with probability $1 - \epsilon$, and a random draw otherwise. For the government the strategy is to choose τ in period t as follows:

i. With probability ϵ the tax rate τ is set equal to one if the aggregate saving is zero, and equal to $\bar{\tau}$ if the aggregate saving is positive.
ii. With probability $1 - \epsilon$ the tax rate τ is a random draw.

The key points to consider are the following:

(i) With probability 1 the government faces positive aggregate savings in each period, no matter what the strategy of the agents is. This follows from the assumption that strategies are totally mixed, and from the law of large numbers for a continuum of random variables.

(ii) The members of the public know that, with probability one, they will face in each period a tax rate equal to $\bar{\tau}$. This follows from the point (ii) above, and the definition of the strategy of the government. So the agents are facing their optimal allocation problem where the production function looks as follows:

i. The capital stock k_t and the flow of public services g_t in period t is small (if all the other players are following the strategy), since savings come only out of the ϵ-size mistakes;
ii. The tax rate is $\bar{\tau}$, so the return to private savings is $AR(\bar{\tau}) > 0$.

We conclude that each agent deviates and saves a positive amount. The equilibrium is therefore not perfect.

Comparison of the Chari-Kehoe setup and ours

We saw above that in the Barro model the autarchic equilibrium in which the government sets the tax rate at one and the public saves nothing is not a perfect equilibrium. In the Chari-Kehoe model, by contrast, the autarchic equilibrium in not only subgame perfect, but it can also easily be shown to be robust in the sense of being perfect.

Consider the following sketch of a proof. In this economy the payoff to each player is determined as follows. In the second period of their lives agents have income equal to $(1-\delta_t)Rk_t + (1-\tau_t)l_t$, where δ_t is the tax rate on capital, and τ_t the tax rate on labor (the rest of the notation is self-explanatory). The *autarchy equilibrium* has $\delta_t = 1$ for any period, while the tax rate τ_t on labor set optimally to provide for the tax revenues to pay the exogenous amount g.

Consider first the decision of the government. If there is no positive saving in the economy (the aggregate capital is zero), then the tax rate in the present period does not affect the current payoff, so it does not produce any one-period gain. If there are positive savings, given that agents will save almost zero in future periods the best tax rate is the maximum rate on capital, with the maximum probability $1-\epsilon$.

Consider now the agents. Expecting the maximum tax rate with high probability in the future, they calculate that a positive saving today will certainly reduce their consumption today, and increase their income tomorrow (in the second period) only in the low probability event of a zero tax rate; hence when the probability ϵ is small enough it is optimal for them to save zero with probability $1-\epsilon$, as claimed.

What explains this difference between the Chari Kehoe setup and ours? Consider the one shot problems, which are obtained by setting the discount rate equal to zero. In Chari-Kehoe the optimal tax rate on capital is one whenever there is positive capital in the economy. In our setup the optimal tax rate in the one shot problem is $\bar{\tau}$ for any initial capital which is strictly positive, and any tax rate otherwise. This explains why a deviation of the public is not important in their model, but it is in ours. Facing a positive saving, the government in their model still wants to tax capital at a maximum rate, while in our model the government wants to tax at the "myopic" rate $\bar{\tau}$.

Value of deviation

If agents expect that after a period t the tax rate $\bar{\tau}$ will be implemented, the Euler equation governing the growth of individual consumption is

$$\frac{c_{t+1}}{c_t} = (\beta R(\bar{\tau}))^{\sigma} \tag{9.54}$$

As a result,

$$c_s = c_t\,(\beta R(\bar{\tau}))^{\sigma(s-t)} \tag{9.55}$$

What is the level of consumption the period of the deviation? Equation 9.39 becomes

$$c_t = \left(1 + \sum_{v=t+1}^{\infty} \prod_{s=1}^{v} (\beta R(\bar{\tau}))^{\sigma} \phi^{-1}(\tau_s)\right)^{-1} \phi(\bar{\tau}) k_t \tag{9.56}$$

Therefore, the value as of period t is

$$\begin{aligned} V^D(k_t) &= \left(\frac{\sigma}{\sigma-1}\right) \sum_{s=t}^{\infty} c_s^{\frac{\sigma-1}{\sigma}} \beta^{s-t} \qquad (9.57) \\ &= \left(\frac{\sigma}{\sigma-1}\right) (\phi(\bar{\tau}) k_t)^{\frac{\sigma-1}{\sigma}} \\ &\times \left(1 + \sum_{v=t+1}^{\infty} \prod_{s=1}^{v} (\beta R(\bar{\tau}))^{\sigma} \phi^{-1}(\tau_s)\right)^{\frac{1-\sigma}{\sigma}} \left(1 - \beta^{\sigma} R(\bar{\tau})^{\sigma-1}\right) \end{aligned}$$

The government must therefore select a sequence of τ's to maximize 9.57. The relevant derivative is

$$\begin{aligned} \frac{\partial V^D(k_t)}{\partial \tau_m} &= (\phi(\bar{\tau}) k_t)^{\frac{\sigma-1}{\sigma}} \left(1 + \sum_{v=t+1}^{\infty} \prod_{s=1}^{v} (\beta R(\bar{\tau}))^{\sigma} \phi^{-1}(\tau_s)\right)^{\frac{1-2\sigma}{\sigma}} \left(1 - \beta^{\sigma} R(\bar{\tau})^{\sigma-1}\right) \\ &\times \sum_{v=m}^{\infty} \left(\prod_{s=1, s\neq m}^{v} (\beta R(\bar{\tau}))^{\sigma} \phi^{-1}(\tau_s)\right) \left(\beta \frac{\phi'(\tau_m)\,(R(\bar{\tau})^{\sigma})}{(\phi(\tau_m))^2}\right) \qquad (9.58) \end{aligned}$$

Therefore, the first order condition for the government's problem is

$$\phi'(\tau_m) = 0 \text{ if } m > t \tag{9.59}$$

Hence, the government's best response to the individual's expectations is indeed to make them self-fulfilling by setting $\tau_m = \bar{\tau}$ if $m > t$. Since the deviation also consisted of setting $\tau_t = \bar{\tau}$, we have that $\tau_m = \bar{\tau}$ if $m \geq t$.

Using this in the expression 9.57 we have

$$\begin{aligned} V^D(k_t) &= \left(\frac{\sigma}{\sigma-1}\right) (k_t)^{\frac{\sigma-1}{\sigma}} \left(\phi(\bar{\tau}) - (\beta R(\bar{\tau}))^{\sigma}\right)^{\frac{\sigma-1}{\sigma}} \left(1 - \beta^{\sigma} R(\bar{\tau})^{\sigma-1}\right)^{-1} \\ &= \left(\frac{\sigma}{\sigma-1}\right) (k_t)^{\frac{\sigma-1}{\sigma}} H^*(\bar{\tau}) \qquad (9.60) \end{aligned}$$

which is the equation we have in the text.

Analysis of the Lagrangean

We denote for convenience

$$H_m \equiv \frac{\partial H}{\partial \tau_m}; X_m \equiv \frac{\partial X}{\partial \tau_m}; Y_m \equiv \frac{\partial Y}{\partial \tau_m} \tag{9.61}$$

so that for any $\tau = (\tau_0, \tau_1, \ldots)$ and any $m \geq 0$,

$$\frac{\partial L}{\partial \tau_m} = H_m(\tau_0, \tau_1, \ldots) + \sum_{i=0}^{\infty} \lambda_i H_{m+1-i}(\tau_i, \tau_{i+1}, \ldots) \tag{9.62}$$

where the λ's are the Lagrange multipliers. The necessary condition for the (third best) optimality is

$$\frac{\partial L}{\partial \tau_m} = 0 \text{ for every } m \geq 0. \tag{9.63}$$

But notice:

$$H_0(\tau) = \left(\frac{\sigma - 1}{\sigma}\right) \phi(\tau)^{-\left(\frac{1}{\sigma}\right)} \phi'(\tau) XY \tag{9.64}$$

and

$$H_m(\tau) = \phi^{\left(\frac{\sigma-1}{\sigma}\right)} [X_m Y + XY_m] \tag{9.65}$$

Let us now consider the expression for the Lagrangean when τ_t is equal to a constant for every t. We drop the argument τ for simplicity of notation, and we find that

$$\frac{\partial X}{\partial \tau_m} = \left(\frac{1-\sigma}{\sigma}\right) X^{\left(\frac{1-2\sigma}{1-\sigma}\right)} \left(\sigma \frac{R'}{R} - \frac{\phi'}{\phi}\right) \left((\beta R)^\sigma \phi^{-1}\right)^m \left(1 - \left((\beta R)^\sigma \phi^{-1}\right)\right)^{-1} \tag{9.66}$$

while the other term is

$$\frac{\partial Y}{\partial \tau_m} = (\sigma - 1) \frac{R'}{R} \left[(\beta R)^\sigma R^{-1}\right]^m Y$$

If we substitute these into 9.63 and factor out the common term

$$\left(\frac{\sigma - 1}{\sigma}\right) \phi^{\left(\frac{\sigma-1}{\sigma}\right)} XY$$

we find that 9.63 is equivalent to

$$-\left(\sigma \frac{R'}{R} - \frac{\phi'}{\phi}\right) \sum_{i=0}^{m-1} \lambda_i \left((\beta R)^\sigma \phi^{-1}\right)^{m+1-i} + \frac{\sigma R'}{R} \sum_{i=0}^{m-1} \lambda_i \left((\beta R)^\sigma R^{-1}\right)^i + \lambda_m \frac{\phi'}{\phi} = 0$$

If we substitute an exponential λ solution of the above equation, with $\lambda_i = \lambda^i$, we obtain

$$-\left(\sigma \frac{R'}{R} - \frac{\phi'}{\phi}\right) \frac{\lambda^m - \left((\beta R)^\sigma \phi^{-1}\right)^{m-1}}{\lambda - \left((\beta R)^\sigma \phi^{-1}\right)} + \frac{\sigma R'}{R} \frac{\lambda^m - \left((\beta R)^\sigma R^{-1}\right)^{m-1}}{\lambda - \left((\beta R)^\sigma R^{-1}\right)} + \lambda^m \frac{\phi'}{\phi} = 0. \tag{9.67}$$

It is easy to see that the only exponential solution of the above equation must satisfy the condition on λ:

$$1 > \lambda > \left((\beta R)^\sigma R^{-1}\right) \tag{9.68}$$

The condition $1 > \lambda$, in particular, follows from the fact that the Lagrange multipliers have to be summable. In addition, if the condition 9.68 is satisfied, then in the limit as $m \to \infty$, λ^m dominates $\left((\beta R)^\sigma \phi^{-1}\right)^{m-1}$ and the equation 9.67 reduces to

$$-\left(\sigma\frac{R'}{R}-\frac{\phi'}{\phi}\right)[\lambda-((\beta R)^\sigma\phi^{-1})]^{-1}+\sigma\frac{R'}{R}[\lambda-((\beta R)^\sigma R^{-1})]^{-1}+\frac{\phi'}{\phi}=0. \quad (9.69)$$

We have now to check that there exists a solution in λ of the above equation, where λ satisfies the additional condition 9.68. Let us define the function $\Phi(\lambda)$ as

$$\begin{aligned}\Phi(\lambda) \equiv & -\left(\sigma\frac{R'}{R}-\frac{\phi'}{\phi}\right)\left(\lambda-\frac{(\beta R)^\sigma}{R}\right)+\sigma\frac{R'}{R}\left(\lambda-\frac{(\beta R)^\sigma}{\phi}\right) \\ & +\frac{\phi'}{\phi}\left(\lambda-\frac{(\beta R)^\sigma}{R}\right)\left(\lambda-\frac{(\beta R)^\sigma}{\phi}\right) \end{aligned} \quad (9.70)$$

Note that λ^* solves 9.69 if and only if $\Phi(\lambda^*)=0$.

In what follows we focus only on the case of $\rho<0$, so that $\bar{\tau}>\tilde{\tau}$. An analogous proof exists for the converse case. If $\rho<0$. We prove that a λ as required exists by observing that Φ is a continuous function of λ and that

$$\Phi\left(\frac{(\beta R)^\sigma}{R}\right)<0; \Phi(1)>0. \quad (9.71)$$

The first inequality follows from direct substitution, which gives:

$$\Phi\left(\frac{(\beta R)^\sigma}{R}\right)=\left(\frac{(\beta R)^\sigma}{R}\right)(\sigma R')\left(\frac{1}{R}-\frac{1}{\phi}\right)$$

a non-positive number since $R'\le 0$ and $R\le\phi$; for the second, we have:

$$\begin{aligned}\Phi(1) = & -\left(\frac{\sigma R'}{R}-\frac{\phi'}{\phi}\right)\left[1-\left(\frac{(\beta R)^\sigma}{\phi}\right)\right]^{-1}+ \\ & \left(\frac{\sigma R'}{R}\right)\left[1-\left(\frac{(\beta R)^\sigma}{R}\right)\right]^{-1}+\frac{\phi'}{\phi}.\end{aligned}$$

The derivative of H^* is now:

$$\begin{aligned}\frac{dH^*}{d\tau} \equiv & -\left(\frac{\sigma R'}{R}-\frac{\phi'}{\phi}\right)\left(\frac{(\beta R)^\sigma}{\phi}\right)\left[1-\left(\frac{(\beta R)^\sigma}{\phi}\right)\right]^{-1}+ \\ & \left(\frac{\sigma R'}{R}\right)\left(\frac{(\beta R)^\sigma}{R}\right)\left[1-\left(\frac{(\beta R)^\sigma}{R}\right)\right]^{-1}+\frac{\phi'}{\phi}.\end{aligned}$$

Now we take the difference:

$$\Phi(1)-\frac{dH^*}{d\tau}=\frac{\phi'}{\phi}$$

which is positive, because both ϕ and ϕ' are positive; also $\frac{dH^*}{d\tau}$ is positive. We conclude that $\Phi(1)>0$, and our claim is proved.

We can also show that the λ^* is unique, and that there is no λ that solves $\Phi(\lambda) = 0$ for $1 > \lambda > \left((\beta R)^\sigma R^{-1}\right)$ if the condition given by 9.71 fails. For this purpose it suffices to show that

$$\Phi'(\lambda) = \frac{\phi'}{\phi}\left(1 + 2\lambda - \frac{(\beta R)^\sigma}{R} - \frac{(\beta R)^\sigma}{\phi}\right) > 0 \tag{9.72}$$

over the interval $1 > \lambda > \left((\beta R)^\sigma R^{-1}\right)$. Notice however that $1 + 2\lambda - \frac{(\beta R)^\sigma}{R} - \frac{(\beta R)^\sigma}{\phi} > 0$ because $\lambda > (\beta R)^\sigma R^{-1} > (\beta R)^\sigma \phi^{-1}$. Therefore sign $\Phi'(\lambda) = \text{sign}\frac{\phi'}{\phi} > 0$, since we are in the case where $\rho < 0$. Now it is clear by inspection that if 9.71 fails there is no λ^* such that $\Phi(\lambda^*) = 0$ for $1 > \lambda^* > \left((\beta R)^\sigma R^{-1}\right)$. The argument is the same for $\rho > 0$ except for appropriate modifications of signs and inequalities.

References

1. Barro, R.J. (1990) Government spending in a simple model of endogenous growth. *Journal of Political Economy* 98(5), Part 2: S103–S125
2. Barro, R.J., Gordon D.B. (1983) Rules, discretion and reputation in a model of monetary policy. *Journal of Monetary Economics* 12: 101–122
3. Benhabib, J., Rustichini, A. (1996) Social conflict and growth. *Journal of Economic Growth* 1: 125–142
4. Benhabib, J., Velasco, A. (1996) On the optimal and best sustainable taxes in an open economy. *European Economic Review*40: 135–154
5. Benhabib, J., Rustichini, A. (1995) Optimal Taxation without Committment. CORE DP
6. Chamley, C. (1986) Optimal taxation of capital income in general equilibrium with infinite lives. *Econometrica* 54(3): 607–622
7. Chamley, C. (1985) Efficient taxation in a stylized model of intertemporal general equilibrium. *International Economic Review* 26(2): 451–468
8. Chari, V.V., Kehoe, P.J. (1990) Sustainable plans. *Journal of Political Economy* 98: 783–802
9. Chari, V.V., Christiano L.J., Kehoe, P. (1994) Optimal Fiscal Policy in a Business Cycle Model. *Journal of Political Economy* 102(4): 617–652
10. Jones, L., Manuelli, R.E., Rossi, P. (1993) Optimal taxation in models of endogenous growth. *Journal of Political Economy*
11. Judd, K. (1985) Redistributive taxation in a simple perfect foresight model. *Journal of Public Economics* 28: 59–83
12. Kydland, F.E., Prescott, E.C. (1977) Rules rather than discretion: The time consistency of optimal plans. *Journal of Political Economy* 85: 473–491
13. Lucas, R.E., Stokey, N. (1983) Optimal fiscal and monetary policy in an economy without capital. *Journal of Monetary Economics* 12: 55–93
14. Marcet, A., Marimon, R. (1994) Recursive contracts. Working paper, Universitat Pompeu Fabra, Barcelona
15. Ramsey, F.P. (1928) A mathematical theory of saving. *Economic Journal* 38 543–559
16. Stokey, N.L. (1991) Credible public policy. *Journal of Economic Dynamics and Control* 15: 627–657

Are "Anti-Folk Theorems" in repeated games nongeneric?

Roger Lagunoff[1], **Akihiko Matsui**[2,3]

[1] Department of Economics, Georgetown University, Washington DC 20057 USA. (e-mail: lagunofr@gunet.georgetown.edu; www.georgetown.edu/lagunoff/lagunoff.htm)
[2] Faculty of Economics, University of Tokyo, 7-3-1 Hongo, Bunkyo-ku, Tokyo 113-0033, Japan
[3] Institute of Policy and Planning Sciences, University of Tsukuba, Ibaraki 305-8573, Japan (e-mail: amatsui@e.u-tokyo.ac.jp)

Abstract. Folk Theorems in repeated games hold fixed the game payoffs, while the discount factor is varied freely. We show that these results may be sensitive to the order of limits in situations where players move asynchronously. Specifically, we show that when moves are asynchronous, then for a fixed discount factor close to one there is an open neighborhood of games which contains a pure coordination game such that every Perfect equilibrium of every game in the neighborhood approximates to an arbitrary degree the unique Pareto dominant payoff of the pure coordination game.

1 Introduction

The central result in the theory of repeated games is the Folk Theorem.[1] According to this result, any stage game profile of payoffs that strictly dominates players' minimax payoffs is sustained by a Perfect equilibrium of a repeated game with discounting if players are sufficiently patient. While there are many versions of the Folk Theorem depending on the monitoring and timing structure of the game, they all have this key feature: payoffs of the game are fixed while the discount rate is freely varied by the modeler to achieve the desired payoff profile. There is no persuasive reason that this must be the case. Indeed, in reality, it is often the case that the discount rate r is pinned down by exogenous data such as the market rate of interest. Even patient agents should take this into

The main result of this paper comprises Theorem 3 in an earlier working paper: Lagunoff and Matsui (1995). Some other results in that paper were published in Lagunoff and Matsui (1997). Numerous helpful suggestions for that paper (and, by extension, the present one as well) came from an AT&T miniconference on Economic Theory. We would like to thank Peter Linhart, Roy Radner, and other participants of that conference. The first author, in particular, is indebted to Roy Radner for the many helpful suggestions and encouragement on this and other projects throughout the author's career. The authors thank an anonymous referee for helpful comments and suggestions.

[1] See Aumann (1981) and Fudenberg and Maskin (1986).

account. Thus, if we state the robustness of the Folk theorem, the result ought to be robust against the order of limits. While we do not claim this is untrue in standard repeated games, we show that the Folk theorem is sensitive to the order of limits if players' moves are asynchronous.

We prove a result that pertains to a class of *asynchronously repeated games*. These are dynamic games with a certain payoff stationarity and where at most one player moves at each decision date. Lagunoff and Matsui (LM) (1995, 1997) and, more recently, Yoon (1999) examine Perfect equilibria of asynchronously repeated games.[2] LM show that if the stage game is one of pure coordination and if players are sufficiently patient, then every Perfect equilibrium payoff is arbitrarily close to the Pareto dominant payoff of the stage game. Consequently, the set of equilibrium payoff profiles is a singleton (up to an approximation).

By contrast, Dutta (1995) and Yoon (1999) prove Folk Theorems for large classes of repeated games, including those with synchronous moves, asynchronous moves, and most everything in between, provided that stage games satisfy certain dimensionality restrictions.[3] Since pure coordination games fail the dimensionality restrictions, Dutta's and Yoon's results suggest that the "Anti-Folk Theorem" of LM is nongeneric. More generally, the results suggest that multiplicity of equilibria in repeated situations is a generic property. This paper proves a result that suggests otherwise.

Specifically, we prove the following. Fix any stage game of pure coordination. Let u^* denote the unique, Pareto dominant Nash equilibrium vector of payoffs. We show that given any $\epsilon > 0$, if players are sufficiently patient, then there is an open neighborhood of the payoff vector of the pure coordination game such that every Perfect equilibrium payoff of the asynchronous repetition of every stage game in this neighborhood is within ϵ of u^*.

Hence, by fixing the level of discounting in advance, one can construct a neighborhood of games whose Perfect equilibria *all* approximate the unique Pareto dominant payoff of the coordination game. The constructed neighborhood contains a positive measure of games that are full dimensional. In this sense, multiplicity of repeated games is not a generic phenomenon. The result also demonstrates that games that approximate team problems described by Marshak and Radner (1972) have desirable outcomes.

The paper proceeds as follows. Section 2 describes the model and defines the class of asynchronously repeated games. The canonical example of an asynchronously repeated game is the two-player alternating move game. A standard reference is Maskin and Tirole's (1988) model of duopolies with inertia or costly upgrading. Letting s_i denote the decision of firm i, and let $\Omega_1 = \{1, 3, 5, \ldots\}$ and

[2] Related models are found in Rubinstein and Wolinsky (1995) and Wen (1998) who examine repeated extensive form games. See also Benabou (1989), Maskin and Tirole (1987, 1988a,b), Haller and Lagunoff (1997), and Bhaskar and Vega-Redondo (1998) all of whom restrict attention to Markov Perfect equilibria of certain asynchronously repeated games.

[3] Strictly speaking, Dutta's result applies to all finite state stochastic games. While many asynchronously repeated games are stochastic games, Yoon's result applies to asynchronously repeated games with a, possibly, nonstationary process determining the set of movers each period.

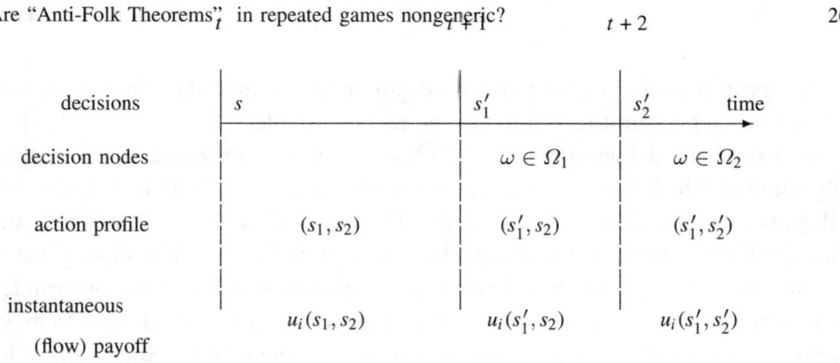

Fig. 1. A play of the game when the firms inherit decision profile $s = (s_1, s_2)$ at date t (even)

$\Omega_2 = \{2, 4, 6, \ldots\}$ denote the decision dates of firms 1 and 2, resp., the timing of the game is demonstrated in Fig. 1 above.

An example of an alternating move game of pure coordination is a situation in which two firms in the same product group desire a uniform accounting standard to simplify their consolidation work. However, they have different closing dates due to the nature of their business, which makes the decision points alternate. Another example is one in which two offices of a company are located in New York and Tokyo, respectively, so that their business hours do not overlap.

To see what our result implies in this context, consider an alternating move repetition of the simple 2×2 pure coordination game below. Our result implies that for any $\epsilon > 0$ and a discount factor close enough to one, a neighborhood of this game exists for which *all* the Perfect equilibria of the nearby games lie in the box $(2 - \epsilon, 2] \times (2 - \epsilon, 2]$. Notably, the stage game Nash equilibrium payoff pair $(1, 1)$ is *not* a Perfect equilibrium in any of the nearby games.

		Player 2	
		s_2^*	$\bar{s}_2$
Player 1	s_1^*	2 , 2	0 , 0
	$\bar{s}_1$	0 , 0	1 , 1

Fig. 2. A pure coordination game

Another timing structure covered by our result is the Poisson revision process. The game is occurs in continuous time, and each individual's decision nodes follow a Poisson process. The decisions are asynchronous since, almost surely, no two individuals can update their actions at the same time. An example of this type is a replacement process, common in evolutive models, in which a player is defined as a lineage rather than a single individual entity. A son inherits his father's position only after the father's death, at which time the son can take his own action and commit to it through the rest of his life.

In Sect. 2 we define more general class of games with repeated interaction, only some of which break the perfect synchronization of the standard model. We call games in this class *renewal games*. Originally described in Lagunoff and Matsui (1995), a renewal game is defined as a setting in which a stage game is repeated in continuous time, and at certain stochastic points in time, determined by an arbitrary renewal process, some set of players may be called upon to make a move. Both standard repeated games and asynchronously repeated games are special cases. The main result is stated in Sect. 3. In that Section we also examine sensitivity to the order of limits in the context of a 2×2 example. Section 4 gives the proof of the main result. Section 5 provides a brief summary and offers concluding remarks.

2 A model of asynchronously repeated interaction

2.1 Stage game

Let $G = (I, (S_i)_{i \in I}, (u_i)_{i \in I})$ denote a normal form stage game where I is the finite set of players, S_i $(i \in I)$ is the finite set of actions for player i, and $u_i : S \equiv \times_{i \in I} S_i \to \Re$ is the payoff function for player $i \in I$. Without loss of generality, assume that $S_i \cap S_j = \emptyset$ for all $i \neq j$. We will call an element of $s = (s_1, \ldots, s_{|I|}) \in S$ a *behavior profile* (or simply "profile"). Given some $\hat{s}_i \in S_i$, let $s \backslash \hat{s}_i = (s_1, \ldots, s_{i-1}, \hat{s}_i, s_{i+1}, \ldots, s_{|I|})$. The tuple of payoff functions is denoted by $u = (u_i)_{i \in I}$. A mixed strategy for i will be denoted by σ_i and has the standard properties: $\sigma_i : S_i \to [0, 1]$ and $\sum_{s_i} \sigma_i(s_i) = 1$. A *mixed profile* is given by $\sigma = (\sigma_i)_{i \in I}$. Finally, a game G is a *coordination game* if its Nash equilibria are Pareto ranked and there is some Nash equilibrium that strictly Pareto dominates every other profile of the game.

2.2 Renewal games and asynchronously repeated games

In this Section, we introduce a framework that encompasses a wide variety of repeated strategic environments. Consider a continuous repetition of a stage game G. After the first decision node, which occurs for all players at time zero, all players' decision points are determined by a semi-Markov process with finitely many states.[4] In the following, revision nodes refer to the decision nodes other than the first one at time zero.

A semi-Markov process is a stochastic process which makes transitions from state to state in accordance with a Markov chain, but in which the amount of time spent in each state before a transition occurs is random and follows a renewal

[4] We can formulate the problem in such a way that the first action profile is chosen by nature as in models of evolution. It will be clear that the following description and results will not be altered by specification of choice at time zero.

process. For the sake of convenience, we separate the process into two parts, a renewal process and a Markov chain. The renewal process, which we denote by ν, determines when the decision nodes (the "jumps") occur; the Markov transition, denoted by p, determines who moves at each node.

Formally, let $X_1, X_2, \cdots$ be an infinite sequence of i.i.d. nonnegative random variables which follow a (marginal) probability measure ν with $E_\nu(X_1) < \infty$ and $\nu(X_1 > \epsilon) > \delta$ for some $\epsilon, \delta > 0$. It is also assumed that $\nu(X_1 = 0) = 0$ so that the orderliness condition for the renewals is guaranteed.[5] Then let $T_0 = 0$ and $T_k = T_{k-1} + X_k = X_1 + \cdots + X_k$ $(k = 1, 2, \cdots)$. T_k is the time elapsed before the kth revision point. At each decision point a state ω is determined from a finite set Ω according to a Markov process $\{Y_k\}_{k=1}^{\infty} \in \Omega^\infty$ where $Y_k = \omega$ $(\omega \in \Omega)$ implies that state ω is reached at time T_k. We denote $p_{\omega\omega'} = Pr(Y_{k+1} = \omega' \mid Y_k = \omega)$ for $\omega, \omega' \in \Omega$. Let $\Omega_i \subseteq \Omega$ denote the nonempty set of states in which player i has a decision node. Let $\Omega_0 \subseteq \Omega$ be the set of "inertial" states in which no player has a decision node. By definition, $\Omega_0 = \Omega \backslash (\cup_{i \in I} \Omega_i)$. We write $\boldsymbol{\Omega} = (\Omega_0, (\Omega_i)_{i \in I})$. We assume that the initial state, denoted by $\omega(0) \in \Omega$, is never reached again. By definition, $\omega(0) \in \Omega_i$ for all $i \in I$. Note that $(\Omega_i \cap \Omega_j) \backslash \{\omega(0)\}$ $(i \neq j)$ may or may not be empty.

Using this semi-Markov process, a typical play of the game is described as follows. In the beginning, a strategy profile s^0 is chosen. Deterministically or stochastically, the first revision time is reached at time T_1. Suppose that ω is chosen by the Markov process, and let $I(\omega) = \{i \in I : \omega \in \Omega_i\}$ denoting the players who can move if nature chooses ω. If player i $(i \in I(\omega))$ takes s_i^1, then the strategy profile changes to $s^1 = s^0 \backslash (s_i^1)_{i \in I(\omega)}$. That is, each time there is a renewal and revision, only the corresponding coordinate(s) of the previous strategy profile is replaced by the revised one, while other coordinates remain unchanged. If we define $(s^k)_{k \geq 0}$ this way, i.e., s^k $(k = 1, 2, \cdots)$ is the strategy profile between T_k and T_{k+1}, then the flow payoff is realized and the discounted payoff for player $i \in I$ will be given by

$$r \sum_{k=0}^{\infty} \int_{T_k}^{T_{k+1}} e^{-r\tau} u_i(s^k) d\tau. \tag{1}$$

Definition 1. *A* renewal game *is a tuple*

$$\Gamma = \langle G,\ \nu, \boldsymbol{\Omega}.\ (p_{\omega\omega'})_{\omega,\omega' \in \Omega},\ r \rangle,$$

where $r > 0$ is a common discount rate, and for all $\omega \in \Omega$ and all $i \in I$, there exists a chain of states, $\omega^0, \omega^1, \omega^2, \ldots, \omega^M$ $(M < |\Omega|)$, with $\omega = \omega^0$ and $\omega^M \in \Omega_i$ such that $p_{\omega^{m-1}\omega^m} > 0$ $(m = 1, \cdots, M)$ (from any state, every player obtains a revision node).

Since the number of states is finite, renewal games have the property that from any state, every player obtains revision nodes infinitely many times, and the

[5] If $\nu(X_1 = 0) > 0$, then the orderliness condition is not guaranteed, i.e., we cannot order the renewals properly since any finite number of renewals occur at the same time with a positive probability.

expected time interval between two revision nodes is finite. Standard discounted repeated games are renewal games which may be described in several ways. One straightforward way is: $\Omega = \Omega_i$, $\forall i \in I$, and $\nu(X_1 = 1) = 1$. However, we wish to specialize further to only those renewal games in which choice is asynchronous.

Definition 2. *An* asynchronously repeated game *is a renewal game in which* $\Omega_i \cap \Omega_j \backslash \{\omega(0)\} = \emptyset$, $\forall i \neq j$.

In asynchronously repeated games, no two individuals have simultaneous revision opportunities. When $\omega \in \Omega_i$, we will write $i(\omega) = i$. Below we list a few examples that we described in the Introduction.

Example 1 (Alternating move game). Let $I = \{1,2\}$, $\Omega = I$, $X_1 \equiv 1$, and $p_{ij} = 1$ if $i \neq j$. Then the decision points are deterministic, and players' revision nodes alternate.

Example 2 (Poisson revision process). Let $\Omega = I$. And let X_1 follow an exponential distribution with parameter $\lambda > 0$, i.e., $\nu(X_1 < x) = 1 - e^{-\lambda x}$, and let $p_{ij} = p_j$ for all $i, j \in I$. Then players' revision points are independent of each other, and player i's decision points ($i \in I$) follow a Poisson process almost surely with parameter λp_i.

Example 3 (ϵ-approximation of the standard repeated game). Let $I = \{1,2\}$, and

$$\Omega = \overbrace{\{\omega_0^1, \ldots, \omega_0^M\}}^{\Omega_0} \cup \overbrace{\{\omega_1^1, \omega_1^2\}}^{\Omega_1} \cup \overbrace{\{\omega_2^1, \omega_2^2\}}^{\Omega_2}$$

Then assume that Y_k's follow the process illustrated in Fig. 2 next side. In the figure, the process proceeds through the inertial states until ω_0^M. At that time the process moves to either player 1's or player 2's decision node with probability 1/2 each. Let $X_1 \equiv 1/(M+2)$. Then if M is sufficiently large, the process approximates the standard repeated game in the sense that each player has a revision opportunity once in a unit of time, and that the two players' decision nodes are very close in timing.

2.3 Recursive structure

One additional assumption that we will make will be to restrict the class of behavior strategies that individuals use. We assume that individuals only condition on the *sequences* of decision points and the actions taken at these points rather than on the time interval between them. This assumption does not restrict the strategy space at all if the renewal process is deterministic (the Markov process can be stochastic) as with Examples 1 and 3 in the previous section, and it significantly reduces the notational burden.

Restricting conditioning events to the "jumps" rather than on time intervals between jumps allows a straightforward recursive representation of individuals' continuation values in the asynchronous model. To formulate this, let $s(t) =$

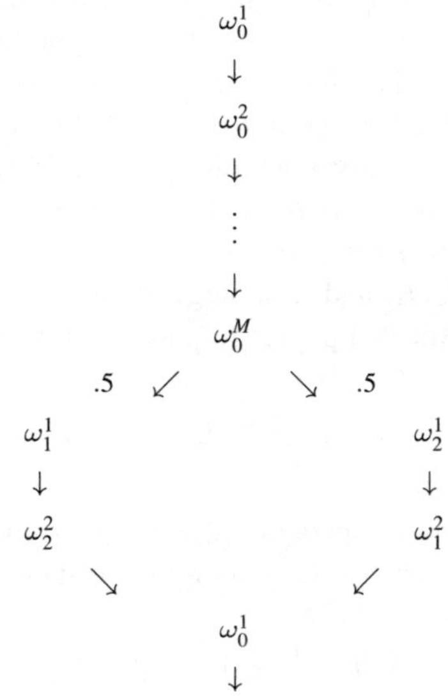

Fig. 3. An ϵ-approximation of the standard repeated game

$(s_1(t), \dots s_{|I|}(t))$ denote the behavior profile at time t, and let $N_t \equiv \inf\{k : T_k > t\}$ denote the number of renewals up to time t. Due to the assumption on X_k's, $N_t < \infty$ holds almost surely. Recall that Y_k denotes the kth Markov state to be reached that identifies the current mover. Then define the space of histories H such that a history $h^t \in H$ is given by $h^t = (y^t, s^t)$ wherever N_t is finite, and

$$y^t = \{Y_k\}_{k \leq N_t},$$

and

$$s^t = \{s(T_k)\}_{k \leq N_t}.$$

The null history is denoted by h^0. Since at most one player switches his action at a time after the initial profile we write $s^t = (s(h^0), s_{Y_1}, \cdots, s_{Y_{N_t}})$ whenever convenient. We let $s(h)$ and $\omega(h)$ denote the current behavior and state at history h, resp., and let $i(h)$ denote the last player whose decision node was reached. We also define $h^{t-} = (y^t, \{s(T_k)\}_{k<N_t})$ so that h^{t-} includes the same information as history h^t except for the behavior profile at time t which may include a new decision by a player. We write H^- for the set of all such *conditioning histories* and denote an element by h^-.

A *strategy* for player i is a history contingent action given by the function $f_i : H^- \to \Delta(S_i)$ where $\Delta(S_i)$ denotes the set of mixed strategies (probability distributions) on the action set S_i. Although this formulation appears to require that i is unable to condition on the current behavior profile, recall that decisions are only made at the “jumps” in the renewal process.

Given a strategy profile f, the play of the game proceeds as follows. At time zero, all the players in I simultaneously take actions, $f_i(h^{0-})$ for $i \in I$. Suppose $T_1 = t_1 = x_1$ and $Y_1 = y_1 \in \Omega_i$. If $i = 0$, nothing changes except the Markov "clock." If $i \in I$, then $h^{t_1-} = (f(h^{0-}); y_1)$, player i's revision node is reached at time t_1, and he takes action $f_i(h^{t_1-})$. History at time t_1 becomes $h^{t_1} = (y_1; f(h^{0-}), f(h^{0-})\backslash f_i(h^{t_1-}))$. Given a strategy profile f and $h \in H^t$ (resp. $h^- \in H^{t-}$), $\{\tilde{s}(f|h)(\tau)\}_{\tau>t}$ (resp. $\{\tilde{s}(f|h^-)(\tau)\}_{\tau\geq t}$) denotes an induced (stochastic) path of action profile after h (resp. h^-).

Given a history $h^t \in H$ and a strategy profile $f = (f_i)_{i\in I}$, we define the conditional discounted expected payoff to player i at time t by

$$V_i(f|h^t) = r\int_t^{\infty} e^{-r(\tau-t)}E\left[u_i\left(\tilde{s}(f|h^t)(\tau)\right)\right]d\tau,$$

where $E[\cdot]$ is the expectation operator. A strategy profile f^* is called a *perfect equilibrium (PE)* if for each $i \in I$, f_i^* is a best response to $(f_j^*)_{j\neq i}$ after every history h^t, i.e.,

$$V_i(f^*|h^t) \geq V_i(f^*\backslash f_i|h^t)$$

for any of player i's strategies f_i.

One immediate result in the asynchronously repeated game is that for almost all histories, mixed strategies will not be used at any revision opportunity. Hence, the mixed strategy minimax payoff which is always an equilibrium of the stage coordination game is not the benchmark here necessarily. Hereafter, we will often denote a pure strategy by $f_i(h^-)$ as well as a mixed strategy.

Given a history $h = h^t \in H$, let $h^t \circ (\omega; s_j)$ denote the concatenated history in which, after h^t, the next state $\omega \in \Omega_j$ is reached, at which player j takes s_j. Given $h^t \in H$, $h^t \circ \omega \in H^-$ is a path such that after h^t, state ω is reached (without specifying the revised action). Using this expression, the value after $h \circ \omega \in H^-$ is given by

$$V_i(f|h\circ\omega) \equiv V_i(f|h\circ(\omega; f_{i(\omega)}(h\circ\omega))).$$

The analysis will make extensive use of the following recursive formulation. The continuation value to i induced by f after history $h^t \in H$ with $\omega(h^t) = \omega$ may be expressed as

$$V_i(f|h^t) = (1 - \sum_{\omega'\in\Omega}\theta_{\omega\omega'})u_i(s(h^t)) + \sum_{\omega'\in\Omega}\theta_{\omega\omega'}V_i(f|\ h^t\circ\omega'). \qquad (2)$$

where

$$\begin{aligned}\theta_{\omega\omega'} &\equiv p_{\omega\omega'}\int_0^{\infty} e^{-rt}d\nu(t)\\ &= \text{expected discounted probability that } \omega' \\ &\quad\ \text{is the first state reached from } \omega.\end{aligned} \qquad (3)$$

2.4 Existence

The following is a standard proof for the existence of perfect equilibria. What is proven here is actually the existence of Markov perfect equilibrium.

Theorem 0. *For any asynchronously repeated game* $\Gamma = \langle G, \nu, \boldsymbol{\Omega}, p, r\rangle$ *there exists at least one perfect equilibrium.*

Proof. Partition H^- into $\wp = \{H^-_{\omega s}\}_{s\in S,\omega\in\Omega}$ such that

$$H^-_{\omega s} = \{h^- \in H^- | \omega(h^-) = \omega, s(h^-) = s\}, \forall\omega \in \Omega, \forall s \in S.$$

Observe that $\wp$ constitutes the "payoff relevant" set of states. Suppose that each player takes a $\sigma(\wp)$-measurable behavior strategy where $\sigma(\wp)$ is the σ-algebra generated by $\wp$. Then the play of the game follows a Markov process, and we can represent a strategy of player i by the "Markovian" function $\psi_i \in [\Delta(S_i)]^{\wp}$. The strategy represented by ψ_i is denoted by f_{ψ_i}.

For each $i \in I$ let $BR^i = \{BR^i_{\omega s}\}_{\omega\in\Omega,s\in S}$ satisfy

$$BR^i_{\omega(h)s}(\psi) = \arg\max_{f_{\psi_i}} V(f_\psi \backslash f_{\psi_i} | h) \tag{4}$$

Letting $BR = (BR_i)_{i\in I}$, equation (4) defines an upper hemicontinuous correspondence $BR : \times_i[\Delta(S_i)]^{\wp} \to \times_i[\Delta(S_i)]^{\wp}$ where $\times_i[\Delta(S_i)]^{\wp}$ is compact and convex. Therefore, by Kakutani's fixed point theorem, there exists ψ such that $\psi \in BR(\psi)$ holds. Standard arguments show that the corresponding strategy f_{ψ_i} is a best response to $(f_{\psi_j})_{j\neq i}$ within the class of *all* strategies after any history h (or, more precisely, after any h^-) since all j, $(j \neq i)$ only vary their behavior over "states" $\omega s \in H^-_{\omega s}$. Hence, f_ψ is a perfect equilibrium. □

As a special case, we will be interested in pure coordination games. A game G is a *pure coordination game* if $u_i = u_j = u$ for all i and j.[6] Let s^* denote the profile that gives each player his highest payoff u^*.

3 Main result

3.1 A theorem

The main result below demonstrates that order of limits matters. The typical Folk Theorem fixes the stage game and then varies r. By contrast, the hypothesis of the Theorem fixes r and then varies G. The former will surely be more familiar to those familiar with the Folk Theorem. However, the latter is more useful if it is the discount rate r, rather than the stage payoffs, which is pinned down by exogenous data such as the rate of interest.

Theorem. *Given* $\epsilon > 0$ *and any asynchronously repeated game* $\langle G, \nu, (p_{\omega\omega'}), r\rangle$ *in which* $G = (I, S, u)$ *is a pure coordination game with* u^* *as the unique Pareto efficient outcome, there exists* $\bar{r} > 0$ *such that for any* $r \in (0, \bar{r})$*, there exists an open subset* $\mathcal{U} \subset \Re^{\times_{i\in I} S_i}$ *with* $u^* \in \mathcal{U}$ *such that in an asynchronously repeated game* $\langle (I, S, u'), \nu, (p_{\omega\omega'}), r\rangle$ *with* $u' \in \mathcal{U}$*, every continuation value in any perfect equilibrium is at least* $u^* - \epsilon$.

[6] This can be weakened so that we require only that $u_i = \alpha u_j + \beta$ for $\alpha > 0$ and $\beta \in \Re$.

3.2 The order of limits: An example

We apply the Theorem to the class of two-player alternating move games where the stage game is of the form G_3 below. In the stage game G_3, $u^* > 2$ and $\alpha, \beta < 1$. Clearly, G_3 is an "impure" coordination game since the costs of miscoordination are not identical. Notice that G_3 satisfies full dimensionality. Using the full-dimensionality of this game, we first fix α and β then vary r to construct a perfect equilibrium of which payoff is bounded away from the Pareto efficient payoff pair, (u^*, u^*). Next, we apply our Theorem to show why the construction fails when, first fixing r, β is varied to be sufficiently close to α.

2

		s_2^*	$\bar{s}_2$
1	s_1^*	u^*, u^*	β, α
	$\bar{s}_1$	α, β	1, 1

G_2: $u^* \geq 2, \alpha, \beta < 1$

Fig. 4.

We construct such an equilibrium in the following way. First, we consider two phases, Phase I and Phase II. Phase I is divided into four subphases given by the following.

$$\underbrace{s^* \to \cdots \to s^* \to}_{k \text{ times}} \quad \underbrace{(\bar{s}_1, s_2^*) \to \cdots \to (\bar{s}_1, s_2^*) \to}_{\ell \text{ times}}$$

Phase I.A Phase I.B

$$\bar{s} \to \quad \underbrace{(s_1^*, \bar{s}_2) \to \cdots \to (s_1^*, \bar{s}_2) \to}_{m \text{ times}}$$

Phase I.C Phase I.D

This is the prescribed path in Phase I. After the last stage of Phase I.D, the system returns to the first stage of Phase I.A. In this construction, k, ℓ, and m satisfy the following:

$$\frac{u^*k + \alpha\ell + 1 + \beta m}{k + \ell + 1 + m} > \frac{u^*k + \beta\ell + 1 + \alpha m}{k + \ell + 1 + m} > 1, \tag{5}$$

and

$$\frac{u^* + \beta\ell + 1}{\ell + 2} < 1. \tag{6}$$

Such k, ℓ, and m exist. Indeed, we choose ℓ large enough to satisfy (6). Then choose m so that $\alpha\ell + \beta m$ is greater than $\beta\ell + \alpha m$, i.e., $\ell > m$ if $\alpha > \beta$, and vice versa. This will guarantee the first inequality of (5). Note that we cannot find such a m if the game is pure coordination, i.e., $\alpha = \beta$. Finally, take a sufficiently large k to satisfy the second inequality of (5).

Phase II is the same as Phase I except that $(\bar{s}_1, s_2^*)$ (resp. $(s_1^*, \bar{s}_2)$) is replaced by $(s_1^*, \bar{s}_2)$ (resp. $(\bar{s}_1, s_2^*)$). That is, Phase II is a mirror image of Phase I with respect to the players. The play of the game begins with the first stage of Phase I.A and stays in Phase I, following the above arrows, unless there is a deviation. If player 1 deviates, then the system moves to an appropriate subphase of Phase II. For example, if player 1 deviates in Phase I.B to take s_1^*, then the system goes to some state corresponding to player 2's move in Phase II.A.

If player 2 deviates, then we have the following transitions:

1. If player 2 deviates in Phase I.A, then player 2's prescribed action in the next move is to return to s_2^*, and player 1 will keep s_1^* until player 2 takes s_2^*. After player 2 returns, the system goes to the last stage of Phase I.A.
2. If player 2 deviates to take $\bar{s}_2$ earlier than prescribed in Phase I.B, then player 1 will keep $\bar{s}_1$ until player 2 takes s_2^*, and then the system moves to the first stage of Phase I.B. If player 2 deviates to keep taking s_2^* in the last stage of Phase I.B, then the system moves to the second last stage of Phase I.B.
3. If player 2 deviates to take s_2^* in Phase I.D, then the system moves to the last stage of Phase I.A. If player 2 deviates to keep taking $\bar{s}_2$ in the last stage of Phase I.D, then the system moves to the second last stage of Phase I.D.

Note that player 2 will have no revision point in Phase I.C. Prescribed actions and the transition in Phase II are the same as those in Phase I except that the roles of the players are reversed.

Now, we are in a position to check that incentive constraints are satisfied for a sufficiently small discount rate $r > 0$. Note that this means we now vary r having fixed payoff parameters α and β. If player 1 deviates in Phase I, his expected payoff converges to

$$\frac{u^*k + \beta\ell + 1 + \alpha m}{k + \ell + 1 + m} \tag{7}$$

as r goes to zero. On the other hand, his expected payoff in Phase I converges to

$$\frac{u^*k + \alpha\ell + 1 + \beta m}{k + \ell + 1 + m},$$

which exceeds (7). Thus, for a sufficiently small $r > 0$, player 1 has no incentive to deviate. To check player's incentive to deviate, we examine three cases indicated in the above construction.

1. Phase I.A: If player 2 deviates, she will get α for a while instead of u^*. Therefore, she has no incentive to deviate there. Even if she keeps $\bar{s}_2$, she will get only $\alpha < 1$.
2. Phase I.B: If player 2 deviates to take $\bar{s}_2$ earlier than prescribed, she will get 1 and then some extra β before the system reaches the stage where she deviated. Since the expected payoff along the equilibrium path exceeds one,

and $\beta < 1$, player 2 has no incentive to deviate. In the last stage of Phase I.B, if she deviates, she will get $\beta < 1$ for two more periods, which does not increase her payoff.

3. Phase I.D: If player 2 deviates to take s_2^* earlier than prescribed, then she gets u^* for one period, β for ℓ periods, 1 for one period, and some α's before the system reaches the original stage where player 2 deviates. From (6), the expected average payoff before the system reaches the same stage is less than one. Thus, player 2 has no incentive to deviate. Finally, in the last stage of Phase I.D, if she deviates, she will get $\alpha < 1$ for two more periods, which does not increase her payoff.

Hence, the strategy profile constructed above is a perfect equilibrium. It should be noted that in a standard repeated game, we do not need this type of complicated construction since the strategy profile that prescribes $\bar{s}_i$ for player $i = 1, 2$ after any history is a subgame perfect equilibrium. On the other hand, it is shown that in an asynchronously repeated game, such a simple strategy does not constitute a subgame perfect equilibrium unless α is sufficiently larger than β. This type of construction is used in other Folk Theorems possibly without synchronous moves and without public randomizing devices. See, for example, Dutta (1995), Wen (1998), and Yoon (1999).

Now suppose that r is fixed in advance of fixing α and β. The problem with this and other constructions is the following. Returning to Inequalities (5) and (6), observe that they are satisfied with a judicious choice of phase lengths k, ℓ and m which depends, in turn, on values α and β. In particular, for a r bounded away from 0, payoffs in (5) only approximate actual dynamic payoffs in Phase 1. In fact, the LHS of (5) must exceed the RHS by more than $1 - e^{-r}$ times the minimum absolute stage payoff differential. For simplicity, let $z > 0$ denote this differential. Then, the incentive constraint for Phase 1 is given by

$$\frac{u^*k + \alpha\ell + 1 + \beta m}{k + \ell + 1 + m} > \frac{u^*k + \beta\ell + 1 + \alpha m}{k + \ell + 1 + m} + (1 - e^{-r})z$$

which we rewrite as

$$\alpha\ell + \beta m > \beta\ell + \alpha m + (k + \ell + 1 + m)(1 - e^{-r})z. \tag{8}$$

Instead of having to only satisfy $\alpha\ell + \beta m > \beta\ell + \alpha m$ as before, we now require that (8) be satisfied. Letting $\alpha = \beta + \varepsilon$, (8) becomes

$$\varepsilon(\ell - m) > (k + \ell + 1 + m)(1 - e^{-r})z$$

which is clearly violated for ε sufficiently small.

4 Proof of the main result

Take as given an asynchronously repeated game $\langle G, \nu, (p_{\omega\omega'}), r\rangle$ in which $G = (I, S, u)$ is a pure coordination game, and $s^* \in S$ is the unique Pareto efficient outcome. Also take $\epsilon > 0$ as given. Any affine transformation of u will give the same result in the following analysis. We set $\bar{r}$ so as to satisfy

$$\min_{\substack{(\omega_0,\omega_1,\cdots,\omega_N)\in\Omega^{N+1}\\ 2\le N\le|\Omega|-1}} \left\{ \frac{\theta_{\omega_0\omega_1}\cdots\theta_{\omega_{N-1}\omega_N}}{\theta(\omega_0,\cdots,\omega_N)} : \theta_{\omega_0\omega_1}\cdots\theta_{\omega_{N-1}\omega_N} > 0 \right\}$$
$$> 1 - \frac{\epsilon}{3|I|}\frac{1}{u^* - \min_s u(s)},$$

where

$$\begin{aligned}\theta(\omega_0,\cdots,\omega_N) &= 1 - \sum_{\ell=1}^{N} \Pi_{n=1}^{\ell-1}\theta_{\omega_{n-1}\omega_n}\sum_{\omega'\neq\omega_\ell}\theta_{\omega_{\ell-1}\omega'}\\ &= 1 - \sum_{\omega'\neq\omega_1}\theta_{\omega_0\omega'} - \theta_{\omega_0\omega_1}\sum_{\omega'\neq\omega_2}\theta_{\omega_1\omega'}\\ &\quad - \cdots - \theta_{\omega_0\omega_1}\cdots\theta_{\omega_{N-2}\omega_{N-1}}\sum_{\omega'\neq\omega_N}\theta_{\omega_{N-1}\omega'}.\end{aligned}$$

Such an $\bar{r}$ can be found since both $\theta_{\omega_0\omega_1}\cdots\theta_{\omega_{N-1}\omega_N}$ and $\theta(\cdot)$ converge to $p_{\omega_0\omega_1}\cdots p_{\omega_{N-1}\omega_N} > 0$ as r goes to zero. Also, let $\underline{\theta} = \min\{\theta(\omega_0,\cdots,\omega_N) : \theta_{\omega_0\omega_1}\cdots\theta_{\omega_{N-1}\omega_N} > 0\}$. Fix $r \in (0,\bar{r})$.

Consider a neighborhood of u given by $\mathcal{U} = \{u' \in \Re^S \mid \forall s \in S,\ |u_i'(s) - u_i(s)| < \eta/4\}$ where η satisfies

$$0 < \eta < \frac{1}{2}\min\left\{u^* - u^{**},\ \frac{\epsilon}{2|I||\Omega|},\ \frac{\epsilon}{3(|I|+1)}[1 - \int_0^\infty e^{-r\tau}d\nu(\tau)]\right\},$$

where $u^{**} = \max_{s\neq s^*} u(s)$, i.e., the second highest payoff. In the following, we consider an asynchronously repeated game $\Gamma' = \langle (I,S,u'),\nu,\boldsymbol{\Omega},(p_{\omega\omega'}),r\rangle$ with $u' \in \mathcal{U}$.

Now, fix a perfect equilibrium f of Γ'. For each $i \in I$, each $s \in S$, and each $\omega \in \Omega$, we let $\underline{V}_{i\omega}^s = \inf_{s(h)=s,\omega(h)=\omega} V_i(f|h)$, and $\underline{V}_i^s = \inf_{s(h)=s} V_i(f|h)$. Note that $\underline{V}_i^s = \min_{\omega\in\Omega}\underline{V}_{i\omega}^s$.

For any $\delta > 0$ there exists $h \in H$ such that $s(h) = s^*$ and

$$\underline{V}_i^{s^*} > V_i(f|h) - \delta,\ \forall i \in I. \tag{9}$$

The continuation value for player $i \in I$ after h is given by

$$V_i(f|h) = \left(1 - \sum_{\omega\in\Omega}\theta_{\omega(h)\omega}\right)u_i'(s^*) + \sum_{\omega\in\Omega}\theta_{\omega(h)\omega}V_i(f|\ h\circ\omega). \tag{10}$$

If $\omega(h) \in \Omega_0$, then $s(h\circ\omega) = s^*$ and therefore, $V_i(f|h\circ\omega) \geq \underline{V}_i^{s^*}$. Observe also that since f is a perfect equilibrium strategy profile, it must be the case that for all $\omega \in \Omega_j$ $(j \in I)$,

$$V_j(f|\ h\circ\omega) \geq V_j(f|\ h\circ(s_j^*;\ \omega)) \geq \underline{V}_j^{s^*} \tag{11}$$

where the second inequality holds due to the definition of $\underline{V}_j^{s^*}$. Since $|u(s) - u_i(s)| < \eta/4$, $|V_j(f|h) - V_i(f|h)| < \eta/2$ holds for all $i, j \in I$, all f and all $h \in H$, and therefore, (11) implies

$$V_i(f \mid h \circ \omega) \geq \underline{V}_i^{s^*} - \eta. \tag{12}$$

Substituting (12) into (10) and using (9), we obtain

$$\underline{V}_i^{s^*} > \left(1 - \sum_{\omega' \in \Omega} \theta_{\omega(h)\omega'}\right) u_i'(s^*) + \sum_{\omega' \in \Omega} \theta_{\omega(h)\omega'} \underline{V}_i^{s^*} - \delta - \eta \tag{13}$$

Inequality (13) implies

$$\underline{V}_i^{s^*} > u_i'(s^*) - \frac{\delta + \eta}{1 - \int_0^\infty e^{-r\tau} d\nu(\tau)}.$$

Since δ is arbitrary and independent of other variables, the definition of η implies $\underline{V}_i^{s^*} > u^* - \epsilon/(|I| + 1)$.

We will now show that for all $k = 1, 2, \cdots, |I|$, after h with $s(h) \in S^k$, its continuation value satisfies

$$V_i(f|h) > \underline{V}_i^{s'} - \frac{\epsilon}{|I| + 1}, \tag{14}$$

for some $s' \in S^{k-1}$ if $r < \bar{r}$. Backward induction implies that (14) holds for all $s' \in S^{k-1}$ if $r < \bar{r}$. Once we show (14) for all s' and k's, we verify that $0 < r < \bar{r}$ implies that for all history $h \in H$, $V_i(f|h) > u_i'(s^*) - \epsilon$. Moreover, recall that the choice of $\bar{r}$ is independent of f. Thus, the proof will be completed.

Fix $k = 1, 2, \cdots, |I|$ and $\hat{s} \in S^k$. By the definition of $\underline{V}_{i\omega}^{\hat{s}}$ $(\omega \in \Omega)$, there exists $h_\omega \in H$ such that $s(h_\omega) = \hat{s}$, $\omega(h_\omega) = \omega$, and

$$\underline{V}_{i\omega}^{\hat{s}} > V_i(f|h_\omega) - \frac{\epsilon\underline{\theta}}{3(|I| + 1)|\Omega|}. \tag{15}$$

We have

$$V_i(f|h_\omega) = \left(1 - \sum_{\omega' \in \Omega} \theta_{\omega\omega'}\right) u_i'(\hat{s}) + \sum_{\omega' \in \Omega} \theta_{\omega\omega'} V_i(f \mid h_\omega \circ \omega'). \tag{16}$$

Since f is a perfect equilibrium, for each $\omega' \in \Omega_j$ with $j \in I$,

$$V_j(f \mid h_\omega \circ \omega') \geq V_j(f \mid h_\omega \circ (\hat{s}_j; \omega) \geq \underline{V}_{j\omega'}^{\hat{s}}, \tag{17}$$

where the second inequality holds by the definition of $\underline{V}_{j\omega}^{\hat{s}}$. Similarly, if $\hat{s}_j \neq s_j^*$, then

$$V_j(f \mid h_\omega \circ \omega') \geq V_j(f \mid h_\omega \circ (s_j^*; \omega)) \geq \underline{V}_{j\omega'}^{\hat{s} \backslash s_j^*}, \tag{18}$$

Also, by the definition of $\underline{V}_{i\omega'}^{\hat{s}}$ for each $\omega \in \Omega_0$, we have

$$V_i(f \mid h_\omega \circ \omega') \geq \underline{V}_{i\omega'}^{\hat{s}}, \ \forall \omega' \in \Omega_0. \tag{19}$$

Since $|u(s) - u_i(s)| < \eta/4$, then $|V_j(f|h) - V_i(f|h)| < \eta/2$ holds for all $i, j \in I$, all f, all s, and all $h \in H$, and therefore, (17) and (18) imply

$$V_i(f|\, h_\omega \circ \omega') \geq \underline{V}^{\hat{s}}_{i\omega'} - \eta, \tag{20}$$

and

$$V_i(f|\, h_\omega \circ \omega') \geq \underline{V}^{\hat{s}\backslash s_j^*}_{i\omega'} - \eta, \tag{21}$$

respectively. Substituting these inequalities into (16), we obtain

$$V_i(f|h_\omega) \geq \left(1 - \sum_{\omega' \in \Omega} \theta_{\omega\omega'}\right) u_i'(\hat{s}) + \sum_{\omega' \in \Omega} \theta_{\omega\omega'} \underline{V}^{\hat{s}}_{i\omega'} - \eta. \tag{22}$$

Inequalities (15) and (22) imply

$$\underline{V}^{\hat{s}}_{i\omega} \geq \left(1 - \sum_{\omega' \in \Omega} \theta_{\omega\omega'}\right) u_i'(\hat{s}) + \sum_{\omega' \in \Omega} \theta_{\omega\omega'} \underline{V}^{\hat{s}}_{i\omega'} - \frac{\epsilon\underline{\theta}}{3(|I|+1)|\Omega|} - \eta. \tag{23}$$

Since i was arbitrarily chosen, (23) holds for all $i \in I$. By definition, $\underline{V}^{\hat{s}}_{i\omega_0} = \underline{V}^{\hat{s}}_i$ for some ω_0. Take such ω_0. There exists $i \in I$ such that $\hat{s}_i \neq s_i^*$. Then there exists a chain $\omega_0, \omega_1, \ldots, \omega_N$ with $N < |\Omega|$ and $\omega_N \in \Omega_i$ such that $p_{\omega_{n-1}\omega_n} > 0$ for all $n = 1, \cdots, N$. Sequentially substituting ω_n ($n = 0, 1, \cdots, N$ in place of ω in (23) and applying (21), we obtain

$$\begin{aligned}
\underline{V}^{\hat{s}}_i \;\geq\; & (1 - \textstyle\sum_{\omega' \in \Omega} \theta_{\omega_0\omega'}) u_i'(\hat{s}) + \displaystyle\sum_{\omega' \neq \omega_1} \theta_{\omega_0\omega'} \underline{V}^{\hat{s}}_{i\omega'} \\
& + \theta_{\omega_0\omega_1} \left[\left(1 - \sum_{\omega' \in \Omega} \theta_{\omega_1\omega'}\right) u_i'(\hat{s}) + \sum_{\omega' \neq \omega_2} \theta_{\omega_1\omega'} \underline{V}^{\hat{s}}_{i\omega'} \right] \\
& + \cdots \\
& + \theta_{\omega_0\omega_1} \cdots \theta_{\omega_{N-2}\omega_{N-1}} \left[\left(1 - \sum_{\omega' \in \Omega} \theta_{\omega_N\omega'}\right) u_i'(\hat{s}) + \sum_{\omega' \neq \omega_N} \theta_{\omega_{N-1}\omega'} \underline{V}^{\hat{s}}_{i\omega'} \right] \\
& + \theta_{\omega_0\omega_1} \theta_{\omega_{N-1}\omega_N} \underline{V}^{\hat{s}\backslash s_i^*}_{i\omega_N} - \frac{\epsilon\underline{\theta}}{3(|I|+1)} - \eta|\Omega|.
\end{aligned} \tag{24}$$

Using $\underline{V}^{\hat{s}}_{i\omega} \geq \underline{V}^{\hat{s}}_i$ ($\forall \omega \in \Omega$), we have

$$\underline{V}^{\hat{s}}_i \geq \left[1 - \frac{\theta_{\omega_0\omega_1} \cdots \theta_{\omega_{N-1}\omega_N}}{\theta(\omega_0, \cdots, \omega_N)}\right] u_i'(\hat{s}) + \frac{\theta_{\omega_0\omega_1} \cdots \theta_{\omega_{N-1}\omega_N}}{\theta(\omega_0, \cdots, \omega_N)} \underline{V}^{\hat{s}\backslash s_i^*}_i - \frac{2\epsilon}{3(|I|+1)}$$

Thus, for all $r < \bar{r}$,

$$\underline{V}^{\hat{s}}_i > \underline{V}^{\hat{s}\backslash s_i^*}_i - \frac{\epsilon}{|I|+1},$$

where, by construction, $\hat{s}\backslash s_i^* \in S^{k-1}$. □

5 Concluding remarks

This paper proves that when moves are asynchronous and for a fixed discount factor close to one, an open neighborhood of any pure coordination game exists with the property that all Perfect equilibria of games in the neighborhood will approximate the unique Pareto dominant payoff. The key distinction between this assertion and the Folk Theorem lies in a switch in the order of limits. In the statement of the typical Folk Theorem, a stage game is fixed while the discount factor is varied. Here, the discount factor is fixed while the stage game is varied in a neighborhood of a pure coordination game.

The result demonstrates the robustness of an "Anti-Folk Theorem" in a prior paper, Lagunoff and Matsui (1997), for pure coordination games. At the same time, the present result demonstrates, in our view, a potential weakness of Folk Theorems: multiplicity of equilibria in games of sequenced moves may be sensitive to changes in the order of limits. Ultimately, these robustness issues will only be resolved by complete characterization of equilibrium outcomes over all stage games, discount factors, and timing structures.

References

Aumann, R. (1981) Survey of repeated games. In *Essays in Game Theory and Mathematical Economics in Honor of Oskar Morgenstern*. Bibliographisches Institut, Mannheim

Bhaskar, V., Vega-Redondo, F. (1998) Asynchronous choice and markov equilibria: Theoretical foundations and applications. mimeo

Benabou, R. (1989) Optimal price dynamics and speculation with a storable good. *Econometrica* 57: 41–80

Dutta, P. (1995) A folk theorem for stochastic games. *Journal of Economic Theory* 66: 1–32

Fudenberg, D., Maskin, E. (1986) The folk theorem in repeated games with discounting or with incomplete information. *Econometrica* 54: 533–556

Haller, H., Lagunoff, R. (1997) Markov Perfect Equilibria in Repeated Asynchronous Choice Games. Revised: January, 2000. mimeo, Georgetown University

Lagunoff, R., Matsui, A. (1995) "An 'Anti-Folk Theorem' for a Class of Asynchronously Repeated Games. CARESS Working Paper #95-15, University of Pennsylvania

Lagunoff, R., Matsui, A. (1997) Asynchronous choice in repeated coordination games. *Econometrica* 65: 1467–1478

Marschak, J., Radner, R. (1972) *The Economic Theory of Teams*. Yale University Press, New Haven

Maskin, E., Tirole, J. (1987) A theory of dynamic oligopoly, Part III: Cournot competition. *European Economic Review* 31: 947–968

Maskin, E., Tirole, J. (1988a) A theory of dynamic oligopoly, I: Overview and quantity competition with large fixed costs. *Econometrica* 56: 549–570

Maskin, E., Tirole, J. (1988b) A theory of dynamic oligopoly, II: Price competition, kinked demand curves and fixed costs. *Econometrica* 56: 571–600

Wen, Q. (1998) A folk theorem in repeated sequential games. mimeo, University of Windsor

Yoon, K. (1999) A folk theorem for asynchronously repeated games. mimeo, Korean Society Development Institute

Rubinstein, A., Wolinsky, A. (1995) Remarks on infinitely repeated extensive-form games. *Games and Economic Behavior* 9: 110–115

Trust and social efficiencies

Robert W. Rosenthal

Department of Economics, Boston University, 270 Bay State Road, Boston MA 02215, USA
(e-mail: rosenthal@bu.edu)

Abstract. In a variant of the repeated prisoner's dilemma, if extra costs are associated with the verifications built into strategies that could otherwise produce Pareto efficient equilibria, the attainment of efficient play becomes problematical. Evolutionary-game versions of this dilemma are studied here in an attempt to understand the difficulties societies face in maintaining efficient interactions mediated by trust.

1 Introduction

This paper touches on several themes that have recurred in Roy Radner's distinguished research record. One is the search for efficient organizational forms for firms and for societies more generally. A second is the use of game-theoretic models to explore social problems. A third theme is the explicit incorporation in formal models of the limited abilities of humans to accomplish what is in their interests. Indeed, he was a pioneer on the subject of bounded rationality, and his work formed the primary inspiration for my own interest in the subject.

The paper uses an evolutionary, rather than a utility-maximizing, paradigm to represent the opportunism that arises in many social situations. It begins with the simple premise that, other things equal, societies possessing higher endemic levels of trust can operate more efficiently than can less trusting societies, but that such trust creates the potential for opportunistic behavior by individuals, which in turn erodes trust. Combatting such opportunism may therefore be a legitimate goal of public policy, but how best to achieve that goal is not obvious.

I am grateful to Douglas Gale, Joel Guttman, Hsueh-Ling Huynh, Glenn Loury, John Nachbar, Debraj Ray, and Arthur Robson for enlightening conversations on the subject of this paper; to Parikshit Ghosh and Sumon Majumdar for excellent research assistance; to a referee for helpful suggestions; and to the National Science Foundation for financial support.

The repeated prisoner's dilemma (another Radner subject[1]) has often been used as a paradigm within which to examine such issues:[2] The strategy that always cooperates, independently of the history of play, is viewed as vulnerable to opportunism. The strategy that always defects, despite the fact that it forms an equilibrium when played against itself, is completely untrusting; and the equilibrium payoff such a pair produces is viewed as something that can be improved on. (Indeed, it is hard to think of a population of individuals who behave this way as a society at all.) When the players are sufficiently forward looking, strategies such as "Tit For Tat" (begin by cooperating and continue by imitating the opponent's previous choice at each subsequent round), "Grim" (begin by cooperating and continue to cooperate only if the history to date has been completely cooperative), and many others "trust but verify"[3] and generate equilibria with payoffs higher than those of the always-defect equilibrium.

This is encouraging, but beyond the simple repeated prisoner's dilemma paradigm such strategies are not without their own difficulties: Verification is not generally a costless activity; and if everyone else in a society is trustworthy, verification becomes redundant and a strategy of the form "Trust But Verify" can profitably be replaced by the strategy that always cooperates.[4] So, "Trust But Verify" apparently cannot be relied on as an all-purpose, decentralized solution to the social inefficiencies that are caused by absence of trust, even when individuals are very forward looking.

Society-level collective actions might help to overcome the inefficiencies. The use of social sanctions, for instance, can change the structure of the underlying prisoner's dilemma game, or at least can change the relative magnitudes of the payoff parameters. Such social sanctions are likely to be costly in practice, however, as they must be imposed and enforced continually. Much of what a system of criminal justice does might be interpreted as imposing such sanctions, for example.

The purpose of this paper is to look at these issues through the lens of a simple model similar to the one studied in Young and Foster (1991).[5] Section 2 of this paper begins with analysis of an evolutionary-game model of a society in which individuals are repeatedly randomly matched to play a restricted version of the repeated prisoner's dilemma with payoffs modified to incorporate small verification costs. The evolutionary game has three strategies: Always Cooperate (All C), Always Defect (All D), and Trust But Verify (TBV). It has three equilibria: One, which is stable (locally) in a sense to be described, involves all players using the All D strategy. Another, which is unstable, is a heterogeneous mixture of All D and TBV. The third equilibrium, which possesses a weak kind of stability that is not as persuasive as that possessed by the first equilibrium,

[1] E.g., Radner (1986).

[2] Cf. Axelrod (1984), for example.

[3] The phrase became popular after it was used in a speech by U.S. President Reagan.

[4] This argument is seen frequently in the literature on repeated games played by finite automata. Cf., Chapt. 9 in Osborne and Rubinstein (1994).

[5] Compare also the analysis of the evolutionary game "Matrix V" in Hirshleifer and Martinez Coll (1988).

involves a heterogeneous mixture of All C, All D, and TBV. If successful societies are those within which a significant fraction of interactions are efficient ones mediated by trust, a possibly cost-effective role for collective social action then is to interfere occasionally with the natural population dynamic in order to move the social state away from the domain of attraction of the stable, but very inefficient, All D equilibrium and near to the weakly-stable equilibrium. (Note the difference between such policies and those mentioned in the previous paragraph.) Since any social state other than an equilibrium possessing at least some stability properties must be very expensive to enforce for long, the hope is that the (weak) stability property of this equilibrium might hold down the expense of such a collective action, since the action would need to be taken only when the ambient levels of trust in the society became too low.

Section 3 explores what happens when a small asymmetry is added to the model of Sect. 2. The idea is to see whether the single-population results are robust to nonuniform matching probabilities that could arise, for example, from location-based biases. It should come as no surprise that the addition of asymmetries to a symmetric model permits the existence of additional, asymmetric equilibria. In this asymmetric version of the model, each individual is classified as belonging to one of two groups. All individuals are otherwise identical, however, and are assumed to be completely unaware of, and hence cannot adopt strategies that condition action on, the group to which the current opponent belongs. Within-group matches are assumed to be more likely than across-group matches. Depending on parameter values, new equilibria now arise. In some of these equilibria, the frequencies of the All D strategy are substantially different across the two populations. The social-policy questions become therefore more complicated; unmodeled issues of equity, discrimination, and inter-group jealousies arise. Furthermore, stability analysis of some of the equilibria becomes intractable.

In light of the difficulty of the stability analysis of Sect. 3, I look at a simpler, albeit less well motivated, model in Sect. 4. Here there is again a single population, but players are more likely to be matched with others who use the same strategy as they do themselves. (For example, there might be locational biases in the matching frequencies and locations could be correlated with strategies.) The stability properties of the equilibria of this model are explored and compared to those of the model in Sect. 2.

All of this is discussed further in the concluding Sect. 5.

2 The single-population model

Consider the prisoner's dilemma of Table 1, where $\beta > \alpha > 0 > -\gamma$. ($C$ stands for cooperate and D for defect.) The strategy pair D vs. D is, of course, the unique Nash equilibrium of the one-shot game. If the game is repeated infinitely, with both players having the same discount factor $\delta < 1$ (or if the players maximize the sum of their expected payoffs but the game stops after any round

Table 1.

	C	D
C	α, α	$-\gamma, \beta$
D	$\beta, -\gamma$	$0, 0$

with probability $1-\delta$) and if $\delta > (\beta-\alpha)/\beta$, then, as is well known, in addition to the Nash equilibrium in which both players play D every time no matter what history they have seen (call this strategy in the repeated game All D), there are additional Nash equilibria that generate C vs. C at every round. I will lump Tit For Tat, Grim and all the rest of these together and call any strategy from this class Trust But Verify (TBV). TBV strategies all begin with cooperation and then continue to cooperate after a sequence of complete cooperation. (They differ from each other in what they do after other histories, but these are not relevant for this discussion.)

In practice, TBV strategies are likely to be more difficult to play than All D or All C . They are more complex, and they require that attention be paid to the history of play. So if the population of possible opponents were known to consist only of TBV players, for example, a player might be tempted to simply adopt All C, since it generates the same cooperative sequence against TBV without requiring the additional effort. In order to quantify this tradeoff, I assume from now on that the adoption of TBV involves an ongoing cost represented by subtraction of a small constant κ (> 0) from the player's payoff at every repetition of the one-shot game. In order that TBV not be dominated by All C or All D, κ must be small enough that

$$\delta > \frac{\beta - \alpha + \kappa}{\beta} \quad \text{and} \quad \delta > \frac{\kappa}{\gamma}, \tag{1}$$

which I assume from now on. (Tighter restrictions will be imposed on the size of κ below.)

Suppose now that the members of a large population are repeatedly randomly matched against each other in order to play the repeated prisoner's dilemma. Suppose further that each member of the population is endowed with a (repeated-game) strategy that he uses inflexibly and that strategies which do relatively better against the strategy distribution in the rest of the population at a point in time tend to expand in the population at the expense of those strategies that do relatively worse.[6] To keep matters as simple as possible, I restrict the possible strategies to All C, All D, and TBV. Evolutionary games have proved useful at modelling such situations. The evolutionary game that describes this one is Table 2, where the entries are the payoffs to the row strategy when it is matched with that of the column. (As usual in evolutionary games, payoffs need to be interpreted as reproductive fitnesses.) The rough idea is that for any current distribution of the population across the three strategies, those strategies with higher average

[6] One can think of these changes in the population's relative frequencies as arising from either cultural adaptation or from biological evolution, though the former seems more natural.

payoffs against the current distribution should increase in relative frequency at the expense of those with lower average payoffs.

Table 2.

	All C	All D	TBV
All C	$\frac{\alpha}{1-\delta}$	$\frac{-\gamma}{1-\delta}$	$\frac{\alpha}{1-\delta}$
All D	$\frac{\beta}{1-\delta}$	0	β
TBV	$\frac{\alpha-\kappa}{1-\delta}$	$-\gamma - \frac{\kappa}{1-\delta}$	$\frac{\alpha-\kappa}{1-\delta}$

The most popular equilibrium concept for evolutionary games is ESS (evolutionary stable strategy) which requires that the population distribution, viewed as a mixed strategy in the two-person symmetric one-shot game in which both players face the payoff matrix in Table 2, be a symmetric Nash equilibrium satisfying the additional stability condition that any alternative best response to the equilibrium strategy does worse against itself than does the equilibrium mixture. (Thus, an ESS is stable in the sense that a small perturbation in the relative population frequencies toward one of these alternative best replies creates a tendency, under any dynamic that rewards better-performing strategies at the expense of poorer-performing strategies, for the distribution to return to the equilibrium.) For the game above, it is easy to see that there is a unique ESS, and it is for the entire population to use All D. This is a gloomy result as it seems to mitigate against the emergence of cooperation, but it can be ameliorated somewhat if one is prepared to weaken a bit the restrictions imposed by ESS.

To see why such a weakening might make sense in this case, first note that under suitable parameter restrictions, in particular when κ is sufficiently small, there are two (and only two) additional symmetric Nash equilibria for the symmetric two-person one-shot game: One is the mixed strategy in which All C is never used, All D is played with probability

$$\frac{\alpha - \beta(1-\delta) - \kappa}{\alpha - (\beta - \gamma)(1-\delta)},$$

and TBV is played with the rest of the probability. (Since the expression above is clearly between 0 and 1, one only needs to verify that against this mixture when κ is sufficiently small the expected payoff to All C is less than that to TBV which in turn equals that to All D.) The other symmetric equilibrium strategy is the completely mixed strategy in which All C is played with probability

$$\overline{A} = \frac{(\delta\gamma - \kappa)(\alpha - \beta(1-\delta)) - \gamma\kappa}{\delta^2\beta\gamma},$$

All D is played with probability $\overline{B} = \kappa/\delta\gamma$, and TBV is played with the remaining probability $1 - \overline{A} - \overline{B}$. (For this second mixture to generate an equilibrium, we need to be assured first that $\overline{A}, \overline{B}$, and $1 - \overline{A} - \overline{B}$ are all nonnegative: When κ is sufficiently small, $\overline{B}$ is obviously small and positive; and $\overline{A}$ is approximately

$$\frac{\alpha - \beta(1-\delta)}{\delta\beta},$$

which is strictly between 0 and 1 from (1), as is $1-\overline{A}-\overline{B}$. That the payoffs to all three strategies are equal is easily checked. That there are no other symmetric equilibria is similarly easy to verify.)

I will argue that this last equilibrium has some claim on our attention. To keep the discussion as simple as possible, I will work from now on with an example from the part of the parameter space in which both mixtures form equilibria: $\alpha=2, \beta=3, \delta=2/3, \gamma=3/2$, and $\kappa=1/6$. In this case, the evolutionary game is Table 3;

Table 3.

	All C	All D	TBV
All C	6	$-\frac{9}{2}$	6
All D	9	0	3
TBV	$\frac{11}{2}$	-2	$\frac{11}{2}$

and straightforward calculations produce $(0,5/9,4/9)$ for the first mixture and $(7/24,4/24,13/24)$ for the second.

Call an equilibrium (locally, asymptotically) *stable* relative to a (deterministic, continuous-time, regular [7]) dynamic if all trajectories starting sufficiently close to the equilibrium converge to it. The question is: Which dynamic? Our evolutionary story suggests that at a point in time if a pure strategy has higher expected payoff than does some other pure strategy that is used with nonzero frequency in a particular population mixture, then the difference between their frequencies should be increasing at a rate that is uniformly bounded below by some positive linear function of the payoff difference. Call such a dynamic *monotone*.[8] Since the pure equilibrium in which everyone plays All D is a strict Nash equilibrium, it is clearly stable in any monotone dynamic. At the other extreme, starting from any mixture of the form $(0,5/9,4/9)+(\varepsilon_1,\varepsilon_2,-\varepsilon_1-\varepsilon_2)$, where $\varepsilon_1 \geq 0$, $\varepsilon_2>0$, and $\varepsilon_1+\varepsilon_2<4/9$, it is obvious that All D is the unique best response and hence its frequency must continually grow in any monotone dynamic. So $(0,5/9,4/9)$ is unstable in any monotone dynamic.

For the completely mixed equilibrium, matters are not so clear-cut. Call an equilibrium *weakly stable* if for some monotone dynamic the equilibrium is stable and for some other one it is not.

Proposition 1. *The completely mixed equilibrium is weakly stable in the game of Table 3.*

The proof of Proposition 1 is relatively complicated and is relegated to an Appendix. The idea is easy, however, and can be understood with the help of

[7] By *regular*, I mean only that the dynamic is required to produce well-defined trajectories from all starting states.

[8] Cf., Nachbar (1990), Friedman (1991) and Samuelson and Zhang (1992). Motivated by the emphasis on the replicator dynamics in the evolutionary biology literature (and for technical reasons), more attention is focused in those papers on monotonicity as a natural restriction on changes in growth rate differences rather than simply in frequency differences, as here. In the present context, the notion of monotonicity adopted here seems to me the more natural one.

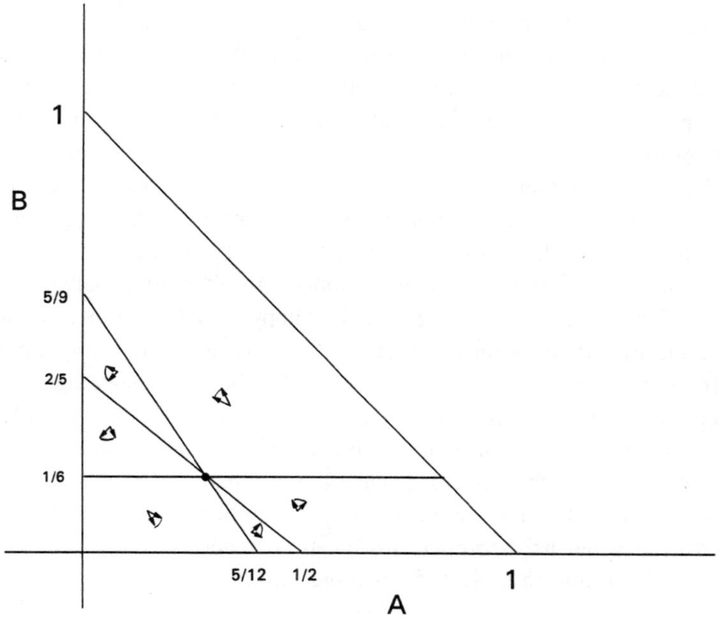

Fig. 1

Fig. 1: Monotonicity requires that the flow diagram be divided into the six pictured regions, together with their respective boundaries, and that the direction of flow inside each region be within the respective depicted ranges. Every trajectory beginning close to the completely mixed equilibrium therefore swirls around it in a counterclockwise fashion. Arguments from elementary geometry then show that the dynamic can be specified so that for starting states sufficiently close to the completely-mixed equilibrium the swirling motion can be either an inward-directed or an outward-directed spiral.

In evolutionary games such as those of this class, recently-developed stochastic stability theories (e.g., Kandori et al. 1993 and Young 1993) select from among equilibria based on notions of long-run occupancy ratios.[9] For the game of Table 3, it is not difficult to see that such theories necessarily select the All D ESS. Despite this, I argue that for social policy attention should still be focused on the completely mixed equilibrium. My reasons for this, however, come from considerations outside of the model at hand: Even if individuals adapt (or reproduce) unthinkingly, as in the usual interpretation of evolutionary models, there can be an understanding of the efficiency gains possible from cooperation at the level of the society as a whole. In this case, policy interventions, such as prohibitively strong sanctions imposed temporarily against the play of D, can move the population to a more cooperative profile. Once there, since the completely

[9] These theories superimpose occasional mutations (or errors) on top of the sorts of deterministic dynamics assumed here in order to shake the system occasionally away from an equilibrium. They then use limits of long-run occupancy ratios of the different equilibria as the mutation rate goes to zero as the selection device.

mixed equilibrium of the model is weakly stable, the society's actual dynamic (which could be much more complicated than in the model, perhaps involving stochastic elements and both inward-swirling and outward-swirling elements) can once again take hold without additional interference, even if only until the actual dynamic pushes the state beyond the basin of attraction of the completely-mixed equilibrium. If the actual dynamic produces a trajectory that, at least initially, resembles one produced by a monotone dynamic for which the completely mixed equilibrium is stable, there is the potential for social benefit.

I have in mind, therefore, a kind of long-term alternation between the two equilibria. Occasional episodes of social collapse, such as those in Somalia, Rwanda, and Bosnia in recent years, last until the society can, through collective action (perhaps assisted from the outside), move the social state again close to the completely-mixed equilibrium. Of course, it would be better to defend this position with an explicit model of a political process having such features, and I am not proposing such a model; I make the argument informally here only to illustrate that interest in the completely mixed equilibrium of this model can be sustained even when its theoretical justification is not as compelling as that of the All D equilibrium. (See Sect. 5 for more on this.)

3 A two-population model

Now modify the evolutionary game of Table 3 as follows. Each individual belongs to one of two unchanging groups having relative sizes r and $(1-r)$, respectively. Suppose that when any member of the second group is matched, the probability that the match is with a member of the first group is λ; and suppose that the probability that any member of the first group is paired with a member of the second group in a match is μ. Then $\lambda(1-r) = \mu r$. Purely random matching would produce $\lambda = r$, so to produce a bias toward within-group matches, I assume $\lambda < r$, which implies $\mu < 1-r$ and

$$\mu + \lambda < 1.$$

In all other respects, the model is as in Sect. 2. In particular, individuals need not even be aware of the existence of groups.

Denote by A here the fraction of the first group employing All C and by B the fraction of the first group employing All D and by a and b the corresponding fractions for the second group. Let X, Y, and Z be the expected payoffs to the three strategies, respectively, for individuals in the first group; and let x, y, and z be the corresponding payoffs for the second group's strategies. Then

$$\begin{aligned}
X &= (1-\mu)\left[(1-B)(6) + B\left(\frac{-9}{2}\right)\right] + \mu\left[(1-b)(6) + b\left(\frac{-9}{2}\right)\right] \\
Y &= (1-\mu)\left[A(9) + (1-A-B)3\right] + \mu\left[a(9) + (1-a-b)3\right] \\
Z &= (1-\mu)\left[(1-B)\left(\frac{11}{2}\right) + B(-2)\right] + \mu\left[(1-b)\left(\frac{11}{2}\right) + b(-2)\right]
\end{aligned}$$

$$\begin{aligned}
x &= \lambda\left[(1-B)(6)+B\left(\frac{-9}{2}\right)\right]+(1-\lambda)\left[(1-b)(6)+b\left(\frac{-9}{2}\right)\right]\\
y &= \lambda\,[A\,(9)+(1-A-B)3]+(1-\lambda)\,[a\,(9)+(1-a-b)3]\\
z &= \lambda\left[(1-B)\left(\frac{11}{2}\right)+B(-2)\right]+(1-\lambda)\left[(1-b)\left(\frac{11}{2}\right)+b(-2)\right].
\end{aligned}$$

Now it is obvious that if

1. $A = a = 0$ and $B = b = 1$, or if
2. $A = a = 0$ and $B = b = \frac{5}{9}$, or if
3. $A = a = \frac{7}{24}$ and $B = b = \frac{4}{24}$,

then the equilibria of the single-population model become equilibria here no matter what λ and μ are. But there are also other equilibria of this model under suitable restrictions on the parameters λ and μ. In the interest of brevity, I list below only those that exist for a full two-dimensional subset of $\{(\lambda, \mu) : \lambda+\mu < 1\}$ and leave the verifications to the reader.

4. For $\lambda \leq 4/9$ and $10\mu + 3\lambda \geq 3$,

$$A = 0, B = 0 \quad \text{and} \quad a = 0, b = \frac{5}{9(1-\lambda)}.$$

5. For $\lambda \leq 4/9$ and $1/6 \leq \mu \leq 5/9$,

$$A = 0, B = 0 \quad \text{and} \quad a = 0, b = 1.$$

6. For $\lambda \leq 1/6$,

$$A = 0, B = 1, \quad \text{and} \quad a = \frac{7}{24(1-\lambda)}, b = \frac{4-24\lambda}{24(1-\lambda)}.$$

7. For $\lambda \leq 5/9$,

$$A = 0, B = 1 \quad \text{and} \quad a = 0, b = \frac{5-9\lambda}{9(1-\lambda)}.$$

8. For $1/6 \leq \lambda \leq 3/10$ and $\lambda \geq 3(\mu-1)/(24\mu-10)$,

$$A = 0, B = \frac{1}{6\lambda} \quad \text{and} \quad a = \frac{10\lambda-3+3\mu}{24\mu\lambda}, b = 0.$$

Obviously, by reversing the roles of λ and μ and of the upper and lower case Latin letters in #4–#8 above, another five categories of equilibria are added.

Extending the stability definitions in the obvious ways so that monotonicity is imposed separately on each group, it is immediately obvious that the equilibria of categories #1 and #5 are stable: In the product of sufficiently small neighborhoods of each of the strategies that is being used exclusively by the respective groups, the motion of every monotone dynamic is back toward the (product of the) respective strategies. Similarly, it is not hard to see that the equilibria of categories

#3, #4 and #7 are all unstable: Whenever B and/or b are higher than their equilibrium values, the motion of every monotone dynamic is toward further increases. For the remaining categories, matters are not so clear-cut. In fact, determining whether or not such equilibria are weakly stable appears to be a formidable task; and I do not know how to accomplish it. The state space is now the product of the two-dimensional simplices, and the class of monotone dynamics is not simple to characterize.

It is nevertheless of interest to notice a few features of the equilibria that are not obviously unstable, at least. In #5, one population plays TBV exclusively, the gains from cooperation within the group outweighing the losses from the cross-group matches but the presence of the All D players in the other population forestalling the use of All C. Overall expected payoffs are higher for both groups than in the single-population stable equilibrium, and are worse for both groups than in the single-population weakly-stable equilibrium as long as $\lambda > 1/6$. (When $\lambda < 1/6$, the second group is better off in the symmetric equilibrium.) Expected payoffs are unequal across the groups, of course.

In #6, the equilibrium is essentially one group playing the stable single-population equilibrium with the other playing a modified version of the weakly-stable single-population equilibrium. Overall expected payoffs for the first group are intermediate between the same two single-population equilibrium payoffs, while for the second group they are equal to those of the weakly-stable single-population equilibrium.

In #8, the interplay across the groups is more subtle. Here the number of All D users in the first group is

$$Br = \left(\frac{1}{6}\right)\left(\frac{(1-r)}{\mu}\right) > \frac{1}{6},$$

so it exceeds the total number of All D users in the single-population weakly-stable equilibrium. The equilibrium payoffs for both groups are intermediate between those of the single-population stable and weakly-stable equilibrium payoffs in the relevant region of (λ, μ)-space. Notice also that some policy prescriptions intended to move the system from this asymmetric equilibrium to the symmetric one of #3 may turn out to be unhelpful in practice; viz., suppose that sanctions are imposed by society when possible on instances of an individual using D when the opponent uses C. The effect of this might be to decrease β slightly in Tables 1 and 2 and the corresponding numbers in Table 3, producing small effects on the equilibrium quantities a and B. But, if the sanctions are applied disproportionally against instances in which the C player is from the first group (e.g., extra money for police temporarily, but they patrol mostly in the neighborhoods where the second group resides disproportionally), it can end up producing the perverse effect of increasing, rather than decreasing, the behavioral differences between the groups.

For the most part, the pattern seems to be that the asymmetric equilibria, whatever their stability properties, achieve part, but not all, of the average welfare gain of the weakly-stable single-population equilibrium over the All D equilibrium. On the other hand, to the extent that the asymmetric equilibria turn out to be "more stable" than the completely mixed symmetric equilibrium, they may actually be advantageous for overall welfare. Whatever the ultimate balance, the analysis of this section suggests that public policies that work toward the homogenization of a society, interpreted as increasing both λ and μ, may have complicated side effects that have not been previously addressed in that they alter the domains on which certain equilibria exist.

4 Nonuniform within-group matches

In this section[10] I consider another variation on the basic model involving a single population but with nonuniform matchings. Here the assumption is that individuals are more likely to be matched with others who use the same strategy. For simplicity, I assume the following form, parametrized by $t \in (0, 1]$: at any time a fixed fraction t of each strategy type is matched only with its own type; the remaining fraction $(1 - t)$ of the population is matched at random. So, for example, if the current population frequency vector is $(A, B, 1 - A - B)$, the probability that a particular All C player is matched with another All C is $t + (1 - t)A$, and is matched with an All D with probability $(1 - t)B$. The expected payoffs, calculated analogously to those in Sect. 2, become

$$\begin{aligned} X &= 6 - \frac{21}{2}(1 - t)B, \\ Y &= 3(1 - t) + 6(1 - t)A - 3(1 - t)B, \\ Z &= \frac{11}{2} - \frac{15}{2}(1 - t)B. \end{aligned}$$

As can easily be checked, there are now five possible equilibria, for different ranges of t.

1. For $t \leq \frac{4}{15}$, $A = 0$, $B = 1$.
2. For $t \leq \frac{4}{15}$, $A = 0$, $B = \frac{5 + 6t}{9(1 - t)}$.
3. For $t \leq \frac{13}{36}$, $A = \frac{7 + 12t}{24(1 - t)}$, $B = \frac{4}{24(1 - t)}$.
4. For $t \geq \frac{1}{3}$, $A = 1$, $B = 0$.
5. For $\frac{1}{3} \leq t \leq \frac{13}{36}$, $A = \frac{3 - 7t}{1 - t}$, $B = \frac{-2 + 6t}{1 - t}$.

The first three of these are obviously extensions of the three equilibria of Sect. 2, respectively, and it is easy to see that the stability properties of the corresponding equilibria of Sect. 2 extend to these directly, at least on the interiors

[10] I am grateful to Hsueh-Ling Huynh for suggesting inclusion of the model of this section.

of the respective ranges of t values. Category #4 is stable for $t > 1/3$; this follows from the strict inequalities involving X. Category #5 is unstable for $t > 1/3$; to see this note that if $A > (3 - 7t)/(1 - t)$, the state is in the basin of attraction of #4.

Although the model here is perhaps less interesting for applications than is the model in Section 3, the functional forms for the equilibria above also hint at the social effects of certain asymmetries. In #3 above, the analogue of the weakly-stable equilibrium of Sect. 2, for instance, A and B both increase with t, so the frequency of TBV declines. Evidently, the asymmetry decreases the usefulness of costly TBV verifications; and the society becomes increasingly like one with two separated subgroups, one trusting and one not. This is somewhat analogous to the #5 equilibria of Sect. 3.

5 Discussion

If the models of this paper depict the salient features of real social phenomena, then it is useful to ask how various society-level interventions can be reflected in the models and the results. One class of such interventions is those that seek to change permanently the payoff structure of the games. For instance, play of D (or play of D when the opponent plays C) could be deemed a crime and permanently subject to sanctions. The stiffer the penalty or the larger the set of resources devoted to detecting and punishing the crime, the larger the effect could be on the entries in the payoff tables. Except at lower dimensional regions of the parameter space, however, marginal changes in the payoff parameters can only move the location of the equilibria marginally. So, to produce major changes in behavior in equilibrium, more-than-marginal changes in payoff parameters are generally necessary. The criminalization example suggests that this might be costly, though not necessarily prohibitively costly. Analysis of models like those in Sect. 2 of this paper might be used for cost-benefit calculations.

A second set of interventions is the class aimed at overcoming the instabilities of preferred equilibria. The idea is that the real world dynamic process is perhaps complicated and perhaps involves stochastic elements, but it might at least resemble those dynamics used in the stability calculations of this paper. When the dynamic process is away from the desired equilibrium, it may be possible and not too expensive to move it back. If the equilibrium possesses at least weak stability, there is then the chance that the process may stay near the desired equilibrium for awhile without the expenditure of additional resources by the society. It is this last point that raises hope at least that interventions from this class can sometimes be cost-effective. As mentioned earlier, if recent social breakdowns such as those in Somalia, Rwanda, and Bosnia[11] are interpreted as movements from a relatively efficient equilibrium to a relatively inefficient one,

[11] By repeating these three unfortunate examples, I do not mean to imply that episodes from other countries' histories cannot be interpreted similarly. On the contrary, I suspect that all human societies face similar dilemmas at one level or another on a regular basis.

then multinational interventions envisioned as temporary can be viewed as being from this class. No doubt the hope of the policy makers involved in the actual interventions is that by temporarily enforcing cooperative interactions among individuals, a pattern of cooperation could be started that could persist in its own dynamic after the enforcement mechanism was removed.

I suggest that the results of Sect. 3 above can be interpreted as cautions against the use of such interventions. Casual observation suggests that differences in behavior, customs, taboos, etc., are widespread and persistent across subpopulations. Similarly, the effect of an intervention is likely to be felt and responded to differently across subpopulations. So, an attempt to move the process from near the All D equilibrium to a neighborhood of the completely mixed equilibrium in the model of Sect. 2, for instance, may move it instead to one of the asymmetric equilibria of the model of Sect. 3 in which only one of the subpopulations has changed appreciably. While this is still a social improvement, it is not the desired one; and, to the extent that inequality breeds mistrust, it may contain additional, unmodeled instabilities. Furthermore, unless the intervention can be targeted at each subpopulation separately, my guess is that subpopulations resist interventions differently and therefore that the asymmetric equilibria are the more likely ones.

Having come this far, let me go on to suggest that if I am right about the asymmetric effectiveness of such interventions, the possibility of asymmetric equilibria can itself be viewed as a kind of meta-social inefficiency. To the extent that it is, it should weigh in positively for social policies that have the effect of decreasing diversity within a society.

In Sect. 3, I did not allow individuals to recognize the group membership of the matched opponent. If this were possible, as seems likely in many applications (for instance, the aforementioned three national tragedies), additional strategies that condition behavior on the opponent's identity become available, and additional assumptions need to be considered about the costs of maintaining such strategies. If these costs are not too large, it seems that still more equilibria will exist.

Finally, I should mention that there are other models of social breakdowns in the literature that involve multiple Pareto-ranked equilibria (e.g., Murphy, et al. 1993), although I know of none that are closely related to the models of this paper.

Appendix

Proof of Proposition 1. For ease of exposition, I use the familiar language of time derivatives, although differentiability plays no role. Let $(A, B, 1 - A - B)$ denote the current population mixture. With the uniformly positive lower bound (which is needed for technical reasons only) replaced by zero, the monotonicity retriction is:

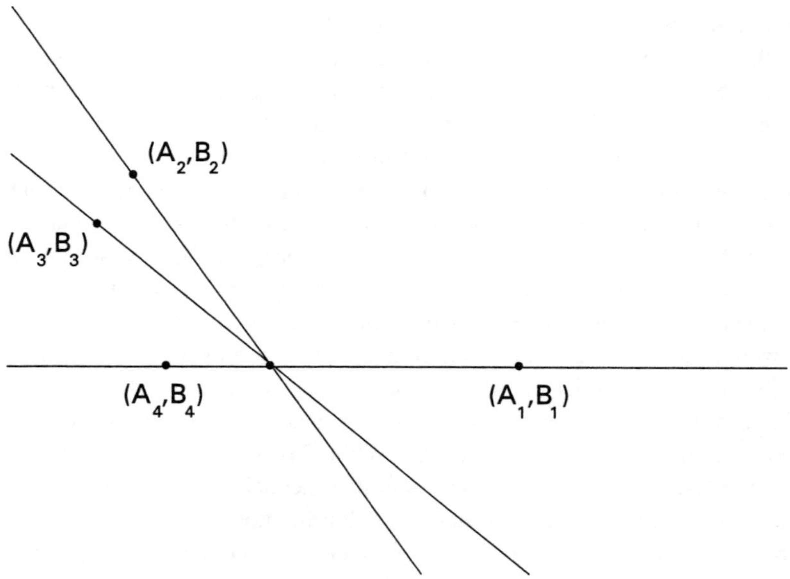

Fig. 2

$$\dot{A} \geq \dot{B} \Longleftrightarrow 6A - \frac{9B}{2} + 6(1-A-B) \geq 9A + 3(1-A-B);$$
$$\dot{A} \geq -\dot{A}-\dot{B} \Longleftrightarrow 6A - \frac{9B}{2} + 6(1-A-B) \geq \frac{11A}{2} - 2B + \frac{11(1-A-B)}{2};$$
$$\dot{B} \geq -\dot{A}-\dot{B} \Longleftrightarrow 9A + 3(1-A-B) \geq \frac{11A}{2} - 2B + \frac{11(1-A-B)}{2}.$$

Simplifying,

$$\dot{A} \geq \dot{B} \Longleftrightarrow 12A + 15B \leq 6;$$
$$\dot{A} \geq -\dot{A}-\dot{B} \Longleftrightarrow B \leq \frac{1}{6};$$
$$\dot{B} \geq -\dot{A}-\dot{B} \Longleftrightarrow 12A + 9B \geq 5.$$

I will first show that there are dynamics respecting these conditions under which $(7/24, 4/24, 13/24)$ is stable.

Suppose we begin at some point (A_1, B_1) on the line $B = 1/6$, with $A_1 > 7/24$, as in Fig. 2. Since $B_1 = 1/6$, we get $\dot{A} = -\dot{A} - \dot{B}$; and since $12A_1 + 15B_1 > 6$, it must be that $\dot{A} < \dot{B}$. Consequently, $\dot{B} > 0$, $\dot{A} < 0$, and $(\dot{B}/\dot{A}) = -2$. The trajectory therefore immediately enters the region characterized by $\dot{B} > -\dot{A}-\dot{B} > \dot{A}$; i.e., in which $\dot{B} > 0$, $\dot{A} < 0$, and $-2 < (\dot{B}/\dot{A}) < -(1/2)$. If A_1 is sufficiently close to $7/24$ and if $(\dot{B}/\dot{A})$ changes sufficiently quickly from near -2 to near $-(1/2)$, then the trajectory hits the line $12A+9B = 5$ (having slope $-12/9$) before it hits $A = 0$. Let (A_2, B_2) be this hitting point. After (A_2, B_2), the trajectory enters the region characterized by $-\dot{A} - \dot{B} > \dot{B} > \dot{A}$, so that $\dot{A} < 0$ and $-(1/2) < (\dot{B}/\dot{A}) < 1$. Again, if A_1 is sufficiently close to $7/24$, the trajectory hits the line $12A + 15B = 6$ (having slope $-(4/5)$) at the point (A_3, B_3) before it hits $A = 0$. After (A_3, B_3), the trajectory enters the region characterized by $-\dot{A} - \dot{B} > \dot{A} > \dot{B}$, where $\dot{B} < 0$ and $-2 < (\dot{B}/\dot{A}) < 1$. Again, if A_1 is sufficiently close to $7/24$, the trajectory hits the line $B = (1/6)$ at the point (A_4, B_4).

If, upon entering each new region, the slope of the trajectory were to change immediately to its new limiting value, then

$$\frac{B_2 - B_1}{A_2 - A_1} = -\frac{1}{2}, \quad \frac{B_3 - B_2}{A_3 - A_2} = 1, \quad \text{and} \quad \frac{B_4 - B_3}{A_4 - A_3} = -2.$$

Combining these with

$$B_1 = B_4 = \frac{1}{6}, \quad 12A_2 + 9B_2 = 5, \quad \text{and} \quad 12A_3 + 15B_3 = 6,$$

we obtain

$$A_4 = \frac{7}{24} - \frac{7}{15}\left(A_1 - \frac{7}{24}\right).$$

Repeating the same argument for the region below the line $B = (1/6)$, we come to the point

$$(A_7, B_7) = \left(\frac{7}{24} + \left(\frac{7}{15}\right)^2\left(A_1 - \frac{7}{24}\right), \frac{1}{6}\right),$$

which is obviously closer to the equilibrium than is (A_1, B_1). Therefore, in any dynamic whose direction approximates that of this limiting dynamic on a neighborhood of the completely mixed equilibrium, the completely mixed equilibrium is stable.

To find a dynamic under which the equilibrium is unstable, start sufficiently close to the equilibrium in the region defined by

$$B > \frac{1}{6}, \quad 12A + 9B > 5, \quad A + B < 1, \quad \text{and } A \geq 0.$$

Notice that if the slope $\dot{B}/\dot{A}$ stays below $-12/9$, the trajectory must hit $A = 0$ before any of the other boundaries of the region. But this means that such a trajectory must pass into the basin of attraction of the All D equilibrium, which implies that the completely mixed equilibrium is unstable.

References

Axelrod, R. (1984) *The Evolution of Cooperation.* Basic Books, New York

Friedman, D. (1991) Evolutionary games in economics. *Econometrica* 59: 637–666

Hirshleifer, J., Martinez Coll, J. (1988) What strategies can support the evolutionary emergence of cooperation?. *Journal of Conflict Resolution* 32: 367–398

Kandori, M., Mailath, G., Rob, R. (1993) Learning, mutation, and long run equilibria. *Econometrica* 61: 29–56

Murphy, K., Shleifer, A., Vishny, R. (1993) Why is rent-seeking so costly to growth. *American Economic Review* 83: 409–414

Nachbar, J. (1990) Evolutionary selection in games: Convergence and limit properties. Mimeo

Osborne, M., Rubinstein, A. (1994) *A Course in Game Theory.* MIT Press, Cambidge, MA

Radner, R. (1986) Can bounded rationality resolve the prisoners' dilemma? In: Mas-Colell, A., Hildenbrand, W. (eds.) *Contributions to Mathematical Economics*. North Holland, Amsterdam, pp. 387–399

Samuelson, L., Zhang, J. (1992) Evolutionary stability in asymmetric games. *Journal of Economic Theory* 57: 363–391

Young, H. P. (1993) The evolution of conventions. *Econometrica* 61: 57–84

Young, H. P., Foster, D. (1991) Cooperation in the short run and in the long run. *Games and Economic Behavior* 3: 145–156

Survival and the art of profit maximization

Prajit K. Dutta[1], **Rangarajan K. Sundaram**[2]

[1] Department of Economics, Columbia University, New York, NY 10027, USA
(e-mail: pkd1@columbia.edu)
[2] Department of Finance, Stern School of Business, New York University, New York, NY 10012, USA (e-mail: rsundar@stern.hyu.edu)

Abstract. We study the relationship between rationality and economic survival in a simple dynamic model, where agents from different populations interact repeatedly through random matching. An explicit criterion ("bankruptcy") determines whether agents survive each interaction; all agents are presumed to be aware of this criterion. Survival in each interaction depends on two factors: the strategies agents adopt when they interact, and the wealth levels they bring to the game. The model is completely symmetric with the only difference between the agents of different populations being their objectives.

We consider the case where there are two populations of agents in which all agents from one group have as their objective, maximizing the *expected profits* from each interaction, while all agents from the other attempt simply to maximize the probability of *surviving* (i.e., not going bankrupt in) the interaction. We show that under the equilibrium dynamics, the proportions of each group in the total population must be bounded away from zero, but the balance is in favor of the survival-probability maximizers in that their numbers as a fraction of total population must always exceed 1/2, and can be arbitrarily close to unity. On the other hand, the fraction of total wealth controlled by the expected profit maximizers must also be at least 1/2, and can asymptotically tend to unity.

1 Introduction

This paper examines the link between rationality and economic survival in the context of a model where agents have differing objectives. Our inquiry is motivated by the question of whether, and in what sense, environments select agents who "adapt;" and the extent to which success in survival can be attributed to

We would like to thank a number of people for helpful comments and suggestions including, especially, Jeff Banks, Ananth Madhavan, Kalyan Chatterjee, and an anonymous referee.

"rational" decision rules such as profit- or utility-maximization. This line of inquiry has, of course, a long history in economics. Our paper is related to at least two strands of the existing literature.

One, beginning with Alchian (1950) and Friedman (1953), adopts the common viewpoint that in a market selection mechanism, realized profitability is a *necessary* condition for survival.[1] On the implication of this assumption for identifying the most "fit" decision rules, there has been less unanimity. Some authors, such as Friedman (1953) and Enke (1951), have argued that competitive forces would lead, in such a world, to the selection of firms that *maximized* profits.[2] When there is perfect knowledge regarding the consequences of different choices by the firms, this appears an uncontroversial assertion. In a world of uncertainty, however, where firms are, in effect, choosing probability distributions over profit levels, the notion of "profit maximization" lacks an *a priori* meaning, since the market selects firms whose *realized* (and not *anticipated*) profits are highest. This problem was pointed out by Alchian (1950), but he did not propose any one criterion as most "rational" or "fit" in such situations. Alchian notwithstanding, it would be fair to say that economic theory has subsequently, and rather uncritically, reinterpreted the Friedman argument as identifying the maximization of *expected* profits with fitness, and as the criterion to be adopted in the marketplace.[3]

One problem with this branch of the literature has been the absence of a formal model within which its conclusions may be examined.[4] Certainly, the *a priori* connection between "rationality" and "expected profit maximization" is not obvious. In any reasonable economic model, firms must be assumed to have knowledge of the selection mechanism. A "rational" firm would presumably incorporate knowledge of this mechanism into its decision calculus, and there is no reason at all to expect, under these conditions, that the firm will choose expected-profit maximization as the "best" criterion. It is important to point out that giving firms knowledge of this selection mechanism, and allowing them to incorporate it into their decision process, creates no problems under certainty, for, here, maximizing profits and maximizing the probability of survival are (by definition!) the same.

A second strand of the literature, that on "evolutionary games," originating with Maynard Smith (1982), models more explicitly the interaction among alternative strategies within the context of a game and studies the long-run fitness

[1] For example, "...those who realize positive profits are the survivors; those who suffer losses disappear." (Alchian, 1950, p.213)

[2] To quote Friedman (1953) "Unless the behavior of businessmen in some way approximated behavior consistent with the maximization of returns, it seems unlikely they would be in business for long."

[3] Undoubtedly, one reason behind the the popularity of the expected-utility (or expected-profit) maximization hypothesis lies in the analytical tractability of models in which all agents pursue such goals.

[4] However, see Blume and Easley (1988) and Dutta and Radner (1999).

of different strategies. A typical evolutionary game model[5] has the following structure. The population of agents is divided into groups on the basis of the strategies the agents adopt, with all agents within a group playing the same strategy. Agents are then randomly matched. In each period, the group or groups whose strategies fare better than the population average are then assumed to grow in size (more precisely, their proportion in the population increases). The aim is then to examine whether there are strategies which are "evolutionarily stable," i.e, that survive this selection mechanism. This literature has resulted in important insights into selection mechanisms and the problems of obtaining "stable" strategies. As a theory of economic evolution, however, it suffers from at least three shortcomings. First, in much of this literature, agents' strategies are exogenously fixed: players do not actively seek to adapt or react to the strategy choices of those with whom they are matched.[6] In particular, they do not take cognizance of the survival mechanism into account when making their choices. Secondly, the rule determining survival is somewhat arbitrary. Third, there are no market features in these models (such as, say, market shares or wealth shares). Thus, while who survives is determined, the question of asymptotic control of the market, a logically different issue from which group's numbers are preponderant in the limit, cannot be examined.

Our aim in this paper is to study a simple dynamic model that is rich enough to admit the following important features:

1. There is an explicit survival criterion, and all agents are aware of this criterion.
2. There are different kinds of agents who interact with each other at regular intervals. Some agents simply try to maximize the probability of surviving each encounter, while others maximize the expected level of profits from the interactions.
3. Each member of each group is also characterized by his wealth level[7] at any point in time, so that there are two dynamic processes that evolve together: the proportion of each type in the overall population, and the wealth share of each type in the overall wealth.

Our model will have the appealing feature that one group of agents – the survival-probability maximizers – will, *ceteris paribus*, have a greater probability of survival, but conditional on survival, the wealth level of the other group – the expected-profit maximizers – will be higher.

Our aim is then to track the performance of the two groups over time along two dimensions. First, how do the proportions of the two groups in the overall population change over time? Second, how do the proportions of total wealth controlled by each group change over time? We adopt the position at the outset

[5] See, e.g., Friedman (1988) or the *Journal of Economic Theory* Symposium Issue on Evolutionary Games (August 1992).

[6] Some models of evolutionary learning (e.g., Canning, 1990) provide agents with endogeneous decision-making power. Here, typically, agents' actions have to be best-responses to some conjectured population strategies.

[7] Wealth in our model is a proxy for market power.

that the "fitness" of a strategy in the marketplace must be measured along both dimensions. A strategy that leads to "survival" while getting swamped in growth by other strategies, is not "fit" in any sense in which economists would wish to use that word.

The details of the model we study borrows much from both branches of the literature discussed above. From the first, we adopt the notion of "bankruptcy" as determining the condition of failure; survival therefore entails avoiding bankruptcy. From the second, we import the idea of dividing the population into different types of agents, and the matching specification. More formally, we consider a world with large populations of two types of agents, who interact repeatedly over a number of "rounds." In any round, agents from each type are randomly matched into pairs. Each pair then plays a "bankruptcy" game, the outstanding feature of which is that not all risk can be hedged (there is real uncertainty). In this game, players pick actions that jointly determine the parameters of the stochastic process governing the growth rate and evolution of their wealth levels. The game terminates when one player has become bankrupt, i.e., when his wealth level reaches zero. The bankrupt agent then leaves the game, while the surviving agent takes his wealth level at this point into the next round.

Agents from the two populations are presumed to have different preferences. In particular, we assume that those of the first type choose their strategies to maximize their expected wealth level at the end of each round (in our model this is analogous to maximizing expected profits from each encounter); while agents from the second population simply maximize their probability of surviving (*i.e.*, not going bankrupt in) each round.

Our main conclusions may be summarized as follows. First, when the environment is "symmetric" (either group faces exactly the same possibilities and payoffs, the only difference being their objectives), expected profit-maximizers never fare better than survival-probability maximizers on population share, and often do strictly worse. On the other hand, expected-profit maximizers fare at least as well as survival-probability maximizers on wealth share, and sometimes do strictly better. In particular, when the stage-game is "linear," they do as well on the wealth-share dimension, but strictly worse on the population share dimension. When the stage game is sufficiently non-linear, they do strictly better on wealth share, even though they do worse on pupulation share.

Secondly, symmetry is important for a fair comparison. If the model is asymmetric (i.e., the environment favors one group or the other), much depends on who has access to the superior technology. If the environment facors the expected-profit maximizers (no matter how slightly), they can come to dominate the market along both dimensions, in population-share as well as wealth-share; but exactly the opposite is true if the environment tilts towards the survival-probability maximizers. Finally, if wealth generation is subject to increasing returns, then we find that expected-profit maximizers can come to control the entire market wealth even if their share in the population falls below 50%.

The two papers closest to ours are Dutta and Radner (1999) and Blume and Easley (1988). The Dutta-Radner paper asks exactly the same question as the current one: (under what conditions) does a market whose selection mechanism is bankruptcy select an entrepreneur with profit-maximizing preferences? The conclusion reached by that paper is even more stark than the one we uncover here: in the Dutta-Radner model, every profit-maximizing entrepreneur goes bankrupt in finite time with probability one, but there are survivalists who survive forever with positive probability. Hence, after a long period of time, the proportion of the population that is maximizing profits is essentially zero. Moreover, the wealth share of profit-maximizing entrepreneurs also goes to zero.

The model in the Dutta-Radner paper differs from the current one in one important respect: unlike here, there is no product-market interaction in that model (although there is capital-market interaction since every firm has to come to a common capital market to get funded). Once funded, each firm is run independently – or equivalently, is run in a competitive product market. Hence the differential performance of profit-maximizers versus survivalists is driven not by relative differences in riskiness of choice (as in the current analysis) but rather by absolute differences. In particular, the key insight of the Dutta-Radner paper is that a profit-maximizing entrepreneur would never want to build up arbitrarily large cash reserves (since doing so compromises the profits that can be distributed to shareholders). On the other hand, a survivalist entrepreneur would adopt a dividend payout policy that allows for arbitrarily large reserves. From a long-term survival point of view, a cash reserve that is finite-sized must necessarily get run down to zero in finite time.

The Blume and Easley paper also investigates the "survival" of "profit-maximizing" agents. However, their model is a pure gambling model with no production and hence their agents are more analogous to consumers, some of whom pursue expected utility maximization while others do not. Moreover there is no bankruptcy in the model. Hence, the worst that can happen to an agent type is that their wealth share can decrease over time (although their population share, by definition, must remain unchanged). Blume and Easley show that under a variety of scenarios it is entirely possible that the wealth share of expected profit maximizers sink to zero. They were not able, however, to establish which behavioral rules would necessarily do better than the expected utility maximizers.

The remainder of this paper is organized as follows. Section 2 describes our model and motivates the stage-game structure that we use. Section 3 analyzes the "linear" game, both with and without symmetry. Section 4 completes the analysis by looking at non-linear extensions of the model.

2 The evolutionary game

This section is divided into two parts. In Subsect. 2.1, we outline the basic structure of the evolutionary game that we study in this paper. Section 2.2 then presents the specific questions of interest.

2.1 The basic structure

We consider a model with two populations of agents, denoted I and II, each with a continuum of members. The initial measure of each population is normalized to unity. Members of either population are characterized at each point in time by their wealth levels. The initial wealth level of each member of each population is fixed at some $y > 0$.

In each period $t = 0, 1, 2, \ldots$, of an infinite horizon, agents of the two populations are matched into playing a symmetric stage game that we sometimes refer to as a "bankruptcy game." The action space for either player in this game is a non-degenerate compact set $K \subset \mathbb{R}$. These actions may be thought of essentially as constituting the players' choice of "risk levels" in the game; this interpretation of K will become clear shortly. The outcome of the game decides two things: the player who "survives" the game, and the wealth level of the surviving player at the end of the game. This outcome, in turn, depends on two factors, *viz.*, the actions the players take in the game, and the wealth levels they bring to the game. More formally, letting k_i denote the action choice of the type-i player, and y_i that player's wealth level at the start of the game, the outcome of the game is determined by four functions $(\rho_1, \rho_2, h_1, h_2)$ where $\rho_i(y_1, y_2; k_1, k_2)$ specifies the probability that player i "survives" the game (i.e., does not go bankrupt), and $h_i(y_1, y_2; k_1, k_2)$ specifies the terminal wealth level of player i in the event that he survives. The bankrupt player (say j) then exits the game, while the survivor i moves into the next round with the wealth level $h_i(\cdot)$.

Additional structure will be required of the functions ρ_i and h_i in the sequel. We will require the conditions A1–A4 listed below. The first two assumptions are symmetry conditions on the game. (On the importance of symmetry, see Sect. 3.3 below.) The third assumption involves the natural condition that, *ceteris paribus*, the probability of success (as also the terminal wealth contingent on winning) is increasing in own wealth. Finally, Assumption A4 makes clear the interpretation of actions as choices of risk levels: it asserts that, *ceteris paribus*, a higher action results in a lower probability of survival, but, contingent on survival, also results in a higher wealth level. In conjunction with A3, this assumption creates the tension that forms an important component of our model: a, less risky action today implies a greater probability of survival this period (i.e., in the *short run*), but also results in a lower rate of growth of wealth, which, by A3, reduces *long run* survival prospects.

A1 $\rho_1(y_1, y_2; k_1, k_2) = \rho_2(y_2, y_1; k_2, k_1)$.
A2 $h_1(y_1, y_2; k_1, k_2) = h_2(y_2, y_1, k_2, k_1)$.
A3 For each i and for all fixed $(y_j; k_1, k_2)$, the functions ρ_i and h_i are increasing in y_i.
A4 For each i, and for all fixed $(y_1, y_2; k_j)$, ρ_i is decreasing in k_i, while h_i is increasing in k_i.

Returning to our description of the stage game, the players of population I (whom we will also refer to as "expected-profit maximizers") aim to maximize their expected profits from each interaction, i.e., to solve, given k_2

$$\max\{\rho_1(y_1,y_2,k_1,k_2)\cdot h_1(y_1,y_2,k_1,k_2)\mid k_1\in K\} \tag{1}$$

Members of the second population (whom we call the "survival probability maximizers"), on the other hand, have as their objective simply maximizing the probability of surviving each encounter. That is, they solve, given k_1,

$$\max\{\rho_2(y_1,y_2,k_1,k_2)\mid k_2\in K\} \tag{2}$$

Let $K_1(y_1,y_2;k_2)$ and $K_2(y_1,y_2;k_1)$ denote, respectively, the solutions to the optimization problems of players 1 and 2. As always, a *(Nash) equilibrium* of the game is a strategy pair which is such that no player can benefit from unilateral deviation, *i.e.*, a, pair $\kappa(y_1,y_2)=(\kappa_1(y_1,y_2),\kappa_2(y_1,y_2))$, such that for each (y_1,y_2), we have $\kappa_1(y_1,y_2)\in K_1[y_1,y_2;\kappa_2(y_1,y_2)]$ and $\kappa_2(y_1,y_2)\in K_2[y_1,y_2;\kappa_1(y_1,y_2)]$.

This completes the description of the stage game. The following section utilizes this structure to identify the questions of interest.

2.2 Equilibrium dynamics and fitness

Throughout the paper, to keep equilibrium dynamics tractable, we will assume that all members of a given population use the same strategy. Let $\kappa(y_1,y_2)$ be some equilibrium strategy pair. The selection κ together with the initial (common) wealth level y determines the evolution of per capita wealth levels of the survivors in each population as follows (here, as in the sequel, we suppress dependence of these objects on κ and y):

$$\begin{aligned} y_{i0} &= y \\ k_{it} &= \kappa_i(y_{1t},y_{2t}), && t=0,1,2,\ldots \\ y_{it} &= h_i(y_{1t-1},y_{2t-1},k_{1t-1},k_{2t-1}), && t=1,2,\ldots \end{aligned}$$

The conditional probability ρ_{it} of a type-i player surviving into period-$(t+1)$ given survival upto period-t is also determined:

$$\rho_{it}=\rho_i(y_{1t},y_{2t},k_{1t},k_{2t}), \qquad t=0,1,2.... \tag{3}$$

Identifying the probability of a member of a population surviving with the fraction of that population which survives, the fraction p_{it} of population i which survives into period t is:

$$p_{it}=\prod_{\tau=0}^{t-1}\rho_{i\tau} \tag{4}$$

Thus, the relative share p_{t+1} of population I in the total population at time $(t+1)$ (viz., the ratio of population I to population II at that point) is:

$$p_{t+1}=\frac{p_{1\,t+1}}{p_{2\,t+1}}=\left(\frac{\rho_{1t}}{\rho_{2t}}\right)p_t \tag{5}$$

while the ratio s_t of the wealth controlled by population I to that controlled by population II is:

$$s_t = \frac{p_{1t}y_{1t}}{p_{2t}y_{2t}} = \left(\frac{y_{1t}}{y_{2t}}\right)p_t \tag{6}$$

The sequences p_t and s_t form the focus of our study in this paper. To state the precise questions of interest requires a little more notation.

Let P_∞ and S_∞ denote the set of all limit points of the sequences $\{p_t\}$ and $\{s_t\}$, respectively. Note that the sequences $\{p_t\}$ and $\{s_t\}$ (as also, therefore, P_∞ and S_∞) depend on the equilibrium strategy pair $\kappa(.)$. We will sometimes highlight this dependence by writing $P_\infty(\kappa), S_\infty(\kappa)$, etc.

A strategy κ_1, for population I will be called a *fit* strategy against κ_2, if it is the case that either $\inf P_\infty(\kappa_1, \kappa_2) > 0$, or $\inf S_\infty(\kappa_1, \kappa_2) > 0$. This definition of fitness is really a minimal one: a strategy is fit as long as it does not lead to total failure. (By our symmetry assumptions, fit strategies always exist – every strategy is fit against itself.)

As a stronger definition, a strategy κ_1, for population I will be called a *most fit* strategy against κ_2 if the following condition holds: there exists no other strategy $\widehat{\kappa}_1$ such that $\widehat{p} \geq p$ and $\widehat{s} \geq s$ for all $\widehat{p} \in P_\infty(\widehat{\kappa}_1, \kappa_2)$, $p \in P_\infty(\kappa_1, \kappa_2)$, $\widehat{s} \in S_\infty(\widehat{\kappa}_1, \kappa_2)$, and $s \in S_\infty(\kappa_1, \kappa_2)$, with at least one strict inequality for some $(\widehat{p}, p)$ or $(\widehat{s}, s)$. In words, κ_1 is most fit against κ_2, if there is no other strategy for Population I all of whose limit points dominate all of those under (κ_1, κ_2), with strict inequality somewhere.

Finally, the strategy κ_1, will be termed an *unbeatable* strategy for Population I, if it is a most fit strategy against *any* strategy κ_2 for Population II.

Analogous definitions of "fit," "most fit," and "unbeatable" strategies hold for population II. We note the important point that (once again, by the symmetry assumptions), the sets of fit, most fit, and unbeatable strategies for the two populations coincide. So, for instance, a strategy κ_i is a fit strategy for Population i against a strategy κ_j for population j if, and only if, κ_i is a fit strategy for Population j when Population i adopts κ_j.

Of course, the fitness of a strategy confers no equilibrium properties on it whatsoever; in particular, it can be the case that (κ_1, κ_2) are a, pair of strategies that are fit against each other (or most fit against each other, or even unbeatable), but that do not constitute a Nash equilibrium pair.

Indeed, our focus in this paper is primarily on the relationship between fitness and equilibrium. Specifically, we are interested in the following questions. When is it the case that equilibrium strategy profiles are also fit (or most fit or unbeatable) against each other? In particular, when is this true for Population I (the expected profit maximizers)? Conversely, when do most fit strategies (and, especially, unbeatable ones) constitute an equilibrium? Finally, when is it the case that, in equilibrium, one side comes to dominate the market from the wealth angle ($S_\infty = \{\infty\}$) or the population angle ($P_\infty = \{\infty\}$)?

3 A linear model

In this section, we present a first analysis of the evolutionary game of Sect. 3, by considering some restrictions on the functions ρ_i and h_i. These restrictions arise out of a simple extension to a two-person setting of the much-studied framework of one-person bankruptcy problems. We detail this procedure in Sect. 3.1 below. We term the model of the evolutionary game thus obtained the *linear model*, in part because the functions h_i and $\rho_i h_i$ depend linearly on y_1 and y_2. In Sect. 3.2, we then analyze the consequent evolutionary game dynamics. Finally, Sect. 3.3 discusses the consequences of introducing asymmetry into the underlying model.

3.1 The bankruptcy game

A vast literature in statistics and probability (and also economics) has examined the following one-person bankruptcy problem (see, e.g., Karatzas and Shreve 1988, or Dubins and Savage 1957). An agent begins with a wealth level of $y > 0$. This wealth evolves according to the process

$$dy = m\,dt + v^{1/2} dW_t \tag{7}$$

where W is standard Brownian motion. The process terminates and the agent *fails* at the first T at which $y(T) = 0$. The agent is presumed to have some control over this process (say, over the instantaneous drift m or the variance v), and selects his strategy to maximize some desired objective, such as the expected time to failure.

A two-person version of this problem, that can be viewed as a *symmetric bankruptcy game* in which players' actions simultaneously determine (a) the probability of bankruptcy of each player, and (b) the wealth level of the non-bankrupt player at the time of the other's bankruptcy, may be obtained by modifying this problem as follows. Let $K \subset \mathbb{R}$ be a non-degenerate compact set with lower endpoint $\min K$ and upper endpoint $\max K$. (K represents the players' (common) choice of actions in the game.) Let $g : K \times K \to \mathbb{R}_{++}$ be any continuous and symmetric function that is strictly increasing in its first argument and strictly decreasing in the second.

Suppose now that player 1's wealth level y_1 evolves according to some exogenous process as above:

$$dy_1 = v^{1/2} dW_t \tag{8}$$

(for purposes of symmetry, we have set m to zero), while given the action choices (k_1, k_2) for the players, player 2's wealth level evolves according to

$$dy_1 = -g(k_1, k_2) dy_2 \tag{9}$$

That is, each dollar lost by player 2 results in a gain of $\$g(k_1, k_2)$ to player 1, while each dollar lost by player 1 results in a gain of $\$[1/g(k_1, k_2)]$ to player 2. Assume that g is multiplicatively symmetric, i.e., $g(k_1, k_2) \cdot g(k_2, k_1) = 1$ for all

$(k_1, k_2) \in K \times K$.[8] The game terminates at the first T (if any) at which some player becomes bankrupt, i.e., at the first T at which $\min\{y_1(T), y_2(T)\} = 0$.

Simple calculations yield the following. Fix an action pair (k_1, k_2). Let (y_1, y_2) represent the players' initial wealth levels at the start of the bankruptcy game. Then, given (y_1, y_2, k_1, k_2), the terminal wealth level of player 1, contingent on player 2 going bankrupt, is:

$$h_1(y_1, y_2, k_1, k_2) = y_1 + g(k_1, k_2)y_2 \tag{10}$$

while the corresponding figure for player 2 is:

$$h_2(y_1, y_2, k_1, k_2) = y_2 + y_1/g(k_1, k_2) \tag{11}$$

Note that player i's wealth level remains between 0 and $h_i(y_1, y_2, k_1, k_2)$ as long as the bankruptcy game is being played; the moment i's wealth level hits zero, he is bankrupt. Conversely, j goes bankrupt if i's wealth level reaches $h_i(y_1, y_2, k_1, k_2)$. From basic stochastic calculus, it follows that the probability of hitting one or the other boundary is one; and that the probability that player $i (= 1, 2)$ survives (i.e., that player $j \neq i$ goes bankrupt) is:

$$\rho_i(y_1, y_2, k_1, k_2) = \frac{y_i}{h_i(y_1, y_2, k_1, k_2)} \tag{12}$$

These values for the terminal wealth and survival probabilities yield a natural interpretation of the action levels k_i as choices of "risk levels" given our assumptions on g: *ceteris paribus*, the terminal wealth h_i that will result contingent on success increases with k_i, but so also does the probability of failure ρ_i. In particular, assumption A4 is met. It is simple to verify that so also are assumptions A1–A3.

The functions h_1, h_2, ρ_1, ρ_2, as given by (10)-(12), together with the monotonicity restrictions on g, complete the description of the stage game. We now turn to the implications of this structure for the evolutionary game of Sect. 2.

3.2 Equilibrium and its properties

We begin with a description of the equilibria of the stage game. The following result, that establishes the existence of (a multitude of) equilibria in this game, is an immediate consequence of the properties of g and the forms of the functions ρ_i and h_i:

Proposition 3.1. *For any (y_1, y_2, k_1, k_2), we have $K_1(y_1, y_2; k_2) = K$, and $K_2(y_1, y_2; k_1) = \{\min K\}$. Thus, given any (y_1, y_2), the pair $(k_1, k_2) \in K \times K$ constitutes an equilibrium at (y_1, y_2) if, and only if, $k_2 = \min K$.*

[8] Note that in this case we have $g(k, k) = 1$ for all $k \in K$.

Proof. For any fixed $(y_1, y_2; k_1, k_2)$, (10) and (12) imply $\rho_1 h_1 = y_1$, which is independent of k_1. Thus, any $k_1 \in K$ is a best-response for the player from population I to any k_2 at any (y_1, y_2). That $K_2(y_1, y_2; k_1) = \{\min K\}$ follows immediately from the fact that ρ_2 is decreasing in k_2. □

Thus, any equilibrium selection $\kappa(y_1, y_2)$ must have $\kappa_2(y_1, y_2) = \min K$, but $\kappa_1(y_1, y_2)$ is completely unrestricted. Nonetheless, there is enough structure in the model to completely characterize equilibrium dynamics. Fix any equilibrium selection $\kappa(.)$. Recall that p_t denotes the period-t ratio of the population of type 1's to that of type 2's, while s_t is the period-t ratio of the wealth controlled by type 1's to that controlled by type 2's. Recall also that $P_\infty \subset \mathbb{R}_+$ and $S_\infty \subset \mathbb{R}_+$ denote the set of limit points of the respective sequences. Let $\overline{g} = g(\max K, \min K) > 1$. We will prove the following:

Proposition 3.2. *In any equilibrium κ, we have $S_\infty = \{1\}$, and $P_\infty \subset [1/\overline{g}, 1]$.*

Proof. Let (y_{1t}, y_{2t}) denote the sequence of per capita wealth levels from y under κ, and let $(k_{1t}, \min K)$ denote the corresponding sequence of actions. For notational ease, also denote by g_t the term $g(k_{1t}, \min K)$.

Then, $y_{10} = y = y_{20}$, while for $t \geq 0$, we have $y_{1t+1} = y_{1t} + g_t y_{2t}$, and $y_{2t+1} = y_{2t} + y_{1t}/g_t$. It follows that for all $t \geq 0$,

$$\frac{y_{1t+1}}{y_{2t+1}} = g_t \tag{13}$$

Now note that, by substituting from (10) and (11) into (12), we obtain

$$\frac{\rho_1(y_1, y_2; k_1, k_2)}{\rho_2(y_1, y_2; k_1, k_2)} = \frac{y_1}{g(k_1, k_2) y_2} \tag{14}$$

Therefore, $\rho_{10}/\rho_{20} = 1/g_0$, while for $t \geq 1$,

$$\frac{\rho_{1t}}{\rho_{2t}} = \frac{y_{1t}}{g_t y_{2t}} = \frac{g_{t-1}}{g_t} \tag{15}$$

Using the recursive definition of the p_t sequence from (5), we obtain, as a consequence, for $t \geq 0$:

$$p_{t+1} = \frac{g_{t-1}}{g_t} \frac{g_{t-2}}{g_{t-1}} \cdots \frac{g_0}{g_1} \frac{1}{g_0} = \frac{1}{g_t}. \tag{16}$$

It follows immediately that for any $t \geq 0$,

$$s_{t+1} = \left(\frac{y_{1t+1}}{y_{2t+1}} \right) p_{t+1} = g_t \frac{1}{g_t} = 1 \tag{17}$$

establishing one part of the result.

The other part is a simple consequence of the relation above that $p_{1t+1}/p_{2t+1} = 1/gt$: since $k_{2t} = \min K$ for all t, we have

$$g(k_{1t}, k_{2t}) \in [g(\min K, \min K), g(\max K, \min K)] = [1, \overline{g}]$$

Thus, the set of limit points of the sequence $\{1/g_t\}$ (which is P_∞) is contained in $[1/\overline{g}, 1]$. □

Proposition 3.2 establishes that in this simple model, the expected profit maximizers cannot come to dominate the market on either front, when they are faced with agents who simply maximize the short-run probability of survival. Indeed, more is true. Since $S_\infty = 1$, and $P_\infty \leq 1/2$, many (in fact, in some sense, most[9]) equilibrium strategies for Population I are not even most fit strategies:

Proposition 3.3. *An equilibrium strategy κ_1 for Population I is a most fit strategy against the strategy κ_2 specified by $\kappa_2(y_1, y_2) = \min K$ for all (y_1, y_2) if, and only if, the resulting sequence k_{1t} satisfies $\lim_{t\to\infty} k_{1t} = \min K$.*

Proof. If Population I also plays the strategy κ_2, we will have $g_t = g(\min K, \min K)$ for all t, resulting in $P_\infty = S_\infty = 1$. If Population I plays any strategy κ_1 such that, under (κ_1, κ_2), $k_{1t} \nrightarrow \min K$, then, along some subsequence, we must have g_t converging to a limit $\gamma > 1$. Then, $1/\gamma \in P_\infty(\kappa_1, \kappa_2)$, so κ_2 dominates κ_1 against κ_2, so κ_1 cannot be a most fit strategy.

Remark. It is easy to see that given *any* pair of strategies (κ_1, κ_2) in this model, we must have $S_\infty = 1$. Thus, the fitness of one strategy against another must be measured only along the lines of how limit population proportions are affected. It is thus immediate that $\kappa_1(y_1, y_2) \equiv \min K$ is an *unbeatable* strategy for either population. □

To sum up, in the model considered in this section, the total wealth of the expected profit maximizers never grows fast enough for them to come to dominate the market on the wealth front, while their population shares, when they play the survival probability maximizers, is bounded above by $1/2$. Their equilibrium strategies are "typically" not most-fit strategies against their opponents' strategies, except in exceptional circumstances such as the conditions outlined in Proposition 3.3. (This is true even if they are not playing survival probability maximizers, obviously.) On the other hand, it is the case that the unique equilibrium strategy for the survival probability maximizers is also an "unbeatable" strategy.

3.3 A remark on the importance of symmetry

A number of assumptions guaranteed symmetry in the game considered above, including the conditions that the wealth process of player 1 has zero drift, and that the odds-function g is symmetric. The purpose of this section is to point out that if these symmetry assumptions are weakened, the conclusions of the model could change dramatically, since a systematic bias now enters the model.

We illustrate this process by considering a slight modification in the background stochastic process that was used to motivate the bankruptcy game. To elaborate, suppose, instead of (8), the evolution of player 1's wealth level is given by

$$dy_1 = m dt + v^{1/2} dW_t \tag{18}$$

[9] Recall that any strategy is an equilibrium strategy for player 1

where the drift m is not necessarily zero. The rest of the structure is exactly as in Sect. 3.1; in particular, we continue assuming that the wealth levels of players 1 and 2 are related by

$$dy_1 = -g(k_1, k_2)dy_2 \tag{19}$$

where g has the same properties as in Sect. 3.1. Note that m could be as close to zero as desired, so we could be very "close" to the model of Sects. 3.1–3.2.

Standard arguments from stochastic calculus show that when $m > 0$, the probability $\rho_1(y_1, y_2; k_1, k_2)$ of player 1 going bankrupt first, given $(y_1, y_2; k_1, k_2)$, is given by:

$$\rho_1(y_1, y_2; k_1, k_2) = \frac{1 - e^{-\lambda y_1}}{1 - e^{-\lambda(y_1 + g(k_1, k_2)y_2)}} \tag{20}$$

where $\lambda = 2m/v$; while in the case $m < 0$, we have:

$$\rho_1(y_1, y_2; k_1, k_2) = \frac{e^{\theta y_1} - 1}{e^{\theta(y_1 + g(k_1, k_2)y_2)} - 1} \tag{21}$$

where $\theta = -2m/v$. The functions h_1, and h_2 remain unaltered from Sect. 3.1; and as there, we again have $\rho_2 = 1 - \rho_1$.

Note that for $i = 1, 2$, h_i is increasing in k_i, while ρ_i is decreasing in k_i. Thus, the actions k_i continue to represent levels of risk: higher returns require accepting a lower probability of survival. Also, it is still the case that h_i is increasing in y_i. Thus, assumptions A3 and A4 are met, and since the functions h_i have not changed, so also is A2. Assumption Al is however violated, since the probabilities of survival are no longer symmetric.

The following result establishes that, in contrast to the zero drift case, the set of equilibrium strategies when $m \neq 0$ is quite small.

Proposition 3.4. *When $m > 0$, the unique equilibrium action pair at any (y_1, y_2) is given by $(k_1, k_2) = (\max K, \min K)$. When $m < 0$, the unique equilibrium, action pair at any (y_1, y_2) is given by $k_1 = k_2 = \min K$.*

Proof. We prove the Proposition for the case $m > 0$. The case in $m < 0$ is handled analogously. Fix any (y_1, y_2). First consider player 1's response problem for fixed $k_2 \in K$:

$$\max_{k_1 \in K} \left(\frac{1 - e^{-\lambda y_1}}{1 - e^{-\lambda(y_1 + g(k_1, k_2)y_2)}} \right) (y_1 + g(k_1, k_2)y_2) \tag{22}$$

This is equivalent to solving

$$\min_{k_1 \in K} \left(\frac{1 - e^{-\lambda(y_1 + g(k_1, k_2)y_2)}}{y_1 + g(k_1, k_2)y_2} \right) \tag{23}$$

Since $(1 - e^{-\lambda x})$ is a concave function of x, the ratio $(1 - e^{-\lambda x})/x$ declines in x. Thus, minimizing (23) requires maximizing the denominator, or selecting $k_1 = \max K$.

That player 2 always wishes to play $\min K$ follows simply from the fact that ρ_2 is decreasing in k_2. □

More interestingly, we can also show that equilibrium dynamics are now determinate as regards both population- and wealth-shares; indeed, they are not only determinate, they also result in extreme predictions regarding limit population– and wealth–shares that depend only on whether m is positive or negative. Namely, if $m > 0$ (i.e., the drift favors the expected profit maximizers), then in the limit this population must both (a) control all the wealth and (b) be preponderant in numbers in the overall population; while if $m < 0$, a similar conclusion is true of the survival probability maximizers:

Proposition 3.5. *If $m > 0$, then in the unique equilibrium, $P_\infty = S_\infty = \{+\infty\}$, while if $m < 0$, then in the unique equilibrium, $P_\infty = S_\infty = \{0\}$.*

Proof. For notational ease, let $\overline{g} = g(\max K, \min K)$. Denote by $(y_{1t}(m), y_{2t}(m))$ the resulting sequence of equilibrium wealth levels when the drift is m. We have for all $t \geq 0$,

$$\begin{aligned} y_{1t+1}(m) &= y_{1t}(m) + g_t(m)y_{2t}(m) \\ y_{2t+1}(m) &= y_{2t}(m) + y_{1t}(m)/g_t(m) \end{aligned}$$

where $g_t(m) = g(m) = \overline{g}$ if $m > 0$, and $g_t(m) = g(m) = 1$ if $m < 0$. It is trivial therefore that in both cases, we have for all $t \geq 1$, $y_{1t+1}(m) = 2y_{1t}(m)$, and $y_{2t+1}(m) = 2y_{2t}(m)$. Thus, we obtain

$$\begin{aligned} y_{1t+1}(m) &= 2^t(1 + g(m))y \\ y_{2t+1}(m) &= 2^t(1 + 1/g(m))y \end{aligned}$$

In particular, we have $y_{1t}(m)/y_{2t}(m) = g(m)$ for all $t \geq 1$.

First, suppose $m > 0$. We suppress dependence on m. Using $y_{1t} + g_t y_{2t} = y_{1t+1} = 2y_{1t}$ in (19), we obtain

$$\frac{\rho_{1t}}{\rho_{2t}} = \frac{1 - e^{-\lambda y_{1t}}}{e^{-\lambda y_{1t}} - e^{-2\lambda y_{1t}}} = e^{\lambda y_{1t}}$$

Therefore,

$$p_{t+1} = \prod_{\tau=0}^{t} \frac{\rho_{1t}}{\rho_{2t}} = e^{\lambda \sum y_{1\tau}} = e^{(2^t-1)\lambda(1+\overline{g})y},$$

and since $2^t \to \infty$ as $t \to \infty$, $p_{t+1} \to \infty$, establishing one part of the result.

To see the other part, note that $y_{1t}/y_{2t} = \overline{g}$ for all $t \geq 1$. So,

$$s_{t+1} = \frac{p_{1t+1}y_{1t+1}}{p_{2t+1}y_{2t+1}} = p_{t+1}\frac{y_{1t+1}}{y_{2t+1}} = p_{t+1}\overline{g},$$

and s_t also goes to infinity with t.

The results for $m < 0$ are established analogously, and are omitted.

4 A generalization of the linear model

The analysis of the previous section appears to depend on the "linearity" of the underlying structure. It is tempting to think that if h_1 or $\rho_1 h_1$, were to depend non-linearly on (say were convex in) y_1, the result that $S_\infty = \{1\}$ could not arise, and, in fact, with sufficient convexity, one might even obtain $S_\infty = \{+\infty\}$. In this section, we show, using a simple generalization of the linear model, that this intuition is partly correct.

So let $\alpha \in \mathbb{R}_{++}$. We will consider a family of models parametrized by α, in which the case of $\alpha = 1$ corresponds to the linear model. As in the linear model, let $g(k_1, k_2)$ be any function on $K \times K$, which is strictly increasing in k_1 and strictly decreasing in k_2. We begin by replacing the definitions of h_i given by (10)-(11) with

$$h_1(y_1, y_2; k_1, k_2) = (y_1^\alpha + g(k_1, k_2) y_2^\alpha)^{1/\alpha} \tag{24}$$

and

$$h_2(y_1, y_2; k_1, k_2) = (y_1^\alpha / g(k_1, k_2) + y_2^\alpha)^{1/\alpha} \tag{25}$$

Secondly, we replace the definition of the functions ρ_i given by (12) with

$$\rho_1(y_1, y_2; k_1, k_2) = \frac{y_1^\alpha}{y_1^\alpha + g(k_1, k_2) y_2^\alpha} \tag{26}$$

and

$$\rho_2(y_1, y_2; k_1, k_2) = \frac{g(k_1, k_2) y_2^\alpha}{y_1^\alpha + g(k_1, k_2) y_2^\alpha} \tag{27}$$

Note that when $\alpha = 1$, this model coincides with the linear model. We begin our analysis with the following:

Proposition 4.6. *If $\alpha < 1$, the unique stage game equilibrium strategies at any (y_1, y_2) are $(k_1, k_2) = (\max K, \min K)$, while if $\alpha > 1$, the unique equilibrium strategies at any (y_1, y_2) are $(k_1, k_2) = (\min K, \min K)$.*

Proof. Consider first player 1's best-response to k_2 at some (y_1, y_2). Player 1 solves

$$\max\{y_1^\alpha [y_1^\alpha + g(k_1, k_2) y_2^\alpha]^{\frac{1-\alpha}{\alpha}} \mid k_1 \in K\} \tag{28}$$

When $\alpha < 1$, then $1 - \alpha > 0$, and the maximand is increasing in k_1, since g is. Thus, $k_1 = \max K$ is the unique solution here. If, on the other hand, $\alpha > 1$, then the maximand is decreasing in k_1, and the unique solution is $k_1 = \min K$.

That player 2's optimal strategy is to always play $\min K$ follows simply from the fact that ρ_2 is decreasing in k_2. □

Proposition 4.7. *If $\alpha < 1$, then $S_\infty = \{\overline{g}^{(1-\alpha)/\alpha}\} > 1$, and $P_\infty = \{1/\overline{g}\} < 1$, where $\overline{g} = g(\max K, \min K)$. If $\alpha > 1$, then $S_\infty = P_\infty = \{1\}$.*

Proof. First consider the case $\alpha < 1$. At any (y_1, y_2), we have,

$$\frac{\rho_1(y_1, y_2; \max K, \min K)}{\rho_2(y_1, y_2; \max K, \min K)} = \frac{1}{\overline{g}}\left(\frac{y_1}{y_2}\right)^{\alpha} \tag{29}$$

while

$$\frac{h_1(y_1, y_2; \max K, \min K)}{h_2(y_1, y_2; \max K, \min K)} = (\overline{g})^{1/\alpha} \tag{30}$$

Thus, for $t \geq 1$, we have

$$\frac{\rho_{1t}}{\rho_{2t}} = \frac{1}{\overline{g}}\left(\frac{y_{1t}}{y_{2t}}\right)^{\alpha} = \frac{1}{\overline{g}}\left(\frac{h_{1t-1}}{h_{2t_1}}\right)^{\alpha} = 1 \tag{31}$$

This means that for $t \geq 1$,

$$p_{t+1} = \frac{\rho_{1t}}{\rho_{2t}} p_t = p_t, \tag{32}$$

while for $t = 1, p_t = \rho_{10}/\rho_{20} = 1/\overline{g}$, so $P_\infty = \{1/\overline{g}\}$.

Moreover, we also have for $t \geq 1$

$$s_{t+1} = p_{t+1}\frac{y_{1t+1}}{y_{2t+1}} = p_{t+1}\frac{h_{1t}}{h_{2t}} = \overline{g}^{(1-\alpha)/\alpha} \tag{33}$$

This completes the proof for the case $\alpha < 1$. When $\alpha > 1$, then, in equilibrium, $g(k_1, k_2) \equiv 1$, and it is easy to see from this that we must have $p_t = s_t = 1$ for all t. □

Proposition 4.2 suggests that expected profit maximization can be a good thing in general: if $\alpha < 1$, then members of population 1 fare no worse along either the population or wealth dimension than members of population 2, while if $\alpha > 1$, they come to control more than 50% of the aggregate wealth in the limit. Indeed, this proportion increases towards 100% as $\alpha \downarrow 0$, even as their fraction of the population share remains bounded away from zero.

From a technical standpoint, it is easy to see what drives these results. When $\alpha < 1$, then Proposition 4.1 establishes that the equilibrium strategy profile is $(\max K, \min K)$, so $\overline{g} = g(\max K, \min K) > 1$. Moreover, conditional on survival, player 1 will have a higher wealth level than player 2, so we have $y_1 > y_2$ in every period after the first. When these conditions are used in the definitions (24) and (26), a simple picture emerges. As $\alpha < 1$ decreases towards zero, the payoff h_1 contingent on survival increases indefinitely, but while the survival probability decreases monotonically, it remains bounded above zero. Thus, lower values of α aid wealth accumulation more than they reduce survival probability, and this helps members of population 1.

Ultimately, what these results – and those of the previous section – show is that much depends on the precise specification of the environment, but expected profit maximization generally does well overall. Expected profit maximization involves more risky strategies than merely seeking to stay alive. If this increased risk is more than compensated for in terms of wealth accumulation (which occurs when $\alpha < 1$), then expected profit maximizers can not only be expected to survive, they will even come to dominate from a wealth standpoint. If the compensation is merely adequate (as happens when $\alpha = 1$), then expected profit maximizers can only hold their own from a wealth-share standpoint. Finally, if the compensation is less than adequate ($\alpha > 1$), then expected profit maxiization involves an in-built defense – the equilibrium strategy profile changes, ensuring that wealth and population shares never fall below their initial levels.

5 Conclusions

Conventional economic theory makes frequent use of the hypothesis that firms seek to maximize expected profits, even though under uncertainty it is *realized*, and not *anticipated*, profits that determine a firm's survival. In this paper, we look at the justifiability of this hypothesis in an evolutionary sense using a simple dynamic framework. The trade-off captured by our model is that expected profit maximization involves strategies that are more risky than merely seeking to survive to the next period; however, contingent on survival, they lead to greater wealth accumulation which in turn improves *future* survival prospects.

We employ two criteria to judge the efficacy of expected profit maximization strategies: the fraction of the limit population who are expected profit maximizers, and the fraction of the aggregate wealth controlled by this segment. Overall, our results are mixed. From a population share standpoint, we find that expected profit maximization does not always do well: the limiting fraction of expected profit maximizers may be small. However, from the (perhaps more important) wealth share standpoint, they never do badly, and in some cases even come to dominate along this dimension. This suggests that the typical appeal to expected profit maximization may be justified at some level.

Balancing this, our results also indicate that the predictions of the model are sometimes quite sensitive to the precise specification of the environment, in some cases perhaps more sensitive than is comfortable. Thus, one cannot lightly extrapolate our results to a reality which is far more complex than in our model. In the final analysis, our results suggest that while there is reason for some optimism that the expected profit maximization may prove "fit" from an evolutionary standpoint, much reasearch remains to be done.

References

A. Alchian (1950) Uncertainty, evolution, and economic theory. *Journal of Political Economy* 58: 211–221

Blume, L. and D. Easley (1992) Evolution and market behavior. *Journal of Economic Theory* 58(l): 9–40

Dutta, Prajit K. and Roy Radner (1999) Profit maximization and the market selection hypothesis *Review of Economic Studies* 66: 769–98

Enke, S. (1951) On maximizing profits: A discussion between Chamberlin and Robinson. *American Economic Review* 41: 566–578

Friedman, D. (1988) Evolutionary games: An introduction for economists. mimeo, University of California, Santa Cruz

Friedman, M. (1953) *Essays in Positive Economics*. University of Chicago Press, Chicago
Symposium Issue on Evolutionary Game Theory *Journal of Economic Theory* 57(2), August 1992
Karatzas, I. and S. Shreve (1987) *Brownian Motion and Stochastic Calculus*. Springer, Berlin Heidelberg New York
Maynard-Smith, J. (1982) *Evolution and the Theory of Games*. Cambridge University Press, Cambridge